THE
LANDSCAPE
OF
BRITAIN

History of the British Landscape

General editor: MICHAEL REED

Industry in the Landscape, 1700–1900
Marilyn Palmer and Peter Neaverson

THE
LANDSCAPE
OF
BRITAIN

from the beginnings to 1914

Michael Reed

London

First published 1990
by Routledge
11 New Fetter Lane, London EC4P 4EE

First published in paperback 1997

© 1990 Michael Reed

Printed in Great Britain by
T.J. International Ltd, Padstow, Cornwall

British Library Cataloguing in Publication Data

Reed, Michael
The landscape of Britain.
1. Great Britain. Landscape
I. Title
719'.0941

ISBN 0–415–01297–X (hbk)
ISBN 0–415–15745–5 (pbk)

to
Hilarie

Contents

Illustrations

Plates

Figures

Acknowledgements

The author of a book of this kind must of necessity run up enormous debt to scholars, students, and members of the public generally, and I am no exception. Any references here, however fulsome, can never compensate adequately those who have given so generously of their learning, time, and patience, from that unknown passer-by who pointed out to me the best place from which to take the photograph of Brindley's Mill, Plate 70, through those generations of students who have courteously listened whilst I have tried out some of my more outrageous ideas, to my wife, whose patience and encouragement have been beyond price. The dedication of this book is an entirely inadequate discharge of my debt to Mrs Hilarie Bateman who, with imperturbable patience and good humour, initiated me into the mysteries of word-processing and hence materially assisted me in the preparation of the final text.

I wish to thank the following for their kindness in allowing me to use their photographic and other material: Cambridge University Committee for Aerial Photography, Plates 11, 12, 15, and 19; Mr Peter Reed, Plates 14 and 30; Mr Mark Lawrence, Plate 33; M. Jean-Claude Lenoir, Plate 22; Mr Michael Bateman, Plates 47 and 67; Dr J. Richards, Plate 34; Mrs Velda Henman, Figures 11 and 14; and Northamptonshire County Record Office, Figure 13.

Note on radio-carbon dates in Chapters 1 and 2

The correlation of radio-carbon dates with calendar or solar years is a matter of controversy. The following symbols have been used, and they must be interpreted only within their own terms of reference:

bc   radio-carbon years before Christ

BC   calendar or solar years before Christ

bp   radio-carbon years before the present

Introduction

The theme of the landscape historian is the evolution of that external physical world in which men and women have carried on the everyday business of their lives from the remotest periods of prehistory down to the present. He must of necessity leave on one side those of a more speculative turn of mind who would suggest that the external world does not exist. At work and at play, at home and at prayer, successive generations of men and women, by making use of the opportunities presented to them by their physical environment, have created, moulded, and shaped their world to suit their individual needs and aspirations, and then passed it on, sometimes enriched, sometimes impoverished, to their children, so that the landscape today is a palimpsest, a text upon which men and women have written their own social autobiography, without, however, being able to erase entirely the contribution of their ancestors, and the autobiography which is the landscape is almost always much more truthful than most other autobiographies in that it is written almost entirely unselfconsciously.

The landscape historian has two basic sources: the first is the natural world itself, the world of sunshine and rain, ice and snow, wind and cloud, of grass and trees, plants and animals, whether wild or domestic. Until quite recently an oak tree was as valuable as a field of corn, and attempts to preserve deer and foxes have created their own distinctive forms of land use. Both climate and natural fauna and flora interact, in a most subtle and complex manner, with what may be called the basic skeletal structure of the landscape, namely its rocks, whether sandstones or chalk, granites, quartzes, or shales. From these raw materials geomorphological processes, in motion over incomprehensible aeons of time, have created surface deposits of soils, silts, sands, and clays with which men have to wrestle if they are to grow any part of their food, and by creating stone for building, flint, slate, coal, and iron the same forces present a range of opportunities and resources which can have an impact upon the landscape for generations.

The impersonal forces of the natural world may be likened to the ground bass to some monumental passacaglia. They march on relentlessly, rhythmically, without fear or favour. Their impact upon human society is profound, pitiless, and ineluctable. Within the brief span of a human life their immediate influence may be confined to storms and floods, droughts and earthquakes, events which in themselves can have serious consequences for individual communities of human beings. In the long term climatic change can create bleak moorlands from once prosperous farming communities, and the uplands of Dartmoor, Derbyshire, and north Yorkshire are littered with the evidence. In the very long term they shape and mould the environment with irresistible power. Sea-levels rise and fall, rivers break new courses, mountains crumble. Shipden, recorded in Domesday Book, now lies several miles out to sea off the Norfolk coast, and three terse words from the same record summarize the fate of Dunwich: where there had been two carucates of land, by 1086 there was only one: *mare abstulit alia*. Skara Brae was preserved beneath wind-blown sands and the Isle of Thanet was once a genuine island, separated from the mainland of Kent by a wide stretch of open water; and to put the whole on-going endless process of becoming which is the heart of the natural world into perspective it is sufficient to point out that the period, all too brief in geological terms, since the end of the last ice age, may in fact be nothing more than a short interlude between two ice ages. Perhaps in another ten or twenty thousand years' time the snow on the northern slopes of Ben Nevis will not thaw in the summer. Instead it will start to accumulate, compact into ice and as a glacier begin to make its way slowly and inexorably into the lowlands, crushing everything in its path.

Moving across the ground bass of the natural world are the themes created by the presence of man in society within this world, exploiting for his own ends the opportunities it presents, first for the satisfaction of his basic needs for food and shelter, and second for the fulfilment of his most profound spiritual, cultural, and scientific aspirations. It is important to stress that the natural world provides opportunities rather than obstacles, a positive rather than a negative approach to the infinite capacity of men and women in society to adapt themselves to the harshest environments, as the black houses of the Hebrides reveal in the starkest terms.

It is at this point that the landscape historian turns to the infinite riches of his second source, namely the activities of man in society over time, and all three elements need to be stressed, since the landscape is the product of the interaction of human beings living in organized groupings within a natural environment viewed over a temporal continuum. It is probably not too much of an exaggeration to say that every human activity, however base, grubby, altruistic, or refined, finds its reflection in the external world, and the ways in which many of these human activities have been provided for have created institutions and structures which have proved to be astonishingly durable. Thus the first men to return into the inhospitable tundra landscape that was Britain as the last ice sheets melted must very quickly have imposed order upon an inchoate land by dividing it up into territories and labelling it by means of place-names. Both boundaries and place-names have changed very extensively over time, evidence perhaps of how useful men find them, but it is one of the principal themes of this book that no generation can blot out entirely the contribution of its ancestors to the environment which it has inherited from them, and Ruskin's comments, quoted on p. 339, have a timeless quality about them which serves to reinforce this point. Thus county and parish boundaries have been extensively redrawn in the last 150 years or so, but much still survives from earlier times and it is still possible to find boundaries which have been in use for at least a thousand years; some may well go back into prehistoric times, keeping company with that handful of place-names for which there is no satisfactory explanation save to suggest that they have survived from an earlier, pre-Celtic, linguistic stratum.

The Red Lady of Paviland, discussed on p. 35, is evidence of the antiquity of social organization and religious beliefs, although today we can have but the most tenuous ideas of what these beliefs could have been. Monuments such as Maes Howe and Stonehenge are astonishing evidence of the power of these beliefs over the minds and hearts of men, and in this they are the equal of Westminster Abbey and St Paul's Cathedral. That these beliefs could change, sometimes with devastating effect, is shown by the ruins of Fountains Abbey and the bare simplicity of the Friends' Meeting House at Jordans.

But the landscape is not a collection of prominent but isolated monuments. Nor is it to be confused with scenery, although the development of the appreciation of natural scenery and the attempts made from the nineteenth century onwards to preserve areas of outstanding natural beauty, form part of a significant shift in aesthetic, philosophical, and artistic ideas and tastes that is apparent from the early years of the eighteenth century onwards, a shift in itself an important area of landscape history since it led men deliberately to seek gloomy, untended, savage spots and to build houses and cottages of a matching irregularity as part of the cultivation of the Picturesque. Monastic ruins, once symbols of papal superstition, became instead much admired relics from a simpler, more human, medieval world. All of these attempts to preserve so-called 'natural landscapes' do, of course, rest upon a fallacy. No corner of Britain remains untouched by human activity. The Lake District, the North Yorkshire moors, the Chiltern Hills, are as much a product of generations of human activity as the Black Country, the Rhondda valleys, or the tenements of Glasgow. A study of the reasons why the Cleveland Hills and not Middlesbrough have been made into a national park would be an important contribution to the evolution of the appreciation of scenery, but it would be only a part of the history of the landscape of those two areas.

The landscape historian is concerned neither with isolated, historical monuments, nor with the aesthetics of scenery, but with the total

environment of man in society, so that the meanest back streets in some
grimy industrial town or the most monotonously regular pattern of field
and hedgerow across the Midland Plain are of equal interest to him, since
both are man-made, the consequences of patterns of thought, beliefs, and
aspirations combining with contemporary socio-legal structures and levels
of technology to produce a distinctive contribution to the landscape, a
contribution which has neither blotted out earlier ones nor, in spite of later
changes, in its turn been completely erased. As with the natural world, the
human landscape has been created by the two processes of erosion and
deposition, and it is the historian's task, and his delight, to unravel them
both.

The task of the landscape historian must be twofold. First of all he must
attempt to re-create past landscapes, using the enormously wide range of
evidence of every kind which is now available. In order to do this
successfully he must explore not only the 'how' but also the 'why', the
latter providing at least some insight into the dynamics of change. He
needs to explain how and why some landscape features are more
characteristic of certain periods of time and not others, how and why they
were brought into being, with, wherever possible, some account of the
motives, reasons, and attitudes of contemporaries since these are
enormously influential in determining the structures and functions of
landscape features; and he must explain, too, how and why they were
discarded, changed, altered, demolished, or rebuilt, again with some
account of the motives and reasons of those responsible. Thus, to take an
obvious example, the ruins of Fountains Abbey draw tourists in their
thousands, not least because they are set in a meticulously groomed setting
that appears to be the quintessence of natural tranquillity. The setting is in
fact entirely man-made, being a creation of the eighteenth century. To
enquire for a moment into the lives of the monks who lived there so long
ago leads to the monastic revival of the twelfth century, whilst to ask for an
explanation for its present ruined state must lead in the end into the
innermost recesses of the mind of Martin Luther, whose spiritual
wrestlings found the monastic life redundant.

Secondly, the landscape historian must seek to identify and account for
relic features of past landscapes surviving into those of today, and an
astonishing amount has survived, even from the remotest periods,
although the full significance of much of this is only now beginning to be
appreciated. The evidence for a Bronze Age 'enclosure movement' is now
overwhelming. The evidence itself, in the form of boundary ditches and
banks, has been there since it was first created, but with the passage of time
these banks and ditches became neglected, their purpose was forgotten and
they sank into the background, not only of the physical world, but, much
more importantly, into the background of the mental landscapes of
succeeding generations. It became impossible to conceive that men had

been so resourceful and so numerous so long ago. It needed patient fieldwork and careful reappraisal with a clear eye before convincing explanations of the purpose and the antiquity of these features could emerge. Subsequent reorganizations of the rural landscape have added to this ancient inheritance rather than obliterated it. Large-scale destruction is the legacy only of the years after 1945. It is this endless process of accretion which has created the landscape of the present, giving to it its incredibly rich historical density and making its exploration endlessly fascinating.

Part I

FOUNDATIONS

1

The land of Britain

The foundations of the landscape of Britain were first laid down at the beginning of geological time, so long ago as to be quite incomprehensible in human terms, with the result that nine-tenths of this book is, paradoxically, concerned with a time-span which, in geological terms, is almost as incomprehensibly short. The immensities of geological time, like those of astronomical space, are so great that the human mind cannot make the required gear-change and thus fails to grasp more than a fraction of their significances. Geological structures, shaped by the immense, impersonal forces of geomorphological processes, provide, dispassionately and without bias or prejudice, a wide and varied range of opportunities and determinants which mould, in a thousand subtle, interrelated, and inescapable ways, that brief moment of time which is all that the individual human being is allowed between the cradle and the grave. It is for this reason that, because this book is concerned with man in his environment, this first chapter must look in some detail at the structure of the stage upon which he will act out his all-too-brief life.

The geological structure of Britain is at once comparatively simple and immensely complex. It is simple in that as a crude generalization the oldest rocks lie in the north and the west of the island, younger ones in the south and the east. Within the framework of this oversimple generalization lies a picture of great complexity, evidence of an eventful, sometimes catastrophic, geological history. The rocks which outcrop at the surface, and it is only those that can be shown on a geological map such as that which forms Figure 1, vary enormously in age and have been subject to a number of phases of tectonic deformation, involving both folding and faulting as well as uplift and subsidence, leading to a correspondingly complex pattern of relief. At the same time there is now overwhelming evidence to show

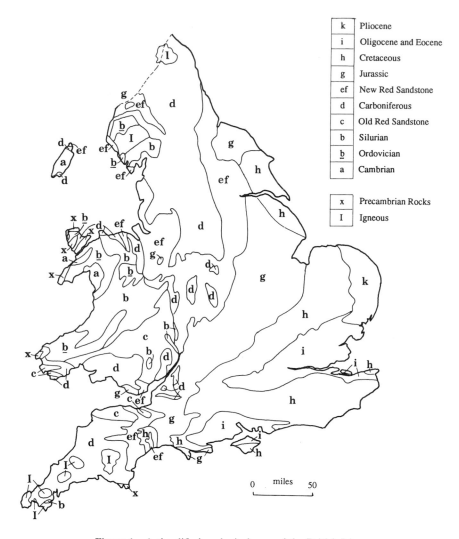

k	Pliocene
i	Oligocene and Eocene
h	Cretaceous
g	Jurassic
ef	New Red Sandstone
d	Carboniferous
c	Old Red Sandstone
b	Silurian
b̲	Ordovician
a	Cambrian
x	Precambrian Rocks
I	Igneous

Figure 1 A simplified geological map of the British Isles

that the blocks of which Britain is today composed were once several hundreds of miles apart and were also, perhaps 400 million years ago, in latitude 30 degrees South. The vast block of continental crust of which they were once part, comprising Europe, Asia north of the Himalayas, Africa, and America, drifted very slowly north across the face of the earth, crossing the Equator somewhere between Lower Carboniferous times, some 340 million years ago, and Permian, about 250 million years ago, to reach modern latitudes about 170 million years ago, by which time it was beginning to split up and the Atlantic Ocean to open out.

			Millions of radio carbon years before the present	
Mesozoic	Quaternary	Holocene	0.012	Post-glacial Growth of peat bogs
		Pleistocene	c. 1.5	Ice Age
	Tertiary	Pliocene	c. 7	
		Miocene	26	
		Oligocene	38	
		Eocene	54	Volcanic activity in N.W. Scotland
		Palaeocene	65	Alpine orogeny
Cainozoic	Cretaceous	Chalk	100	
		Upper Greensand	105	
		Lower Greensand	112	
		Wealden	136	
	Jurassic	Purbeck, Port-land, Kim-meridge, and Oxford beds	162	
		Cornbrash and Oolites	172	
		Lias	195	
	Triassic	Rhaetic Keuper New Red Sandstones Bunter	225	
	Permian	Magnesian Limestone	280	
Palaeozoic	Carboniferous	Upper	325	Hercynian orogeny
	Devonian Old Red Sandstone	Upper	359	
		Middle	370	Caledonian orogeny
		Lower	345	
	Silurian		440	
	Ordovician		500	
	Cambrian		570	
	Pre-Cambrian		pre-600	

Figure 2 Geological succession

As the result of some two hundred years of careful and painstaking study geologists can now agree upon a broad pattern for the succession of geological strata, from the oldest levels at the bottom to those still in the process of formation at the top (Figure 2). This is based first of all upon the comparative study of fossils, the inference being that if identical fossils are to be found in different kinds of rocks from different parts of the country then the strata are likely to be synchronous. It is based secondly upon the hypothesis that rocks are of necessity laid down in chronological succession, so that younger ones overlie older ones, although it quickly became apparent that tectonic deformation can on occasion distort this pattern, sometimes very severely. Estimates of the age of the world and its component rocks are based upon a study of the radioactive decay of certain elements found in the earth's crust, more especially potassium-argon and rubidium-strontium.

Nine-tenths of geological time is taken up with the Precambrian period. A wide range of rock formations was created but they are difficult to correlate because of the almost complete absence of fossils. There are however extensive records of microscopic organisms recovered from some of the earliest known rocks, of which some, in northwestern Australia, may be 3,500 million years old. Simple organic compounds would build up as a result of natural chemical processes, perhaps promoted by unchecked ultraviolet radiation, since the earth's atmosphere then lacked an ozone layer to shade out the high energy radiation in the 2,400–2,900 Angström wavelength which inhibits the DNA molecule upon which life depends. These compounds would only become truly alive in particularly favourable environments, in warm nutrient-rich pools in rock crevices, especially in areas of volcanic activity. Here, bacteria and blue-green algae, through organic photosynthesis, began the long process of creating an oxygen-rich atmosphere. These very primitive living organisms lack a membrane-bound cell nucleus, but once oxygen had reached the level of 1 per cent of the atmosphere, then the development of such a nucleus could take place. This, by providing a centre in which genetic information can be stored and transmitted, constitutes the greatest single advance in organic evolution. It seems to have taken place between 2,000 and 1,000 million years ago. The atmosphere reached its present oxygen levels perhaps 600 million years ago.

The immensely long Precambrian period was marked by phases of volcanic activity alternating with long periods of sedimentation, so that Precambrian rocks include lava and ash as well as sandstones and muds. Rocks of this period form much of Scotland north of the Highland Boundary Fault (see Figure 3), with the gneisses of Lewis among the oldest rocks known anywhere in the world. These were subjected to severe folding before Torridonian sandstones were laid down on top, in their turn to be eroded to reveal once again the gaunt, stark bones of the skeleton of the world.

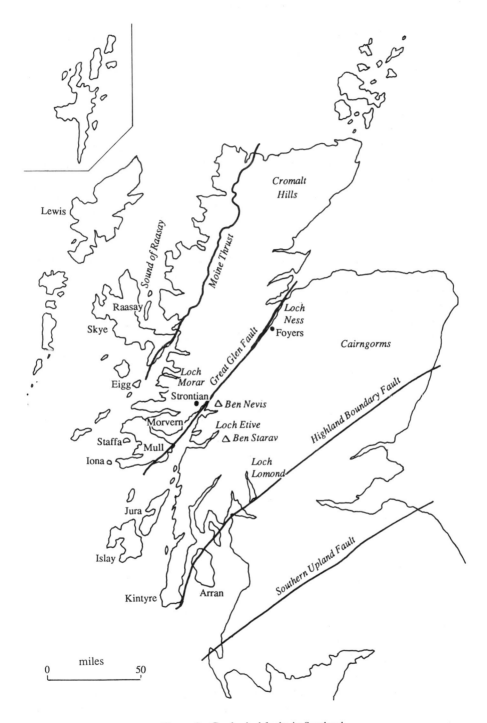

Figure 3 Geological faults in Scotland

1   A Precambrian outcrop on Beacon Hill, Charnwood Forest, Leicestershire.

These heavily eroded Precambrian rocks are the dominant feature of the landscape of northwestern Scotland. They are to be found at the surface only very occasionally elsewhere in Britain, although where they do occur they often create a very distinctive and striking landscape. Much of Anglesey is composed of a complex series of Precambrian granites, slates, and limestones eroded to form a low plateau with many parallels to Lewis, in the Outer Hebrides. The Charnwood Forest, in Leicestershire, is an outcrop of Precambrian slates, grits, and quartzites protruding through the very much later New Red Sandstones. Even more dramatic are the Malvern Hills, the Long Mynd, and Caer Caradoc, in Shropshire, all of Precambrian origin. Other Precambrian rocks are to be found in Pembrokeshire and the Lizard peninsula in Cornwall.

Although some fossils are known in the Precambrian rocks of Charnwood Forest, it is only in rocks from the Cambrian period that they begin to survive in sufficient numbers to be useful for dating and correlation purposes. Those which are particularly common include trilobites, brachiopods, and graptolites. These are marine creatures, and the Cambrian, Ordovician, and Silurian periods were marked by the submergence beneath the sea of the whole of what is now Wales, the Lake District and southern Scotland. Sandstones, slates, originally deposited as muds, and shales were laid down in this sea, with an outburst of volcanic activity producing immense quantities of ash to be added to these marine deposits. This period of volcanic activity is followed by a long period, the Silurian, of quiet deposition of sediments upon a gently subsiding sea-bed. Much of the landscape of North Wales is composed of rocks of these periods, subsequently folded and then eroded to produce the peaks of Snowdonia and Cader Idris, the vale of Festiniog and, between Llanberis and Bethesda, the most important slate quarries in Britain. These rocks re-emerge in central Wales in the region of Builth Wells and Llandrindod Wells.

Ordovician and Silurian slates and shales, grits, and flagstones also make up the oldest rocks of the Lake District. An immense sandwich was formed beneath the sea at this time. What are now called the Skiddaw Slates lie at the bottom. The Borrowdale volcanic rocks were formed next, and a series of Silurian beds, including Stockdale Shales, Coniston Flags, and Bannisdale Slates, were then laid down on top. In succeeding geological eras this sandwich will be uplifted, distorted and then intensely eroded to give the quite distinctive scenery characteristic of each of the slices of the sandwich in the landscape of the Lake District today.

The fossils of the Silurian period include the first fishes with jaws and the first land plants. The period comes to an end with a massive convulsion of the earth's crust when these immensely thick beds of sedimentary rocks were raised out of the sea to form mountain chains. This is the Caledonian orogeny, a succession of movements which produced, where now are the Grampians, a mountain range which was once more massive than the Himalayas, imparting to almost the whole of Scotland, together with the Lake District and much of central and northern Wales, that northeast–southwest grain which is so characteristic of the landscape. This movement produced immense stresses, and a great dome began to crack along a series of lines of weakness, more especially those known as the Highland Boundary Fault and the Southern Uplands Fault. The result was that a great block of land, some 50 miles wide, slowly subsided to form the Central Lowlands of Scotland. These movements broke upon the immovable blocks of gneisses and sandstones that today lie in the northwest Highlands and islands of Scotland, beyond the Moine Thrust (see Figure 3), but as they did so great wedges of ancient crystalline rocks were forced over younger strata to produce the extraordinary geological structures of, for example, the Cromalt Hills. It was also at this time that the great 'sandwich' of the Lake District was uplifted and folded, the pressures and tensions thus created producing fractures and faults, accompanied by the intrusion of great masses of magma welling up from the earth's core, transforming the surrounding rocks by their heat, and, as they cooled, crystallizing the granite, such as the Shap Granite, and other minerals.

The mountain ranges formed in this way were immediately subjected to erosion and the materials thus produced formed Old Red Sandstones such as are to be found in Herefordshire. At the same time marine sedimentation was depositing the sandstones and limestones found over much of Devon and Cornwall.

This period of mountain building was followed by the submergence beneath the sea of large areas of Britain. Carboniferous limestones and Millstone grits, the latter in a great delta covering much of northern England fed by rivers flowing from the landmass which then joined Scotland to Scandinavia, were deposited in this sea, accumulating to great thicknesses. In due course shallow freshwater lagoons and swamps developed in semi-tropical conditions, since the continental mass of which Britain was then part lay some 10 degrees south of the Equator. The lush vegetation of this period provided the raw materials for the Coal Measures. Carboniferous limestones form some of the most attractive and striking scenery in Britain, from the Avon Gorge to Dovedale, and from the Great Orme to Malham Tarn.

Once again a long era of deposition and sedimentation is brought to an end by a period of earth movement and folding. This period, the

2 Dovedale, Derbyshire, a limestone gorge created by the erosive powers of the River Dove.

Hercynian orogeny, produced a series of folds lying east to west, particularly apparent in southern England and south Wales, especially in Cornwall and Devon, the Mendips, the Gower peninsula, and south Pembrokeshire. In the downfolds the Coal Measures were subsequently overlain to produce the coalfields of Somerset, whilst the Coal Measures were eroded from the upfolds. Similar folding separated out the coal basins of the Central Lowlands of Scotland. The Great Glen Fault, although following the northeast–southwest trend created in the earlier mountain-building period, is largely a creation of this Hercynian orogeny. It is an immense lateral shift, of about 65 miles, as a study of the granites at Foyers and Strontian, once part of the same geological structure, has shown.

This period of mountain building is again followed by long eras of sedimentation and deposition, sometimes in freshwater lakes and some-times in arms of the sea. The earliest of these new sedimentary deposits are the New Red Sandstones, formations which can show considerable diversity, from the Bunter sandstones producing the thin poor soils of Sherwood Forest, through Keuper marls and sandstones to the Magnesian limestone scarp, lying today in a long, comparatively narrow belt of countryside along the eastern flank of the Pennines. These are followed by the Jurassic formations, ranging from the limestones which, in Gloucester-shire and Rutland, have produced some of the finest English building stones and thus a distinctive and unmistakable character to their landscapes, to the wide bands of Kimmeridge and Oxford clays, lying to the south and east, again with their own distinctive landscapes, together with the clays and sands of the Wealden basin, laid down in a freshwater lake.

In many ways the culmination of this long period of sedimentation is the submergence of most of England beneath a clear sea in which the skeletons of countless millions of small marine creatures were deposited to form the chalk beds which sweep from Flamborough Head to Beachy Head and the white cliffs of Dover in an immense crescent over southern and eastern England. Much of this chalk has been eroded. It seems very likely, for example, that large areas of Wales were once covered in chalk, although almost nothing now survives, whilst in Scotland only scattered and isolated beds of Jurassic and Cretaceous origins now remain, in Skye, Raasay, Mull, and Morvern for example, as testimony to the immense quantities of material subsequent erosion has removed from the Scottish landscape.

Many of the strata of this long period of deposition form today a series of steep scarps, facing generally northwest, as in the Cotswold scarp in Gloucestershire and the Chiltern scarp of Bedfordshire and Buckingham-shire, with a long dip slope to the south and east, another example of a widespread geological structure imparting an unmistakable grain to the landscape of today.

The close of this period is marked in Scotland by intense volcanic activity, especially in the Western Isles. This activity appears to be associated with the breakup of the immense continental landmass known to geologists as Gondwanaland into its component parts of Europe and America, and the opening out of the Atlantic Ocean as these huge fragments drifted apart. In the island of Mull is one of the most complex and massive series of igneous intrusions known anywhere in the world, producing spectacular mountain scenery. Further centres of volcanic activity produced the splendid peak of An Sgurr, 1,292 feet high, on the island of Eigg, and, on Skye, the largest basalt plateau in Britain together with the spectacular scenery of the Cuillins, where there are no less than twenty peaks over 3,000 feet high. There were several stages in this volcanic activity, and the intense heat and pressure created by the lava flows and igneous intrusions brought great complexity into the structure and nature of the surrounding strata. It is also associated with the creation of a series of long, narrow igneous outcrops, or dykes, often clustering in swarms, about centres of volcanic activity. They sweep in a great arc from the southern part of the Isle of Lewis through Skye, Ardnamurchan, Mull, Islay, Kintyre, and Arran into northern England. The basalt columns, cliffs, and caves of Staffa are part of this formation. A rather similar igneous outcrop, but one which solidified underground rather than at the surface, being exposed by later erosion, forms the cliff upon which Bamburgh Castle is built, the Farne islands, and Whin Sill, along which, on its stretch north of the Tyne, the Romans built Hadrian's Wall.

By this time too the last great period of mountain building, the Alpine orogeny, was under way, so called because it is this period of activity which saw the creation of the Alps of central Europe, over a period of some 70 million years. It now seems likely that this period of mountain building was of only indirect importance in Britain in that it served to reactivate and reinforce east–west folds which had already developed across southern England during the Hercynian orogeny. The folds of the Weald, the London basin, the Isle of Wight and smaller ones across Salisbury Plain and into eastern Devonshire would appear to have originated in this way.

Some 70 million years ago a period of uplift led to the slow emergence of a landmass that is at last recognizable, at least in its main features, as the island of Britain. The rate of uplift was greater in the west than in the east and so a land surface with an eastward tilt was created, and upon this the first recognizable drainage patterns began to take shape, with an eastward-flowing Dee–Trent network, a proto-Thames network and a third based upon the Frome–Solent network. This period of geological evolution, the Tertiary, is marked by very severe denudation across much of Britain, and it is estimated that in some parts of the country, over the dome of the Weald for example, up to 3,000 feet of superimposed deposits were removed from the landscape at this time. The uplift was by no means a simple process, and in the southeastern part of England shallow seas from time to time covered much of the area. At least twelve of these marine transgressions have been recognized in the successive layers of muds, silts, and sediments which they created. At the same time much of the material being removed from exposed land surfaces was being redeposited in these shallow seas. Thus it is clear from sediments to be found in the Hampshire basin that the granites of Dartmoor were now exposed and subject to erosion, and similar sediments in the London basin show that the chalk dome over the Weald was breaking up.

Up to this point we have been concerned with impersonal geomorphological processes of deposition and denudation, whether in fresh water, beneath the sea or on land, mechanical or chemical, reinforced or modified by tectonic movements or igneous intrusions, all working over an incomprehensible time-scale. Minerals and sediments, muds and clays, silts and sandstones have been recycled in successive waves of sedimentation and erosion, or metamorphosed under intense heat and pressure. Within the limited capacity of the human mind to grasp the time-scale involved this slowly moving pattern of change can at times be confusing and bewildering. This in itself is a not unacceptable impression, since the patterns of change were immensely complex, and many yet remain to be more fully and more accurately explained.

Nevertheless, two points need to be made at this stage. First of all none of the changes outlined in preceding paragraphs ever succeeded in erasing totally the evidence of previous change, so that somewhere in Britain there is evidence of every step in the chain of events which has produced the landforms of today, from the most ancient gneisses in the Isle of Lewis to medieval silts and sediments in the fens. Secondly these processes still continue today, although they operate so slowly as to be scarcely perceptible over the minute time-span which is recorded human history. These processes have therefore produced the foundations of the stage for human activity, but they must themselves now recede into the background as we turn our attention increasingly to the resources, opportunities, and challenges which their results present to the human beings who are about to appear upon the scene. But before these human beings do appear, another impersonal, natural phenomenon comes to the fore to exercise an increasingly important influence over the environment. This is climate.

We have hitherto been able largely to ignore any climatic factors that there might have been at work upon the geomorphological processes outlined in the preceding paragraphs, save to point out that the lush vegetation from which the coal measures were formed is likely to have flourished in a tropical climate. It is now clear however that climatic fluctuations can exert considerable influences over the shaping of landforms, and when mean temperatures fall sufficiently far as to create permanent ice sheets then its influence as exercised by means of the ice becomes overwhelming. Although there are indications of a Precambrian glaciation on a worldwide scale, it is only for the last 2 million years, during which period some 32 per cent of the earth's land surface has at some time been glaciated, that there is really extensive evidence to show just how important glaciation can be in moulding landforms.

It is in the nature of any one stage of glaciation to remove much of the evidence for the existence of its predecessors, and minor fluctuations in climate can further complicate the picture by creating local advances and retreats of individual glaciers. In spite of much painstaking research the history of the successive glaciations of Britain still remains uncertain and there is still controversy over the limits and duration of successive stages and their correlation with evidence from Europe and North America. There is however growing evidence of two very early glaciations, the Baventian, some one and a half million years ago, and the Beestonian, approximately half a million years ago, but their extent over Britain must at present remain largely conjectural. A more temperate period followed, a period known as the Cromer Interglacial since much of the evidence for it is to be found in lake deposits which now form the coastal cliffs between Cromer and West Runton. Materials found in the sediments of this lake show that many of our trees – pine, yew, oak, beech, elm, birch, and hazel – were already present.

The furthest extent of the glaciers occurred some 270,000 years ago. This is the Anglian glaciation, so called because much of the evidence for its existence is to be found in the glacial till of East Anglia, particularly the Cromer and Lowestoft boulder clays. The extent of this glaciation is shown on Figure 4 and its southern margin is at present generally accepted as the southern limit of glaciation in Britain. In other words England south of the Thames together with the southwestern peninsula has never been glaciated, although it is a region which has been subjected to the intense cold of periglacial conditions.

The Anglian glaciation was followed by some 40,000 years of a more temperate oceanic climate, a period known from its type site, some brick pits at Hoxne in Suffolk, as the Hoxnian interglacial. Here was a lake in which pollen from the surrounding trees and plants was laid down in the sediments on its bottom. There are comparable deposits at Marks Tey, near Colchester. Pollen grains are almost indestructible, and each plant produces a quite distinctive pollen grain, so that they serve almost as plant fingerprints. The pollen grains can be identified under the microscope. It is from this evidence that a picture of the surrounding vegetation emerges. A mixed forest developed, first of all of birch followed by pine, to which oak, elm, alder, lime, and hazel were in due course added, and at a later stage silver fir, spruce, and hornbeam, together with some plants no longer to be found in Britain, including a water fern, *Azolla Filiculoides,* found now only in America. At one period there was a marked reduction in the number of trees, and a landscape of grassland and herbaceous plants is

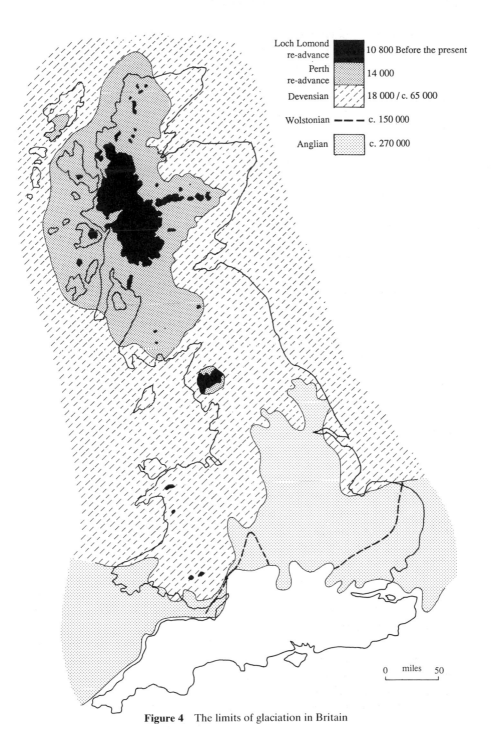

Loch Lomond re-advance		10 800 Before the present
Perth re-advance		14 000
Devensian		18 000 / c. 65 000
Wolstonian	— — —	c. 150 000
Anglian		c. 270 000

Figure 4   The limits of glaciation in Britain

recorded. From this level also come some of the oldest human artefacts so far known in Britain, and at Marks Tey charcoal has been found in the contemporary lake sediments. Had a deposit of this kind been dated to the Neolithic period it would have been added to the rapidly growing number of sites providing clear evidence of man's ability to interfere with his environment on a large scale and over a long period of time, but it is Lower Palaeolithic, and at present it is difficult to accept that men at this time had such mastery, so the interpretation of this site remains at the moment conjectural.

Some 200,000 years ago the ice returned once more to Britain, a glacial period known from its type site at Wolston, in Warwickshire, as the Wolstonian. Its extent and duration are not exactly known, but it seems to have covered much of the midlands, perhaps as far south as the Chilterns, and it may well have lasted for some 50,000 years, slowly giving way to a long warm period during which, at its maximum, temperatures in the summer may on average have been up to 3 degrees Centigrade higher than they are today. This is the Ipswichian interglacial, again named from its type site, although there are also very well known river sands from Trafalgar Square in London which have yielded a detailed picture of what conditions were like at the height of this interglacial. Plant, mollusc, and beetle remains all point to a warmer climate than that of today, and the fauna included *Elephas antiquus,* rhinoceros, and hippopotamus. There is the distinct possibility that so much ice melted during this interglacial period that the sea-level rose sufficiently to cut Britain off from the rest of Europe, thus preventing the return of the silver fir, a tree extinguished in Britain during the previous glacial and one which has not returned since.

Some 65,000–70,000 years ago the plant communities of the Ipswichian interglacial began to break up as the climate turned colder and the glaciers once again returned. This glaciation is called the Devensian in Britain and it correlates very closely with the Weichselian glaciation of northern Europe. Its type site in this country is at Four Ashes, in Staffordshire. More is known about this glaciation and its breakup than about any other, not least because it is the last and the latest, and its evidence remains comparatively undisturbed. It is from this time too that a further powerful tool becomes available to students. This is radio-carbon dating, which has an accurate, effective span of just about 70,000 years. Its application over the last twenty-five years in archaeology and palaeo-ecology has revolutionized our knowledge of the past.

The extent of the Devensian glaciation in Britain is marked by the limits of the Newer Drift (see Figure 5), although it is clear that conditions in the glacier-free areas of southern Britain were very harsh, with permafrost and periglacial soil disturbances. It is also now clear that this glaciation was not a period of uninterrupted intense cold, but that there were several interstadials, that is periods when temperatures ameliorated sufficiently to

Free of glacial drift

Limit of the
Newer Drift

Southern limit
of Old Drift

0   miles   50

Figure 5   The limits of the Old and New Glacial Drift

allow some vegetation to appear but not enough to permit the formation of the temperate deciduous woodland that would be found in a full interglacial. From Chelford in Cheshire, for example, there is evidence of a cool interstadial some 60,000 years ago, with a vegetation of pine, spruce, and fir, together with their associated beetles, such as today would be found in northern Finland, and a similar interstadial, based on evidence from terrace gravels of the River Salwarpe, near Upton Warren in Worcestershire, shows a vegetation that would be characteristic of southern Sweden today, although the mammoth, bison, reindeer, and woolly rhinoceros also found at Upton Warren have long disappeared from Scandinavia.

The Devensian ice at its maximum extent, perhaps 18,000 years ago, swept in one huge unbroken mass from Greenland to the Plato Putorana in north central Siberia, and the southern North Sea was an ice-dammed lake with a river draining southwestwards through what is now the Straits of Dover and the English Channel to reach the sea far to the west of Brittany and Land's End. By about 15,000 years ago the ice was in full retreat. This seems to have been checked for a while in what is called the Perth Re-advance (see Figure 4) although it would appear that this was not a return everywhere to full glacial conditions. By about 12,700 years ago the whole of Britain may have been free of ice, a period of climatic improvement known as the Allerød interstadial. There was a sudden fall in temperatures about 11,500 years ago and the glaciers began to reappear in the western Highlands of Scotland, to reach their maximum extent about 10,800 years ago, a period known as the Loch Lomond Re-advance. Temperatures then rose almost as rapidly as they had fallen so that the last ice sheets had gone by about 10,000 years ago.

The speed of our gallop through time is now slowing down dramatically. At the beginning of this chapter hundreds of millions of years were dismissed in a line or two, and then the pace slowed to tens of millions of years. The last paragraphs have been concerned with the last million years, a period in which there have been at least four long periods of intense cold with almost the whole of Britain submerged beneath ice sheets which must on occasion have been several thousands of feet thick, and over the last hundred thousand years we have seen temperatures oscillate quite rapidly to give cool periods with coniferous forests like those to be found in Scandinavia today. Several interglacial periods have lasted at least twice as long as the 10,000 years which have elapsed since the last ice sheets vanished from Britain, and, as we shall see in a moment, mean annual temperatures have continued to fluctuate quite widely ever since. In other words we may well be living in yet another interglacial, perhaps, for all we know, a comparatively short one in geological terms, and at some time in the not-too-distant future the glaciers may well start to form again on the northern flanks of Ben Nevis and begin to make their inexorable descent into the lowlands.

Glaciation is one of the most obvious ways in which climate is reflected in the landscape, since ice and frost unleash an entirely new set of geomorphological processes on to the moulding of landforms. We shall look at these processes at work in a moment, after we have brought the story of the British climate down to the present.

It appears that mean annual temperatures continued to rise steadily to reach a climatic optimum between seven and five thousand years ago. The climate was both warmer and drier than it is today, with the mean July temperature 2 or 3 degrees Centigrade higher, bringing with it a longer growing season and the cultivation of upland areas of Britain. There was then a slow deterioration to a wetter, cooler climate, with a sharper fall between about 1000 BC and 50 BC. By the beginning of the Christian era the climate was again improving, to reach the medieval optimum between about 950 and 1200 AD, and once again the margins of cultivation were pushed up the hillsides. From the end of the thirteenth century the Little Ice Age gripped Europe. The wet cold summers of 1313–17 and 1433–8 led to famine on a European scale, and those of the 1590s brought severe shortages in Britain and a reference in *A Midsummer Night's Dream*. The 1690s were also years of harsh weather, crop failures, and famine in Scotland. The winter of 1564–5 was the longest and most severe for over a century and there were severe winters in 1684, 1708–9, and in 1740. Rivers froze over and frost fairs were held on the Thames. By the end of the seventeenth century the growing season had been shortened by from three to five weeks, and permanent snow is recorded in the Cairngorms throughout the seventeenth and for much of the eighteenth century. There was a series of great storms throughout the Little Ice Age. Extensive peat cuttings near the coast were flooded by the sea during one of these, to form the Norfolk Broads. Sand dunes blown in from the sea overwhelmed the fertile farmlands of Culbin, on the southern shores of the Moray Firth, in the late seventeenth century, and Leland, writing in the early sixteenth century, records the disappearance of several Cornish churches beneath coastal dunes.

The climate once again showed some improvement during the second half of the nineteenth century, to reach a minor optimum between 1933 and 1952, to be followed by further cooling, especially since 1960, and a shortening of the growing season by about ten days a year, largely the consequence of wet cold weather in the spring, that of 1986 being the coldest for fifty years.

Climate is a factor in man's relationship with his environment which can be all too easily overlooked. Climatic fluctuation, when combined with variations in altitude and aspect, can influence profoundly the vegetational cover, including that part of it grown to satisfy human needs, even over quite short distances. A south-facing valley slope will have a longer growing season than the slope facing north on the other side of the valley, whilst the higher slopes on both sides will be both cooler and have shorter growing seasons. The mean temperature is reduced by 1 degree Fahrenheit for every 300 feet in altitude, and the growing season is reduced by ten days for every 260 feet. The prevailing winds in Britain are from the southwest, and the highest ground in Britain is to be found in the north and the west. The result is that the highland areas of Britain also have the heaviest rainfall, up to 200 inches in a year in the wettest places in northwest Scotland and the Lake District, the longest snow cover, the most cloud and the least sunshine of any part of Britain. This means that the only cereal crop that will grow and ripen is oats, that soils are often poor and acidic because the rainfall leaches out the nutrients, so that large areas of upland

Britain are given over to coarse pasture, and that the winters are so harsh that livestock cannot survive outside, and so has to be brought into byres and pens. The east of England is both drier and warmer than the west and north. In East Anglia rainfall can be as little as 20 inches in a year, and in the Breckland it was so dry in the seventeenth century that the vegetation could not cover the ground and there were extensive sand blows. Around the coasts of Britain the sharp increase in windiness combined with the effects of salt spray mean that trees are often stunted and deformed, or, as in much of Cornwall and the Outer Hebrides, they are almost entirely absent save in the most favoured spots. There are of course very wide local variations within this very generalized picture, so that unique local combinations of aspect, altitude, and topography produce widely differing microclimates over very short distances.

Climatic fluctuations which are insufficient to bring about an ice age can nevertheless profoundly affect man's relationship with his environment. Worsening weather in the later middle ages drove men and women down from the uplands where they had once been able to cultivate their fields, and at the same time contemporaries were compelled to leave their villages on the lowland clays or risk sinking into a quagmire of mud caused by excessive rainfall.

Thus, if the underlying geological structure of Britain is the first of the great, impersonal building blocks from which the landscape is made, then climate is perhaps the most significant of the independent factors which have gone into its shaping over time.

We must now retrace our steps to look at the impact of the successive ice ages upon the underlying geological structure of the landscape by studying first of all the impact of the ice upon existing landforms; second, those created by the ice; third, the soils which have evolved upon these landforms, and finally the animals and plants which have colonized these soils.

The ice of slowly but inexorably moving glaciers can exert enormous forces to erode and mould the landscape over which it passes. It can be so thick as to cause the land itself to sink beneath the superincumbent weight. It can scour a landscape clean of soil and loose rocks, exposing very ancient land surfaces which in turn it will scratch, abrade, and polish. The materials thus picked up become embedded in the sole of the glacier, and this, by acting like very coarse sandpaper, serves to speed up these processes. Pressure and low temperatures can search out weaknesses and faults in the underlying rocks, exploit them and force out pieces of rock, a process which can develop very extensively as successive faults appear. To these processes of gouging, plucking, abrading, and polishing performed by the ice itself must be added depositional ones as the ice melts, dumping often vast quantities of debris to be dispersed, sorted, or bypassed by meltwaters.

These processes can profoundly affect landforms and can also remove almost all trace both of preglacial landforms and the effects of earlier glacial and interglacial conditions. As Figure 4 shows, almost the whole of Britain north of the Thames has been subjected to the effects of glaciation, but its imprint is not everywhere immediately apparent. The last, Devensian, glaciation was less extensive than previous ones, its furthest limits being marked by the boundary between the Older Drift and the Newer. The area of the Older Drift remained free from ice during the last glaciation with the result that earlier glacial landforms, such as drumlins, kames, eskers, and moraines, have been extensively remodelled by other erosional processes, although thick spreads of glacial till and outwash gravels still remain.

The landscape of the Newer Drift bears much more extensive and widespread evidence of the power of the glaciers to mould and shape the landscape. Those glacial deposition landforms already mentioned – eskers, kames, drumlins, and moraines – are very common in the lowland areas of the Newer Drift, whilst upland areas bear the evidence of the erosional power of glaciers, and nowhere in Britain more obviously than in the western Highlands and islands of Scotland.

The main north–south mountain watershed of the Highlands, from Sutherland to Mull, is breached by over thirty major glacial troughs. Loch Ness, 754 feet deep and 23 miles long, with valley sides rising steeply to 1,500 feet, is one of the largest glacial troughs in Britain. Loch Morar, another great trough, is 1,017 feet deep, whilst near Ben Starav the glacial trough is more than 4,000 feet deep, from the top of Ben Starav itself to the floor of Loch Etive. Several of these glacial troughs stretch well beyond the present coastline. The Sound of Mull is a submerged trough, whilst the Sound of Raasay, 1,062 feet deep and the greatest depth in British coastal waters, is another. Many of these troughs are U-shaped and others are V-shaped, whilst yet others, Glen Nevis for example, have both profiles in alternation, dictated by the differential powers of successive rock formations to resist glacial erosion.

The landscape of western Scotland is also marked by large numbers of ice-formed corries, or cirques. These are valley heads which have become filled with snow. This becomes compacted into ice which in its turn cuts into the back wall by plucking, at the same time gouging out the floor as it starts to move out and downhill to form a glacier. When the ice melts some material is dumped at the lip of the corrie to dam in a small lake or lochan, as in the corries of Coire an-t-Sneachda, Coire an Lochain and Lochan Uaine, in the Cairngorms. Sometimes two corries are formed back-to-back and the dividing rock is reduced to a thin sharp-crested precipice, or arête, as has occurred in the Cuillins for example. In the corries on the northeastern slopes of Ben Nevis snow frequently lasts the summer. It will be from here that the glaciers will re-emerge should the mean annual temperature ever fall permanently by more than about 3 degrees Centigrade.

3 The Grey Mare's Tail, in the heavily glaciated Moffat Water Valley, Dumfriesshire.

The eastern Highlands of Scotland are generally less affected by glacial erosion than the western, although the river Dee rises in a deep ice-eroded trough in the Cairngorms, and several of its tributaries also occupy glacial troughs, Glen Geusachan and Glen Luibeg for example, and Glen Derry.

A similar pattern is to be found in the Southern Uplands, where the western hills are quite severely glaciated with numerous corries and a number of U-shaped valleys, of which Moffat Water is a splendid example. Here the waterfall of the Grey Mare's Tail plunges over 700 feet from a hanging valley, itself created by glacial action, and draining Loch Skene, a lake impounded by glacial moraine and lying in an upland basin surrounded by corries. In the eastern Southern Uplands, however, the hills are less obviously glaciated, although in the lowland area of the Merse of Berwick there are large spreads of glacial boulder clay, outwash and drumlins, which are elongated mounds of glacial debris, often occurring in very large numbers and orientated in the direction of the ice flow. Drumlins are also to be found in the valley of the Clyde and in lowland Wigtownshire. A rather similar feature but on a large scale is the crag and tail formations to be found in the Central Lowlands. The crag, or hill, is composed of a highly resistant rock mass, often a volcanic plug, which has stood in the path of the glacier, giving some protection to the tail which slopes gently away on the downstream side. Edinburgh castle stands on such a crag, and the city was built on the line of the tail.

As temperatures began to rise again the ice started to decay. The debris carried in the ice was dumped, and immense quantities of water released. Drumlins appear to have been formed beneath the ice, whilst moraines are composed of huge quantities of unsorted materials dumped at the glacier's snout, and eskers are ridges of materials deposited by meltwaters. At the same time as the ice melted, its weight was removed from the land surface, causing it to rebound. This is isostatic uplift. In due course the melting water returns to the sea, causing sea-levels to rise. This is eustatic sea rise. The two processes do not always synchronize. Sometimes there are extensive marine transgressions. At one period only 5 miles of land separated the Firths of Clyde and Forth, and whale skeletons have been found to the west of Stirling. In other periods successive movements of isostatic uplift have raised coastal beaches above sea-level, to create the spectacular raised beach gravels on the western side of Loch Tarbet, on the island of Jura.

Glacial dumping can block drainage, creating moraine-blocked lakes and lochs. Only glacial moraine separates Loch Lomond from the sea, whilst the parallel Roads of Glen Roy represent the successive shore lines of a series of ice-dammed glacial lakes. Glacial meltwaters eroded extensive networks of channels and eskers, creating an often chaotic landscape of humps and hollows as they sorted, sifted, and transported the glacial till. A striking example of such a landscape is to be found at Coir'a'Cheud-chnoic, on the shores of Glen Torridon. Meltwaters could also create extensive fans of sorted and graded sands and gravels. One outwash spread near Blair Gowrie covers 10 square miles.

We have taken several paragraphs to study the effects of glaciation on the landforms of Scotland. This is only appropriate, since it is here that the hand of the ice lies most heavily and most obviously, profoundly affecting very many aspects of Scottish landscape history. Settlement patterns and the organization of the cultivation of the soil will, for example, be intimately shaped and moulded, either by what the glaciers have removed or else by what they have left behind, since over 60 per cent of the Scottish landscape is covered with glacial till. Across the rest of Britain the more obvious glacial landforms are more localized than in Scotland, and in the areas of the Older Drift they are almost entirely absent.

In England it is the Lake District which displays the most heavily glaciated landscape. From a central area of ice accumulation a series of glacial troughs radiate outwards to form the lakes, plugged, as is Windermere for example, by glacial moraines. Just north of the ferry is a flat terrace, evidence of a higher lake level. Glacial debris, augmented by river-borne alluvium, is all that separates Derwentwater and Bassenthwaite, Buttermere and Crummockwater. Derwentwater itself has a very uneven bed of glacial debris, and it is very likely that its islands, Derwent Isle and St Herbert's Island, are in fact a partially submerged esker. Many of the high tarns, Red Tarn for example, Angle Tarn, and Blea Water, lie in ice-formed corries, known locally as coves, whilst corries created two of the best-known features of the Lake District, the arêtes of Striding Edge

4 The boulder-strewn course of Styhead Gill, south of Seathwaite, Cumberland, with grass-covered mounds of glacial drift on the right of the picture.

and Swirral Edge. The boggy moss below Blea Water is all that is left of a once large lake, held up by a moraine dam, now breached and drained by Blea Water Beck. Much of the upper part of Borrowdale was also once a lake, with end moraines at Rosthwaite and Thornythwaite to show where once the glacier snout halted sufficiently long to dump at least part of its load of debris, whilst the footpath from Seathwaite to Stockley Bridge threads its way through a chaotic, tumbled landscape composed of mounds of grass-covered glacial drift.

The glacial troughs often created a series of hanging valleys, usually marked by waterfalls, as where Swindale Forces carry Mosedale Beck some 500 feet down in to Swindale, and Watendlath Beck plunges into Borrowdale. Different glacial erosion is also a prominent feature of the Lake District landscape. The comparative uniformity of the Skiddaw Slates has produced a more rounded topography, whilst the much more varied Borrowdale volcanic rocks, alternately hard and soft, have produced under glaciation an irregular, craggy topography. Finally, lower ground and valley floors in the Lake District are often the sites of drumlin swarms, in the Esthwaite valley for example, in the area to the south of Kendal and in the Eden valley.

The landscape of north Wales has also been dramatically affected by glaciation. A series of corries surrounds Snowdon, creating a distinctive radial pattern of precipitous arêtes, with small lakes filling many of the

5   The rugged landscape of the hard Borrowdale volcanic rocks, a scene near Thirlmere in the Lake District.

6 Pickmere, Cheshire.

corries. A splendid example of a lake-filled corrie is Llyn-y-cae, on Cader Idris, and there is another at Cwm Idwel, where the lake is dammed in by a crescent-shaped moraine perched on the lip of the rock basin. Many of the valleys show the over-deepened U- and V-shaped profiles so characteristic of glacier troughs – the Pass of Llanberis for example, the Cwellyn valley, Nant Gwynbant and Nant Ffrancon.

In England the southern limits of the Newer Drift are marked by the Cheshire Plain, the Vale of York and the Lincolnshire coastlands. The Cheshire Plain is thickly covered with boulder clay intermingled with spreads of outwash sands and gravels, with many of the hollows in this glacial till filled with small lakes or meres, Pickmere for example. The Vale of York was once an ice-dammed lake, its southern edge being marked by the dry morainic ridge which, standing above the marshy lowland of the valley of the Ouse, provides the site for the city of York itself. A similar glacial lake filled the valley of the Trent as far south as Nottingham, and another lay on the eastern side of the Lincoln Cliff and extended far into the fens, to lay the foundations of the seaward silts and inland peats that characterize the structure of the low-lying lands which today drain into the Wash.

In the lands of the Older Drift the effects of glaciation are far less obvious, but no less important. Boulder clays, sands, and gravels which are glacial, but Wolstonian, not Devensian, in their origins, provide much of the surface deposits of England north of the Thames, profoundly influencing settlement patterns, land usage, and agricultural practices over wide areas, but with an almost infinite variety, so that one corner of a field can be a sticky morass of boulder clay and another a well-drained patch of glacial sand.

Even where the ice never penetrated, however, conditions of intense cold would have created a tundra landscape stretching for many miles beyond the edges of the glaciers themselves. The action of frost in these periglacial conditions would have been particularly powerful. Alternate freezing and thawing shattered the granite tors of Devon and Cornwall. It would also break up soil and rock on slopes, and gravity would bring masses of loosened materials sliding down, like some muddy, half-frozen avalanche, to come to rest in a valley bottom. This process of solifluction is almost certainly responsible for the deposits of combe rock which fill the dry valleys of the chalklands of southern England. It also created the frost-riven edges or 'scars' of the Millstone grits and Carboniferous limestones of the Pennines. Strong winds blowing across land surfaces bare of vegetation would remove the finest particles, to redeposit them as loess, a soil structure to be found in many areas of southern England.

The last glaciers and ice sheets probably took less than a thousand years to melt away, and by about ten thousand years ago the land of Britain was completely free of ice. The regions of the oldest rocks, the north and the west, had been profoundly affected by the erosional powers of the ice, so that, paradoxically, the oldest rocks show the youngest landforms. Valleys of great depth had been gouged out in Snowdonia, the Lake District, and the western Highlands. The complex folds of the Grampians had been planed down to leave a region of high plateaux dissected by valleys. The ancient rocks of the Outer Hebrides had been reduced to a gaunt, bare surface only a little above sea-level. Everywhere vast quantities of rock, soil, and surface debris had been stripped away, crushed and flattened under the enormous weight of the ice, transported, sometimes over great distances, to be dumped as the glaciers thawed, and then sorted, graded and yet further dispersed by the rushing meltwaters from the glacier's edge.

If the mountains of Scotland, Wales, and the Lake District show the erosional powers of the ice, then everywhere else in Britain north of the Thames reveals its depositional powers, whilst the region south of the Thames shows the capacity of frost over long periods to shape land-forms. Glacial till, an agglomerate of silts, clays, muds, sands, gravels, and loose rocks, from pieces the size of a thimble to massive boulders weighing many tons, was plastered over much of lowland Britain and in numerous valley floors and plateau tops in upland Britain. Sometimes it was a heavily impacted, unsorted mass producing a chaotic landscape of humps and hollows. Sometimes, especially where meltwaters had been at work, it was sorted, graded, and smoothed down, whilst solifluction would bring masses of mud and rock slithering down valley slopes to collapse on the valley floor, there to be further sorted and dispersed by other geomorphological processes.

Figure 6 The Highland and Lowland Zones

Aeons of geological time have provided the underlying structures of the British landscape. The enormous powers of the glaciers have shaped them into the landforms of today. They have combined to produce an island which may be divided into two broadly contrasting regions, the Highland Zone and the Lowland Zone (see Figure 6). The Highland Zone, lying in the north and west of the island, is a region of mountains, thin acidic soils, and a harsh climate, although it is important to appreciate that, compared with those of European landforms, British altitudes are low. Uplands are generally considered to begin at 700 feet above sea-level, mountains at 2,000 feet, and the highest point in Britain, Ben Nevis, is only 4,406 feet above sea-level, whereas Mont Blanc, the highest mountain in Europe, is well over 15,000 feet, nearly four times as high. The Lowland Zone, a region of low, rounded hills, deep fertile soils, and a more smiling climate, forms the south and the east of the island.

Generalizations of this kind conceal much local and regional variation, and it is impossible to draw a firm dividing line between the two regions. Nevertheless the terms Highland and Lowland Zones provide convenient shorthand expressions covering a range of differences which have existed in one form or another since the Bronze Age. The Lowland Zone, lying nearest to Europe, has been quick to receive and adopt new ideas, ideas which have penetrated the Highland Zone only very slowly and often only when they have been adapted to suit its own range of conditions. The contrasts between the two regions are very real, and have influenced profoundly the evolution of their respective landscapes.

With the structures and forms of Britain in being, the story of their moulding into the landscape of today begins, and it is not too much of an exaggeration to say that this story takes its origins at the dripping, thawing snout of a glacier, some 10,000 years ago.

It is very likely that Scotland and almost the whole of Wales were entirely devoid of life of any kind at the height of the last glaciation. Beyond the edges of the glaciers, however, in the lands of the Older Drift, was a rich and varied Arctic flora and fauna, and the caves at Creswell Crags in Derbyshire, in a gorge formed by the action of surface drainage working on the Magnesian limestone and first occupied during the Ipswichian interglacial, some 100,000 years ago, were inhabited on a seasonal basis by a small community of men and women living in an Arctic environment of the harshest kind.

Once the great thaw had set in, then life would return very quickly to the bare surfaces exposed by the melting ice. Plants and animals would colonize the open ground as soon as conditions were right, and each group would pave the way for its successors. Mosses, lichens, grasses, and sedges would colonize the bare glacial till. Their demands for nutrients and root-hold, together with their own organic remains, would combine with chemical and physical weathering processes to produce the first soils, in

7   One of the cave entrances at Creswell Crags Gorge, on the borders of Nottinghamshire
and Derbyshire.

which larger plants could gain a foothold. It is most important to
appreciate that the soil itself, as with every other facet of the total
landscape, has its own history. Very many historians and archaeologists
still tend to think that modern soil classifications, such as those carried out
by the Ministry of Agriculture, can be projected back into the past. This is
patently not true. Modern soil structures cannot be used to explain
settlement patterns and agricultural practices in the past since it is clear
that the soils of today are themselves the end-product of some 5,000 years
of cultivation. Soils are dynamic systems in which change is governed by a
range of factors at work over time, factors which include climate, relief,
parent material, and the impact of plants and animals. This last, the biotic
factor, is probably the most important at work in the conversion of the raw
parent materials into soils. As we have seen, much of Britain is covered

with glacial till, a material which may vary enormously in constitution, structure, and depth. This is the basic parent material with which plants and animals have to work. Micro-organisms, insects, and worms working with and through plant remains of every kind, attack the fabric of the topmost layers of the raw mineral parent material, creating the humus A level of a typical soil profile. The soluble complexes, especially of iron and aluminium, created in the A level are then leached out by percolating water to be redeposited as a separate B horizon between the humus and the C horizon, the parent material. As the accumulating soils become deeper and richer so they are colonized by a succession of plants until a climax vegetation is reached, which in Britain is mixed deciduous woodland. Continuous woodland cover provides excellent drainage. A mature oak tree gives off several gallons of water a day by transpiration through its leaves. This cover reduces exposure to winds, gives a leaf litter rich in animal life, including earthworms, and reduces the splash or impact effect of raindrops. Trees bring up nutrients from the C horizon through their root systems and these are returned to the soil through leaf fall. But the rich brown earth soils beneath mature woodland evolve only very slowly and their pedogenic equilibrium is finely balanced. Interference with the vegetational cover on any scale can tip this balance towards soil degradation, waterlogging, podsolization, the development of acid mor and the appearance of heath and bog, and these developments are often irreversible. As we shall see in the next chapter, it is men, going about their everyday lives, who have removed this vegetational cover, and they began this work some 7,000 or 8,000 years ago.

It is unlikely that Britain was entirely free of vegetation, even at the height of the last ice age. Sediments from the former glacial kettle hole which is now Blelham bog, near Windermere, date from 12,000 to 13,000 years ago, and show a late-glacial Arctic alpine vegetation that included *dryas octopetala,* lichens, algae, *Cladocera, Rumex,* willow, juniper, dwarf birch, reeds and sedges. As conditions improved an open tundra landscape was colonized by birch and pine, followed by hazel, oak, and elm, with alder in suitably damp places, and ash on limestone. The more warmth-loving lime, beech, and hornbeam arrived last. By 9,700 years ago birch and hazel were established at Din Moss, in Roxburghshire, to be followed by oak and elm over the next thousand years. By 9,000 years ago birch and hazel woodland was established in Caithness and Skye. By 7,500 years ago the forest cover had reached its optimum. Mixed deciduous woodland was to be found everywhere up to at least 2,500 feet, with a belt of scrub for the next 500 feet until natural open grassland began at about 3,000 feet. Only those areas in which it was physically impossible for trees to grow were open – marshlands, cliffs, the seashore, the sugar limestones of Upper Teesdale. In other words, at its maximum the forest covered the open fells of the Lake District, the bleak Yorkshire and Derbyshire moors, the mountains of Wales and the Highlands of Scotland up to about 2,500 feet. Even the Isle of Lewis and the windswept coasts of Cornwall were wooded, with birch-hazel scrub the vegetational climax on Orkney.

There was of course much local variation in the nature and composition of this woodland, depending upon micro-environments which could vary from one valley side to the next. The British flora is to be seen as an outpost of the much wider and larger European flora, almost all of it migrating here before the last land link with Europe, a flat marshy bridge from Lincolnshire to north Germany, was finally severed about 7,800 years ago. Vegetational distribution is influenced by a complex interplay of climate, altitude, and aspect, together with soil or edaphic factors, and it is probably better to think in terms of a series of vegetational climaxes rather than one which was to be found throughout Britain. In Scotland, for example, the natural woodland climax was pine forest rather than deciduous woodland. Of this natural climax woodland, whatever its composition, nothing now survives. Abernethy Forest, in Inverness, is perhaps now the nearest approach to the natural Scottish pine forest, and on Creag Fhiaclach, in the northwestern Cairngorms, at an altitude of 1,900 feet, there is one of the few semi-natural altitudinal limits of sub-alpine scrub to be found anywhere in Europe. Elsewhere in Britain today, the vegetation has everywhere been modified by human activity, although some plant communities, largely left alone for several hundred years, have come to resemble semi-natural communities. Very occasionally relics of an older vegetation survive. In Upper Teesdale and Craven are the last relics of a sub-alpine vegetation. Here *dryas octopetala,* alpine bartsia, the hair sedge, alpine foxtail, alpine forget-me-not, bitter milkwort, and the dwarf birch, *betula nana,* retain a precarious foothold, and have done so since the last ice age.

As the immediate postglacial tundra gave way to woodland, so the fauna of Britain also changed. Herds of reindeer, bison, horse, and giant Irish elk were replaced by forest animals, red deer, the wild boar, and the aurochs. Once again, however, it is human interference which has destroyed the larger, the more dangerous and the more spectacular animals. Reindeer were still to be found in Caithness in the tenth century, and the last wolves were killed in the Monadhliath Mountains and Speyside in 1743. The lemming and the northern lynx disappeared from Scotland at the beginning of the Christian era. The last brown bear was killed in the tenth century, whilst the beaver survived in the Highlands of Scotland until the sixteenth century, and the wild boar until about the same period. Kites and ravens were common over England until the eighteenth century, when polecats were still to be found in Chiltern woodlands. The great bustard inhabited Salisbury Plain until 1810, and the last native Large Copper butterfly was taken from Bottisham Fen in 1851.

The recolonization of the land as the ice thawed took place very quickly, and men were among the earliest animals to appear in the bleak, open landscapes. Their coming gives to the history of the landscape an entirely new dimension, since it is human beings, living and working in social groups, who will from now on constitute the single most important factor at work in its evolution. Almost from the first men have had some capacity to shape and mould their environment for themselves, their stone axes and their use of fire being much more powerful tools than is generally appreciated. As their technology develops so too does their mastery over their environment, with two very important interrelated consequences. Men could live within a few miles of the glacier's edge, and the 'last frontier' in Britain melted away as the glaciers melted. Nowhere in Britain has been either unoccupied for very long or allowed to remain in a 'natural' state for very long since that last thaw took place. Nevertheless, the environment which successive generations of men and women have constructed for themselves over the last ten thousand years could only have been built from the raw materials which it has been the object of this chapter to describe.

2

The first men

The first chapter of this book was concerned with the evolution of the fundamental structures of the landscape of Britain. We have seen these structures evolve over inconceivably long periods of time to reach their present forms, and we have been able to tell their story with no more than a sidelong glance at men, not least because men have made no contribution whatsoever to the evolution of the British landscape down to the stage where we left it at the end of the last chapter. But with these structures established, we must now turn our attention to those men and women who, by going about the everyday business of their lives, have moulded and shaped these structures into an inhabitable environment. To this environment successive generations have each made their own distinctive contribution without erasing entirely that of their predecessors, so that the landscape of today resembles a palimpsest from which even the most ancient texts can be recovered, at least in part, and provided we know where to look and what to look for.

The story of the earliest men in Britain is surrounded with difficulties and controversies because the evidence is so fragmentary and has been so much altered by the effects of recent glaciations. There is now however reasonably firm evidence from Westbury-sub-Mendip of the presence of men in Britain before the onset of the Anglian glaciation, and more controversial evidence from Kent's Cavern, near Torquay, and from Fordwich, in Kent. The Anglian glaciation was the most extensive over Britain, reaching to the river Thames, and so it is very unlikely that there was any permanent settlement by human beings anywhere in Britain whilst it was at its height.

For the Hoxnian interglacial there is much more substantial evidence of the presence of men, from sites at Hoxne itself, from Clacton-on-Sea in

Essex and from Swanscombe in Kent. Indeed it has been suggested that during this interglacial the southeastern corner of England provided so favourable an environment that it was densely inhabited by groups of hunters and gatherers, communities which seem to have had a distinct preference for sites beside large sheets of water, whether lakes or rivers. It is impossible to measure their power over their environment, but on occasion it may have been considerable. The presence of charcoal in sediments from both Hoxne and Marks Tey has already been mentioned, and it may well represent fires started deliberately in order to drive game. The site at Clacton has yielded a wooden spear, and one at Stoke Newington sharpened birch poles. Clearly the stone tools of these men were quite capable of felling trees and shaping wood. A human cranium recovered from late Hoxnian levels at Swanscombe seems to show that these men were almost certainly *Homo cf. sapiens,* but their relationship to modern man, *Homo sapiens sapiens,* remains at present unclear.

These men are so shadowy, and they lived so long ago, that nothing of their handiwork has survived the effects of later glacial and other geomorphological processes, but their presence in the landscape, beyond the veil of the Devensian glaciation, deserves more than just a fleeting glance, not least because they almost certainly occupied the southeastern corner of Britain for a longer period of time than has elapsed since the end of the Devensian glaciation.

The climate has fluctuated since Hoxnian times with what seems, in geological terms, bewildering rapidity, causing the ice sheets and glaciers to ebb and flow with astonishing speed. In human terms, of course, these movements were scarcely perceptible, and men and women lived out their lives almost unaware of the long-term changes taking place in their environments. As the glaciers advanced, men would have been compelled to retreat, but so slowly that ancient hunting grounds, engulfed by the ice, would have been a matter of legend rather than practical experience. As the ice thawed, they would have returned, sometimes only in summer hunting parties, sometimes to take up permanent residence in caves and rock shelters. Successive layers from Kent's Cavern show how some very favoured sites have been occupied, deserted, and reoccupied over thousands of years, although no British cave can show the artistic treasures of some of the caves of northern Spain and southwestern France.

The last glaciation, the Devensian, seems to have reached its greatest extent some 18,000 to 15,000 years ago. It seems very unlikely that there were any permanent communities of men and women in Britain during this long period of time. However, at the Paviland Cave in the Gower peninsula, the Reverend William Buckland found in 1823 the skeleton which has ever since been known as the Red Lady of Paviland. In fact it was a young man. He had clearly been deliberately buried, and his body covered with powdered red ochre. The skeleton is still preserved, and a radio-carbon date obtained from collagen attached to one of the bones gives 16510±340 bc, a date when the Devensian glaciation was at its height, although the Gower peninsula was itself probably free from ice. In spite of the seeming precision of the radio-carbon date there are a number of anomalies about this cave site which cannot at present be satisfactorily resolved. What is interesting about it, however, is what it reveals of human mental preoccupations. Death and burial must have been of real significance, with all that this implies of religious beliefs and values, of supporting rituals and of wider social and political contexts. What these beliefs were we have no way of discovering, but of the existence of sophisticated patterns of human values and behaviour at so remote a period in the past there can be no doubt.

As the Devensian glaciers retreated for the last time and plants and animals recolonized the bare ground, so men also returned to occupy or reoccupy caves as soon as conditions became at all tolerable. Kent's Cavern, Wookey Hole, Creswell Crags, Kirkhead Cave in Lancashire, Victoria Cave near Settle, Kendrick's Cave near Llandudno, Fox Hole Cave in Staffordshire were all occupied or reoccupied in the last stages of the last glaciation, although on present evidence at any rate it would seem that men did not make the crossing into Orkney until about 5000 BC. This brings to an end any kind of moving 'frontier' of human occupation that there might have been across the landscape of Britain. Men have lived everywhere in Britain since the end of the last ice age and there have been no geological or geographical restrictions which they have not at some time been able to overcome. Any apparent connection between the distribution of known occupation sites from any period of British history, from prehistoric to medieval, and such topographical factors as soil type, is purely fortuitous, depending as it does upon the survival and the discovery of such sites and upon the differential activities of archaeologists.

The climatic amelioration which brought about the end of the last ice sheets also set in train considerable changes in the lifestyles of the men and women who occupied the new lands. As the open tundra vegetation gave way to closed woodland so the herds of reindeer, horse, elk, and mammoth were replaced by woodland animals such as red deer, wild boar, and aurochs. This change called for new tools and weapons, and at the same time stimulated the exploitation of new resources of food and shelter. Stone axes capable of felling trees were made, arrows were tipped with small flint arrow heads, harpoons were made from bone and antler, and a wide range of stone implements was made for scraping, cleaning and preparing animal skins. There seems to have been much local experiment and environmental adaptation in all this.

This long period of change, from about 10000 to about 5000 BC is traditionally labelled the Mesolithic period, although it is a label which has often been questioned and which many archaeologists would like to discard. Several thousand sites from this very long period are now known throughout Britain, the great majority only from assemblages of stone tools and waste, sometimes in very large quantities. This is because any organic remains of these people will be preserved only in very favourable conditions, particularly where the site has become waterlogged, thus preventing the decay of organic materials such as wood and bone. The most famous Mesolithic site in Britain, at Star Carr, not very far from Scarborough, is one of these.

Here, a group of men and women, perhaps about twenty-five in all, settled at the edge of what was then a lake. A platform of birch brushwood was built over a reed bed. The birch trees had been felled with axes. Radio-carbon testing of samples of the wood gives dates of 7607 and 7538 bc. Part of a wooden paddle was found, as well as rolls of birch bark which would have provided the resin with which to attach arrow heads to their shafts. Large numbers of bones and antlers from red and roe deer, elk, aurochs, and pig, as well as part of the skull of a dog, were recovered from the site. Many of the antlers had had splinters carefully removed for working up into tools and implements, and many red deer frontlets had been perforated, protuberances smoothed away and the weight reduced so that they could be tied to the heads of men. Such head dresses would almost certainly have been used for ritual or magical purposes and perhaps also as lures when men were actually hunting.

Careful analysis of the red deer antlers from Star Carr suggests that this was a seasonally occupied campsite, inhabited between October and April each year. What were its occupants doing for the rest of the year? Current thinking suggests that they moved into the uplands of the Pennines, perhaps to follow the migrating red deer. Studies of red deer in natural conditions today point to seasonal changes in their patterns of behaviour. In the summer they disperse into small groups over extensive upland ranges, congregating in large numbers over much smaller, lowland territories in the winter months. Men would have followed them. Nearly a thousand sites are now known in the Pennines. Many could have served as summer camps, and evidence is accumulating to suggest that in these summer hunting grounds men were not content to remain passive hangers-on to the coat-tails of the red deer herds, but were able and willing to take active steps to manage them. The burning of woodland produces a crop of succulent new shoots that grazing animals find particularly attractive. Improved food supplies mean more and heavier animals. That such fires were being deliberately started across wide areas of the Pennines and the North Yorkshire moors seems from present evidence to be incontrovertible. Such burning would have to be carefully controlled. It would be wasteful if too large an area was cleared since the deer would not venture too far from cover. The optimum diameter seems to be about 400 yards. The effects of such burning are temporary and wear off in as little as

five years, so that a regular cycle of repeated burnings can be envisaged. At
Soyland Moor, in the central Pennines, pollen analysis has revealed a long
period of forest burning and grazing, leading, between about 5950 and
5200 bc, to the appearance of a grass sward in the place of woodland. Very
similar clearances are to be found on Glaisdale Moor, where at North Gill
the charcoal layer was 2 inches thick, at Bonfield Gill Head on Bilsdale
East Moor, and elsewhere in the uplands of northeastern England.

Such activities produced numerous and repeated breaks in the forest
canopy, and could in time lead to permanent change in the environment.
Repeated burning leads to soil degradation. Soil structures are permanently damaged and they become increasingly acid, with lower nitrogen
status. Leaching creates a bleached layer by the removal of iron, which is
redeposited as an impermeable 'pan'. This yet further impedes drainage
and seals off the subsoil since tree roots find it almost impenetrable. The
regeneration of tree roots is prevented, and bog and heather develop
instead, the litter from heather only serving to aggravate soil degradation.
The beginnings of many British heaths and moorlands are to be found in
the activities of men, and it is of very great significance that almost all of
the Mesolithic sites discovered in the Pennines lie at the interface between
the mineral soil and the peat. Men were already beginning to modify
permanently their environment.

The melting of the last glaciers returned immense quantities of water to
the sea. This led to considerable fluctuations in sea-levels, both from
isostatic uplift as the land itself recovered from the weight of the ice and
from eustatic sea rise as the returning waters overtook the rising land.
There is much evidence to show that men were exploiting the resources of
the shoreline wherever possible. Some sites are now to be found only when
the tide is unusually low, whilst others are on raised beaches well above
today's sea-levels, and implements dredged from the bed of the North Sea
serve to underline the reality of the land bridge between Britain and
northwestern Europe.

Large middens of sea shells and other food debris are to be found on
several sites around the coasts of Britain. At Culver Well, Isle of Portland,
in Dorset, the midden is largely composed of limpet and winkle shells.
Another site at Westward Ho! in Devon contains oyster, mussel, and
limpet shells, as well as the bones of deer, pig, and hedgehog. Organic
materials here have been dated to 5200 bc. Some of the most interesting of
these shoreline sites are to be found in caves near Oban and on the
neighbouring islands off the west coast of Scotland, including Oronsay.
Shell middens here have yielded the remains of limpets, crab, scallops,
oysters, cockles, whelks, periwinkles, and mussels, together with many
bone and antler implements and a number of cowrie shells in each of which
two holes had been carefully bored, almost certainly so that they could be
strung together to form a necklace. On the island of Risga, at the mouth of

Loch Sunart, is a large midden which has yielded stone and bone implements including harpoons, awls, pins, and fish hooks; the shells of mussels, oysters, scallops, razor shells, limpets, and whelk; the bones of a wide range of fish, including tope, grey mullet, haddock, and conger eel; the bones of red deer, wild boar, otter, grey seal, and rorqual, as well as the bones of many sea birds, including gannet, cormorant, razor bill, red-breasted merganser, and the great auk. The implication that men at this time were capable of off-shore fishing from boats is reinforced by finds from a site on the east coast of Scotland, at Morton, Tentsmuir Sands, Fife. Here the bones of large codfish have been found, and a dug-out canoe has been found on the banks of the river Tay, at Friarton, Perth.

The exploitation of the abundant wild life of the forests, woodlands, sea-shores, cliffs, and coastal waters of Britain was well within the technology then available. Modern studies of those hunter-gatherer communities still surviving today would suggest however that food plants formed a greater part of the diet of prehistoric men than did animal life. The broken shells of hazel nuts are to be found, sometimes in very large numbers, on almost every Mesolithic site in Britain. Other plant remains are very much more difficult to identify since they are only rarely preserved, but it is very likely that a wide range of bulbs, roots, berries, mushrooms and other fungi, nuts, and seeds formed part of the diet of men and women of this time. The site at Morton has yielded seeds of corn spurry, chickweed, fat-hen, and orache, all of which were once food plants.

Just occasionally the sea would yield a rich bonanza. During one marine transgression the sea extended much further up the Firth of Forth than it does today. Whales were sometimes stranded on the shore. Implements of antler have been found in association with the remains of whales at Airthrey, Blair Drummond, Meiklewood, and Causewayhead. The carcasses of these animals must have provided a feast of gargantuan proportions.

Finally there is, from a number of sites, fragile and sometimes rather ambiguous evidence of huts or other shelters. At Whitcomb Hill, Winfrith Heath, in Dorset, an egg-shaped outline has been found, in a dense scatter of stones. It has been interpreted as the outline of a hut, together with a post-stump in a hole. Other post holes have been identified at Abinger, at Morton, where pits and stake holes were very numerous, and at Broom Hill, Braithfield, Hampshire, from which a date of 6565 ± 150 bc has been obtained. The form and purpose of these structures must remain very uncertain at present. They could have been huts, lean-to shelters, or even posts and rails from which to hang drying or smoking fish and meat.

For half of the time between the end of the last ice age and the present the land of Britain was populated by men and women who, from generation to generation, lived in the ways outlined all too briefly in the preceding paragraphs. Modern science has revealed that in geological

terms this was a period of rapid change, in climate, in sea-levels, and in
vegetational cover. Within the all-too-brief span of an individual human
life, however, these changes would have gone almost unnoticed. Only the
slow accumulation of experience over several generations would have
prompted adaptation to a scarcely perceptible environmental change.
None the less such adaptation did take place, and very successfully, calling
for a range of skills which today have been forgotten, as anyone who has
ever tried to strike a flake from a flint or decide whether or not to eat what
looks like a mushroom will very quickly appreciate. For 5,000 years men
and women were able to exploit a wide range of plant, animal, and mineral
resources, and their use of fire gave them the power to modify permanently
large tracts of their landscape. It seems that Iping Common, in Sussex, has
been open heathland for several thousands of years because Mesolithic
men burnt off the woodland cover, and it has never regenerated. Of their
social organization and their mental patterns we can know nothing. That
they were sophisticated and complex in ways that would be quite alien to
those of men of the late twentieth century there can be little doubt.

About 7,800 years ago the last land bridge linking Britain with the
European continent was severed as a consequence of a rise in sea-level.
This had important long-term effects. Plants and animals could no longer
migrate naturally to Britain. They would henceforth have to be brought by
men in boats. Men also could no longer move freely to Britain from
Europe, and from then on, however intimate the links and however short
and easy the voyage, ideas have always suffered a 'sea change' whilst
making the crossing.

By the middle years of the fifth millennium BC it is clear from the
archaeological record that important changes are taking place in Britain. A
society which has been based for millennia upon a hunter-gatherer outlook
is being replaced, and probably quite rapidly, by one based upon the
cultivation of crops and the raising of domestic animals. A Mesolithic
culture was giving way to a Neolithic one, again a label which is losing
much of its meaning. How far the new developments were indigenous to
Britain and how far they were based upon ideas brought in by immigrants
from Europe, it is difficult to tell. Sheep, goats, and cereals must have
come from the continent since wild stock from which cultivars could be
created did not exist in Britain. But the aurochs and the wild boar did, and
may have contributed to domesticated cattle and pigs. If the new ideas,
animals, and seed corn did come from the continent, then they could only
have come by boat, and it would not be unreasonable to expect to find the
earliest evidence of the Neolithic in the southeastern corner of Britain,
with a slow diffusion north and west. But in fact the earliest Neolithic
settlement so far discovered in the British Isles is at Ballynagilly, in County
Tyrone, Northern Ireland, with a radio-carbon date within the range
3795–3675 bc, which may be calibrated to approximately 4580 BC, and

there are other very early dates from Scotland and Yorkshire. Thus it seems very likely that the new ideas spread very rapidly and from more than one landfall.

A society which is based upon agriculture is profoundly different from one which is based upon hunting and gathering. If men are to plant crops then fields have to be cleared, the ground has to be prepared to receive the seed and fenced in to protect the growing crops from grazing animals and, most important of all, if men are to reap what they have sown then they have to build themselves permanent shelters in which to live whilst they wait for harvest time. A more settled way of life permits more complex patterns of social organization to emerge. There is evidence for all of these developments still to be seen in the landscape today.

Neolithic men came into a landscape which was still largely wooded. We have seen something of the efforts of earlier men to control their environment by burning the woodland. This may have been carried out systematically in many localities and it may have led to the permanent disappearance of the woodland in some of these localities. This is most likely in those districts where the woodland was most fragile, at the edge of its natural limits in upland areas, and over base poor soils in lowland ones. It is of course impossible to quantify the extent of this clearance, or even to locate it at all precisely.

The attack of Neolithic men on the woodland was much more sustained, much more widespread and much more successful. Radio-carbon dated pollen records from sites in the Lake District, where forest clearance near Barfield Tarn led to soil erosion, in Cambridgeshire, Norfolk, Somerset, the Wye valley, in Shropshire, Upper Teesdale, Durham, Yorkshire, mid-Wales, Gwynedd, the Grampians, the Howe of Cromar, and Dartmoor all reveal clearings made in the woodland, sometimes large, sometimes small, sometimes permanent, sometimes only temporary. Cereal pollen appears, and that of open grassland as well as the pollen of weeds nowadays associated with cultivated land, whilst the pollen of trees shows a decline. This is particularly noticeable for the elm, and there is still considerable uncertainty as to whether or not this elm decline was natural or brought about by human activity. On the one hand it may be the consequence of climatic fluctuation or of disease. On the other hand elm leaves and bark undoubtedly provide very acceptable and nutritious food for livestock, so that the decline may have been caused by excessive lopping of branches, thus preventing the formation of the seed from which the next generation of trees will develop. There is at present no certain answer to this problem.

Sometimes the trees were felled, sometimes the woodland was burned. It seems very likely that there was a period of 'slash and burn' exploitation, when areas of woodland were cleared and cultivated for a few years before a new clearing was made and the old one abandoned. Sometimes the woodland regenerated in the old clearing, sometimes the pressure of grazing livestock prevented this. Within a comparatively short space of time, perhaps less than a thousand years, a new, very much more varied, landscape had been created over Britain, a mosaic of cultivated fields and open grassland interspersed with patches of woodland, upland bog, much of it of man's own making because of his interference with the vegetational cover, and lowland marsh. Woodland was still dense and extensive, but there is evidence to show that some, at least, was managed. Wooden trackways built through the marshes of the Somerset Levels contain such large quantities of regular-sized hazel poles that they could only have been produced by coppicing, the systematic felling of shoots from the roots, or stools, of trees when they have reached an appropriate size, having been protected, at least in the initial stages, from the attentions of grazing animals. The demand for timber as opposed to coppiced wood must have been equally as great. At Meldon Bridge, near Peebles, a massive timber palisade, 500 yards long, cuts off a promontory of some 20 acres. The individual timbers were immense, 2 feet in diameter, 15 feet long, some weighing more than 2 tons. This structure would have taken the trees from about 8½ acres of woodland. The southeast end and the sides of the mound of one of the long barrows of the Giants Hills, in Lincolnshire, were revetted with massive split tree trunks, and the house at Ballynagilly, measuring 21 by 19 feet, was made of split oak planks set in trenches. These are but isolated examples of Neolithic structures of wood. Sustained demand for large timbers like these would quickly have made a permanent impact upon woodland resources.

Only a handful of field boundaries certainly to be dated to the Neolithic period have so far been identified, but pollen analysis and the study of carbonized remains from occupation sites and of the impressions of individual grains found on Neolithic pottery all show that emmer wheat, naked six-row barley and hulled six-row barley were being grown, and it seems likely that einkorn wheat and bread wheat were also being cultivated. Cross-ploughing furrows, produced perhaps with an ard plough, have been found under the South Street long barrow, with a radio-carbon date of 2810±130 bc, perhaps 3650–3540 BC.

The actual extent and location of individual clearings must remain conjectural but there is now considerable evidence to show that large tracts of the chalklands of southern England were clear of woodland, tracts which must be measured in tens if not hundreds of square miles. It is very likely that large areas elsewhere in Britain were also clear of trees.

The domesticated animals of Neolithic men included cattle, sheep, goats, pigs, and dogs. There is some controversy as to whether the native wild cattle, the aurochs, could have been the source of the domesticated cattle of this era, but at present this is thought to be unlikely. Domesticated pigs were probably allowed to forage for themselves in the woods, so that interbreeding with wild boar would have been quite common. Surviving skeletons of pigs show them to have been small and with the long snout characteristic of wild pigs. Goats and sheep could only have been brought by sea, and both were very small in comparison with modern breeds, the sheep being very similar to the Soay sheep of today. Dogs had been at least semi-domesticated since Mesolithic times if not before, and there was as yet very little to distinguish them from the wolves from which they were descended.

At present all the evidence points to Neolithic men and women as having lived in isolated farmsteads or small hamlets. Houses were round and of timber construction, probably with thatched roofs. Where timber was absent then stone was used. On both Orkney and Shetland a number of houses built entirely of stone have been found. The most famous of these is the group of eight houses at Skara Brae. All save one were huddled around a central connecting alleyway. Individual houses were squarish, up to 20 feet across, with a single doorway giving access to the central passageway. Each house had a central stone hearth, with a peat fire. Against the back wall was a stone dresser, and in more than one house the excavators found pottery still in place. Beds made of thin stone slabs were situated on either side of the door. The actual bedding was probably of skins. Several houses had clay ovens beside the hearth. The houses were built of stone and corbelled upwards for about 10 feet and then roofed over, possibly with turf, using some precious timber as rafters. At Stanydale, Shetland, fragments of wood recovered from the Neolithic settlement turned out to be spruce, and so they must have been picked up on the shore as driftwood, borne across the Atlantic from North America. Over seventy rather similar houses are known on Shetland, where they tend to be oval rather than squarish in shape. Several are clearly associated with fields, at Scord of Brouster and at Stanydale for example, marked off with dykes made from the stones which would have been collected from the surface of the ground before it could be cultivated. Carbonized grains of barley have been found, and the bones of sheep and cattle.

Men and women may have lived in small communities at this time, but this did not prevent them from organizing themselves into groups capable of undertaking constructional works on the grand scale. Enormous effort seems to have gone into the building of burial mounds, known from their shape as long barrows. The earliest for which at present there is a radio-carbon date is at Lambourn, in Berkshire, dated to 3415±180 bc, perhaps 4340 BC. Long barrows vary considerably in size and structure. Some are little more than 70 feet long, others are nearly 400 feet. The great majority have the long axis orientated more or less to the east. Ditches seem to be an integral part of the structure. They usually run parallel to the long sides, occasionally the two are linked by a semi-circular ditch at one end, but they are never completely surrounded by ditches. Most are sited on low hills and false crests so that they would have been clearly visible from the surrounding lowlands. Study of the soils buried beneath them when they were built, and especially of the remains of snail shells found in these soils, reveals that their sites were already open grassland, and there is evidence of former occupation sites beneath those at Bishop's Cannings and West Overton in Wiltshire. Some are clearly grouped with reference to other monuments and many lie within sight of one another. Those round the Dorset cursus stretch altogether for 20 miles, whilst the cursus to the north of Stonehenge, consisting of two parallel lines of bank and ditch some 110–45 yards apart and running for nearly 1¾ miles across country in an almost straight line, has long barrows at both ends. Such alignments must imply large-scale planning in a landscape almost devoid of trees.

Not all long barrows contained primary burials and so they may have had a significance wider than the purely funerary. Many do contain burials however, and these were often in mortuary chambers, usually built of wood. There is much evidence to show that the bodies here interred had been stored elsewhere immediately after death and that the mortuary chambers were used for a very long time, that at West Kennet being in use for at least a thousand years. As new burials took place then it seems that the older remains were cleared to one side, and rather unceremoniously at that. We can only speculate upon the religious beliefs which called for such monuments and the political organization which could bring gangs of men together to labour, perhaps for years on end, armed only with antler picks and wicker baskets, to build and then to maintain these structures.

In all nearly 300 long barrows are known. The majority are grouped in the Salisbury Plain region, an area clearly of considerable significance in prehistoric times if the number, size, and complexity of its monuments is any guide; but there are outliers along the Chilterns into East Anglia, in Lincolnshire, and in Yorkshire.

In the west of England, the Cotswolds, much of Wales, and in Scotland, another kind of monument is to be found. This is the megalith. Every true megalithic tomb has the burial chamber constructed of massive slabs of stone, often roofed with equally massive capping stones. To simplify a very complex story, megalithic tombs can be divided into two principal types: passage graves, in which a round burial chamber is approached by a stone-lined corridor or passage, and gallery graves, in which the corridor is absent. Both kinds, when completed, would have been covered with a mound of soil or stones. Save for one splendid example in Anglesey, at Bryn-Celli-Ddu, passage graves are almost entirely absent from England and Wales but are to be found in large numbers in Ireland and Scotland. Chambered tombs in Scotland are essentially coastal in their distribution, being found in Galloway, in Argyll and Bute, the Hebrides, in Sutherland and Caithness, around Inverness, and in the Northern Isles. Their construction seems to have taken place over a period of at least 2,000 years, and many are composite buildings in that they were added to and rebuilt, again over a very long period of time. Much detailed, scholarly research has gone into their study and many localized groupings can be recognized. It now seems likely that they take their origins from a common tradition of small, simple funerary chambers built of stone, a tradition to be found in the lands bordering the Irish Sea, rather than from any more distant origin in France or the Mediterranean lands. One of the earliest and most splendid of passage graves to be found anywhere in Britain is that at Maes Howe, in Orkney. Here, beneath a mound some 24 feet high and 115 feet in diameter, is a chamber approached by a passageway about 36 feet long. The chamber itself is 15 feet square, with three further cells lying off it, each nearly 3 feet above the floor of the main chamber. The walls rise vertically for about 4 feet 6 inches and then begin to converge in overlapping courses constructed of slabs of stone laid with astonishing skill and accuracy, helped by the nature of the Orcadian sandstone which splits easily along its bedding planes to produce uniform flags. Both large and small slabs were used, some weighing up to 3 tons, all carefully dressed using stone hammers and mauls. The roof is buttressed by a monolithic slab of stone at each of the four corners of the central chamber. A very similar chamber tomb is to be found at Cuween Hill, Orkney. When it was first explored, in the nineteenth century, the skulls of twenty-four dogs were found on the floor of the chamber. We can only guess at their significance. An even more astonishing example of Neolithic skill in working in and with stone is the Dwarfie Stane, on Hoy, in the Orkneys. Here a small chamber with two side cells has been hewn out of an immense, isolated block of sandstone. The entrance was sealed with a large boulder, still to be seen.

Gallery graves are a feature of the western regions of England and Wales, with an isolated group in Kent. Again they appear to differ widely in their construction, but basically they consist of a burial chamber or chambers, sometimes approached by a long passage, all built of huge slabs of stone and roofed with immense cap stones weighing many tons. The burial chamber itself could be re-opened and it often contained numerous burials. Over thirty disarticulated skeletons were found in the chambers in the impressive West Kennet tomb, which is over 340 feet long and contains five burial chambers at its eastern end.

Megalithic tombs have often been pillaged in the past, either for their contents or for their building materials, so that many now stand bare of their mounds, like gigantic three-legged stools of stone. One of the best preserved is Hetty Pegler's Tump, not far from Nympsfield in Gloucestershire, and that at West Kennet is equally well preserved. Wayland's Smithy, in Berkshire, is a much more seriously damaged example, and at Kit's Coty House, in Kent, three huge uprights capped with a fourth have no more than a pale, ploughed-out shadow of the mound which once covered them.

These long barrows, whatever their form and methods of construction and whatever their purpose, are the oldest man-made monuments still visible in the landscape of the late twentieth century.

But long barrows are by no means the only surviving monuments of the late Neolithic period. Large numbers of other kinds, circular and linear, of earth or stone, sometimes of great size and complexity, are known throughout Britain, and more especially in its western regions. They are difficult to date, since organic remains from which radio-carbon dates may be recovered are rare, and their purposes are frequently obscure. The enormous expense involved in their construction could only have been justified by the religious and social importance which must have been attached to them; medieval cathedrals are perhaps the nearest parallels. Some may have been built to further astronomical observations, but the wilder flights of the fancy of some modern commentators cannot be taken too seriously.

The most numerous, the most complex, and the most impressive group of these monuments is to be found in Wiltshire, and Stonehenge is the most astonishing of them all. Its construction took place in several distinct phases, spread over at least a thousand years. In the first phase a bank and external ditch were built, 320 feet in diameter, with a single entrance on the northeast. Material from this ditch has yielded a radio-carbon date of 2180±105 bc. Inside the area thus marked out is a circle, 288 feet in diameter, composed of pits about 3 feet deep and anything up to 6 feet in diameter, features known as the Aubrey Holes. Also thought to be part of this phase is the Heel Stone, an upright sarsen lying beyond the entrance. The second phase saw the transport of the bluestones from the Prescelly Mountains in southwestern Wales and their erection into double circles in the middle of the area enclosed in the first phase. A radio-carbon date from this phase gives 1620±110 bc. At about the same time an avenue of parallel banks and ditches was constructed, leading in a great sweep from the northeastern entrance through more than 50 degrees to reach the bank of the Avon, nearly 2 miles away. This phase was followed quite quickly by the third phase, which involved the almost complete rebuilding of the monument. Such bluestones as had been erected were dismantled and their sockets filled in. Instead, some thirty dressed upright sarsen stones of great size were brought from the neighbourhood of Avebury and erected to form a circle 98 feet in diameter, the upright stones being linked by lintel stones held together by mortise and tenon joints. This circle enclosed a horseshoe of five trilithons, that is pairs of stones capped with lintels, some 22 feet high. This work may have taken place around 2000 bc. It was followed by the erection of some bluestones in what was probably an oval setting. This was later dismantled and the stones were re-erected into a circle and horseshoe echoing the plan of the sarsen stones. This phase may not have been completed much before about 1100 BC.

Stonehenge is unique in Europe. Even today, in spite of the crowds of visitors, the cars and coach parks, the fencing and the barbed wire, it cannot fail to impress. Its meaning for those who planned and built it and its impact upon the minds of those who saw it when it was finished and had not yet lost its significance, can only be guessed at. Their values and beliefs have left a permanent memorial in the landscape of today.

Stonehenge, known as such since at least the twelfth century, has given its name to a distinctive class of prehistoric monument. From the Nine Maidens near Land's End, to the Ring of Brodgar on Mainland Orkney, some seventy henge monuments are known, but only Stonehenge itself has the horizontal lintel or 'hanging' stones from which the word 'henge' derives. Essentially, these monuments consist of a circular bank with an internal ditch and one or two entrances. That at Avebury is exceptional in having four. Most contain timber or stone constructions, sometimes of great complexity. At Woodhenge there were six concentric rings of massive timber posts within an encircling bank enclosing an area 250 feet in

8 Castlerigg, near Keswick in the Lake District, a Neolithic stone circle some 110 feet in diameter and composed of thirty-nine irregularly-shaped upright stones.

diameter. At Avebury a bank and internal ditch enclose 28 acres within which is first of all an outer circle of stones and then, within this, two free-standing stone circles. The monument now known as Long Meg and Her Daughters, near Penrith in Cumberland, consists of a single upright stone set in a circle of fifty-nine further free-standing stones, whilst the Ring of Brodgar, mentioned above, consisted originally of sixty upright stones, of which twenty-seven still survive, and the henge monument at Winterbourne Bassett is composed of two concentric circles of stones with a single free-standing stone set at the centre.

Henge monuments remain among the most impressive and the most mysterious of all man-made structures in the landscape, even today. Even more mysterious is Silbury Hill, the largest man-made hill in Europe. It is 550 feet in diameter and 135 feet high and seems to have been constructed at about the same time as the first phase of Stonehenge, 16 miles away to the south. Silbury Hill stands a little to the south of the henge monument at Avebury and there is the possibility of some ceremonial or ritualistic link between them, but in spite of careful excavations the purpose of Silbury Hill remains unknown.

Henge monuments are permanent visible testimony to the diffusion of ideas, values, and beliefs in Neolithic times, even if we can never know what these ideals were. Other, more prosaic finds from archaeological sites yield evidence of long-distance trade in a wide range of artefacts. Pottery made by hand without the use of a potter's wheel is found in the earliest Neolithic sites. Both regional and local styles of pottery emerge, and also other styles with a very wide distribution over Britain. One particular style, or rather grouping of styles, known as Groved Ware, is found on sites in Wiltshire, Yorkshire, the Pennines, and Orkney. Yet other pottery, found on sites from Devon to Wiltshire, is made from a gabbroic clay found only on the Lizard peninsula in Cornwall. It has been suggested that this pottery was made on site by a group of professional potters and then distributed through a trading network based upon barter. Similarly, stone axes also entered a long-distance trading network. The most widely distributed of stone axes are those made from porcellanite found at Tievebulliagh, Rathlin Island, in County Antrim. They have been recovered from as far afield as Orkney and Kent, and from Lancashire to Dorset. Axes made from stone found at Great Langdale, in the Lake District, have been found in Cornwall, Northern Ireland, Scotland, and East Anglia, and axes from a site in Pembrokeshire have been found from Devon to East Anglia.

Flint was an important raw material for the manufacture of tools and implements, although it was by no means the only type of stone employed for this purpose. Flint mines were being exploited at Church Hill, Findon, Sussex, by 3390±150 bc, perhaps 4340–4250 BC. At Easton Down, in Wiltshire, a flint-mining complex of about ninety shafts, over an area of about 40 acres, was being exploited by about 2530 BC. Shafts, about 10 feet in diameter, reached the flint seams at about 10 feet below the solid chalk surface. The tools used to dig out the shafts were red deer antler picks and ox shoulderblade shovels. Once brought to the surface the flint was worked up into polished axes on the site, and large quantities of chips, flakes and unfinished axes together with some finished ones were found in the surface debris. The most famous Neolithic flint mines, however, are those at Grimes Graves in Norfolk. Here, at Weeting, near Brandon, an area of heathland nearly 40 acres in extent is pock-marked with the humps and hollows of over 360 mining shafts and their associated spoil heaps. Mining was in full swing here by about 2000 BC.

Pottery and axes made of flint and other stone are of great interest in themselves as examples of the artefacts used by men and women during the normal course of their everyday lives. They are even more interesting for what they can tell us indirectly about the organization of human life and the perception which men had of their environment. Men were well aware that mined flint was a much better raw material than any which might be picked up on the surface, and they knew of its association with chalk. They knew of the special qualities of the greenish-grey volcanic tuff to be found as loose scree on Pike of Stickle, Scafell, Scafell Pike, and Glaramara. The bluestones of the Prescelly Mountains must have had some peculiar significance to make them worth the enormous effort involved in transporting them to Stonehenge. All this reveals both a sophisticated

9 A tree, probably an alder, dug out of the peat of the Bedford Level, near Ramsey in Huntingdonshire, in 1987.

10   A 'landscape of dereliction': the desolate, highly acidic Lady Clough Moor,
near Glossop.

knowledge of natural resources and a complex social organization. By the
fifth and fourth millennia BC the landscape of Britain was thoroughly
explored and widely settled, with a rich and subtle network of relationships
between man, society, and the environment.

It is clear from the archaeological record that important changes were
taking place in Britain during the course of the third millennium BC. First of
all, from the second half of the millennium the climate was deteriorating,
slowly and erratically at first and then quite quickly. At the climatic
maximum summer temperatures were perhaps as much as 3 degrees
Centigrade higher than they are today. The climate was warm and dry. The
mountain tree-line may have been as much as 1,000 feet above that of
today. Settlement was possible in the Somerset Levels and in the fens of
Cambridgeshire and Lincolnshire, and also throughout the upland districts
of Britain, from Bodmin Moor to the Grampians. Woodland clearance in
the uplands was extensive, both for arable and for pasture. However, as
the climate deteriorated the long-term effects of the removal of the tree
cover came to exercise ever-growing influence over human activity.
Increased rainfall in what were already the wettest regions of Britain led to
soil degradation, waterlogging and the spread of blanket bog. Stratifi-
cations visible in peat bogs of upland Britain today reveal the fluctuations
of this climatic deterioration. A band of dark, highly humidified peat shows
a period of slow peat growth as conditions became drier, whilst bands of
lighter-coloured fresh peat reflect wetter conditions and rapid peat

accumulation. The peat often dried out sufficiently to allow trees, especially birch and pine, to colonize the surface, but they were killed off when the peat began to grow again. The stumps of birch and pine trees are common in many upland peat bogs today, at Lady Clough Moor and Tintwhistle Knarr in the southern Pennines for example, where there are many large trunks embedded in the peat, including oak, birch, and pine.

Climatic factors entirely beyond the control of man, working on the environmental weaknesses created by his destruction of the tree cover, compelled him to abandon his upland settlements, creating over much of Highland Britain what has very aptly been called a 'landscape of dereliction', although today we attach so much value to its scenic qualities that we make National Parks and Areas of Outstanding Natural Beauty out of it. The pressures, economic and social, created during the last two millennia by this abandonment of the uplands underlie many of the changes taking place during this long period. It is also during this period that the Highland/Lowland dichotomy becomes increasingly apparent and increasingly significant.

Second, a distinctive pottery form appears, known from its shape as Beaker Ware. Its presence was once thought to indicate the coming of a new wave of immigrants, perhaps Celtic-speaking, into Britain, but this view is being increasingly questioned. Beakers may however have some new ritualistic significance since they seem to appear just as a profound shift was taking place in funerary traditions and practices, a shift from inhumation to cremation and from burial in long barrows to burial in round barrows and in due course in cemeteries containing hundreds of cremation urns. Thousands of round barrows are known, many still visible in the landscape today, many more long since ploughed out and known only from aerial photographs. There are large numbers on the Mendips, hundreds on the Cotswolds, one every 1.81 square kilometres in the section of the Great Ouse valley near Milton Keynes and 10,000 on the North Yorkshire moors. At the same time, or at least within the same millennium, so coarse is our knowledge of the chronology of prehistory, the circles of stone, the great henge monuments of Stonehenge and Woodhenge, together with Silbury Hill, were all reaching the peak of their development.

Third, metal working appears in the second half of the third millennium BC, first of all copper, and then bronze and gold. In due course an entirely new range of tools, weapons, and implements appears, although stone ones long continued to be made and used. Trees are now more easily felled with metal axes, and at the same time the demand for wood to fuel the furnaces in which the ores were smelted added yet a further dimension to the pressures on the woodland.

Fourth, there is now overwhelming evidence to suggest that Britain was almost everywhere densely settled, divided into territorial units and laid out into fields and farms, and this well before the end of the third

millennium BC. Aerial photography, field walking and rescue archaeology
have led to the accumulation of a mountain of evidence, the great bulk of
which still remains to be properly analysed and fully digested, and of which
only a minute proportion, well under 1 per cent, has been excavated. It is
of course impossible to estimate at all accurately the population of Britain
at this time, but such is the evidence for occupation sites that it may be
seriously suggested that there may have been 2 million people living in
Britain by the opening years of the second millennium BC.

Very many settlements and occupation sites are now known. Almost all
houses were circular in shape, built of timber with a diameter of
approximately 20 feet, usually with a central supporting post and an
off-centre hearth. Very frequently these buildings were surrounded with a
bank and ditch or a wooden palisade. Sometimes they were isolated,
sometimes there was a small group, perhaps as many as nine or ten,
arranged rather haphazardly within the enclosure. During the last
millennium BC larger structures were appearing, with a diameter of 50 feet
or more. Buildings of this size have an inner circle of post holes. These may
have been used to provide further support for the roof, or they may
represent an inner wall, giving an inner, open courtyard to the structure.
Such buildings, of whatever kind and with many local variations in detail,
are known the length and breadth of Britain for the last two thousand years
of prehistory, from Blackthorne in Northamptonshire, Little Woodbury in
Wiltshire, Itford Hill in Sussex, and Hod Hill in Dorset to High Knowes in
Northumberland, West Plean in Stirling, West Brandon in County
Durham, Llandegai in Caernarvonshire, and Walesland Rath in Pem-
brokeshire.

Excavated occupation sites often reveal a maze of pits and holes, the
interpretation of which is often difficult and occasionally controversial.
Sometimes the post holes seem to represent a small rectangular building.
These are usually interpreted as granaries, raised on posts out of the way of
damp and rats. Other pits were clearly used for the storage of grain, and
this can be done very successfully provided the pit is made absolutely
airtight by means of a clay cap. This airtight environment allows the carbon
dioxide given off by the grain to accumulate to such a level that it inhibits
germination and kills bacteria and any other animal that might gain entry.
If the seal was broken then the grain would have to be used quickly or it
would deteriorate very rapidly. Both seed corn and grain for human
consumption can be kept in both ways. Perhaps their use was complementary rather than exclusive.

There is also for the last two millennia BC very extensive evidence of
large-scale land division. Smallish plots of land, about 200 by 150 feet and
roughly rectangular in shape, marked off by banks and mounds, have long
been known over wide areas of the chalk downlands of southern England.
Only very recently, however, have they been plotted accurately on a large

scale and then studied carefully. It is now apparent that, beneath the irregularities of individual plots, there is an underlying overall regularity. The small plots can be seen as subdivisions of much larger tracts of countryside laid out and defined by continuous boundaries, often with a

11 Fyfield Down, Wiltshire, a prehistoric planned landscape of rectilinear enclosures laid out on a northeast–southwest orientation.

northeast–southwest axis, and this planned landscape ignores physical features, extending for miles on end. Both Overton Down and Fyfield Down have blocks of fields laid out in this way. They are separated by the Valley of Stones. This is crossed by a single ditch joining the two areas, which, in spite of their physical separation, share the same northeast–southwest orientation. Blocks of land laid out in a similar fashion have been recognized in Hampshire, Wiltshire, Dorset and Sussex, the fenlands, the valley of the Warwickshire Avon, the middle and upper Thames valley, and the area around Grassington in Yorkshire. On Dartmoor large blocks of land are divided up by stone or earth banks, known as reaves, running more or less straight for miles across the countryside. On Spitchwick Common over 3,000 acres of land are divided up in this way.

These are the oldest planned landscapes which can be recognized today. At least two more will be superimposed upon them, the elaborately structured open-field villages of medieval Britain and the ruler-straight roads and field boundaries of the eighteenth-century Parliamentary enclosure commissioners. Only for the last do we have any detailed knowledge of the motives and processes involved, but the evidence on the ground for a Bronze Age 'enclosure movement', with all that this implies of social control, organizing capacity and surveying skills, is now incontrovertible.

Arable cultivation and field systems in the uplands of the Highland Zone seem to show less evidence of planning on a large scale. Stanshiel Rig, in Dumfriesshire, is an area of banks, plots, and occupation sites extending to 65 acres. Other areas are known on Middleton Muir in Perthshire, and The Ord, Laing, in Sutherland, seems to be part of an extensive system bordering the Moray Firth. Some upland areas contain extensive cairn fields, over 800 on Danby Rigg for example, and over 200 acres on Green Crag Slack, in the Pennines, about 400 cairns at Barnscar in Cumberland, and about 130 on Ramsley Moor, near Holmesfield in Derbyshire. The cairns themselves are essentially heaps of stones which appear to have been collected from the surface of the ground as it was cleared of hazel and alder scrub in order to bring it into cultivation. Some cairns are linked by rough stone walling to produce small irregular enclosures.

Houses in the Highland Zone were also built of stone. At Chysauster, in Cornwall, is a group of nine large stone-built houses opening from a central curved passageway. Each house has an open central courtyard with the rooms leading off. Similar courtyard houses are known from the second level of occupation at Jarlshof, in Shetland. Cattle were stalled inside these dwellings. Men and cattle will continue to share the same buildings, often separated by nothing more than a shallow step, until the end of the eighteenth century and beyond.

From about 1400 BC society in Britain appears to have been passing through a long period of crisis and stress. The linear and circular monuments, henges, circles and avenues, whether in stone, wood or earth, were abandoned. It is unlikely that this could have taken place without a crisis in the beliefs and values which surrounded them, since so much time and effort had been lavished upon their construction. Everything points to a religion that was at once subterranean and celestial. To suggest that this crisis was precipitated by climatic deterioration may at first appear over-fanciful, but much evidence points in this direction. Many stone monuments in the uplands are now half-buried in peat, and this has clearly developed since the monuments were erected. Increased cloud would have made many circles and alignments unworkable because their astronomical bearings would have been invisible. Upland occupation sites were being abandoned as the land was overwhelmed in blanket bog. This may have created the pressures compelling the fortification of lower settlements. Hill forts, at Grimthorpe in Yorkshire, Dinorben in Denbighshire and perhaps at Mam Tor in Derbyshire and Kaimes in Midlothian, were all built before the end of the second millennium BC. Finally, so many of the finest examples of Bronze Age metal work have been recovered from rivers,

12   Maiden Castle, Dorset. The site was occupied in Neolithic times and later used as a burial ground. The massive fortifications which dominate it today were constructed only in the last century BC. A late Roman temple was in due course built inside the ramparts.

lakes, and bogs that to see them as propitiatory offerings to water gods is a
reasonable interpretation of the evidence, and the worship of water gods
has continued ever since, even if it has been superficially Christianized, as
in the annual well-dressing ceremonies at Tissington and at Tideswell, in
Derbyshire.

'Hill fort', with its implications of a defended site on a hill top, is a rather
misleading term to apply to a new type of construction which is appearing
in the landscape before the end of the second millennium BC. About 3,000
hill forts are known in Britain, but more than half cover less than 3 acres
and so are little more than farmsteads surrounded with bank and ditch.
Many are on lowland sites, and many could not have been defended for
any length of time because they contain no permanent water supply.
Nevertheless, other hill forts have massive and extensive fortifications,
with complex lines of defence, whether of earthen bank and ditch with
wooden palisade, or more elaborate box-like structures composed of a
double row of wooden posts, strengthened by lacing with horizontal
timbers, the gap between the two rows being packed with soil and rubble,
often the spoil excavated from the forward ditch. In the north and west the
timbers were replaced with stone walls, often carefully constructed without
the use of mortar, and battered towards the top. Some hill fort sites were
being used before the fortifications themselves were constructed, and some
show several stages of building and rebuilding. At their largest, as at
Maiden Castle in Dorset, they represent the most substantial constructions
in the landscape since the completion of Stonehenge.

There is now a growing body of evidence to suggest that in the last
centuries BC a process of selection was taking place among the large
number of hill forts which by that time was in existence. Some were falling
into disuse, whilst others, clearly of growing importance, were being
provided with increasingly elaborate defences, and their interiors were
filling up with buildings. This is almost certainly part of the process of the
crystallization of territorial divisions, as hill forts appear to become the
focal points of dependent territories. Hill forts in the Welsh Marches, at
Credenhill, Croft Ambrey, and Midsummer Hill, contain unmistakable
evidence of planned internal occupation. Excavation at Danebury, in
Hampshire, has revealed four rows of timber buildings arranged along
streets. There is similar evidence of planned internal settlement from
Maiden Castle. Chalbury in Dorset, defended by a single rampart of stone,
contained nearly a hundred substantial round buildings, with stone wall
foundations and paved floors. Hod Hill, also in Dorset, may have had as
many as 270 houses within its walls, nearly as many as there appear to have
been at Eildon Hill in Roxburghshire, where there may have been as many
as 2,000 inhabitants. Such concentrations of people supported communities of craftsmen, potters, weavers, smiths, and metal workers. The
presence of currency bars, at South Cadbury for example, points to trade.

13 The north front of the Eildon Hills, near Melrose.

In other words these focal points were rapidly taking on the functions of towns, and some became tribal capitals – Traprain Law for the Votadini, Eildon Hill for the Selgoviae, Maiden Castle for the Durotriges. The fact that a number, South Cadbury, Maiden Castle, Heathrow, Middlesex, and probably Danebury in Hampshire, contain structures best interpreted as temples, only serves to reinforce the view that at least some hill forts were developing as major foci for a wide range of the sympathies and values of the inhabitants of the surrounding countryside.

Thus it seems very likely that by the late second century BC much of the south and west of Britain, in a broad belt from Sussex westwards through the Welsh marches and into Lowland Scotland, was dominated by strongly fortified hill forts with densely occupied interiors commanding what would appear to be dependent territories of perhaps 30 or 40 square miles in extent. The pattern may well be different in the Midlands and East Anglia, where hill forts certainly seem to be less numerous, but this is a supposition based upon ignorance rather than careful study and so speculation at this stage would be less than helpful.

In the southeast, however, important new developments appear to have been taking place, especially in the 150 years before the Claudian invasion. Urban or proto-urban settlements have been recognized which were not based upon hill forts but upon areas, sometimes very large ones, marked out by a complex series of linear earthworks. Caesar seems to have applied the word *oppidum* to such settlements, and it is a word which historians of today have found very useful. The earthworks at Camulodunum enclose an area of 12 square miles, with several areas of nucleated settlement and much evidence of imported luxury wares, especially wine and pottery, from Rome. At Wheathampstead, in Hertfordshire, massive earthworks almost enclose an area of about 100 acres, an area which shows every sign of dense settlement. This site then seems to have been abandoned early in the first century AD and instead occupation begins at Verulamium, some 5 miles away to the southwest, within an area enclosed by a ditch and palisade, and again showing evidence of intensive occupation and much trade in imported Roman luxury goods. Similar urban, or urbanizing, centres have been recognized at Canterbury, Silchester, Winchester, and Selsey. At Silchester and Winchester the sites in due course become Roman towns. At Selsey an altogether larger area was enclosed, again with a series of linear earthworks, and the town of Chichester was established in the northern part of the enclosure. Other enclosed areas showing evidence of incipient urban development have been recognized at Stanton Harcourt in Oxfordshire, at Dragonbury in Lincolnshire, and at Hengistbury Head, which seems to have been a flourishing port.

Thus in some areas of southeastern Britain urbanization appears to have been taking place at centres away from established hill forts, whilst further to the west it seems to have remained focused on well-established hill forts such as Maiden Castle, Hod Hill, Hambledon Hill, and South Cadbury. Archaeology allows us only to glimpse these processes actually in operation. It cannot explain why or how they were taking place and it may well be that our interpretation of the evidence is entirely mistaken, since there are no documents from which we can check our hypotheses. There is, however, evidence, including accounts by Roman authors such as Julius Caesar and Tacitus, to suggest a strongly hierarchical society in pre-Conquest Britain, with warrior, priestly, and peasant classes sharply distinguished. We know the names of several tribes and of their kings. Both hill forts and *oppida* would certainly fit as centres of tribal authority, with a ruling class rapidly developing an insatiable taste for the more luxurious trappings of Roman civilization.

The picture is yet further complicated by another profoundly important technological development. By about 600 BC it is clear that the use of iron is becoming familiar to smiths and other metal workers. It does not however replace either bronze or stone, and it is several centuries before it becomes at all common. Iron-smelting furnaces make yet heavier demands upon the woodland and iron axes are even more efficient for felling trees, thus hastening still further the disappearance of the woodland. The way in which the use of iron was introduced remains uncertain. There have always been close links between Britain and the continent ever since the last land bridge was overwhelmed by the sea, and the links have worked both ways, with raiders and traders making the sea-crossing in either direction, and some remaining permanently, perhaps not always intentionally. But movements of this kind do not mean migration on any scale, and it seems very unlikely that there was any substantial movement of people into Britain much before the first half of the last millennium BC. By about 300 BC Britain had become largely Celtic, a transformation which may have been a very long process and which was probably completed by absorption and adaptation rather than by large-scale invasion and destruction. The last two centuries before the Roman conquest saw further waves of settlers, one perhaps about 100 BC and a second, more complex and probably more substantial, between Caesar's expeditions of 55 and 54 BC and the Claudian invasion of AD 43.

This chapter has been concerned with the history of the landscape for four-fifths of the time which has elapsed between the end of the last ice age and the present. It is a period for which modern science and archaeology have revolutionized our knowledge in the last thirty years. It is now clear that prehistoric Britain was very much more densely settled at a very much earlier period than was until quite recently thought possible. Trees were being felled, fields cleared and cultivated and profoundly significant funerary monuments were bring built in the fifth millennium BC, all providing indirect evidence of complex social patterns and religious beliefs. The human landscape of Britain has a very long history indeed and some of the more substantial evidence for this early history is to be seen in the landscape of today. The Roman occupation, which forms the subject for the next chapter, opens a new era in that for the first time documentary evidence is available to complement and supplement the archaeological evidence, but the Romans came into a thickly settled landscape that had for several thousands of years supported a sophisticated and highly complex society.

3

Roman Britain

The expeditions of Julius Caesar in 55 and 54 BC and the invasion and conquest of Britain by the Romans in AD 43 mean that for the first time there is documentary evidence to assist us in the interpretation of the landscape. This evidence is, and will remain for centuries, fragmentary, slight, and as difficult to interpret as the archaeological evidence which has been our sole guide so far. It does however provide us with a second, independent and complementary guide, and the two, taken together, do reduce considerably the risks of misinterpretation.

As we saw in the concluding paragraphs of the previous chapter, the Romans came into a densely settled landscape peopled by a society with an elaborate political structure and an increasingly sophisticated taste for the luxuries of the Roman world. It is clear too that at least some settlements in the southeast of Britain were of a size and complexity that would merit the name of town rather than village, and it is very likely that this spontaneous, British, urbanization would have continued to develop in its own ways even if the Romans had not brought their own civilization with them.

The Roman military conquest was not completed overnight, and indeed it was never completed for Scotland. The invasion forces comprised about 40,000 men under the command of Aulus Plautius, brought from the governorship of Pannonia, on the Danube, for the purpose. The Emperor Claudius joined the army on the Thames. He was in Britain for only sixteen days, but according to one historian he was able to lead his troops into Colchester before returning to Rome. Meanwhile the future Emperor Vespasian had been pushing westwards, where, according to Suetonius, he fought thirty battles and captured more than twenty *oppida*. Excavations at the eastern entrance to Maiden Castle have uncovered a cemetery

Figure 7   Roman Britain

containing the bodies of the British defenders killed in the Roman assault, and at Hod Hill, also in Dorset, a Roman fort was built in the northwestern corner of the large Iron Age hill fort, using the Iron Age ditches and banks on two sides. There is no evidence of an assault upon the gates but large numbers of ballista bolts have been found in the houses within the fortifications. The close positioning of many of these bolts suggests that they had been fired from a Roman siege tower. This would have been built of wood, and would have needed to be at least 50 feet high, but this would have been well within the capacity of Roman military engineers.

By the middle years of the century much of the south and west of Britain was firmly under Roman control. A legionary fortress was built in Exeter a little after AD 55, and there was a permanent fort at Nanstallon, near Bodmin, by the same date. By AD 60 there was a legionary fortress at Lincoln for Legio IX and another for Legio XIV at Wroxeter, with Legio II at Exeter and Legio XX, having left Colchester, at Usk. It now seems very likely that the Fosse Way, running from Lincoln through Leicester to Cirencester, was not in any sense a frontier but rather a cross-country communications link, joining the roads which radiated out from London and the southeast. Cirencester seems from the first to have been an important crossroads, and the continuation of the Fosse Way to Exeter now appears to have been a later addition.

This is not the place for a narrative of the Roman conquest of Britain. It is sufficient to say that the conquest of Wales had been completed by about AD 79. Four years later, when Agricola was governor, Legio XX was moved from Wroxeter to Inchtuthil, on the Tay, where a fortress was built to serve as the base for his campaign in Scotland. This site is one of the most important in the Roman world, excavation and aerial photography having revealed unrivalled detail about the construction of a single-period legionary fortress. Building work began in 83, with timber-framed buildings and a turf and gravel rampart. This latter was quickly replaced with a stone wall. The fortress was dismantled and abandoned in about 87, the Roman engineers carefully concealing almost three-quarters of a million nails for the twentieth-century excavators to discover.

A very large marching camp, covering 144 acres, was discovered in 1975 at Durno-Bennachie in Aberdeenshire. It has been suggested, on circumstantial evidence, that the ground between this camp and the conspicuous peak of Bennachie was the site of Agricola's victory of *Mons Graupius,* in which he destroyed for a generation the power of the Caledonian tribesmen. He then went on to build a string of forts from Inchtuthil to Drumquhassle Ridge, south of Loch Lomond, in order to confine the tribesmen to the Highlands. He also gave much attention to consolidating Roman authority in southern Scotland, and forts were built at Gatehouse of Fleet, for example, and at Loudon Hill, with a particularly large one at Newstead, on a site overlooking the Tweed, with the three peaks of the Eildon Hills visible away to the southwest to give it the name of *Trimontium.* This was an important staging point on Dere Street, and in addition to the usual square fort covering over 14 acres, fortified enclosures were also built, probably to shelter convoys which would have come up from the south. Newstead continued to be occupied long after the Romans had abandoned the rest of southern Scotland, and it may have been here that the Emperor Septimius Severus assembled his army before invading Scotland in AD 208.

Early in the second century AD the northern border of Roman territory in Britain probably lay along the Stanegate Road, using the Tyne–Solway gap, with watch-towers and small forts, such as that at Haltwhistle Burn in Northumberland, strung along it. In 117 the Emperor Trajan died. His conquests in Dacia and Mesopotamia pushed the boundaries of the Roman Empire to their furthest limits, and he was probably content to allow southern Scotland to be abandoned. He was succeeded by Hadrian, who gave up Trajan's eastern conquests in order to concentrate on consolidating and defending existing frontiers, first of all on the Rhine–Danube line and secondly in Britain, which he visited in 122. Almost immediately work began on the great wall which still bears his name. When finally completed, after years of work and many changes of plan, it was to be the finest and most elaborate defensive line in the Roman Empire. The Stanegate Road runs nearly at the foot of the Tyne–Solway gap. The new wall follows the northern edge of the gap, with splendid views out to the north. From Newcastle in the east to the crossing of the River Irthing the wall was planned in stone, 10 Roman feet wide. The final section to Bowness-on-Solway was at first built of turf, but very soon rebuilt in stone. There was a wide ditch in front of the wall, and a fort every mile, with two watch-towers evenly spaced in between. During building the wall was extended at each end, to Wallsend-on-Sea in the east and well down the Cumberland coast in the west. The wall itself snaked across the countryside, especially along the Whin Sill outcrop, with its precipitous north-facing escarpment. Behind the wall, in long straight sections, lies the Vallum. This is a ditch, 20 feet wide, 10 feet deep, with a flat bottom 8 feet wide. Thirty feet from each edge is a spoil mound revetted with turf, so that the entire work is 120 feet across. It seems to have been designed as a boundary defining the rear of the military zone and preventing any stealthy or unauthorized approach to the rear of the wall.

The wall had not long been finished when, following the death of Hadrian in 138, the new Emperor, Antoninus Pius, ordered the reoccupation of southern Scotland. This meant a new frontier barrier across the narrow central isthmus, from the Forth to the Clyde, a barrier known today as the Antonine Wall. At the same time a line of forts as far north as the Tay was reoccupied. The Antonine Wall was constructed of turf on a foundation of stones. It was only two-thirds as thick as Hadrian's Wall, although its forward ditch was more substantial. Forts were built along it, one of the largest, at Balmuildy, covering over 4 acres, and one of the smallest, Rough Castle, little more than 1½ acres. When completed the Antonine Wall had a greater concentration of forts than did Hadrian's

Wall, and therefore it was probably more heavily manned, but its life-span was much shorter as it seems to have been finally abandoned shortly after the death of Septimius Severus in 211.

Before the end of the second century German pirates were raiding the southeast coast of Britain. This led in due course to the building of coastal defences, a network of fortifications from Brancaster in Norfolk round to Portchester in Hampshire and Carisbrooke in the Isle of Wight. They were not all built at once, the later ones showing increasing sophistication and increasingly massive defences as the Roman army was forced onto the defensive. The earliest fort may well be that at Reculver, built early in the third century, perhaps about AD 210, with those at Brancaster and Burgh perhaps a little later. All three had masonry walls with earthen banks behind. Towers were added to Burgh only whilst it was being built. The site at Richborough was refortified in about 280 AD. This was one of the principal landing points for the Claudian invasion and it was for long the main entry point from the continent into Britain. An immense triumphal arch was erected here in about AD 85. It was perhaps 70 feet high and stood on a concrete platform nearly 30 feet thick. This marks the beginning of Watling Street, the main Roman road to London. In about AD 280 the site was refortified. The great arch was demolished and its concrete platform was used for the *principia*, that is the headquarters building of a new fort, which was provided with stone walls over 10 feet thick and 20 feet high,

14   Burgh Castle, the Roman coastal fort of *Gariannum*, Suffolk.

with projecting towers. Much of this fort still remains, although subsequent coastal changes mean that it is now about 2 miles from the sea. The fort at Pevensey seems to have been built even later, perhaps about AD 335. These forts do not seem to have been built to an overall plan, and the office of *comes litoris Saxonici,* 'count of the Saxon shore', was not created until the late third century, so the functions of these forts may have been more complex than simply that of coastal defence.

We have spent some time looking at Roman military structures because they survive in the British landscape today as the most striking evidence of the Roman occupation. Hadrian's Wall and the forts at Portchester and Burgh would be substantial remains anywhere in the Roman world. They are the largest surviving above ground in Britain. Such works are also astonishing testimony to the engineering and surveying skills of the Romans, their command of resources and their ability to mould their environment.

There has been room here to name only a few of the most conspicuous Roman military structures still to be seen today. Very many more, vexillation forts and marching camps for example, survive as lines of grass-covered banks and ditches, or else as nothing more substantial than crop marks whose full significance can be spotted only from the air. The Roman occupation was a military conquest, and military structures would have been their first contribution to the landscape. They made many more, and much more subtle and long-lasting ones, during their four hundred years here.

If military structures of every kind are the most conspicuous of the contributions of the Roman army to the landscape of Britain, then the roads which its engineers also laid out have proved to be more permanently useful. A network of roads was constructed as the conquest proceeded in order to secure communications and supplies for the advancing troops, and it is possible to detect the progress of the conquest from a study of the pattern of some of the roads. Thus Watling Street seems to have been built in three stages: the first was aligned from London to a site on the Fosse Way, where in due course a settlement, *Venonis,* grew up. The second stage led, on a changed alignment, to Wroxeter, and in due course a third stage went on to Chester.

Long-distance alignments were laid out with great skill, a skill which must have relied upon careful surveying and accurate maps. Thus Stane Street, from London Bridge to Chichester, runs dead straight for its first 12 miles out of London, aligned accurately on the eastern gate of Chichester, whilst a road running southeast out from Leicester is aimed directly at Colchester, 100 miles away. However, once the alignment of a road was decided upon it was by no means always built dead straight. Its actual course followed the most practicable route, from one sighting point, usually a hill top, however modest, to the next. In hilly and mountainous country plateau top routes were preferred, so that the road avoided valleys and the dangers of ambush. This often meant quite steep ascents by means of zigzags until an open line could be reached.

Main roads were solidly constructed, with foundations of large stones and gravel surfaces, the whole often raised on a bank or agger, with ditches on both sides to serve as drains. In addition there were many miles of unmetalled side roads and lanes. Main roads were provided with mile posts, and along those used by the imperial postal service, the *cursus publicus,* staging posts were established where travellers could find refreshment, accommodation and a change of horses. Many miles of these main roads are still recognizable today, striding straight across the countryside. Some are still roads of the first importance: Watling Street for example, now the A5, and the length of the Fosse Way from Lincoln to Leicester, now the A46, and Akeman Street, the busy A41 road from London to Aylesbury. Yet other Roman roads are now quiet. Thus the Fosse Way southwest from Leicester is used today as a main road only over quite short stretches. For the remainder of its length it is not even a B road. Nevertheless it still provides the most pleasant, the easiest, and the least crowded road from Leicester to the southwest, save for its length from a point northeast of Shipston-on-Stour to one southwest of Cirencester, when it is the A429.

Roman roads were clearly conspicuous features in the landscape and they were used extensively as boundary markers as estates were subdivided and new administrative units created, especially, as we shall see in the next chapter, during the Anglo-Saxon period. Thus Watling Street forms much of the boundary between Warwickshire and Leicestershire, and a number of parishes in north Buckinghamshire also use it for their boundaries. Ermine Street, running north from London to the Humber, is used for long stretches as the A14 and the A1, and often abandoned altogether, as north of the B6403/A17 junction, west of Sleaford, to Lincoln. North of Lincoln and almost dead straight for over 15 miles, it is used as a parish boundary marker for almost the whole of this distance. One consequence of this is that a combination of straight lanes, or even straight hedgerows, with ancient parish boundaries, can lead in many instances to the discovery of long lost Roman roads, particularly minor ones, and especially if the place-name element 'street' occurs in the vicinity since this seems to be the name almost invariably applied by the English to a Roman road.

The Roman military conquest took nearly forty years to complete, and it was a further forty years before the northern frontier was firmly established. It took a similarly lengthy period before the programme of 'Romanization', deliberately introduced by the Roman governor Agricola, began to have any impact, even at a superficial level, upon the everyday lives of the majority of the inhabitants of Roman Britain. As we saw in the preceding chapter, Britain at the time of the Roman conquest was densely settled, with occupation sites ranging from isolated farmsteads through hamlets and villages to places that were towns in all but name. Certainly in the southeast agriculture must have been well above subsistence levels, providing surpluses for export. The Roman conquest brought a number of powerful stimuli into the rural landscape. First of all the army itself, perhaps 40,000 men, was a great consumer of agricultural products of every kind: grain, meat, hides, and skins. It also needed large quantities of timber, pottery, and metal goods, as witness the nails at Inchtuthil. Its demands were met by purchase, requisition, or taxation, but whatever means were employed the inhabitants of rural Britain found themselves prodded or persuaded into producing more. The Roman occupation introduced a money economy, and the demands of the army together with its assorted motley of camp followers of every kind, traders, merchants, and civil servants, created the opportunities for Romano-British farmers to produce for an insatiable market.

Second, the construction of a network of roads vastly improved communications, so that much more distant markets could now be exploited, and not only throughout Britain but also across the length and breadth of the Roman world. Third, in spite of rebellion and civil war, extortion, inflation, and corruption, the Roman occupation brought peace and stability for decades on end, together with a codified and generally impartial legal system and the use of writing for the recording of contracts and agreements. Only in the most exceptional circumstances were people allowed to bear arms of any kind, a rule enforced throughout the entire period, and no Roman villa in Britain shows any clear trace of fortification. The *pax Romana* was very real.

By the end of the first century AD the long-term benefits of the Roman occupation were beginning to make themselves felt. Romano-British farmers, with money in their purses, began to replace their round, timber-framed farmhouses with ones in the Roman style. Such farmhouses have been known to generations of students of Roman Britain as villas, but they raise considerable problems of definition and use, problems to which there can be no satisfactory answers. The term villa should be applied to a country house or farmstead which shows some acceptance of a Roman lifestyle. This means in particular that it has been rebuilt in rectangular form and that Roman furnishings, painted plaster, mosaics, baths and masonry such as tiles and dressed stone have been incorporated. Many villas overlie Iron Age farmsteads. Many were not abandoned until the late fourth or early fifth centuries. We must therefore also expect much building, alteration, patching and rebuilding, sometimes peculiar to the individual site, sometimes reflecting broader changes such as the burst of activity which seems to have taken place on a wide scale in the early fourth century.

Over 750 villas are known, with the great majority in the south and east

15   The unexcavated Roman villa at Little Milton, Oxfordshire.

of Britain and noticeable concentrations around smaller towns. They vary enormously in size, complexity of layout, and lavishness of appointment. Many are simple rectangular buildings of timber-framed construction. A handful, of which that at Fishbourne is the best-known example, vic with any known elsewhere in the Empire in size and luxury. The first are probably the houses of working farmers, or perhaps bailiffs or tenants, the second are the country retreats of men of enormous wealth. At Little Milton, in Oxfordshire, is a simple rectangular villa, about 75 feet long, of six rooms and a flanking corridor. It remains unexcavated, being known only from aerial photographs. At Chedworth, on the other hand, is one of the largest of British villas. It has a long history of additions and rebuilding, in which it is by no means unusual. At its greatest extent, probably in the later fourth century, it comprised three wings, surrounding a courtyard. The north wing was 325 feet long, the west 225 feet. The length of the third, the south wing, remains unknown but it was certainly built on a similar scale. By this time too a series of fine mosaics had been added to the principal rooms and its bath house was supplied with water from a spring a little to the northwest. This spring was provided with a Nymphaeum. It was probably at first the shrine of a water nymph, but in due course it acquired Christian significance and the sacred Chi-Rho monogram was engraved on three of its stones.

Little Milton and Chedworth have one feature in common. They were at the centre of working farms. Unfortunately we have no conclusive evidence as to how large their estates were or how they were cultivated and managed, although we do know a great deal about the crops and animals to be found on Roman farms. Nor do we know if there were any tenants, farmers, or labourers or what their tenurial relationships were. Very occasionally it may be possible to detect field boundaries which would appear to be associated with the villa, as at Barnsley Park in Gloucestershire for example, but again the exact relationship between the two observed features in the landscape of today cannot be certainly established.

Villas were self-contained establishments in very much the same way that seventeenth- and eighteenth-century country houses were. There is evidence of fulling, tanning, building, and carpentry work, all providing goods and services for the household. There is also evidence that at least part of the building and furnishing of a villa was entrusted to professional craftsmen: masons, tilers, glaziers, plasterers, and mosaicists. Mosaics have always been one of the chief features of a villa, at least in the eyes of many eighteenth- and nineteenth-century excavators, whose principal objective seems to have been plunder rather than anything else. Some certainly are splendid and fascinating pieces of workmanship, even today. Thus the mosaic of Orpheus and the Beast, still at the villa at Woodchester, is at once the largest mosaic in northwestern Europe, made up of over one and a half million *tesserae,* and a remarkable work of art. Close study of such mosaics has revealed the existence of several workshops which could provide mosaics to order from pattern books. The most important of these workshops seems to have been at Cirencester.

Very few villas have been properly excavated, and even fewer have had their subsidiary and farm buildings excavated. Thus the functions of individual rooms often remain uncertain and controversial save for the most obvious ones such as kitchens, dining-rooms, and baths, where it is not unusual to find that coal has been used to stoke the furnaces.

However, close study of large numbers of villa plans, not only from Britain but also from northwestern Europe, has suggested that many may in fact have contained two, occasionally three, living units. Thus at Newton St Loe in Wiltshire, Beadlam in Yorkshire, Folkestone, and Llantwit Major there are two houses lying more or less at right angles around a courtyard. At Gayton Thorpe in Norfolk there were two laid out side-by-side until they were eventually joined by a small linking block. The three wings at Chedworth may be interpreted as three houses, again surrounding a common courtyard, and both Chedworth and Folkestone had two bath houses. It may not be too fanciful to see here, behind the superficial Romanized veneer of porticos, mosaics, and painted plaster, provision for one of the most important institutions of Celtic society, namely the extended family or kinship group, with two or more related family units occupying distinct parts of the same building complex but working the estate in common. We shall find a very similar phenomenon in the Welsh 'unit' houses of the sixteenth and seventeenth centuries, arrangements which it may not be implausible to see as the outcome of the workings of partible inheritance. In this way the most abstract rules of human society find their reflection in the landscape.

The villa, however, is only one part of the rural landscape, although it may well have been the most prominent. There were in addition many thousands of other occupation sites, ranging in size from isolated farmsteads on the one hand to nucleated settlements on the other, presenting to historians the insoluble problem of drawing a line between a large village and a small town. The great majority of these settlements are but continuations into the Roman period of sites which had been occupied, sometimes for generations, in the years preceding the conquest. It is customary to call them 'native' settlements but this is misleading since it would appear to draw a racial distinction between them and the 'Roman' villa, a distinction which existed only in a minority of cases since it is generally believed that the great majority of villas were occupied by people of Romano-British origin. It is probably better to think of this kind of occupation site as being a settlement showing a lesser degree of 'Romanization' than the conventional villa, although the dividing line between the two can be a matter of controversy in individual cases. Thus at Woodcutts, in Dorset, is an isolated farmstead within a ditched enclosure with a history that spans the entire period from the late pre-Roman Iron Age to the end of the fourth century AD. A similar farmstead at Rotherly Down in Wiltshire remained in occupation for over 300 years. 'Romanization' in either case did not go very far. At Rotherly Down there was towards the end of the period of occupation a substantial timber building, rectangular in plan. At Woodcutts there is evidence of painted plaster work, although no masonry buildings are known. On West Overton Down, also in Wiltshire, there is a series of hut platforms. Excavation of two of them revealed cottages, one about 30 by 20 feet the other barely 12 feet square. Occupation debris included painted plaster and some roof tiles, but it is assumed that the walls themselves were of timber construction. At Ewe Close, in Westmorland, evidence of 'Romanization' is even slighter. Here is a stone-built 'native' settlement, spread over some 1½ acres, 850 feet up in the limestone fells to the south of Penrith. It seems to have begun as a large circular house set in a more or less rectangular enclosure. A second enclosure, also containing circular houses, was added at a later stage, and a third, much larger enclosure, then followed, with a circular building and at least three rectangular ones, perhaps the first traces of 'Romanization'.

These are just a handful of examples of isolated farmsteads. Nucleated settlements, of almost infinite variety of plan, are equally widely distributed. At Grassington in Yorkshire there are over 150 acres of more or less rectangular fields, with a number of scattered circular houses showing only the loosest nucleation. Surface finds, particularly of broken shards of pottery which may have come from domestic middens spread over the fields as manure, suggest occupation from the second to the fourth centuries AD. One of the best-known Romano-British villages is at Chisenbury Warren, in Wiltshire. Here is a long street village with more than eighty house platforms and a triangular 'green' at each end. At Kingscote in Gloucestershire, a site extending over 50 acres has evidence of at least seventy-five buildings, rectangular house platforms and a great deal of occupation debris dating from the first to the fourth century AD, including limestone building slabs, bronze brooches and bracelets, glassware, a stone quern of Niedermendig lava, and a great deal of pottery, including some from the Rhineland. The site lies in fields known as the Chessalls, and another 25-acre site at Lower Slaughter is called Chessels. Both names come from an Anglo-Saxon word meaning 'heaps of stones'. Clearly sufficient remained visible above ground to impress the English when they came into the region. The site at Lower Slaughter has revealed both round and rectangular houses, pottery from the late Iron Age, painted wall plaster, a forge and the use of coal.

At Salmonsbury, near Bourton-on-the-Water, is a defended settlement of some 56 acres. It was occupied both before and after the enclosing banks and ditches were built, and at least one rectangular house, measuring 14 by 38 feet, was built over an Iron Age circular one. A similar picture of rectangular houses showing every sign of occupation during the Roman period and lying over circular Iron Age ones is to be found on a 20-acre site near Lechlade. An even more interesting site is to be found at Wycomb, in Whittington, Gloucestershire. Here is a 28-acre site showing evidence of occupation from Mesolithic times. A straight road is lined with buildings on either side for at least 600 yards, and there is evidence of building in side roads as well as a structure which has been interpreted as a temple. Are we, here at Wycomb, as well as at Lechlade and at Salmonsbury, looking at small towns rather than villages, with that at Salmonsbury having its roots in the late Iron Age?

The distinction between a village and a town is one of very considerable importance and one which we can no longer avoid trying to make. A variety of criteria can be, and have been, used to point the difference: population density, legal status, structures of local government, economic, social, political, and cultural functions. It is clear however that these criteria are not always particularly helpful and that they change over time. Towns certainly have more inhabitants than villages, but until the end of the eighteenth century the great majority of towns in Britain were very small, and some had fewer than a thousand inhabitants. Secondly, legal status is no satisfactory guide. Manchester had no formal charter of incorporation before the nineteenth century, but Langport Eastover did, and yet Manchester was undoubtedly a town, whereas the claims of Langport Eastover to urban status can be questioned. It is instead to function that we must look. A place becomes a town when it begins to act as a distribution centre for goods and services to neighbouring places, thus becoming a focal point for a district, no matter how narrowly circumscribed that district may be. It also requires that a significant proportion of its working inhabitants should be engaged in non-agricultural activities, making and providing goods and services rather than growing crops and looking after animals. Probably the minimum number needs to be about a third of the working population. This means that although a sizeable number of people will be engaged in agriculture the place will nevertheless rank as a town. We shall see during the course of this book that the breaking away of the town from the country is a long-drawn-out process, scarcely completed before 1914.

The urban/rural dichotomy is of the greatest importance, because it is towns that provide the opportunities for occupational specialization and innovation. Their shops and markets make food and other necessities readily and easily available for cash, giving men and women the opportunity to become tailors, shoemakers, goldsmiths, booksellers, and so on, without their having to grow their own grain or keep their own sheep. At the same time their demands for foodstuffs and raw materials stimulate agricultural development and thus provide the income through which farmers may in their turn make increasing use of the facilities offered in towns. The processes are interrelated in a most subtle and complex fashion and can vary in their intensity over time. It seems very likely for example that there was only the most attenuated urban life in Britain in the two centuries after the collapse of Roman power, whilst it seems equally likely that those developments in hill forts and *oppida* in southern Britain in the last two centuries BC described in the previous chapter were the consequence of the crystallization of increasingly specialized patterns of demand and supply.

This discussion of the distinction between town and country may seem rather arid, but it is of the greatest importance since it heralds the appearance in the landscape of a new social organism with unparalleled powers for change.

The concept of the city state was at the heart of the Roman world and the Empire was but an extension of the city of Rome. If a conquered territory had no towns then their provision was of the first priority if its inhabitants were to become Romanized to any degree. When the Romans began the conquest of Britain they found nothing which they could recognize as a town although, as we saw in the previous chapter, there were nucleated settlements which were incipient towns. One of the first acts of the Roman authorities once the tide of conquest began to move away from the southeast was to found a *colonia* at Colchester. It was established on the site of the now abandoned legionary fortress. The first inhabitants were discharged Roman soldiers, most probably from Legio XX. Each veteran was given a house plot within the new town together with a further, larger, plot, its size depending upon his rank, in the surrounding countryside. Thus the first Roman town had its roots deep in the countryside, and townsmen were both traders and farmers. We shall see burgesses cultivating their strips in the open fields around their town until the end of the nineteenth century. Only in 1875 were the open fields of Stamford enclosed, and it was not until 1927 that the burgesses of High Wycombe lost their right to graze livestock in the Rye, where once a Roman villa stood.

The *territorium* around this new *colonia* was probably quite extensive, obtained by confiscating the lands of the British inhabitants, an act which may have contributed to the ferocious rebellion of Boudicca in AD 60 and the massacre of its citizens. Only two other Roman towns were founded in this way, as *colonia*, that is chartered towns with extensive rights of self-government from the first. These were Gloucester and Lincoln, both established as such before the end of the first century. It is very likely, although uncertain, that Verulamium had also been chartered as a *municipium*, a lower status than that of *colonia*, by the same time. It is also likely that London had also been granted the status of a *municipium* by the end of the century and that it was promoted *colonia* by the fourth century. York followed a rather similar pattern. A legionary fortress was founded on the south bank of the Ouse at the end of the first century. A civilian community began to grow on the north bank. This may have been chartered as a *municipium* by the end of the second century and was certainly a *colonia* by AD 237.

Thus there were in Roman Britain only six chartered towns, with their own governing bodies and their own surrounding, subordinate lands or *territoria*. These were not however the only towns. There were first of all about two dozen *civitates*. As the conquest moved north so local administration was handed over to civil authorities. The Romans everywhere and as a matter of course turned to existing political structures to provide the framework for local government and in Britain these structures were the pre-conquest tribal territories. Each territory, with only very little change – the territory of the Atrebates was divided into two for example – was then considered to be a *civitas,* with its own carefully prescribed rights and duties. Each *civitas* required an administrative centre and in due course they slowly appeared. It is important to appreciate that these towns, now frequently called *civitas* capitals by historians, had no separate legal entity to mark them off from their territory. The *civitas* was both town and country, and what for the moment may be called its administrative centre was founded and developed by the local British tribal aristocracy with the consent, encouragement, and assistance of the Roman authorities. They are, like the villas described in earlier paragraphs, a manifestation of the process of Romanization of the British population, but they were built by and for British inhabitants.

There were eventually over twenty urban centres to the *civitates* into which Roman Britain was divided. Each is unique, but they also have certain characteristics in common.

First, they all show evidence of deliberate planning. The principal streets were laid out upon a regular, gridiron pattern, creating blocks, or *insulae,* of land upon which individual proprietors in due course put up their houses and shops. Two main streets crossed the town, intersecting at right angles. They were the *cardo maximus* and the *decumanus maximus*. In one of the four *insulae* adjoining this crossroads was to be found the forum and basilica. The forum was a large open space which could be used for public assemblies and as a market-place. It was surrounded on three sides by porticos, behind which were probably rows of shops and offices. The whole of the fourth side was taken up with the basilica. In the side facing the basilica there was an elaborate entrance to the whole complex. The basilica itself was a long aisled hall in which judicial and administrative affairs were conducted by the local magistrates, together with offices and rooms for council meetings, and a shrine for statues of the deified Emperors and of local gods. Here was the political, legal, and spiritual heart of the entire *civitas,* and it was these functions that entitle places of this kind to be called towns.

The main streets of the town were made up with gravel. When they needed repair fresh layers were put down. Gradually the street levels rose and later generations of shopkeepers found themselves with a considerable step down from street level into their premises. In Cirencester one of the

16 The Jewry Wall, once part of the Roman baths at Leicester.

principal streets, Ermine Street, rose 9½ feet during the course of 350 years, and at least twenty-four different surfaces have been recognized during recent excavations.

Every chartered town and *civitas* centre in Roman Britain was provided with a supply of water, brought in by means of an aqueduct or conduit from some source outside the town. The gentler topography of Britain means that such splendid Roman aqueducts as the Pont du Gard in southern France were not necessary. Those in Britain still called for considerable skill in their planning and construction. That for Dorchester led water from the river Frome in a very carefully sited and graded channel falling only 25 feet in 11½ miles, bringing nearly 60,000 cubic metres of fresh water into the town every day. Once in the town this water was distributed through the principal streets by means of pipes of wood, lead, or stone. Sometimes, as in Gloucester and York, drinking basins were provided at street corners, and sometimes private shops and houses received a piped supply, as at Wroxeter and Verulamium, but the bulk of the water went into the public baths. Here was a suite of rooms, kept at varying temperatures by furnaces, in which bathers went from a dressing room through an unheated room into a warm room and then into a hot room, followed by a cold plunge as the final stage in what was clearly an important ritual, lying at the centre of the social life of the town. These public baths were often large, imposing buildings. They had to be. It has been estimated that as many as 500 people a day could have used those in Leicester.

Once the water was flowing through the aqueduct it could be stopped only with the greatest difficulty. This meant that an adequate network of sewers had also to be provided to carry the waste water away. Of all the towns of Roman Britain perhaps Lincoln had the most substantial sewers. Built of stone, at their maximum they were 5 feet high and 4 feet wide and were provided with manhole covers so that they could be cleaned and repaired.

The frontages to the streets in the centres of the new towns were quite quickly built up with houses and shops. The building plots were long and rectangular, with the short side facing onto the street, a pattern we shall meet again when we look at the revival of towns in the tenth century and the planting of new ones from then on into the fourteenth. The first properties were often timber-framed, with wattle-and-daub walls and tiled roofs. Interior walls were often plastered and then painted, whilst floors were of concrete or wood, and occasionally mosaic, and windows were glazed. Many of these premises were both house and workshop, and goods which were made on the premises were sold over the counter of the shop at the front, facing onto the street. In this way a pattern of urban living was established in which the shopkeeper lived over and behind his shop, a pattern which has not entirely disappeared from the towns of Britain even today.

An immensely wide range of goods, drawn not only locally but also from the far ends of the Roman Empire, could be bought in the shops of the towns of Roman Britain. It is often difficult to be sure of the trade carried out at any one time in any particular shop, since goods like fruit and vegetables are perishable and leave little trace, and in any case shopkeepers died, sold up or otherwise cleared out their old stock and started new lines in much the same way as shopkeepers today. Nor is there evidence of every kind of shop from every Roman town, but neither is there any evidence to show that any particular trades were excluded from, or confined to, any one town. Thus what follows is an amalgam of fragmentary evidence drawn from several Roman towns across the whole time-span of the Roman occupation.

There were pottery and glassware shops, selling goods made all over Britain, the Rhineland, Gaul, and even Egypt. There were wine shops, drawing their supplies from what is now Bordeaux, as well as Spain, southern Italy, and the Rhine. Oysters were sold in the forum at Caerwent, but oyster shells turn up so frequently and in such large numbers on any and every Roman archaeological site that is excavated that the production, supply, transport, and sale of these shellfish must have been particularly well organized, extending to most corners, urban and rural, of Roman Britain. There were coppersmiths, goldsmiths, and blacksmiths, sculptors, masons, and glaziers. In Leicester one glassworker also carried on the highly dangerous and illegal business of smelting down the debased coins of the later period of the Empire in order to recover the silver. If he were caught, then the consequences for him could have been extremely unpleasant.

There were shops selling shoes and cutlery. Tailors, butchers, tanners, and dyers were to be found. The whole range of trinkets and toys that turn up as a matter of course in Roman excavation sites, things like brooches, pins, tweezers, rings, little glass bottles, mirrors, combs, knives, writing tablets, and samian pottery of every kind, shape, and decoration, were bought and sold in the shops of the towns of Roman Britain, to find their way in due course and in greater or lesser profusion into the remotest and most isolated 'native' farmstead. The money for their purchase came from the sale of grain and cattle to the butchers and bakers in the towns where the dishes, glassware, and bronze rings were bought.

As shopkeepers, traders, and merchants grew rich they began to extend and improve their houses, and the growing range of amenities in towns together with their obligations as magistrates drew in what may be called the country gentry to buy and build town houses for themselves. We shall see the same phenomenon occurring in towns in the seventeenth century. Much rebuilding took place. Masonry walls replaced timber and wattle, and so central heating could be introduced. Larger houses were built round a courtyard, which was laid out as a garden. Mosaics, painted plaster, and other decorative work was popular and often of a very high standard, and occasionally the largest town houses had their own bath houses.

A number of Roman towns had amphitheatres: Dorchester, Silchester, Chichester, Cirencester, and Carmarthen certainly did, York and Leicester may have done, and there were purely military ones at the legionary fortresses at Caerleon and Chester. In Britain at any rate amphitheatres were of earthen construction, with wooden or masonry walls, and seats arranged in tiers. They were usually built on the outskirts of a town because of the space required, and it has been estimated that most of those in Britain could have seated all of the inhabitants of the town to which they were attached and still leave room for visitors from the surrounding countryside. The one at Cirencester could probably have seated between eight and nine thousand people. It was composed of an earthen bank over 130 feet thick and nearly 30 feet high, enclosing an elliptical arena measuring 160 by 130 feet. Masonry walls replaced earlier timber revetments in the late second century. There is the distinct possibility that in the immediate post-Roman period it was fortified, as happened for example to the amphitheatres at Nîmes and Arles.

Only three theatres are known in Roman Britain, at Canterbury,

17 The Newport Arch, Lincoln, once part of the North Gate of the Roman town.

Verulamium, and at Gosbecks Farm, Colchester, although the latter, lying outside the *colonia,* is not really an urban theatre at all. Theatres elsewhere in the Empire were very frequently associated with temples or shrines, and the same appears to be true for those so far recognized in Britain, except at Canterbury perhaps, where the evidence for any religious association is less certain. No circuses have yet been identified anywhere in Roman Britain.

Neither chartered towns nor the administrative centres of *civitates* were fortified when they were first built, and the addition of walls to the towns of Roman Britain is a long, complex and only partially understood process which can be discussed only very briefly here. Both Verulamium and Silchester were provided with earthen banks and ditches within a few years of the invasion, although it remains uncertain why they should have been singled out in this way. By the end of the century the two abandoned legionary fortresses which had served as the bases for the new *colonia* at Lincoln and Gloucester had had their timber and earthen fortifications rebuilt in stone, and it seems likely that Colchester followed suit early in the next century. The crisis provoked by the bid for power of the governor in Britain, Clodius Albinus, in 193 led to extensive plans for the fortification of towns, Cirencester, Exeter, London, Dorchester, and Verulamium for example, although because of the need for speed much of the work took the form of earthen banks and ditches. This work was continued more slowly and more carefully for much of the first half of the third century, so that by the opening years of the fourth many settlements, large and small, had been provided with defences.

The last stage in the fortification of towns in Roman Britain came in the last decades of the fourth century when, after the barbarian invasions of 367, Theodosius was making strenuous efforts to restore order to Britain. Walls were strengthened, new ditches cut, and towers or bastions were built from which, it is generally thought, Roman artillery, that is catapults firing arrows, were deployed to cover the walls.

Many walled towns were very small. Hardham, Alfoldean, and Iping are all less than 4 acres in area, and Horncastle is less than 6 acres. At the other extreme the largest town in Roman Britain, London, had a fortified area of 330 acres, and the second, Cirencester, an area of 240 acres. The town walls did not however always include all of the built-up parts of a town. Some areas remained, or developed, outside the walls to become suburbs.

The towns we have been looking at so far are those which have all the characteristics of the traditional view of what a Roman town should look like: gridiron street plans, forum and basilica, large public baths, stone walls and massive gate towers. It is however becoming increasingly clear that these characteristics are to be found in only a minority of those places in Roman Britain which may be called towns, namely those *coloniae* and *municipia* which were chartered towns, together with the capital towns of the *civitates*, in all about thirty places. There were in Roman Britain many more places which were clearly small towns although it is at present an impossible task to give a comprehensive list of them all, not least because in the present state of our knowledge we are unable to draw a convincing line between them and villages. A number were walled: places like Great Chesterford, Towcester, Alchester, Kenchester, Mildenhall, Leintwardine, Ancaster, Mancetter, and those mentioned in the previous paragraph (Horncastle, Hardham, Alfoldean, and Iping). Many others, Hockwold for example, show no signs of defences, and yet they appear sometimes to extend over areas larger than those of some fortified places. Some show at least minimal efforts at town planning, as at Alchester, Catterick, and Godmanchester, but none show any evidence of forum, basilica, or public baths, and where the principal crossroads does appear to be present, as at Brancaster for example, there is also evidence from aerial photographs to show unplanned and haphazard streets and lanes developing behind the main streets. At Kenchester a main road runs straight through the middle of the place, from east to west, but the internal street pattern within the walled area of about 22 acres is entirely irregular. At Irchester, in Northamptonshire, an area of about 20 acres was enclosed within an earthen bank and ditch late in the second century. This was later cut back to take a stone wall. The internal street plan is very irregular with no main through road of any kind, and similar irregular building continued to take place outside the walls on both east and south sides until the end of the fourth century. At Chesterton, in Cambridgeshire, is the largest of the walled 'small' towns of Roman Britain, extending over an area of about 44 acres. Its backbone is formed by the straight line of Ermine Street, on its way from London to Lincoln. Apart from this the internal street plan developed in a very irregular fashion. The town seems to have risen to prosperity as the centre of the large-scale pottery industry which grew up in the valley of the Nene from the middle of the second century, an industry which had an enormously wide and insatiable market for its wares. An unfortified industrial suburb to the town grew up on the north bank of the Nene and eventually extended over about 69 acres.

Towns were at once the most distinctive and the most important single contribution made by the Romans to the evolution of the landscape of Britain. A fully developed institution was thrust upon an Iron Age society in which urbanization was only in its initial stages. This gap gives to Roman towns a certain air of artificiality at first, but this is rapidly lost as the Romano-British inhabitants quickly adapted themselves to the demands made upon them by the new, urban, way of life. However, this first flush of towns in Britain lasted less than four centuries, since organized municipal life seems to have come to an end by the last decades of the fifth century and Roman municipal institutions made no contribution to the government of medieval towns. Squatter occupation, however, seems to have continued in a number of towns and it is a measure of the skill of Roman planners and engineers that only two major Roman urban sites are unoccupied today, Silchester and Wroxeter, and even here it is only a matter of short-distance migration to Reading and Shrewsbury respectively. Thus the first major contribution of Roman towns to the long-term history of the landscape has been in the choice of their sites. The second has been the line of the town walls. These have exercised a major constraint on town growth and development until comparatively recently, and they have proved to be much more influential upon medieval and modern town morphology than the gridiron pattern of streets, which has almost everywhere been lost.

It is one of the principal themes of this book that the landscape has engraved upon it evidence from the earliest times of the activities and preoccupations of men, from their most mundane and yet fundamental needs for food and shelter to the expression of their most profound spiritual aspirations. We saw in Chapter 2 that the landscape of today still contains much evidence of the activities and aspirations of those prehistoric men whose lives make up four-fifths of the time which has passed since the end of the last ice age. What appear to be their religious monuments, from Stonehenge to Maes Howe, still have power both to astonish and to move. We can however have but the vaguest and most generalized picture of the ideals, beliefs, and values which lay behind the construction of such monuments.

In this chapter we stand on the threshold of history in that we now have some documents in which men record their values and beliefs. These documents are themselves far from numerous and present their own problems of interpretation. There are also very few from Britain itself, so that we often have to rely upon material from other parts of the Roman Empire, with the inherent danger that such material relates only to its place of provenance and that to use it to shed light upon matters in Britain may be positively misleading. Nevertheless with all these reservations made, we do now for the first time have documents which can be made to yield at least some insight into the mental preoccupations with which men built and rebuilt their external, physical world during the four centuries of the Roman occupation.

The pattern of religious beliefs in Roman Britain exhibits the same characteristics as all the other features of the landscape: continuity with the past, complexity of practice in the present, processes of change linking past, present, and future. The people of Roman Britain at the time of the conquest worshipped a wide range of gods and spirits that clearly had many connections with the practices to be found in Gaul at the same time, and it is equally clear that these patterns of belief had only the broadest ideas in common, so that there was much local variety. A great deal of importance was attached to water, particularly springs and wells, and also to sacred enclosures, especially in woods. The Roman state was remarkably tolerant and so many Celtic gods were identified, more or less, with some figure from the classical Graeco-Roman pantheon. Thus at Caerwent there were dedications to Mars Lenus and to Mars Ocelus, where we may be looking at the assimilation of one or more Celtic deities to the Roman god Mars. At the same time the Roman gods themselves were worshipped, as witness inscriptions to Minerva and Neptune at Chichester. An important development that took place in Roman religious practices in the years after the conquest was the growth in the cult of the Emperor, more especially when deified. The most notable example of this is to be found at Colchester, where a great temple was completed and dedicated to Claudius, almost certainly a little after his death. Thirdly there were a number of importations into the Roman world of mystery cults from the East. An altar dedicated to Serapis is known in York, a temple to Isis in London and one dedicated possibly to Osiris in Rochester. All three of these gods are Egyptian in origin. All of these Eastern religions are outweighed by two further ones, Mithraism and Christianity.

Numerous temples and shrines to every religious sect are known throughout Roman Britain. The great majority are comparatively small and simple, and many show striking evidence of continuity of use from late Iron Age times into the Roman period. On the other hand purely classical temples modelled on those traditional to Rome and Greece were almost unknown in Roman Britain. The largest seems to have been that already mentioned, dedicated to Claudius and built in Colchester. It was constructed on a podium, 105 by 80 feet, itself built over vaults which can still be seen beneath the keep of the Norman castle which now occupies the site. At the front was a portico rising on columns perhaps 30 feet high and approached by a broad flight of steps. The temple itself housed the statue of Claudius. All public ceremonies took place outside the temple at the front in a large courtyard where stood the principal sacrificial altar. It must have been a splendid and imposing building when it was first finished. It was destroyed during the rebellion of Boudicca, but it is very likely that it was rebuilt.

Another large classical temple was erected at Bath, with the hot spring and its attendant baths, now the King's Bath, extending from its southeastern corner. Its dedication to Sulis Minerva is a further example of that conflation of Roman and Celtic deities already mentioned. The hot waters rising from the spring were then, as now, considered to have magical and curative properties and many dedications from people from all conditions in life have been found. Other classical temples are known at Verulamium and Corbridge, and a smaller one at Wroxeter.

Much more common in the landscape were temples which have been called Romano-Celtic by modern historians because they have been found throughout the Celtic parts of the Empire. They are generally fairly small and square in shape, although both circular and polygonal ones are known, as at Weycock Hill in Berkshire. It seems most likely that in all three kinds there was a central shrine which may have risen tower-like above the roof of the surrounding portico or ambulatory. The shrine itself was the home of the god, containing perhaps an altar and a statue. There was no provision for public acts of worship. Instead it was left to the individual to perform such acts as he thought fit, with personal sacrifices and gifts. There may have been processions round the shrine, hence the portico, and the whole building may itself have been set within an enclosure, whether the earthworks of a hill fort as at Maiden Castle, or one specially constructed for the purpose. It has been suggested that the shrine at Gosbecks Farm, near Colchester, was built close to a sacred tree, and trees and groves were certainly important in the beliefs of the Romano-British population. The word for such a sacred grove, *nemeton,* survives even today in such place-names as Nympsfield, in Gloucestershire, and the various Nymets and Nymptons in Devon. Nymet Rowland is on the River Yeo, a tributary of the Taw and itself formerly known as the Nymet. Bishops Nympton and

Kings Nympton lie some 5 miles apart, separated by the River Mole, a river also once called the Nymet. About 5 miles away to the southwest of Nymet Rowland is a Roman fort at North Tawton, to which the Roman place-name *Nemetostatio* has been very tentatively applied. At Nettleham in Lincolnshire, a dedication to Mars Rigonemetos, meaning 'king of the sanctuary' has been found. *Aquae Arnemetiae,* now Buxton, would appear to show spring and grove associated together, and Arnemetia seems to have been a goddess in her own right, her name being found on an altar stone from Brough-on-Noe in Derbyshire. *Medionemetum* is a Roman place-name that must lie somewhere in Scotland, and it has been suggested that it can be identified with the unusually striking shrine known as Arthur's O'on, at Larbert, in Stirlingshire. Another Roman place-name, *Vernemetum,* meaning 'very sacred grove', has been identified with the Roman settlement near Willoughby-on-the-Wolds in Nottinghamshire, whilst a tentative emendation of an otherwise corrupt Roman place-name to *Nemetobala* has been equally tentatively suggested for the large and important temple complex built inside an Iron Age hill fort at Lydney, in Gloucestershire. The old gods have still not yet entirely disappeared from the landscape.

Roman law forbade burials in towns, save of children under ten days old, who had no legal existence, and so Roman cemeteries are to be found in the countryside, and especially along roads leading out of towns. Extensive cemeteries are known outside Canterbury for example, and outside Colchester and York, whilst the cemetery at Poundbury, just outside Dorchester-on-Thames, may have contained anything up to 5,000 burials. Burial was either by cremation or inhumation, and there could have been a wide variety of rites to accompany either of these practices. In very broad terms cremation was the principal form of burial in the first and second centuries, slowly giving way to inhumation thereafter, although there was a long period of overlap and it is very unlikely that the spread of Christianity influenced this change, at least at first. It was usual to bury objects with the deceased throughout the entire Roman period, a practice which may have become less common towards its end, but again the influence of Christianity is likely to have been slight. Individual burials were sometimes marked by upright tombstones. These often contain biographical details about the deceased, giving us fascinating glimpses into the lives of ordinary Romano-British people, many of whom were not in fact Romano-British at all but had come from all parts of the Empire, from Syria or Thrace for example. Those families who could afford it were buried either in a mausoleum or else under an earthen mound or barrow. At Keston, in Kent, a buttressed wall of masonry enclosed a circular space about 27 feet in diameter, with access by means of a door. It is very likely that the interior contained niches in which the cinerary urns were placed. At least eight rectangular mausolea are known in the cemetery at Poundbury, and at Stone-by-Faversham, in Kent, a Roman mausoleum was incorporated into the chancel of the medieval church, now ruined.

Burials in earthen mounds or barrows were, if the richness of the grave goods which have been found is any guide, confined to the wealthy few, to what may be called, without too much sense of anachronism, the country gentry. Roman burial mounds are generally larger than prehistoric round barrows and have a much steeper profile. At the Bartlow Hills, Ashdon, in Essex, four large Roman burial mounds survive from what was once a group of eight. Burials seem to have been made in wooden coffins, although one may have been in a tile-built burial chamber. Unfortunately, of the eight, one was destroyed before 1586 and three in 1832, whilst the remaining four were tunnelled into at about the same time. Sadly, almost all that was found has since been destroyed by fire. Two similar burial mounds are at Thornborough, in Buckinghamshire. They also were excavated in the nineteenth century. The more important of the items then found are now in the Fitzwilliam Museum in Cambridge. The Bartlow Hills mounds have at least three villas in the district, and those at Thornborough lie close to a complex site which included a temple, with villas also near by.

Inhumation burials took place either in wooden or in lead coffins and it was not unknown for these coffins to be further enclosed in stone sarcophagi, and occasionally liquid gypsum was poured in. This set and thus retained a mould of the body. There are yet more unusual rites. Almost everyone buried in the cemetery at Puckridge was provided with a pair of hobnailed boots, a practice also found in the cemetery at Curbridge, in Oxfordshire, and in that at Guilden Morden in Cambridgeshire. Close to the cemetery near the amphitheatre at Cirencester a building has been found housing a forge and over 2,000 shoe nails. Perhaps it was felt that the deceased needed a good pair of shoes for his journey into the underworld.

Even more difficult to explain are those burials where the body has been dismembered. The Curbridge cemetery just referred to has also yielded three skeletons with their skulls placed between their feet, and the cemetery at Dunstable contained dismembered skeletons, together with two with boots placed beneath the knees.

We can only guess at the significance of these rites. The presence in the landscape of today of the burial mounds at the Bartlow Hills and at Thornborough, and they are by no means the only ones, are silent reminders of values and beliefs, patterns of thought and moral attitudes which were undoubtedly sincerely held, as witness the effort that must have gone into the construction of the mounds in the first place. We can recover only the vaguest outlines of many of these beliefs, although what we do know would indicate that we would find many of them almost impossible to accept. The grief of Flavia Flavina over the death of her daughter, Julia Iverna, at the age of 16, as recorded on a memorial stone at Caerleon, strikes a chord even in the late twentieth century to show that we

18   The Mithraeum at Brocolitia, Carrawburgh, Northumberland.

share a common humanity, even across the centuries. We should find it
very much more difficult to accept the need to dismember the body of a
deceased relative at the time of burial.

Two eastern cults remain to be discussed: Mithraism and Christianity.
Mithraism was a version of the Persian creed of Zoroaster, in which the
god of light wages an eternal battle against the powers of darkness, good
against evil. It was of course much more complex than this and much was
veiled in mystery. It did however demand adherence to a strict code of
personal conduct, and, by imposing severe and testing initiation rites, it
always remained an exclusive, men only, sect. It did, however, have a
widespread following in Roman Britain if the distribution of its surviving
temples is any guide. A Mithraeum was built outside the fort at
Carrawburgh towards the end of the second century, and another in
London perhaps at about the same time. Others are known at Caernarvon,
Housesteads, the three legionary fortresses of York, Chester, and
Caerleon, and, possibly, at Leicester, Verulamium, Colchester, and
Gloucester. A Mithraeum was, usually, a small, rectangular, aisled
building. The one at London, at 60 by 25 feet, is rather on the large side,
and that at Housesteads was in a cave. The internal darkness of all Mithrae

would have served to heighten the aura of suspense and mystery that surrounded the rites. There were seven grades of initiates, each stage having its own ceremonies and ordeals, in which the sunken trough near the entrance to the Mithraeum at Carrawburgh may have had a part to play. That at Carrawburgh is further evidence of the toleration of the Roman authorities towards a wide range of religious cults, since it is not far from a shrine dedicated to the *Genius Loci,* the Nymphs and the well of the water-nymph Coventina, the centre of what seems to have been a very popular cult.

The Mithraea at both London and Carrawburgh show clear evidence of the destruction of their sacred objects on at least two occasions, when some were defaced and yet others carefully buried. The Mithraeum in London was re-floored and used again during the course of the fourth century, perhaps, it has been suggested, as a Christian church, perhaps for the shrine of some other non-Christian cult. In either case the careful burial of sacred objects may be interpreted as a deliberate purification of the building as part of its conversion to a new faith.

The early origins of Christianity in Britain remain obscure, and there is very little firm evidence at all for the presence of the faith before the fourth century, when we know that three bishops from Britain attended the Council at Arles in 314. There are numerous articles of jewellery and plate known which bear Christian symbols, especially the Chi-Rho monogram, including the splendid hoard of plate found in 1975 in the small town of Chesterton, and there are a number of mosaics and wall paintings of the same kind, particularly the magnificent mosaic discovered at Hinton St Mary in 1963 and what is most likely to have been a private chapel in the villa at Lullingstone, but of the presence of Christianity beyond the circles of the wealthy gentry there is very little evidence. There are several buildings in towns, including Lincoln, Colchester, Canterbury, Ver- ulamium, and Silchester, which have been tentatively identified as Christian churches, of which that at Flaxengate, Lincoln, probably has the best claim, but such identifications are still controversial. The uncertainties may be due to the fact that the church as a distinctive building type had not yet emerged. If practice elsewhere in the Empire is any guide then British bishops would have had their cathedrals in towns. But a cathedral was no more than a suite of rooms set aside for worship within the bishop's house, with only the decorations and furnishings of these rooms to distinguish this house from any other private dwelling, thus making the identification of a church particularly difficult. Nevertheless, Christianity was being practised in Britain before the end of the Roman period, and will continue to be practised somewhere in the island down to the present.

The Roman occupation swept Britain into the orbit of a literate, urban, Mediterranean civilization, a civilization which added towns, roads, and villas to an already ancient, fully explored, and densely settled landscape.

However, the long-term contribution of this civilization to the British landscape was, in spite of its achievements, strictly limited and very uneven, being largely confined to the sites of towns and the lines of roads, not least because in a number of respects its impact upon Britain was rather superficial. Thus the inhabitants of Roman Britain did not adopt Latin universally, and so, when Roman civilization collapsed the incoming barbarians were able to impose their own language, rather than adopting that of the inhabitants, as happened in France.

On 31 December 406 a horde of barbarians, Alans, Suebi, and Vandals, crossed the Rhine. At about the same time the army in Britain mutinied, choosing in quick succession Marcus, Gratian, and then Constantine III to be Emperor. By the end of 407 the last of these three had crossed over into Gaul and had been sufficiently successful in his bid for power for the Emperor Honorius in Rome to recognize him as Augustus. His success was short-lived. There were widespread barbarian attacks on Britain, the army in Spain under Gerontius revolted, Constantine found himself besieged in Arles, and in 410 Alaric and the Huns sacked Rome itself. The historian Zosimus describes how the people of Britain were brought to the point where they revolted from Roman rule, refusing to live by Roman law, expelling Roman officials and setting up their own administration. It seems very likely that this revolt took place in 409, and it may be said to mark the formal end of the Roman occupation of Britain. The rescript of the Emperor Honorius, of the year 410, alleged to have been addressed to the cities of Britain urging them to look to their own defences, may not in fact have been sent to Britain at all, but may instead refer to Bruttium, in Italy.

No one at the time, however, could conceive of the idea that Roman authority would not again be restored in the near future. After all, there had been ambitious usurpers enough from Britain for at least two centuries, none of whom had had any permanent success. Thus in the short-term the events of 409 had nothing extraordinary about them. In the long-term of course they were of the greatest significance, creating a power vacuum that would eventually be filled from an entirely unexpected quarter. In the meanwhile there were between five and six million people living in Britain with next year's harvest to think of.

Part II

MEDIEVAL BRITAIN

4

People:
English, Scots, and Welsh

If there was indeed a revolt in Britain in 409 then it is very likely that only a comparatively small number of people actually left, since most army units had already gone. The departing handful of administrators and civil servants left behind them a densely settled landscape which supported sophisticated political, social, and economic structures and a high level of material prosperity based upon a market economy, although this last was by now ravaged by inflation and a debased coinage which in any case was about to disappear. Such a revolt implies leaders, and it is very likely that they emerged from the Romano-British aristocracy. The Celtic substratum of Roman Britain must have quickly reasserted itself to fill the power vacuum, since the veneer of Romanization was very thin. It is likely that Latin was quite widely spoken in the towns, which were very much Roman creations, and there is much evidence from graffiti on tiles, pottery, wall plaster and the like of a knowledge of both written and spoken Latin among the working population, although it was the Vulgar Latin of the western Empire rather than the formal, classical language of Caesar and Cicero. In the country its use was probably confined to those country gentry with a taste for Virgil. Celtic, however, was spoken everywhere. We may find some supporting evidence for this in the nature of the surviving place-names from Roman Britain. At least 350 names, whether of natural features such as rivers, or man-made ones like forts and towns, are known, but fewer than 25 are in fact Latin, the rest being British in origin, although taken over by the Roman authorities and dressed up to look like Latin, together with a handful which may belong to an older, pre-Celtic, linguistic stratum, including the root which lies behind the name of London.

The greater part of the inhabitants of Britain at the time of the Roman conquest spoke British, a language of the Brythonic group of Celtic languages, spoken over much of western Europe from what is now Portugal to the Rhine, a group known as P-Celtic. In Britain this language, from the fifth and sixth centuries, evolves into modern Welsh and Cornish, being taken at the same time by migrants into Armorica, there to become Breton. Another form of Celtic, Q-Celtic, or Goidelic, was spoken in Ireland. This is the basis for Irish, Manx, and Scots Gaelic, since it was taken into Scotland by Irish settlers from the fifth century onwards. In Scotland north of the Forth–Clyde line the situation was more complex and certainly today much more obscure. Here the people known to the Romans as *Caledonii* spoke a language in which Brythonic elements were imposed upon an older, non-Indo-European language.

Britain north of Hadrian's Wall had seen little of the Romans beyond an occasional trader and some limited military incursions, with the result that Roman influence was slight. This means that in many respects society in northern Britain developed as it would have done south of the Wall had it not been for the Roman occupation. Farmsteads continued to be circular in shape and of timber-frame construction. At Scotstarvit, in Fife, for example, three successive timber-framed round houses were built within a ditched enclosure, and another circular house, this time within a rectangular enclosure, has been excavated at Greencraig, also in Fife. Here was a house with a low turf and stone wall surmounted with a timber superstructure. At West Plean, in Stirlingshire, two successive circular timber-framed houses show every sign of habitation from late Bronze Age times into the first century AD, and at Kilpheder, on South Uist, is a circular stone house in the same tradition.

A variation on the circular house which is peculiar to what is now Scotland is the crannog. This is a house built on an artificial island made by dumping huge quantities of stones and boulders into shallow water. When the platform thus created broke the surface of the water immense stakes and piles were incorporated into it, and a circular house was built on top, the whole being connected to the mainland by a causeway just below water-level. One, in Milton Loch, to the west of Dumfries, was exposed when the level of the water in the loch was lowered in 1953. Excavation revealed occupation during the first and second centuries AD, although there is evidence from other crannogs to indicate occupation well into the medieval centuries, long after the original buildings had rotted away. One of the more picturesque crannog islands is that at Strathcashell Point, some 30 yards out from the shores of Loch Lomond.

Another form of defended homestead peculiar to Scotland is the broch. Nearly 600 are known, almost all of them lying beyond the Highland Line, with over a hundred in Caithness. A broch is a tower, of drystone construction, the walls about 15 feet thick and the interior area anything from 30 to 40 feet in diameter. Few are more than 20 feet high, although the one at Dun Telve, Inverness-shire, is, even now, 33 feet high, and this

19 An aerial view of the broch on Mousa, in the Shetlands. The ruin in the rectangular enclosure is a house, the old Haa.

in spite of its having been robbed over the centuries for building stone, a fate which has overtaken many of the others. The most famous, the largest and the best-preserved broch is that at Mousa, in the Shetlands, and this is 40 feet high. There was but a single door into a broch, and a staircase and other chambers were constructed in the thickness of the walls. They are often difficult to date individually, but in general terms they were being built in the last centuries BC and occupation in some cases, as at Dun Cuier, on Barra, continued on and off into the seventh century AD.

Another form of fortified homestead is that now known as a dùn. A massive drystone wall perhaps 16 feet thick enclosed an area as much as 70 feet in diameter. A fairly well-preserved one at Kildonan Bay, Kintyre, seems to be an early Iron Age building. It was then deserted, to be reoccupied for a long period in medieval times. Large numbers of small dùns are known in the Hebrides, such as that at Dun Buidhe, on an islet off Benbecula, but they remain almost entirely unexplored. Larger dùns seem to shade off into hill forts, of which there are large numbers south and east of the Highland Line. Several show evidence of internal structures, and at least two, Traprain Law and Eildon Hill, have every appearance of being centres of proto-urbanization, developing along very similar lines to those centres in southern England described in the previous chapter. Hill forts continue to be built, rebuilt, deserted, and reoccupied for several centuries, as at Burghead in Morayshire, for example, where a substantial hill fort continued to be occupied until the ninth century.

In AD 297 the peoples living north of the Antonine Wall are called *Picti* for the first time, with no indication as to the origin or meaning of the term, and no evidence for any population movement. The origins of the Picts have caused much controversy, but their first appearance in a documentary record need have as little connection with their history as a reference for the first time in Domesday Book has to the history of an English village.

Widely distributed over eastern Scotland, from the Tay to the Moray Firth, with outliers in Skye and the Shetlands, are sculptured stones generally thought to be Pictish in origin, the earliest dating perhaps from the fifth century AD. They incorporate both animal designs and abstract symbols, including a crescent with an applied V-shaped rod and a double disc with an applied Z-shaped rod. Again there has been considerable controversy but little certainty surrounding the interpretation of these stones. In due course Christian symbols were incorporated, with little apparent sense of incongruity, and some have inscriptions in the Ogam alphabet. The earlier, pre-Christian carvings, known as Class I, are usually on roughly dressed stones and boulders with the symbols incised upon them, as, for example, the Boar Stone at Knocknagael, Inverness-shire. The Christian, Group II, stones are carefully dressed stone slabs with the symbols carved in relief, often with very great skill, as witness the splendid example, nearly 9 feet high, in the grounds of the Manse at Glamis.

Pictish language and Pictish institutions persist until the ninth century, leaving behind large numbers of place-names of which a number, including those incorporating *lanerc* (clearing), *carden* (thicket) and *pert* (copse), would appear to have some reference to land clearing, whilst the most controversial element, *pit,* seems to indicate a portion or share of land. *Pit* place-names in particular are thickly distributed in the same areas of Scotland as the Pictish symbol stones, namely from the Tay to the Moray Firth, and all the evidence taken together points to a densely settled landscape extensively cleared and divided up into estates.

The linguistic melting-pot of Roman Britain received yet further ingredients. Groups of Germanic soldiers were undoubtedly being introduced into Britain long before the beginning of the fifth century. Some 5,500 Sarmatians, from the Danube frontier, were settled in Britain in the neighbourhood of Ribchester before the end of the second century. A Germanic king, Crocus, with a cohort of Alamanni, was in Britain at the time that Constantine the Great was proclaimed Augustus, and another Alamannic king, Fraomar, was transferred to Britain in 372, by which time there were large contingents of Alamanni and of Franks in the Roman army. Cemeteries containing cremations in hand-made pottery urns showing distinctive Germanic decoration have been recognized at Sancton in Yorkshire, at Elkington in Lincolnshire, at Lackford in Suffolk, in Leicestershire, along the upper reaches of the Thames, and near Winchester. The burials in these cemeteries date from the middle to the end of the fourth century. It has been suggested that the cemetery known at Caistor-by-Norwich occupied a site within the rectangular street plan of *Venta Icenorum* which had been deliberately cleared for use as a barbarian cemetery as early as the late third century, and then used on an increasing scale from the mid-fourth, with cremation urns showing startling parallels with those to be found in cemeteries in northwestern Germany.

Thus it is clear that Germanic people of a wide range of tribal origins were settled in many parts of Britain long before the collapse of Roman authority. Many garrisoned the coastal forts described in the previous chapter, something which may go a little way to explain the high survival rate of the Latin names for these places. It is very likely that some at least would have had to acquire a working knowledge of Latin and it may have been in this way that a number of Latin words which subsequently became Old English place-name elements were adopted. These include 'camp' from *campus*, 'port' from *portus*, 'wic' from *vicus*, the unique use of *faber* in Faversham, *cohors*, which lies behind Dovercourt, and *crocus*, which lies behind the first element in Croydon. Altogether much more frequent are 'ceaster' from *castra* and 'straet' from *strata*.

Nevertheless, immediately after the collapse of Roman authority it was the Romano-British aristocracy who filled the power vacuum, continuing to rule in much the same way as they had done for centuries. We catch a glimpse of them in an account of a visit to Britain in 429 of St Germanus, bishop of Auxerre, sent to combat the Pelagian heresy, led in Britain by Agricola, the son of a bishop, with the backing of local magistrates, described as 'conspicuous in their wealth, brilliant in their dress, and surrounded by a crowd of fawning supporters'. Much less certain is the role of a shadowy figure called Vortigern, a name which means 'high king', although the extent and nature of his authority is unknown. It seems very likely that somewhere about 430, under renewed attacks from Picts and Scots, he brought in Saxons to help in the defence of Britain, settling them in the eastern part of the country. In due course, these Saxons, their numbers swollen by fresh waves of settlers, rebelled against their British masters. A long period of fighting and disorder followed, during which the even more shadowy figure of king Arthur may perhaps be discerned, until somewhere before 500 the British defeated the Saxons at the battle of *Mons Badonicus,* the site of which remains unknown. This was followed by a lengthy period of comparative peace until the Saxon conquest was renewed in the 570s, so that by 600 the Saxons were in control of almost the whole of lowland England. It is however important to distinguish military conquest from peaceful settlement. There was certainly no concerted plan on the part of the English to conquer Britain, and indeed to use the word

English can in itself be misleading since the people subsumed under this word had no sense of national identity and were divided themselves into a number of warring kingdoms. There is instead a great deal of linguistic evidence to suggest long periods of peaceful intercourse between Romano-British inhabitants and Saxon settlers. It was the slow, persistent infiltration of the countryside by small groups of peasant farmers which created Anglo-Saxon England out of Roman Britain rather than the exploits of raiding war-bands.

The fifth and sixth centuries also saw the emergence of separate kingdoms in what is now Wales and Scotland. In Wales there were extensive settlements of Irish in the southwest, where place-names of Irish origin are particularly numerous, and, less extensively, in the northwest. Brychan, of Irish descent, became ruler of the kingdom of Brycheiniog, in due course to become Breconshire. Two major kingdoms emerged in north Wales, Gwynedd and Powys, the latter in itself a particularly interesting name since it is a corruption of the Latin *pagenses,* the plural form of the name given to the simplest districts of rural administration during the Roman occupation. In south and central Wales kingdoms were smaller, more numerous, more short-lived and far more uncertain in their origins and extent: Ceredigion, Brycheiniog, Dyfed, Glywysing and, among the smaller ones, Gower, Gwent, and Ergyng. Maelgwyn was king of Gwynedd until 547. A tradition first given written form only in the ninth century suggests that his great-grandfather Cunedda came into north Wales with his eight sons from Manaw Gododdin, now the region between the Forth and Northumberland. On the death of Cunedda his kingdom was divided among his sons, who gave their names to their shares, Ceredig to Ceredigion for example. But the tradition lacks any other confirmation and is to be treated with caution.

In southern Scotland three kingdoms emerged. Rheged was centred in the southwest, and stretched into Cumberland. Its name is preserved in that of Dunragit, in Wigtownshire. Its kings seem to have derived their lineage from Magnus Maximus, a successful Roman general who, crossing over from Britain in 383, managed to establish himself as Emperor at Trier for a while. The most prominent of the kings of Rheged was Urien, whose struggle against the English is recorded in a cycle of poems attributed to a Welshman, Llywarch Hen. Rheged disappears early in the seventh century, partly at least because the English from Northumbria had reached the Solway and partly because Oswy, king of Northumbria, married the daughter of Urien.

North of Rheged, stretching into the Clyde valley, was the kingdom of Strathclyde. This had a much longer history, and it may for a time have extended into the English Lake District following the collapse of Northumbria. Strathclyde seems finally to have disappeared as a separate kingdom by about 1000. The third kingdom, Gododdin, in the eastern

Lowlands, disappeared before the advancing English of Northumbria, who had reached the southern shores of the Firth of Forth by the opening years of the seventh century.

Scotland north of the Forth–Clyde line was divided into two kingdoms. By far the larger part was in the hands of the Picts. The other kingdom occupied much of what is now Argyllshire. This area was settled by the Scots from Ireland in the fifth century, becoming the kingdom of Dal Riada. By about 850, owing to the efforts of Kenneth mac Alpin, the Scots of Dal Riada had largely absorbed the very much larger kingdom of the Picts, giving their name to the whole of north Britain and bringing with them their own version of Celtic, which seems very quickly to have replaced the Pictish language throughout what may now be called Scotland.

In 787 the Vikings made their first recorded attack on England, landing on the coast of Dorset. In 793 they plundered Lindisfarne. Viking is an all-embracing term for the Scandinavians who by this time were breaking out of their homelands. The Swedes turned most of their efforts to the east, navigating the great rivers of Russia and finding their way to Constantinople. It was principally the Danes who descended on England, devastating the country far and wide, extinguishing monasticism and almost destroying the English state, which was saved only by the efforts of Alfred the Great. The Norwegians settled in the Shetlands and the Orkneys before the end of the eighth century, and were in Lewis and Skye a little later. They sacked the monastery on Iona, settled in Galloway, the Isle of Man and the eastern coast of Ireland, from where in due course they came to settle in Cheshire and the Lake District. In England the Danes became so numerous in Yorkshire, Lincolnshire, Leicestershire, Nottinghamshire, and Derbyshire that king Edgar recognized the Danelaw as an autonomous region with its own laws and customs, a region stretching from the Thames to the Tees. From 1016 England, under king Cnut, was part of a wider Danish empire, until in 1042 Edward the Confessor became king. In 1066 the Norse connection was resumed, but indirectly, when William of Normandy conquered England. By this time, however, the Norsemen who had settled in northern France, giving their name to Normandy, spoke French, thus introducing the last linguistic element into the landscape.

In the Northern Isles the new settlers almost completely replaced the old language with their own, although both Yell and Unst appear to be survivors from an older place-name stratum. It is Viking names for topographical features, fields, farms, and settlements which have come down to the present. The political ties with Norway and then Denmark survived until 1469, and the language, Norn, continued to be spoken on Foula until the end of the nineteenth century. Similar place-name evidence suggests heavy Norse settlement in Lewis, Skye, and in Caithness. The Norsemen in the Northern and Western Isles almost certainly took part in the colonization of the Faroes and of Iceland, then uninhabited, and also raided Norway itself until the Norwegian king, Harald Fairhair, put a stop to it.

The preceding paragraphs contain a garbled and grossly oversimplified account of the long slow crystallization of kingdoms out of the confusion and uncertainty created by the collapse of Roman power. It is a long, complex process for which documentary sources are few and fragmentary, making it very difficult and sometimes impossible to keep track of the ever-shifting patterns of kings and kingdoms throughout Britain for the very long period of time from 400 to the Norman Conquest in 1066. It is however a period of immense importance in the shaping of almost every facet of the landscape.

First of all successive waves of barbarians, pirates, military adventurers, and peasant farmers brought with them their own languages. These sometimes completely replaced the languages of the indigenous inhabitants, as in the Northern Isles where Norn replaced Pictish, or over most of Scotland, where Scots Gaelic came to prevail, or in England, where English supplanted both British and Latin. Sometimes the new language had a considerable impact upon the old: British absorbed nearly a thousand words from Latin, and the early English settlers also adopted some words, especially place-names, from both British and Latin. Other, later, settlers, were themselves absorbed. Thus the Norsemen of Cumberland and the Danes of Lincolnshire did not long continue to use their own languages. Norman French was spoken in aristocratic circles and in the royal courts of law until the end of the fourteenth century, and indeed it continued to be used as a technical legal jargon until 1730. Others disappeared much more slowly. It seems likely that Cornish was last spoken as a living language in the last years of the eighteenth century, whilst yet others, Welsh and Scots Gaelic, continue to this day. English took a number of forms, of which Lowland Scots must count as one, but English dialects never became distinctive patois, as happened to French in a number of the regions of France.

This bewildering linguistic variety has had its greatest impact on the landscape through the medium of place-names, which must rank with boundaries as the most important intangible components of the landscape. As we have seen, a small handful of place-names may well be immensely old, coming from a pre-Celtic language stratum. Celtic place-names are very common in Scotland, Wales, and southwestern England, whilst the great majority of river names the length and breadth of Britain are Celtic, with the probability that some may well be older. In some parts of Scotland, Lewis for example, and the Northern Isles, Norse place-names predominate, whilst in Cardiganshire there are large numbers of Irish place-names. In Cumberland and in Leicestershire, Norse and Danish place-names are numerous, whilst scattered over most parts of Britain is a thin sprinkling of French names, Beaulieu and Belvoir, Mountsorrel and Beachy Head.

However, in spite of their seeming antiquity, place-names are, like every other facet of the landscape, themselves subject to change over time although, again like every other facet, the processes making for change never succeed in sweeping the board completely clean. Thus Wenlock was once *Wininicas* and Derby was called *Northworthy*. *Cronuchomme* becomes Evesham, *Streoneshalh* becomes Whitby, and what was once called *Gumeninga hearh* is now Harrow, whilst it was only during the course of the eleventh century that *Beodrichesworth* came to be known by its modern name of Bury St Edmunds. Occasionally documents survive which enable us to see these processes of change at work. Two parts of an estate called *Aescesbyrig,* in Berkshire, had been granted to Wulfric by 958, and in due course they took his name, Wulfric's tun, now Woolstone. Later, the third part was granted to Uffa, coming to be called Uffington. As a result the old name of the estate dropped out of use. A similar story is to be told for an estate by the River Coln, in Gloucestershire. It was granted in about 730 to Leppa and his daughter Beage. The estate then took on the name of the new lord, or rather lady, becoming known as *Beagan byrig,* to give Bibury today. Place-names could change more than once. In 788 King Offa granted land called *Duningcland,* near Eastry, in Kent, to the thegn Osberht. In 824 the Archbishop of Canterbury gave land at Shelford to Christchurch, Canterbury. A description of the bounds of the estate mentions Eastry on the east and *Osberhtinglond* on the south. It seems reasonable to suggest that the estate of *Duningcland* had taken the name of its new lord. This new name has in its turn been replaced. It is perhaps now clear from these examples that we must expect considerable fluidity in the nature and structure of place-names.

The great majority, over three-quarters, of place-names in England are English in origin, and the majority of these, with perhaps the exception of field names, had been created by the end of the eleventh century. The study of place-names has been revolutionized in the last twenty years, and many of the old certainties have gone, including the belief that -*ing* place-names were among the earliest to be formed, and the opinion that the majority of the seemingly straightforward topographical names are in themselves not particularly interesting. Instead, it is now apparent that it is much more difficult to construct a chronology of place-names, and that even when this has been done it does not imply a chronology of settlement, first because, as we have seen, place-names can change with successive changes in lordship, and second because it is very likely that place-names were given to estates rather than to occupation sites within estates. Further, intensive study of the hitherto largely neglected topographical names has revealed first of all an astonishingly subtle awareness on the part of the English peasant farmer of every bend and twist in the topography of the landscape, and second the intriguing possibility that it is these place-names which form the earliest stratum of English place-names. The result is that it is now possible for late-twentieth-century landscape historians, by comparing closely the different names given, well over a thousand years ago, to seemingly similar topographical features, to see the landscape with at least something of the same sharp perception and keen eyesight as that of the first English settlers.

The English had a wide range of terms for almost every topographical feature, and if they did not then they were not above borrowing what was probably to them almost a technical term for a feature which they had not hitherto encountered. There are, for example, at least seven terms for a stretch of moving water. The word *ea* seems to have been applied to rivers of some size. It gives rise to such place-names as Eton and Eaton, and it may well be that these are settlements with some rather specialized function in relation to the river within a larger estate. We shall see this possibility occurring in respect of other names in a moment. Next are the elements *burna*, *broc*, and *bæce*, which appear to be applied to streams smaller than those worth designating *ea*, with *bæce* being applied to a stream in a fairly well-marked but not dramatic valley, a description which fits admirably the stream which flows through Beachampton in north Buckinghamshire, a place-name which incorporates this element. Thus for the modern observer yet another dimension is added to the landscape of this quiet village.

But the *bæce* at Beachampton is quite large when it is compared to those called *rith*, *lad*, or *sic*, with the probability that the last two were terms applied to man-made drainage ditches, whilst a *dic* is likely to be even smaller. A perambulation of the boundaries of an estate at Chetwode-Hillesden, again in north Buckinghamshire, was made in 949. The description of the boundaries includes a *lytle ridig*, a *sic*, a *dic*, and a *lytlan dic*. The differences between a little stream, a sike, a ditch and a little ditch, for this is what the terms mean, are today scarcely discernible to the blunted perception of a myopic townsman, but to a tenth-century countryman they were clear and self-evident.

The English had an equally rich vocabulary to describe wetlands: *fenn, merse, mor,* and *mos*. Again the subtle differences between these various kinds of marshland often elude the modern observer, not least, of course, because many areas which once were marshland have long since been drained, such as that *fenn* which once lay where Fenchurch Street, in London, is now to be found. Interestingly, *fenn* is in fact a very rare place-name in the region of Lincolnshire and Cambridgeshire now called the Fens, whilst *mor* is a word which has slowly changed its meaning. It seems to have been used at first to describe a low-lying marsh, and it must have been employed in this way for Chesham Moor, a marshy area of the Chess valley in Chesham. Later, *mor* came to be applied to barren uplands, to give the present 'moor', although many of these in fact contain large areas of ill-drained peat bog. Both *mersc* and *mor* give rise to place-names and it is not unlikely that the Marstons and Mortons which derive from these elements had, like the Eatons, some specialized function relating to the exploitation of the marshland within a larger estate.

Yet further place-names reveal a keen perception on the part of the English of slight differences of slope and aspect to hills and valleys. *Denu* implies a long, sinuous valley, of which the Hambleden valley in south Buckinghamshire is a good example. Two further words, however, *cumb* and *dun*, were, it is generally thought, borrowed from Celtic. *Cumb* was very likely adapted from the Primitive Welsh word which eventually gave 'cwm' to modern Welsh, to end up as 'coomb' in English. A valley called a *cumb* was generally shorter and broader than a *denu*, more bowl-shaped and with steeper sides. *Dun* is probably another word borrowed from Celtic, where the British form, *duno*, was one of the most important elements in the surviving place-names of Roman Britain. It gives the Welsh 'dinas', and the modern English down, as well as numerous place-names ending in -don. It seems to be applied particularly to a hill which has a summit suitable for some kind of occupation site. Both *cumb* and *dun* may well have been borrowed by the English to describe topographical features which they had not encountered before their arrival in Britain. That they could take such terms over from the Romano-British population and employ them with precision, as they so obviously appear to have done, is yet another indicator of long periods of peaceful intercourse between the two peoples. However and wherever the English acquired these two words they certainly applied them with a marvellously keen eye for topographical subtleties, making the exploration of that broad band of country lying to the north and west of the Chiltern scarp in Oxfordshire and Buckinghamshire, where such place-name elements are particularly common, a fascinating and rewarding exercise in the study of the niceties of hill slope and size, valley shape and length.

Place-names are one of the most important features of the landscape to crystallize out of the long centuries of confusion which followed the collapse of Roman authority in Britain. As we have seen, some of them are among the oldest features of the landscape. Others are evidence of the successive groups of men and women, linguistically and culturally widely diverse, who have, all unselfconsciously, made their own contribution to the palimpsest that is the landscape. Yet other place-names, by revealing a close awareness of the subtleties of topography, are perhaps evidence that the apparent confusion of the post-Roman centuries is misleading and that the majority of men for the majority of their lives were preoccupied with their fields and their farms, their harvest and their livestock. Place-names are also an intangible feature of the landscape in that they cannot be touched, or even seen save on maps and signposts, and yet they have been created since time immemorial and for very practical purposes.

Another, equally intangible, element in the landscape also emerges from these confused post-Roman centuries, one which is quite as important as place-names. Boundaries serve to divide land up into units which can be exploited for a very wide range of purposes, and the units themselves range in size from single house plots to kingdoms. They are sometimes visible on the ground in the shape of walls, hedges, fences, and ditches, often inconspicuous in themselves but marking off areas of widely differing land use, even as between one unit and its immediate neighbours. Thus the lands of one village could, in the seventeenth century, lie in broad open fields with scarcely a hedge in sight, whilst all around it the fields of its neighbours were enclosed and parcelled up into little patches, divided one from the other by hedges and ditches, an altogether different landscape separated from the first only by a boundary. Thus boundaries can mark off entirely opposed social and economic codes of practice affecting almost every aspect of human life. They delineate estates and parishes, counties, townships, wapentakes and lathes, boroughs, dioceses, hundreds, rapes and deaneries, cantrefs, commotes, and kingdoms. Some change rapidly. Local government reorganization in 1974, far-reaching though it was, was only one stage in an almost continuous process. Other boundaries are very ancient indeed and are deeply engraved, not only on the landscape but also in the hearts and minds of men, so that change can prompt very strong emotional reaction, as witness the outcry at the abolition of Rutland as part of the reorganization of 1974.

Most animals and birds have a strong territorial instinct, as the squabbles between sparring blackbirds in spring is noisy evidence, and man is no exception. Even the most footloose of nomads do not wander aimlessly, but move regularly across a known and recognized territory, even though its boundaries may not everywhere be exactly and firmly delineated. It is most likely that those groups of Mesolithic men and women described in Chapter 2 had each a recognizable territory, whilst the sophisticated social structures that must have lain behind Stonehenge and Maes Howe must also have had a territorial basis. Some of the oldest territorial divisions that can be recognized today are those field boundaries on the chalk downlands of southern England described in Chapter 2. Some archaeologists would claim to be able to identify other boundaries dating from the second millennium BC. Thus the Snilesworth area of northeastern Yorkshire has lines of well-preserved round barrows marking local watersheds and what appear to be occupation sites in the intervening valleys. Could the upland barrows be boundary markers? Certainly there are linear earthworks which seem to reinforce the boundaries, and the practice of siting burial mounds on boundaries is found in pre-Christian Ireland and among the pagan Anglo-Saxons, whilst modern township boundaries in the area do follow the suggested boundaries remarkably closely. The evidence is of course only circumstantial and the postulated links must remain for ever non-proven, but the weight of evidence for the intensive occupation of every part of Britain by the third millennium BC is now overwhelming, and with it must go the inescapable corollary that the land surface by that time must have been marked off into units of widely varying size, from house plots upwards, and of equally varied purpose, with the possibility that a small handful of such boundaries has survived in a recognizable form down to the present.

It was not Roman practice to introduce wholesale change into the territorial organization of conquered provinces, and in Britain as elsewhere throughout the Empire tribal territories were accepted as units of government. The *civitas* capitals which have been recognized in Roman Britain were, as we saw in Chapter 3, the administrative centres for such tribal territories although we do not know their exact boundaries. Interesting attempts have been made to identify smaller units, as for example the estate of the villa at Withington in Gloucestershire, but the evidence is again only circumstantial and the case, in the absence of documentary confirmation, must remain not proven.

The re-introduction of written documents into England after the collapse of Roman power is undoubtedly connected with the mission of St Augustine to convert the English to Christianity and the desire of the Church to have some permanent record of its title to the lands which were given to it, but whether such documents owe their origin to St Augustine in 597 or to Archbishop Theodore in 669 is still a matter for controversy. There are, nevertheless, a handful of documents surviving from before 700 which are undoubtedly genuine. They reveal that England was already divided up into a complex hierarchy of units, great and small. A grant made in about 672 to the monastery at Chertsey, in Surrey, illustrates this. It is made by Frithewald, of the province of the men of Surrey, and sub-king of Wulfhere, King of the Mercians, this in itself implying a political hierarchy. The grant is of 300 *manentes,* forming an estate which was bounded by the the Thames, an ancient ditch called *Fullingadic,* and the bounds of the adjoining province of the Sunningas, of which Sonning, in Berkshire, is an echo. The estate had various names: Chertsey, Thorpe, Egham, Chobham, Eaton in Chobham, Molesey, Woodham in Chertsey, and *Hunewaldesham,* a lost place in Weybridge. There was in addition a detached portion lying by the port of London, where ships come to land. A *manens* was, like a hide, sulung, virgate, carucate, ploughgate, oxgang, or bovate, a unit of assessment that once almost certainly had some relationship to an actual area of land, although what this area was could vary considerably over time and space. It was also very quickly adopted as a unit for the payment of royal dues and taxes, and as such the assessment of an actual piece of land in numbers of units could be varied by the king from time to time, either as a favour or else as a reflection of changing economic fortunes, the fiscal hide becoming 'a lame compromise between a unit of area and a unit of value'. It was noted, for example, in a document from the reign of King Edgar, who died in 975, that the assessment of Chilcomb, in Hampshire, and a property of the Old Minster at Winchester, had been reduced, by good and wise kings, from a hundred hides to one. The system shows great variation from one part of Britain to the next and becomes increasingly complex as units are broken up, assessments changed and the rents and services which once were paid in kind were commuted for cash. What is of the greatest significance, however, is the obvious complexity of the organization of the landscape as soon as documents make their appearance, and this is as true of Wales and Scotland as it is of England.

It is one of the theses of this book that the landscape is never wiped clean. How old then is the complex organization of the landscape that emerges from the first historical documents, dating from the latter part of the seventh century? If the landscape has indeed never been wiped entirely clean since the end of the last ice age then it is equally true that each generation has made its own unique contribution to it. We have seen earlier in this chapter that some place-names may survive from a pre-Celtic linguistic stratum, and that although the great majority of the place-names of England are English, there are significant numbers of Celtic, Scandinavian, and French ones as well. It is very likely that the complex territorial organization of Britain is made up in much the same kind of way, the real problem being the unravelling of the successive additions and at the same time taking into account those which have disappeared altogether, in much the same way as place-names have disappeared from use, leaving only fossils embedded in ancient documents to confuse and mislead later generations of readers.

It is also clear from the earliest documents, not only that there were very large estates divided into smaller units which could have a variety of names, but also that these estates had clearly defined boundaries, were already fully exploited within the technological levels of the time, and were also already actively being divided up, granted away and amalgamated. Thus Ceadwall, King of Wessex, granted 60 hides of land in Farnham in about 686 to found a monastery. The land lay not only in Farnham but also in Binton and Churt, with the rest assigned to their own places, including *Cusanweoh,* a name which is now lost, with everything belonging, including fields, woods, meadows, pastures, fisheries, rivers, and springs. A charter of 738 granted ten sulungs at Stoke, formerly called *Andscohesham,* and itself another example of a place-name which has changed, in a *regio* called *Hogh*, now Hoo in Kent, to the cathedral at Rochester, whilst another of 778 granted only half a sulung at Bromhey, also in Kent, to the same cathedral. *Regiones,* or provinces, are ancient territorial divisions known from most parts of Anglo-Saxon England and they may have originated in tribal settlements, but almost nothing further is known about them.

Documents survive in increasing numbers from the early years of the eighth century to provide a growing body of detailed evidence of change in the patterns of territorial organization, although unfortunately they survive very unevenly, there being no early ones for the four northern counties of England or for Scotland. They reveal a network of large estates composed of a number of subdivisions which make renders in services and goods to an estate centre. They also reveal these estates being broken up into their constituent parts, the further subdivision of these parts and the commutation of ancient renders in kind into cash payments. At the same time the boundary descriptions become increasingly detailed so that it is possible to recognize the unit of land upon the ground today and to walk its bounds as people must have done a thousand years ago.

Thus a group of charters dating from the middle years of the tenth century all grant an estate in Wiltshire called simply *Eblesburnan,* but it is clear from their boundary perambulations that in fact a large estate is being broken up into smaller units which are today called Bishopstone, Coombe Bisset, Stratford Tony, Odstock, and Homington, all strung along the River Eble, whilst another charter of 955 granted an estate called Chalke, a unit which included seven parishes although documentary evidence for this subdivision has not survived.

Another charter, of the year 903, states that it is a replacement for a document which had been lost by fire. It records the grant of an estate at *easteran Hrisanbyrge* and it includes a detailed perambulation of the bounds of this estate, which corresponds with the ancient parish of Monks Risborough in Buckinghamshire. The perambulation begins in the south and progresses in a clockwise direction, much of it being marked by hedges, lanes, and roads which can still be followed today. One of the most striking features of this boundary is the reference to the Black Hedge, a botanically rich hedgerow which strides across the Chiltern scarp for nearly 4 miles and is so thick that in places a footpath runs through the middle. Here is the living, tangible evidence of an ordered, regulated landscape and of a boundary which was probably old when the document was drawn up.

Nearly 800 of these boundary perambulations survive from the Anglo-Saxon period, the great majority from the tenth century. They provide an immense amount of detail about the landscape as seen through the eyes of those who rode or walked it so long ago, but the one feature of the landscape which comes through most clearly of all is the existence of the boundaries themselves and that from the first appearance of written documents at the end of the seventh century. Very often these units evolve into ancient ecclesiastical parishes, for reasons which we shall examine in

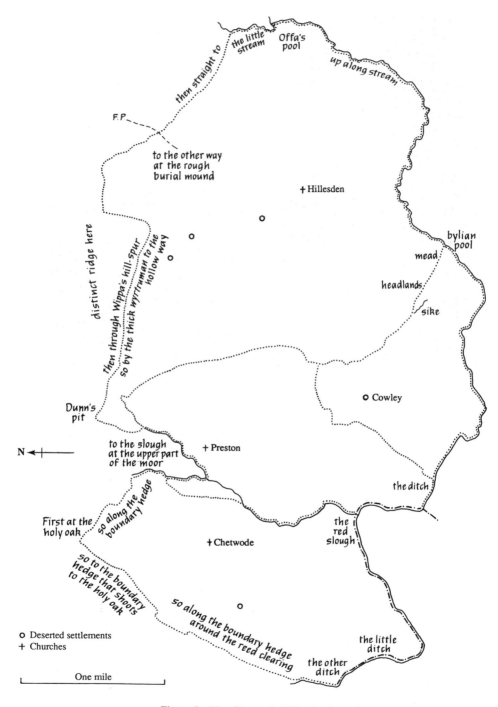

the little
stream

then straight to

Offa's
pool

up along stream

F.P.

to the other way
at the rough
burial mound

+ Hillesden

○

○

bylian
pool

mead

distinct ridge here

then through Wippa's hill-spur

so by the thick myrtrtman to the
hollow way

○

headlands

sike

○ Cowley

Dunn's
pit

N ←—┼—

to the slough
at the upper part
of the moor

+ Preston

the ditch

so along the boundary hedge

First at the
holy oak

the
red
slough

so to the boundary
hedge that shoots
to the holy oak

+ Chetwode

so along the boundary hedge
around the reed clearing

○

the little
ditch

○ Deserted settlements

+ Churches

the other
ditch

One mile

Figure 8 The Chetwode/Hillesden boundary

20 The Hillesden/Chetwode boundary hedge (see Figure 8).

more detail in Chapter 6. The oldest parish boundary which can be recognized in this way is that of Woodchester in Gloucestershire, described rather briefly in a document to be dated between 716 and 745, although there is some evidence for an even older one, at Minster in Thanet, in Kent.

Boundaries are obviously among the oldest elements in the landscape and, with place-names, constitute two of the most important means through which men impose order upon an inchoate environment. By the end of the Anglo-Saxon period it is clear from surviving documents that England was divided into a very large number of territorial units, themselves ordered hierarchically, and that everywhere was named from shires down to individual trees and ditches. In many respects the great survey which is Domesday Book, compiled in 1086, is a summary of the changes which had taken place in the organization of the English landscape in the four hundred years between the era of the first documents, namely the last decades of the seventh century, and its compilation. It reveals first of all much detailed information about the organization of estates, great and small and, second, something of the extent to which ancient patterns of organization had disintegrated by 1086.

There is evidence from all over Britain of very large estates made up of a central manor or *caput* together with subordinate or dependent parts, called sokes, berewicks or appendices. In England and in Scotland such estates are sometimes called 'shires', a term not to be confused with the more modern counties. Thus there is evidence for a Tottenhamshire and a Walthamshire. Southern Buckinghamshire may once have formed a separate shire with its meeting-place at Skirmett, a place-name in which the word 'shire' appears in Scandinavian guise. There is firmer evidence for Blackburnshire, in what is now Lancashire, as well as for Hallamshire, Hexhamshire, Mashamshire, and so on. In Wales the basic unit was called a cymwd, or commote, two of which made up a cantref.

The presence of these big estates in England is sometimes betrayed by their large fiscal assessments, although we must not allow ourselves to be deceived by small ones since that estate at Chilcomb mentioned above as having its assessment reduced from a hundred hides to one also had eleven dependencies. Spaldwick, in Huntingdonshire, is assessed at 15 hides. Only a subsidiary document to Domesday Book, one known as the *Inquisitio Eliensis*, mentions its three berewicks of Stow, Barham, and Easton. Bridlington, in the East Riding of Yorkshire, had two berewicks and fourteen sokes. Southwell, in Nottinghamshire, had twelve berewicks, not named in Domesday Book but listed in a charter of 958. Leominster, in Herefordshire, still had sixteen members at the time of Domesday Book, but a further twenty-three used to belong to it. Hitchin, in Hertfordshire, had a dozen dependencies, including Hexton, which King Harold had forcibly attached to it. Tring, also in Hertfordshire, had had several dependent berewicks, but the Count of Mortain had taken several of them away, including Pendley, Wigginton, and Dunsley, and it is also recorded that Little Gaddesden had formerly been a berewick of Berkhamsted.

The *caput* of an estate organized in this way acted as the collecting point for a wide range of rents which were paid in kind, whether honey, malt, grain, lambs, sheep, eggs, poultry, even, in Derbyshire, lead. Other rents were paid in services, including carrying services, stabling the king's horses, entertaining his falconers and huntsmen or, as in Hereford, attending the king when he went hunting. The royal household was continually on the move, consuming as it went the accumulated produce in the barns and store houses of the royal manors. The provisions required for the royal court for one night's lodging had, by the time of Domesday Book, long been fixed, being known as *firma unius noctis*, 'one night's farm'. These rents and services could be a considerable burden and many, by the time of Domesday Book, had been commuted for cash, granted away, or simply allowed to lapse. Thus in a charter of 845 Berhtwulf, King of Mercia, granted exemption of 20 *manentes* of the lands of the monastery at Stratford-on-Avon from provisioning the king, the royal huntsmen, horses and falcons and the servants who led the hunting dogs, whilst the Bishop of

Winchester was prepared to give 60 hides of land to King Edward in 904 in order to buy exemption of his great estate at Taunton from the duty to provide one night's entertainment for the king and nine nights for his falconers, to support eight dogs and a dog-ward and to perform various carrying services. Kings Clere, Basingstoke, and Hurstborne Tarrant, all in Hampshire, were, at the time of Domesday Book, still paying the 'one night's farm' which was due from each, whilst Milborn Port, also in Hampshire, paid only three-quarters of 'one night', and Linton, in Herefordshire, paid only a quarter. In Oxfordshire, however, the farm of three nights due from the county had been commuted to £150, and the ancient corn rent, called *annona*, due from the royal manors, which included Bensington, Headington, Shipton under Wychwood, and Kirtlington, had also been commuted for cash payments. Of the king's estate at Leighton Buzzard in Bedfordshire, it was recorded that it paid £22 in money and half a day's farm in grain and honey together with 70s for customary payments for the dogs. Similar partial commutations were also to be found for Luton and Houghton Regis, in the same county.

In Devonshire it was noted that the manors of Tamarton, Sutton, and Walkhampton used to pay 'one night's farm', but no longer did so, and of Whittington in Shropshire, an estate with eight and a half berewicks, it was recorded that it used to pay half a night's farm in the time of King Ethelred, but no longer did so, and the customary due of twelve sheep from Oare, in Somerset, which used to be paid to the king's manor of Carhampton, was also no longer paid. The Count of Mortain seems to have been particularly adept at stopping these ancient customary dues. Cricket St Thomas, also in Somerset, used to pay six sheep with their lambs and a bloom of iron from each freeman to the king's manor of South Petherton, but the Count had stopped this, as he had the payment of twenty-four sheep a year from the manor of Brushford due to the king's manor of Dulverton, also in Somerset. He also seems to have broken up the estate at Tring, in Hertfordshire, by detaching its dependencies.

Multiple estates, organized in this way and drawing upon a wide range of rents and dues paid in kind and in services, were to be found the length and breadth of Britain. Domesday Book reveals that they were widespread over England, but that their ancient organization was in many cases disintegrating. Relics do however persist in many parts of England throughout the medieval centuries. The payment of a bowl of honey from Swanbourne to the manor house at Brill, in Buckinghamshire, persisted until the end of the fifteenth century, and is a relic of the multiple estate which once focused upon the ancient royal manor there. Similarly, commutation of individual services also continued well into the medieval centuries, as when the men of Eynsham, in Oxfordshire, were released in 1105 from the duty of going *ad stabilitatem*, that is of going into the woods to head off the deer when the king went hunting.

The former existence of multiple estates organized in this way accounts for many of the regional and local oddities of the structure of the landscape of medieval England, since it is clear that they disintegrated in a piecemeal fashion, leaving much debris behind as they broke up. In Wales and in Scotland they formed the basis for the organization of the landscape throughout the medieval centuries. Their presence in these parts of the island, regions where Roman and English influence was slight, would suggest that they have a very long history indeed, with roots deep in the pre-Roman period, although it would probably be unwise to speculate further.

The already complex spatial organization of the landscape was made yet more complicated by the emergence of new territorial divisions to meet new political, religious, and social needs.

The hundred was the unit for the administration of justice, both civil and criminal, and for the collection of royal taxes. It was a popular assembly, meeting every four weeks in the open air. There are no clear references to it as an institution before the tenth century but it has every appearance of being very ancient, and it may well have originated as a district liable for the rents and services due from a hundred hides, with later reassessments obscuring the neatness of this pattern. In some counties some of the great royal estates described above had one or more hundreds attached to them: Bensington, in Oxfordshire, had four and a half hundreds attached to it, Kirtlington had two and a half and Shipton under Wychwood had three, a pattern of organization that continued at least until the end of the thirteenth century. The hundred continued to be important as an administrative unit until well into the eighteenth century, since high constables from each hundred were expected to attend county Quarter Sessions, and the inhabitants of the hundred were liable to make good any damage done to turnpikes and navigable rivers as well as that consequent upon the burning of houses, barns, and stacks of hay and corn. In the Danelaw counties of Lincolnshire, Derbyshire, Nottinghamshire, Leicestershire, and the West and North Ridings of Yorkshire, these divisions were known as wapentakes, from the Scandinavian word *vapnatak,* denoting the flourishing of weapons with which the assembled men of the district gave their assent to decisions. There is some evidence to suggest that the wapentakes of Leicestershire, Derbyshire, and Nottinghamshire were themselves subdivided into smaller units called hundreds, but these did not long survive the Norman Conquest.

The administrative subdivisions of Kent and Sussex had other names. In Kent they were known as lathes, of which six are mentioned in Domesday Book, five full ones and two halves. These lathes seem in their turn to have been divided into numerous small hundreds. They may well descend from the ancient *provinciae* into which the once independent kingdom of Kent was formerly divided, and of which that *regio* of *Hogh*, mentioned on

p. 104, was one. In Sussex the subdivisions were called rapes. By the time of Domesday Book there were five, centred on Hastings, Pevensey, Lewes, Steyning, and Chichester. Their creation was probably comparatively recent since their organization is remarkably uniform: each had a castle, with a harbour and a market, all in the hands of a single lord. Each rape probably also had its own sheriff.

Hundreds, wapentakes, rapes, and lathes are subdivisions of shires or counties. In Wessex shires were in existence by the end of the eighth century, apparently originating as blocks of territory dependent upon a town as an administrative centre. Thus Dorset was dependent upon Dorchester, Somerset upon Somerton, and Wiltshire upon Wilton. They may however descend from still older units since their names, *Dornsæte* and *Sumorsæte,* would appear to indicate groups of people rather than territories, and *Wiltunscir* replaces an earlier *Wilsætan,* meaning people by the River Wylye. The midland shires have different origins. Leicestershire, Northamptonshire, Huntingdonshire, Bedfordshire, and Cambridgeshire seem to descend from Danish armies which had settled in the districts, taking what was to become the county town as their headquarters and place of assembly. Other midland shires, Shropshire, Warwickshire, Buckinghamshire, and Oxfordshire for example, were probably the deliberate creations of Edward the Elder as part of his measures to combat the threat posed by the Danes. Their new boundaries rode roughshod over more ancient ones. Shropshire was carved from the lands of the *Magonsætan* and the *Wreocensætan,* for example, and the most easterly portion of the kingdom of the *Hwicce* was incorporated into Warwickshire, whilst other ancient units, the *Cilternsætan* of north Buckinghamshire, the *Stoppingas* around Wootton Wawen, the *Pecsætan* of the Peak District, for example, disappeared altogether. One of the shires thus created at this time, Winchcombshire, was only short-lived, being incorporated into Gloucestershire in about 1016.

Cheshire was also probably created at this time, being first mentioned in 980. Lancashire, however, did not yet exist as such. The lands between the Ribble and the Mersey were administered as six great royal manors annexed to Cheshire, whilst lands north of the Ribble were surveyed in 1086 under Yorkshire. The four northern counties are not described in Domesday Book. The Church of St Cuthbert at Durham had exclusive jurisdiction over what was to become County Durham, although the bishop did not lose his very wide powers until 1836, when the county was formally assimilated into the English county system. Cumberland, Westmorland, and Northumberland were very much debatable lands, and the Scottish border was not fixed until 1237, when the Scottish King Alexander II renounced all claims to lands in the three counties. The Scots did not give up Berwick-upon-Tweed until 1482. Its status long remained anomalous: as late as 1854, for example, a separate declaration of war upon Russia at the outbreak of the Crimean War was made on its behalf.

In Scotland the imposition of royal authority by means of newly created administrative organs on ancient territorial units was a much more protracted process than in England. There is much evidence for the existence of multiple estates in Scotland along the same lines as those just described for England. Tynninghame, in East Lothian, for example, had in 1094 four dependencies, and a clue to the antiquity of estates of this kind may perhaps be found in the fact that the place-name *pit,* already mentioned earlier in this chapter, is very frequently attached to the dependent parts. During the course of the tenth century the English words 'shire' and 'thane' seem to have been adopted into Scotland to describe such estates and their ministerial tenants. During the twelfth century, however, and especially during the reign of David I, the Scottish monarch strengthened his control through new officers, his sheriffs, who come to exercise authority in new, very much larger territories. Thus the ancient Berwickshire was by 1139 only a small part of the new sheriffdom of Berwickshire, and by 1162 the sheriffdom of Lothian, which had incorporated the ancient Haddingtonshire and Linlithgowshire, had itself been divided into three. By 1165 there were sheriffs for Selkirk, Peebles, Stirling, Roxburgh, and Lanark, but the new system spread only very slowly, much power remaining with the great feudal lords such as Fergus, in Galloway, who enjoyed remarkable independence, being referred to as *rex Galwitensium* and *princeps Galwaie,* until in 1160 he retired into the monastery of Holyrood.

The Western Isles were ruled by the king of Man under Norwegian suzerainty until another great lord, Somerled, lord of Argyll, conquered much of the region in 1156–8. It was the seventeenth century before Scotland was finally divided into shires, when between 1631 and 1641 Sutherland, Caithness, and Ross-shire were split off from Inverness-shire.

The boundary between England and Wales remained ill-defined and uncertain for centuries. A long period of fighting between the English advancing from the east and the retreating Welsh led to the settlement of two of the English tribal groups that we have already met, the *Magonsætan* and the *Wreocensætan,* in what is now Shropshire and Herefordshire during the course of the seventh century; and the further expansion of Mercia in the eighth century, especially under King Offa (757–96), led to the construction of a series of banks and ditches in the border regions, of which the most spectacular is that known traditionally as Offa's Dyke. This splendid earthwork stretches, although not continuously, from near Prestatyn in the north to the mouth of the River Wye in the south, where it leaves the ferry crossing of the Severn from Aust to Beachley, in use from prehistoric times until the nineteenth century, on the Welsh side. Offa's Dyke seems to have been essentially a boundary marker rather than a

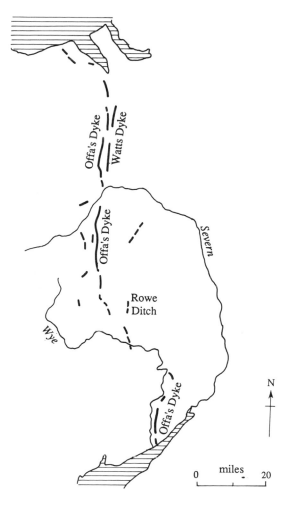

Figure 9 Earthworks in the Welsh Marches

fortification since long sections, in the Clun Hills for example, have the appearance of following a negotiated, compromise line, giving up one hilltop here in order to include another there. Its construction must have called for considerable resources and have taken a long time, and in parts it appears to be incomplete. It is not, however, by any means the only linear earthwork in the Welsh Marches. There are a number of others, such as Wat's Dyke, stretching from the Severn to the Dee somewhat to the east of Offa's Dyke, and probably built slightly earlier, and the Rowe Ditch, to the west of Leominster and again east of Offa's Dyke and so again presumably of an earlier construction.

The frontier thus marked out did not become permanent. English settlers had already made their way beyond it, in the Vale of Radnor, for example, and to the west of the River Wye. After the Norman Conquest the Norman lords, newly established in their estates along the Marches, began to push westwards to acquire yet further lands for themselves. This piecemeal conquest was made easier by the chronic disunity among the Welsh princes, and the Normans made considerable progress, especially along the river valleys and the lowlands of the south and the north. By the time of Domesday Book, Hugh, Earl of Chester, had established castles at Bangor and Caernarvon, Roger of Montgomery, Earl of Shrewsbury, had seized the cantref of Arwystli, in central Wales, and in the south castles had been built at Wigmore, Clifford, Ewyas Harold, Chepstow, and Caerleon. The Domesday survey included large areas of what is now Flintshire under Cheshire, and much of what is now Denbighshire under Shropshire, whilst a great area to the west of the Wye, called Arkenfield, was surveyed, together with the town of Monmouth, under Herefordshire. The king had three churches in Arkenfield, where the priests sang two masses each week for him and also had the duty of carrying his embassies into Wales.

The Normans brought many new features into the Welsh landscape, including feudal land tenures, towns, and a Church organized upon a diocesan basis, but they also took over the traditional Welsh administrative units of cantref and commote, together with many of the customary rents and services which were as characteristic of these multiple estates as they were of those of England and Scotland. This means that many of their ancient boundaries were also adopted, to survive, through many vicissitudes, down to the present.

The Welsh discovered a measure of unity in the twelfth century, more especially under Rhys ap Gruffyd (1155–97) whom Henry II recognized as ruler of Deheubarth. After his death leadership passed to the principality of Gwynedd, until the invasions of Edward I brought it to an end. The Statute of Rhuddlan of 1284 introduced considerable change into the spatial structure of Wales, but it was firmly based in ancient, traditional institutions. The cantrefs of Rhos and Rhufoniog were united to form the new lordship of Denbigh, and that of Dyffryn Clwyd became the lordship of Ruthin. The cantref of Tegeingl became the new shire of Flint. Gwynedd west of the river Conway was divided up into three new shires on the English model: Anglesey, Caernarvon, and Merioneth, but the ancient cantrefs and commotes were retained as subdivisions. New shires were also created for Carmarthen and for Cardigan. The ancient kingdom of Powys had already fallen into two halves. The southern part remained under its Welsh prince, but the northern part was divided into two new lordships, Bromfield and Yale, and Chirk. The rest of Wales remained in the hands of the marcher lords as semi-independent domains, even enjoying, if that is the right word, the right to private warfare among themselves. Many were forfeited to the Crown during the Wars of the Roses, and they finally disappeared with the passing in 1536 of the Act of Union. This introduced English law and administration into Wales and made English the sole language for official transactions of every kind. The lordships were grouped together to form the counties of Denbighshire, Montgomeryshire, Radnorshire, Breconshire, Glamorganshire, Monmouthshire, and Pembrokeshire. Their actual boundaries, however, continued to follow very ancient territorial divisions. Thus Radnorshire was in effect the ancient kingdom of Rhwng Gwy a Hafren. Denbighshire incorporated northern Powys and three cantrefs of the Perfeddwlad, whilst the ancient kingdom of Brycheiniog and the cantref of Buellt were amalgamated to form Breconshire. These new counties were also subdivided into hundreds, but again in most cases it was ancient cantref boundaries which were used. The new wine was poured into some very old bottles.

The themes surveyed in this chapter constitute additions of fundamental importance to the fabric of the landscape. As we have seen, Britain was, by the time of the Roman Conquest, a densely settled and largely cleared island, and had long been so. The Roman occupation brought decades of peace and stability, permitting the further development of existing features and at the same time adding new ones, especially roads and towns. The centuries after the collapse of Roman power must have brought a sudden and rapid drop in the material well-being of the inhabitants of Britain, as well as much chaos, disorder, and instability. It is from this confusion however that some of the basic structures of England, Scotland, and Wales slowly emerge, and this chapter has been concerned with two of them, namely boundaries of every kind, and place-names. Together they form two of the most important elements in any landscape, providing it with form and structure, and reflecting in their own long histories something of the languages and socio-political structures of the successive generations of men and women who, over the course of three millennia, had contributed to its evolution. Although they themselves are intangible, visible only very rarely actually upon the ground itself, the influence that they exert is real, profound, and remarkably long-lasting. Many of those which make their first appearance in the historical record during the centuries covered in this chapter constitute some of the deepest roots to the landscape of twentieth-century Britain.

5

*Places:
fields and farms,
villages and towns*

We can begin this chapter in the same way as we began Chapter 4: 'if there was indeed a revolt in Britain in 409 then it is very likely that only a comparatively small number of people actually left'. But on the morning after the last civil servant had gone men and women still woke up to the routine of their everyday lives. Villas were only slowly abandoned and allowed to fall into decay, and there is evidence of organized municipal life in some towns, Verulamium for example, well into the second half of the fifth century. Roman Britain ended, not with a bang but with a whimper, and it took many years for the long-drawn-out disintegration of the fabric of Roman institutions to make itself felt in the landscape. The nature and extent of the consequent changes have provoked much discussion and controversy among historians and archaeologists but little agreement, save a general appreciation that the transition from Roman Britain to Anglo-Saxon England was a matter of continuity rather than catastrophe. This merely pushes the debate one stage back, since continuity is difficult to define and almost impossible to prove. Germanic settlers came into a landscape crowded with people, with villas and farmsteads, villages, towns, and roads, and yet, as far as we can tell at present, no villa remained in use after the first quarter of the fifth century, the public buildings in towns fell into ruins and appear to have been taken over by squatters, and hundreds of farms were abandoned. On the other hand, if any reliance at all can be placed upon the evidence brought forward in the previous chapter then some institutions, especially multiple estates, appear to have survived in a sufficiently coherent form to leave traces as late as the time of Domesday Book.

Thus there is a paradox to be resolved: on the one hand widespread evidence of material decline and collapse, on the other the very real possibility of continuity in territorial organization. The solution may be found in the nature of the archaeological evidence itself, drawn as it is almost everywhere from sites which have failed, not least because such sites are very much more accessible to archaeologists than those, London, Gloucester, Lincoln, and York for example, which have been occupied more or less continuously ever since. The severe and rapid decline in engineering and commercial skills upon which Roman material prosperity was built seems nevertheless to have been very real, so that many of the inhabitants of post-Roman Britain must very quickly have had to adapt to a very much lower standard of living. There is a limit to which a leaking roof can be patched if roofing tiles are no longer available, and windows have eventually to be blocked up if glass cannot be bought, so that in due course it becomes more convenient to move out altogether into a timber-framed and thatched house which can be more easily maintained. Institutions, however, are much more difficult to displace. Estate boundaries need no repair and rents can be paid by barter, in kind and in services, if there are no coins to be had. Thus the discontinuities may be more apparent than real, the real continuity being found in the ever-present but ever-changing land itself, where the ebb and flow of arable and pasture, wood and marsh, field and farm reflects, as it always has done, changing social and political structures as well as more permanent, basic human needs for food and shelter.

For at least 5,000 years the landscape of Britain has been a kaleidoscopic patchwork of marsh, woodland, arable, pasture, and human settlement, of varying intensity and varying location. Woodland is felled and allowed to regenerate, pasture is ploughed up, arable is abandoned, villages move, cottages are pulled down. Human beings are everywhere, sometimes densely packed, sometimes only very thinly distributed, but their good soils are not those of the late twentieth century and their attractive sites are not ours. Techniques of cultivation change over time, as do the legal codes governing the exploitation of the resources then perceived to be available. These processes have been at work for millennia, but it is only from late in the seventh century AD, nearly 300 years after the collapse of Roman authority, that at last documents begin to survive from which it is possible to describe them within a human time-scale. Marshland, woodland, arable, pasture, and human occupation sites represent patterns of land use, with the level of the intensity of that use determined by the technology available at any given period of time. Let us look at each in turn.

Marsh, fen, and wetlands were common and widespread over much of medieval Britain. Probably the largest area was the fen district of Lincolnshire, Cambridgeshire, Huntingdonshire, and western Norfolk, but there were also considerable areas in eastern Norfolk where the River Waveney reached the sea. Other areas lay along either side of the estuary of the Thames, the north Norfolk coast, the Isle of Thanet and the marshes of Romney and Pevensey, the Somerset Levels, the mosses of southern Lancashire and its coastline, and the estuary of the Dee. Further, the lower courses of the rivers which flow into the Humber wound their way through extensive areas of marshland. There were also broad tracts along the coasts of the Solway Firth, and Lochar Moss remains largely unreclaimed even today, with extensive coastal marshes between Ruthwell and Glencaple. The mosses of Flanders and Blairdrummond, in the upper Forth Valley to the west of Stirling, were entirely undrained before the middle years of the eighteenth century, and the Howe of Fife and the Carse of Gowrie also remained badly drained marshlands until well into the same century.

We saw in the previous chapter something of the rich technical vocabulary for every feature of the landscape which the English settlers of the fourth and fifth centuries had at their disposal. Surviving place-names of today point to areas of marshland which have long disappeared. The place-name element *eg,* meaning island, seems to have been used most frequently to refer to dry ground surrounded by marshland. A group of such place-names cluster around the River Ock and its tributaries in northwest Berkshire, pointing to extensive, badly drained marshlands, places such as Charney, Goosey, Hanney, Pusey, and Tubney, with Mackney, Cholsey, Hinksey, and Chimney on the Thames and Witney on the Windrush, all in the same region. A charter of about 970 refers to *bulunga fen* in the immediate vicinity of Westminster Abbey, the site of which was once known as Thorney, the island covered with thorn bushes.

Marshlands were not however desolate wildernesses, in spite of the story of St Guthlac, who wrestled with demons in the fens amidst 'black water overhung by fog'. He was guided by a local fisherman called Tatwine to the remote island of Crowland, probably in about the year 700. The cell that he and his two companions established there became the nucleus for Crowland Abbey, which could still be reached only by water as late as the thirteenth century.

Instead, marshlands everywhere supported a complex and sophisticated way of life that was finely adapted to the exploitation of the very rich resources that marshland contains. Large areas dried out in the summer months so that cattle and sheep could be turned out to graze, even if they had to be taken by boat to their grazing grounds. Winter flooding brought much fine silt, and this kept the pastures in good heart. The intricate network of river channels provided ample opportunities for fishing, and few were without fish traps and weirs. Many kinds of freshwater fish were caught, especially eels, which, in the fens of Lincolnshire and Cambridgeshire, became almost a unit of currency. Wildfowl were almost as important, whilst rushes and sedges were regularly harvested to provide roofing thatch and bedding, and large tufts of coarse grass, called hassocks, were collected to make kneeling on the stone floors of churches more comfortable. Along the coasts salt was manufactured by allowing sea-water to evaporate in specially constructed pans.

There is documentary evidence of this rich and complex way of life from the earliest times. A charter of 774 granted a *mansio* on the west bank of the River Lyme, near its mouth, to Sherborne Church, in order that salt could be obtained, both as a seasoning for food and for ritual use. In about 1022 King Cnut granted fisheries at Upwell and Outwell to the Abbey of Bury St Edmunds together with 4,000 eels from Lakenheath. The great abbeys of East Anglia kept fishing boats in the fenland meres, and these are described in Domesday Book. Thus Bury St Edmunds Abbey had a boat with a draw net at Soham, worth 4s a year, whilst the Abbot of Ely's boat on the same mere was worth 30s. Thorney Abbey had fishing boats on Whittlesey Mere and on Trundle Mere. This last has now been so well drained that all that is left is a shadow on an aerial photograph. There were a number of fishermen in Wisbech, paying rents in eels together with 24s in fish tribute. At Wilburton in Cambridgeshire, 16d was due from rushes, whilst in Lincolnshire the marsh of Axholme was said to measure 10 leagues by 3 and there were 330 acres of marshland at Old Sleaford. Records of the Abbey of Ely list roach, perch, barbel, salmon, and pike as well as eels in the catches of their fish weirs, and geese, goosanders, herons, ducks, and Dartford warblers among the birds which were trapped and snared. The Abbey of St Benet Holme was already, in the twelfth century, grazing sheep over its marshes and exploiting the thick deposits of peat which were to be found all over eastern Norfolk. It has been estimated that some 900 million cubic feet of peat were removed from these cuttings in the course of three centuries. By the end of the fourteenth century they had been flooded, to form the Norfolk Broads of today.

Exploitation also meant reclamation. Generations of peasant farmers, sometimes on their own initiative, sometimes at the instigation of their landlords, especially the monasteries, embanked and ditched, drained, cleared and improved. The fenlands of Lincolnshire and Cambridgeshire divide into two: towards the sea lie the silt lands, several feet above the coastal marshes and also above the inland peat fens. East of Spalding lies the wapentake of Elloe. Intensive study of the documentary evidence has made it possible to trace the reclamation of the marshlands by the fen dwellers in the period from about 1150 to about 1300. On the seaward side a succession of banks and sluices added new lands, about 16 square miles in all, with an elaborate organization of dyke reeves to see to the maintenance of the all-important sea walls. Their achievement on the fenland side was even more dramatic, some 90 square miles of land being reclaimed here. Their progress south is marked by a series of fen banks: Austen Dyke, probably built before the Norman Conquest, Old Fen Dyke, built about 1160–70, Hassock Dyke, of between 1190 and 1198, Asgar Dyke, about 1203–8, and then Common Dyke, completed by about 1240.

The work was done entirely by the fenland communities themselves, although the land when drained was held by individuals who could use it as they wished rather than it being held in common. In due course new settlements appear: Cowbit and Moulton Chapel early in the thirteenth century, Whaplode Drove, Holbeach Drove, Gedney Hill, and Sutton St Edmund by its end.

A very similar pattern of reclamation can be recognized north of Spalding along the coastlands to Boston and beyond, where the new lands are protected from the sea by a series of massive earthen banks, most of which were completed before the end of the twelfth century.

Much of the new land thus created was used for arable farming, probably less than a third being pasture at the end of the thirteenth century. This reclamation was accompanied by, and perhaps to some extent propelled by, a rapid growth in population. Between 1086 and 1287 the number of recorded households at Pinchbeck, for example, increased elevenfold, and by 1334 the Holland district of Lincolnshire was the wealthiest in England. Marshland certainly did not equate with poverty.

Reclamation was also taking place in the Somerset Levels, much of it under the direction of the Abbey of Glastonbury. It seems very likely that the present course of the River Brue is artificial, the result of a series of diversions and new channels cut at the instigation of the abbey, the largest being the Pilrow Cut, completed in the early fourteenth century. Monastic houses also directed reclamation work elsewhere. Canterbury Cathedral was responsible for 'inning' lands around the Isle of Thanet and in Romney Marsh for example, whilst Battle Abbey was at work in the Pevensey marshes, and the Abbey of Meaux, almost entirely surrounded by marshes in the valley of the Hull River, was ditching and draining during the course of the thirteenth century. All of this work was difficult and expensive, whether to excavate, build, or maintain. It all had to be done with spade and shovel, and there were no mechanical means of pumping water away. Gales and storms could undo the work of decades in a single night. Flooding destroyed the work of the monks of Meaux at Salthaugh Grange and Tharlesthorpe, and caused the monks of Battle to give up arable farming at Barmhorne, in the Pevensey Levels, and turn the land over to grazing.

During the fifteenth century there seems to have been a slackening of effort. Population decline, the consequence of the Black Death in 1348 and later epidemics, together with climatic deterioration, combined to exacerbate the technical difficulties. The only major work seems to have been the construction of Morton's Leam, from Stanground near Peterborough to Guyhirne, a drainage channel 12 miles long, 40 feet wide and 4 feet deep, built to carry the Nene in an almost straight line to Wisbech. The dissolution of the monasteries, completed by 1540, had a serious impact upon the maintenance of the drainage works, since it brought to an end the

21 Mortons' Leam, to the west of Guyhirne, Cambridgeshire.

sustained direction of repair and maintenance work so essential in projects of this nature, and it is the 1630s before attention is once again directed to the draining of marshlands in Britain.

It is almost impossible to exaggerate the importance of wood in pre-industrial Britain. It was the main source of fuel, whether as firewood or as charcoal. It was a principal building material in houses and cottages and for the roofs of churches, castles, and cathedrals. The octagon of Ely Cathedral, built in the first half of the fourteenth century, is a marvellous example of medieval engineering in timber. Almost all the machinery of windmills and water-mills was made of wood. Ships and boats, carts and wagons, ploughs, fish traps and weirs, were all made of wood, as were farm implements and domestic furniture, from bedsteads to spoons. Such a valuable commodity was produced commercially by means of coppicing, a technique which, as we have seen, has been practised since Neolithic times.

Coppicing means careful management if it is to be successful. Other areas of woodland were designated as game reserves, either as Royal Forests or else as private parks and chases. Again the woodland was carefully managed. Thick woods were present in many parts of medieval Britain, but in no sense were they an untamed wilderness.

The extent of the woodland in Britain in the period immediately following the collapse of Roman power is, and must remain, very uncertain. It is very likely that there was very little woodland left in the Romanized part of Britain, and that the disintegration of Roman authority led to considerable regeneration of secondary woodland, something which can take place in less than a hundred years if grazing and other agricultural pressures are removed. A number of place-names point to the survival into the post-Roman period of areas of woodland, including the Celtic names of Arden, Lyme, Kinver, Morfe, Wyre, and Savernake, and the Celtic element for 'wood' in *ced*, which survives today in Chute and in Chetwode, where it was combined with the English word 'wood'. In addition, the Old English place-name element *wald*, meaning forest, was applied to the extensive woodland of Kent, Sussex, and Surrey known as the Weald, and in its form *wold* it may serve to indicate other areas which once were heavily wooded, such as the Cotswolds.

Whatever the actual extent of the woodland, the earliest documents make it clear that it was already carefully parcelled up and exploited, even if it was at a low level of intensity. In 679 Hloththere, King of Kent, granted land in Thanet to Abbot Brihtwold, land which included fields, pastures, marshes, small woods, fens and fisheries as marked off by the well-known boundaries. A charter of 736 says that the woods called Kinver and Morfe belonged to an estate by the River Stour, in Worcestershire, whilst other documents of the same period show that the woodlands of the Weald were already divided up into swine pastures, at Petteridge and Lindridge for example, and at Speldhurst, Marden, and Rusthall. Other documents make it clear that the woodland was also used for hunting. A grant made to the Abbey of Abingdon in 962 included game taken in the king's woods, and another of about the same date mentioned the hedges of the bishop of Worcester's hunt, whilst, as we saw in the previous chapter, a charter of 845 exempted lands of the monastery at Stratford-upon-Avon from the onerous burden of receiving the king's huntsmen, horses, and falcons. It is clear, incidentally, that Edward the Confessor provided well for his huntsman, Edwin, who is recorded in Domesday Book as holding lands in Hampshire and Dorset, whilst Godwine, the royal falconer, had other lands in Hampshire.

It was however left to William the Conqueror to introduce the forest laws into England. The principal object of these laws was to protect the deer and the trees which gave them cover since, as Richart Fitz Neal, Treasurer to Henry II, wrote, the forest was 'the sanctuary and special delight of kings, where, laying aside their cares, they withdraw to refresh themselves with a little hunting'. The animals preserved by the forest laws were the red deer and the fallow deer, together with the wild boar, which was becoming scarce by the thirteenth century. The roe deer was excluded following a legal decision in 1340. The wolf was not protected, and was instead hunted as a pest. Indeed the family of Engaine held lands at Pytcheley, in Northamptonshire, by the service of hunting wolves in the counties of Northampton, Buckingham, Oxford, and Huntingdon, and King John was prepared to pay 5s a head for them. In about 1112 Walter de Beauchamp was granted permission to hunt wolves in all the Royal Forests of Worcestershire, with leave to make traps round his park to capture them, and at about the same time the Abbey of Chertsey was given leave to keep its own hunting dogs to take hares, foxes, and wild cats on their lands, both within and without the Royal Forest.

Royal Forests spread rapidly in the century following the death of William the Conqueror, to reach their greatest extent under Henry II, by which time very large tracts of England were subject to the forest laws, two-thirds of Essex for example, and perhaps half of Northamptonshire, whilst a great belt of Royal Forest swept from the New Forest through the Forests of Fremantle, Pamber, and Eversley, to Windsor. The Forests of Macclesfield and the Peak joined one another on the borders of Cheshire and Derbyshire, and those of Allerdale and Inglewood occupied a large area of central Cumberland. Such areas were not of course everywhere densely wooded. Churches and cottages, fields, farms, villages, and towns were to be found. Beasts of the plough and sheep could be turned into the forest save during the month centred on Midsummer, when the hinds were fawning, although pigs were excluded except between 14 September and 11 November each year. It was always the deer which had priority. Farmers were not allowed to erect fences or plant hedges that would keep the deer out of their crops. Such an encroachment, or purpresture, was punishable by a fine, as were such other encroachments as making a mill pond or a fish pond. The forest laws were undoubtedly harshly administered, and after the death of Henry II the more extreme claims of the Crown were given up. The Charter of the Forest of 1217 permitted the building of mills and fish ponds outside the covert and disafforested the woods afforested by Richard I and John. There were further extensive disafforestations by Edward I in 1301.

The Royal Forests provided the Crown with a considerable revenue, both in kind, including venison and timber, and in cash, whether for licences to enclose and clear patches of woodland, to set up sheep-folds, or as fines levied in the forest courts for breaches of the forest laws. Both Richard I and John sold their forest rights on a large scale to relieve their pressing financial problems. John, for example, disafforested all the Royal Forests in Devon and Cornwall, except Dartmoor and Exmoor, for 7,200 marks and twenty palfreys. We shall see Charles I doing much the same kind of thing for the same reasons in Chapter 7. During the fifteenth century, however, administration of the forests became increasingly lax, and fines imposed in the forest courts for offences like keeping pigs in the woods throughout the year come to look like licences to continue rather than deterrents.

By the end of the fifteenth century the timber in the Royal Forests was becoming more valuable than the deer, and in 1512 a central accounting department for the sale of wood was established in the Office of Surveyors General, although its impact seems to have been slight. Measures to protect the timber were introduced. At Act of Parliament of 1482 permitted the owners of lands in forests and chases to enclose their woodlands against the deer for seven years after each coppicing, an essential step to protect the new growth from grazing animals, and the Statute of Woods of 1543 required twelve standard oak trees to be left on every acre of coppice, and further required that coppices worked on a 14-year rotation should be enclosed for four years and those on a 14- to 21-year rotation for six years.

Occasionally a tract of Royal Forest passed from the Crown into private hands, when it became a chase. Again it was the hunting which was preserved, but this time through the common law rather than the forest laws, and in the interests of the private owner. There were something over twenty chases in medieval England, and although their areas were often individually quite extensive, Needwood Chase in Staffordshire, for example, extended over nearly 8,000 acres, *in toto* they were much less extensive than Royal Forests. There were chases at Whaddon in Buckinghamshire, not enclosed until the 1830s, at Cannock in Staffordshire, at Hatfield, at the point where the boundaries of the West Riding, Nottinghamshire, and Lincolnshire meet, at Malvern, at Enfield, at Copeland in Cumberland, and at Cranborne, in Dorset, where in 1296 nearly 1500 acres were recorded as being within the chase.

Yet a further medieval game reserve was the park. Parks were generally still smaller than forests or chases, and were as much private as royal. A licence from the Crown was required to create a park, such as that granted in about 1125 to the Abbot of Chertsey for his parks at Epsom and Cobham, and licences to impark continued to be issued until the early seventeenth century. Parks were created essentially to preserve the deer, and not only for hunting but also as a useful supply of fresh meat. Their basic need was for good woodland cover. Deer enclosures are known from Anglo-Saxon times, and the term *haga*, which occurs quite frequently in boundary perambulations, may refer to them. It has been suggested, for example, that the *haga* mentioned in a charter of 962 may well refer to the deer park of Hanley Castle, in Worcestershire. Thirty-five parks are recorded in Domesday Book, including those at Costessey in Norfolk,

22 Fallow deer in Bradgate Park, Leicestershire. The park was enclosed before 1247 and has never been landscaped so that it still retains much of the appearance of a medieval deer park.

Stagsden in Bedfordshire, and Ruislip in Middlesex, whilst not only was there a park at Winkleigh, in Devonshire, but also part of the manor was held by Norman the park-keeper. In all, nearly 2,000 parks are known in medieval England. They are often oval or elliptical in shape, and the most striking feature about them, and the most expensive to construct and maintain, is the immense ditch and bank, the latter surmounted by a wooden palisade, which had to be built to keep the deer in. Lengths of such bank and ditch are often still to be seen in the countryside, even today, sometimes still fairly substantial as at Ryehill, Wimborne St Giles, in Dorset, in other cases much denuded and scarcely visible as such, as at Seagrave's Farm, at Penn in Buckinghamshire.

From the sixteenth century onwards deer parks were either abandoned, the deer removed or slaughtered, the trees grubbed up and the land turned down to pasture or arable, so that it is often only the pattern of field boundaries together with insubstantial traces of banks and ditches which today betray the former presence of a deer park, or else they were enlarged, sometimes substantially, to serve as the basis for the carefully landscaped amenity parks of seventeenth- and eighteenth-century country houses.

The story of the Royal Forests in Scotland is somewhat different. They were first established by David I in the 1130s and by the 1150s there were Royal Forests in Selkirk, Traquhair, Pentland, Moorfoot, Stirling, Clackmannan, and Gala. Scottish forest law was less savage than English, with no provision for the mutilation of offenders as there undoubtedly was in England, or for the lawing of dogs, that is the clipping of the toes in their front feet to prevent them pulling down the deer. Much Royal Forest was alienated in Scotland during the fourteenth century but later attemps to revoke earlier grants were largely unsuccessful. In 1455 however Selkirk Forest, now renamed the Forest of Ettrick, reverted to the Crown. By the early sixteenth century the king was setting lands in the Forest to feu farm. Tenants could build houses, make fish ponds, and build bridges. They also had freedom to plough in the customary places, an unconscious admission that it had long been going on. Pressures on Scottish woodland generally were becoming increasingly severe by this time, and successive statutes of the Scottish Parliament made attempts to protect it. One Act, of 1503, claimed that Scottish woods were 'uterlie destroyit', and another, passed in 1579, made it a capital offence on the third conviction for cutting green wood, all to little or no purpose. By this time much of lowland Scotland was almost devoid of trees.

Marshes and woods are only two of the ways in which men can make use of the surface of the land, and they are certainly ways which could be made to yield handsomely for the effort put into them. Topographical variations dictate other forms of land use. Large areas of upland Britain, from Dartmoor to the Cairngorms, were, during the medieval centuries, given up to rough grazing, and it is very likely that climatic deterioration from the fourteenth century onwards made it increasingly difficult to maintain even this form of land use save by transhumance, a system under which livestock is driven up into summer pastures in the hills as soon as the weather permits, and brought back into pens and byres at the onset of winter. Climatic deterioration also pushed the areas of cultivation down the hillsides, and arable land was abandoned, in the Lammermuir Hills for example, and in central Wales and around the edges of Dartmoor.

For the great majority of men bread was the mainstay of their lives, and such was the level of technology throughout the greater part of the medieval centuries that they had to grow for themselves almost the whole of what they would eat, and at the same time provide for the beasts of the plough without whose patient labours their task would have been so much more difficult. In other words, large areas of land had to be devoted to growing crops, especially cereals, and to providing meadow and pasture. To keep the cattle out of the corn, boundaries had to be constructed, whether of stone or turf, earthen banks or ditches, hedges or fences. Even the largest of fields had to be fenced in at some point, so that the very term 'open fields' is in some respects misleading. Sometimes these fields were cultivated for centuries on end. Sometimes they were used for pastures for an equally long period of time. Yet other fields could alternate between arable and pasture within a matter of years, or alternatively change their purpose only once over a couple of centuries. Similarly the boundaries of fields could change, and large fields could be divided up into small ones and small ones thrown together to make large ones. Small-scale piecemeal change is continuous across the rural landscape of Britain. Sometimes it slows to a snail's pace, and stability seems to be the order of the day, an impression which the use of maps, which begin to appear at the end of the sixteenth century, serves only to reinforce, since maps are by their nature frozen moments of time, giving a picture which seems to lie beyond the reach of change. At other periods change accelerates, as in the fifteenth century for example, and in the eighteenth. In order to give substance to these abstract statements, examples are essential, always with the proviso that all examples have their own unique features and that the very act of choosing may be determined by such random factors as the chance survival of documents, compounded by the ignorance of the person making the choice. One example nevertheless may serve to illustrate the discussion so far. Creslow, in north Buckinghamshire, was once a parish of large open arable fields. It was enclosed at some time in the fifteenth century, at a period when it was more profitable to rear sheep for their wool than to grow corn for men, and the arable was turned down to pasture. It has been pasture ever since. The big arable fields were divided up into smaller fields ranging in size from 6 to 99 acres, together with one very large field called the Great Field, of 310 acres, worth, in 1649, £434. These fields can still be seen in the landscape today, marked off by the sinuous field boundaries which characterize enclosure made before the end of the seventeenth century. The Great Field was itself divided into four smaller fields at some time during the course of the eighteenth century, with the straight hedgerows which are so typical of enclosure at that time. Here is the landscape as palimpsest, with change taking place very slowly over a long time-span, at the same time reflecting changes in agricultural practices which are themselves reflections of change within society as a whole.

Fields, in the very broad sense of enclosures made for arable or pastoral husbandry, may be found almost everywhere in Britain up to the 2,000-foot contour, and in some instances, the enclosures about Scottish shielings for example, above that. Processes of change have altered and modified their boundaries and the use which was made of them. Many have been abandoned altogether, especially in the uplands, something which has been taking place since prehistoric times. This kaleidoscopic patchwork of fields has never been entirely still for as far back as it is possible to penetrate, and we saw in Chapter 2 that fields can be recognized, both on the ground and from aerial photographs, which are almost certainly Neolithic in their origins. It is however only in the post-Roman centuries that documents start to survive from which it is possible to discover how these fields were organized and managed. Two problems immediately present themselves.

We saw in Chapter 3 that fields can now be recognized that are almost certainly Roman in their origin, and that some of these fields are rectangular in their shape rather than square. There is also a small but growing body of evidence to show that on occasion Roman boundaries underlie medieval field boundaries, but there is very much more evidence showing Roman boundaries being ignored. The land itself would still have been cultivated, however, since both Romano-British and Anglo-Saxon peasants had to eat. The first problem, therefore, is that there is a discontinuity between Roman fields and early medieval ones which at present cannot be satisfactorily bridged.

The second problem concerns the way in which their cultivation was organized. Some small plots of arable have always been cultivated in severalty, that is by one occupier without reference to a neighbour. But throughout the length and breadth of Britain, from Cornwall to the Moray Firth and from Caernarvonshire to Suffolk, the arable has usually been cultivated in common, with the land itself parcelled out into shares which are not fenced off from one another, with some of the tasks of the agricultural year, such as ploughing, performed on a co-operative basis and the crop regime decided by the community rather than the individual. The plots of the individual farms are distributed throughout the arable of the community and are usually elongated in shape, on occasion nearly a mile in length, sometimes less than 50 yards.

The origins of this system of common or shared land-holding have provoked intense controversy among historians but no satisfactory answers, save that it is now clearly established that the English did not bring it with them from their homelands in northern Germany, first because excavation has proved conclusively that it developed in these homelands long after the period of migration had come to an end, and second because it is now evident that the arable in north Wales and in Scotland, regions well beyond any Anglo-Saxon influence, was also held in shares.

The Laws of Ine, who was King of Wessex from 688 until 726, speak of common meadows and arable shareland. We cannot however assume that all land, even within the same community, was thus held, nor that livestock was turned out to graze over the stubble once the harvest was in. Nor is there any suggestion of communal ownership, rather of what has been called 'a community of shareholders', which is by no means the same thing. It is the tenth century before there is clear documentary evidence of the existence of the open-field system. A charter of 966 refers to arable shareland *(gedal-land)* at Clifford Chambers, in Warwickshire, and another of 961, almost certainly relating to Arlington in Berkshire, speaks of land lying among other lands held in shares, open pasture common, meadow common and ploughland common, whilst a third, of 962, referring to Hendred, also in Berkshire, says that the bounds of the lands are common so that acre lies ever among acre, a phrase echoed in other charters to Drayton and Kingston Bagpuize, also both in Berkshire, and to Linden End in Aldreth, Cambridgeshire, and generally taken to refer to land lying in strips. Another document, of about 900, relating to land at Alton Priors, in Wiltshire, tells of unenclosed heath held entirely in common, and yet another document of 963 mentions not only the right to cut wood in the common copse but also the services of one day's work at haymaking and one at harvest time.

Thus it is very likely that the exploitation of the agricultural resources of midland England on a co-operative basis was well established by the tenth century, although it is equally likely that the complex open-field system did not reach its full maturity before the twelfth. There is also evidence from Wales to suggest that the arable was divided into shares at this time, with individual plots being rectangular in shape, and there is also some evidence to indicate that these plots were re-allocated from time to time, something which appears to be unknown for the arable in England but was widely practised for meadow land until well into the sixteenth century. There is no documentary evidence from Scotland before the twelfth century, when the surviving handful of documents would seem to point to arable land shared out in long strips or rigs, and again there is some evidence to show that these were re-allocated from time to time.

It is often suggested that the origins of land division into strips is to be sought in the rules of partible inheritance, under which a man's property was divided into equal portions among all his sons. Such subdivision undoubtedly took place, and could lead to the reduction of a viable farm into a patchwork of uneconomic plots within a comparatively short period of time. Sir John Wynn of Gwydir, writing in the fifteenth century, described partible inheritance as 'the destruction of Wales'. It continued to be widely practised both in England and in Wales until well into the seventeenth century, in Rossendale in Lancashire for example. It may also be suggested that co-operative farming and the sharing of lands arose from the impossibility of an individual peasant farmer's being able to maintain for his sole use a plough and plough-team, with division of wasteland brought into cultivation by joint effort being shared among those who had taken part. All of these suggestions are reasonably plausible, and all may contain some part of the truth, but it is very unlikely that any one, or indeed any combination, will contain the whole truth; and it is even more unlikely that we shall ever know the full story of the introduction or evolution, or both, of those systems for the co-operative exploitation of the land of Britain which have dominated the rural landscape from at least the seventh century until the end of the nineteenth.

Over about half of England, in a great belt extending from Dorset and Somerset in the southwest to the coastal plains of Durham and Northumberland in the northeast, the open-field system was, by the opening years of the thirteenth century, the dominant form in the organization of the rural landscape, regulating very precisely the ways in which men were to cultivate the land and their access to its resources and to its produce.

There is now much evidence to show that the introduction of the open-field system was a long-term process brought about as a result of the replanning of individual estates, the second great restructuring of the landscape since the first which can at present be recognized, that of Bronze Age times, as described in Chapter 2. This second, medieval, replanning involved the bringing together into one nucleated village of a number of isolated farmsteads and hamlets scattered over an estate, and the re-allocation of the arable shareland into strips divided among two or three great fields. So regularly was this allocation of strips done that each man found himself with the same neighbours wherever his strips lay, and this is recorded in numerous documents from the latter part of the twelfth century and much of the thirteenth. To give just one example. Several documents recording the transfer of land in the village of Steeple Claydon, in north Buckinghamshire, between about 1220 and 1240 show that wherever Thomas de Hampton had strips then Henry de Kaam was his neighbour. Evidence of this planning is still visible on the ground today in the regularity with which house plots line the streets of such villages as Cold Kirby in Yorkshire and Pockley in the Vale of Pickering, a region in which as many as twenty-three out of twenty-nine adjacent villages bear every mark of deliberate planning. Such villages are to be found almost everywhere in England, at Newton Bromswold in Northamptonshire for example, or Isle Abbots in Somerset, whilst other villages have planned extensions, as at Okeford Fitzpaine in Dorset and Newton Longville in Buckinghamshire.

In nucleated villages of this kind the arable was divided into two or three great fields, each of several hundred acres in extent. Each field was in its turn divided into furlongs, and each furlong was composed of a bundle of strips, which were often laid out with close attention to the lie of the land. These strips could vary considerably in size, from under half an acre to two or three acres, occasionally more. If the village arable was divided into two open fields, then one was under crops whilst the other lay fallow. If there were three, then one was sown with winter wheat, the second with spring crops such as peas, beans, and barley, whilst the third lay fallow. Sometimes, of course, there were more than three fields, as at Aston Clinton in Buckinghamshire, where there were nine, or at Islip in Oxfordshire, but very often these fields were managed in groups, or 'seasons', rather than as a large number of independent units.

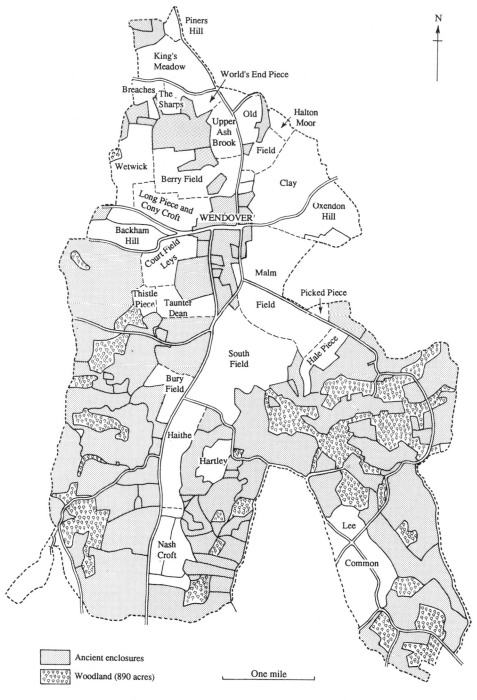

Figure 10 Wendover, Buckinghamshire, before enclosure

This is the traditional picture of the English open-field village. But its aura of permanence and immutability is very misleading. First of all, as we have seen, it is very likely that it came into existence as the result of a deliberate replanning of the layout of an estate by its lord at any time between the tenth and the thirteenth century. Secondly, once laid out, it was itself subject to change. Rising population in the twelfth and thirteenth centuries put increasing pressure upon resources, and one way of producing more grain was by reorganizing two arable fields into three, so that only a third of the arable lay fallow in any one year, rather than half. Such a reorganization seems to have taken place in Thornborough in Buckinghamshire for example, early in the fourteenth century, when the Mill Field was created from furlongs taken from the East Field and the West Field.

Not only could the field boundaries change, but also the furlong boundaries. Study of the layout of the village of Raunds, in Northamptonshire, reveals a pattern of 'long' strips, over 1,000 yards long and running across several furlongs with names like Upper, Lower, and Middle, suggesting that they had been subdivided at some time in the past. Such long strips have also been recognized elsewhere in England, at Wharram Percy and Burdale, both in Yorkshire, for example.

It is also clear that the village itself could 'drift' across the landscape. At Walgrave and at Canons Ashby, both in Northamptonshire, cottages and gardens were once laid out across the ridge and furrow of the arable, and at Burwell in Cambridgeshire, a new settlement, about 300 yards to the north of the old, which itself was an expansion from a nucleus about the village church, developed over a headland between strips in the open fields. At Lower Slaughter in Gloucestershire, however, cottages were built on what was once the village green. Such 'drift' could take place comparatively easily because the houses of the men who cultivated the fields were insubstantial buildings of timber, thatch, and wattle. The smallest of peasant houses were one- or two-roomed cabins, no more than 20 by 15 feet at the largest. These must have been the homes of the poorest members of village society, with little or no land of their own, so that they were entirely dependant upon wages, paid in cash or in kind, by their wealthier neighbours. Larger altogether were the long houses of the tenant farmers, whether villeins, who were legally bound to the lord, paying heavy rents in cash and labour services, or freemen, whose rents were very much lighter. The long house was to be found throughout Britain. It could be anything up to 90 feet long, but rarely more than 15 feet wide. It was divided into two. One half was for the family, the other for their livestock. Sometimes men and beasts were separated by a cross passage, sometimes by a wattle partition, sometimes by only a step. Living conditions must at times have been appalling. In due course, however, the animals were moved out into their own byres and stables, which were grouped more or

23 Reconstructions of the cabins built by English peasants at West Stow, near Bury St Edmunds in Suffolk, a settlement probably abandoned before the end of the seventh century AD.

less into a square to give the farmyard, with the farmer's house occupying one side and with a midden in the centre. This process was taking place in the eleventh century, and it has been traced in detail for the thirteenth by careful excavation at Gomeldon in Wiltshire. It was not completed in the remoter parts of Devonshire and Cumberland before the nineteenth.

The family living quarters were usually divided into two. There was an open central hearth in the first part, and the far end was partitioned off to provide sleeping accommodation. Furniture seems to have been sparse. Houses had stout wooden doors because hinges, locks, and keys have been found on excavated sites, but any windows would have been closed with shutters since glass was very expensive. Floors were of clay or trodden earth. The interiors of these houses seem to have been kept very clean, since excavation has revealed remarkably little domestic rubbish of any kind.

The houses and cottages of the peasant cultivators were almost invariably of one storey, open to the roof. They were built of timber, with thatched roofs, Sometimes they were timber-framed, with posts set in holes in the ground or on sills, either of timber or of stone. Sometimes they were of cruck construction, a technique employing pairs of curved timbers

24   A sixteenth-century cruck-framed cottage at Cossington, Leicestershire.

set in the ground and meeting overhead, with two or more pairs joined by a ridge pole. Timber set directly into or on the ground will eventually rot and so will need to be replaced. Excavation of the deserted village at Wharram Percy, in Yorkshire, has revealed just how frequently this rebuilding could occur. Every thirty or forty years, sometimes more frequently, sometimes less, a new cottage replaced an old one, usually on a slightly different alignment, so that the most permanent feature of the site turns out to be the boundary of the toft in which the house stood rather than the house itself. Gradually, and more especially from the thirteenth century onwards, rebuilding took place in stone, or partly in stone, since the new never entirely replaces the old. At Wharram Percy one cottage had low stone walls levelled off to take timber sills, and another had stone walls up to the eaves.

Of these houses and cottages, in which lived nine-tenths of the population of Britain in the twelfth and thirteenth centuries, nothing now survives above ground. Our knowledge of their construction and layout has had to be pieced together from the meticulous excavation of deserted village sites such as that at Wharram Percy, or Goltho in Lincolnshire, Barton Blount in Derbyshire, Wythemail in Northamptonshire, Hound Tor, and elsewhere.

Rows of timber-framed and thatched cottages, set in open arable fields divided up into furlongs and strips, were not however the only elements of the thirteenth-century village community. Meadows, pasture, and woodland were equally important. Meadow was frequently located in damp hollows and near streams. This meant that there would be a good growth of grass for making into hay. This fodder would then provide for the village livestock during the winter months. The traditional story that most animals had to be slaughtered in the autumn because of the lack of fodder is a myth. Study of the animal bones found in deserted villages shows that most animals were at least three years old when killed. Meadowland was valuable. It was often worth ten or fifteen times the value of arable land. It was usual for it to be divided into strips in the same way as the arable, but these strips of meadowland were re-allotted among the villagers every year, unlike the arable, which formed a permanent farm, however small and however fragmented.

Permanent pasture on the other hand was often provided in the form of waste and common land, frequently reduced by overgrazing to thorn scrub and usually lying at the periphery of the estate. Woodland was also sometimes available, to provide fuel, building materials, and wood for carts and farm implements. Pigs and other livestock were also turned out to graze, and this could in the long term have a deleterious effect upon the woodland by preventing the growth of seedlings and saplings, so that it degenerated into pasture. Yet further grazing would become available after the harvest had been gathered in, when animals were turned out into the stubble, there to find such living as they could until the time came to plough once more. Their droppings may also have made some contribution to the restoration of the fertility of the soil, but this could only have been slight since such droppings were not distributed evenly and in any case many nutrients would have been quickly lost through weathering.

This, the classical open-field system of agriculture, was characteristic of about half of England, the lowlands of the Welsh borders and south Wales throughout the medieval centuries. It has not completely disappeared even today, since it is still practised at Laxton, in Nottinghamshire, and there are other, more fragmentary, remains at Rhosili on the Gower peninsula. There is a wealth of documentation from which the *minutiae* of its organization and day-to-day administration can be studied, and from the last years of the sixteenth century there are splendid maps which portray in vivid detail what must surely have been one of the most complex codes for the exploitation of natural resources ever devised.

There was, however, much variety in the rural landscape of medieval Britain. Indeed in many respects each village has its own unique features

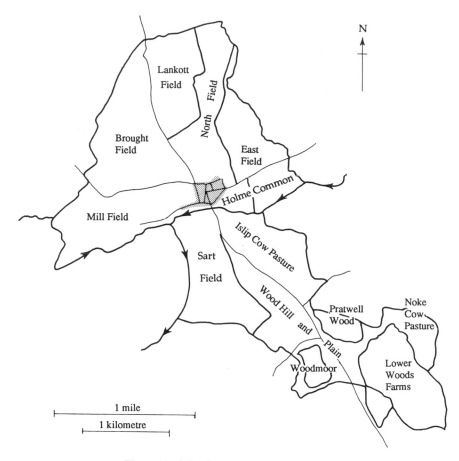

Figure 11   Islip, Oxfordshire, before enclosure

within the very broad generalizations offered above. In Wales, the Lake District and in Scotland there were yet further differences.

The rural landscape of Scotland was characterized by the infield/outfield system. The nucleated village which evolved in England from the tenth century onwards was almost entirely absent from Scotland save in the area from the Firth of Forth to the Northumberland border. Instead Scottish rural settlement took the form of the ferm-toun, a loose grouping of cottages, usually called a clachan in the Highlands. In the immediate vicinity of the ferm-toun lay the arable. The nature of the Scottish terrain meant that it was unusual to find this arable in large blocks. It lay instead in a number of pieces interspersed with moss, coarse grazing, patches of bog, and stony ground. Within the blocks of arable the land was divided up into strips, or rigs. These were often very steeply ridged, sometimes as much as 6 feet from the crest to the hollow, and, where topography allowed, they could also be very long. Each tenant of the ferm had his land scattered throughout the arable in strips. It was cultivated every year. Its only fallow came during the winter months. All the manure of the ferm-toun was spread out over this arable, or infield. Cattle had to be penned during the winter months, in byres or kail yards, and their manure accumulated in great quantities. To this was added domestic refuse of every kind together with, sometimes every year, sometimes every two or three, the soot-laden thatch from the cottages. The whole malodorous mass was spread over the infield. Here, oats were grown each year, save that sometimes a course of bere, or barley, was sown.

The crop from the infield was supplemented by a crop from the outfield. This was a much larger area, of which only a part was cultivated each year. During the summer months the livestock of the ferm-toun was penned on that part of the outfield which it was proposed to cultivate in the following year. This tathing was the only form of manuring applied to the outfield. That part chosen for cultivation was then cropped for as long as four or five years in succession before being allowed to revert to weeds and then grass, and another patch was broken up.

Both infield and outfield were usually surrounded by a head dyke, a substantial wall or bank and ditch. This served to keep the livestock of the ferm-toun away from the growing crops and out on the commons, moors, and wastes where, in the summer months at any rate, they were turned to graze. This rough grazing was often very extensive, running to thousands of acres in some districts. It was supplemented by shielings, summer grazings often at some distance from the ferm-toun, to which the livestock was driven as soon as the weather permitted, there to remain, in the company of their herdsmen, until the winter. A sheep dyke which must be unique in the British Isles is to be found on North Ronaldsay. It completely encircles the island, its purpose being to keep the islanders' sheep on the seashore, where they feed on seaweed.

The Norman penetration of the lowlands of south and north Wales and the Marches brought with it the open-field system as developed in England. In the uplands, and especially in central and northern Wales, ancient forms of rural organization persisted. Our knowledge of these depends upon a collection of legal texts known as the Book of Iorwerth (*llyfr Iorwerth*) of which all the known manuscripts save one date from the thirteenth century. They claim, however, to represent the laws of Hywel Dda who died in about 950, a claim which, in broad terms, is widely accepted. The laws present a highly schematized pattern of estate organization, grouping homesteads and townships into commotes in order to make arrangements for the collection of the rents and services due to the lord or to the king, rents which were almost always paid in kind: loaves of bread, vats of mead, sheaves of oats, pigs, flitches of bacon, and so on. The men who paid these rents were considered either to be free or to be bondmen. Freemen held their land by one form of tenure, bondmen by another. Land held by freemen was called *tir gwelyawg*. This often consisted of a personal holding, *tir priod*, comprising a homestead and parcels of arable lying in one or more open fields, and an undivided share of pasture and waste lands called *cytir*. The personal holding was subject to partible inheritance (*cyfran*), under which at the death of the tenant it was divided equally among all his sons. This subdivision could reduce a well-established family to poverty over the generations. Land held by bondmen, *tir cyfrif*, usually also included arable shareland cultivated in strips. Bond holdings were subject to heavy rents in services and kind.

By the end of the fifteenth century this elaborate system was breaking up. Many holdings of *tir gwelyawg* were too small to be economically viable. Many of the rents on *tir cyfrif* were being commuted for cash, and, as in England, there were very few men left who were personally unfree. They often found themselves unable to pay the new cash rents and were evicted. These trends left the way open for those with money and opportunity to snap up both *tir gwelyawg* and *tir cyfrif* land and consolidate them into new estates, enclosing and improving as they went along. This disintegration of traditional landholding patterns was immensely hastened by an Act of Parliament of 1542 which provided for the abolition of partible inheritance upon the next change of heirs. At the same time estate surveyors, whether working for the Crown or for great landowners such as the Earl of Leicester, began to treat unenclosed land as common land and therefore the property of the lord, ignoring any claim that it was ancient *cytir* and as such deliberately left open and unenclosed. In this way ancient legal structures governing the holding of land collapsed, creating much uncertainty over a long period of time. The slate is never wiped entirely clean, however. Until they were ploughed out in the 1970s strips of land formerly held under these ancient tenures were still visible around the village of Llanynys, in Denbighshire, and as late as 1840 similar sharelands lying in strips survived at Pennant in Merionethshire, to be recorded on the tithe map of that year, with at least part lying some 800 feet up the hillside.

These then, at least in broad outline, are the principal features of the medieval rural landscape. But there was no such thing as *the* medieval landscape, rather a series of ever-changing local and regional landscapes moulded by subtle variations of topography, climate, and social patterns and only loosely linked by a poor communications network in which the great bulk of the traffic went on foot and the fastest traveller could go only as quickly as a galloping horse could carry him. Much has disappeared of these medieval landscapes, but much also remains, often in very unexpected places. Thus many thirteenth-century field boundaries are still to be found on the Chiltern Hills, around Great Hampden for example, to be recognized by their botanically rich hedgerows, whilst others are fossilized in the property boundaries of houses and gardens laid out early in the twentieth century as Beaconsfield New Town was being built. Well over 3,000 deserted medieval village sites are known, the victims of the long-term effects of the Black Death and later epidemics and of changes in international trade and commerce as it became increasingly more profitable during the fifteenth century to rear sheep for wool than to grow corn for men. Open arable fields were enclosed and laid down to pasture. Peasants were evicted from their cabins, which quickly fell into ruins. All that is left today are the grass-grown house platforms, separated by lanes, equally grass-grown, worn down by centuries of traffic, and surrounded on all sides by the ridge and furrow, created by generations of medieval ploughmen patiently cultivating their strips in the open fields. Often all that remains above ground today to indicate where once a village was to be found is an isolated church, the only stone building of the community, standing in melancholy solitude in fields that have not been ploughed for five centuries or more, with sheep and cattle grazing over the ridge and furrow.

Groups of timber and thatched cabins were by no means the only houses to be found in the medieval landscape. A rectangular building was the basic form of accommodation for everyone, from king to peasant, although they varied enormously in size and in quality of construction, according to the rank in society of their owners. Substantial timber-built Anglo-Saxon royal palaces in which a rectangular hall was the principal building are known by excavation at Yeavering in Northumberland, at Northampton, and at Cheddar, whilst a manor house excavated at Sulgrave in Northamptonshire, and to be dated to the last century of the Anglo-Saxon period, had a hall of stone and timber construction separated from its service rooms by a screen, with a kitchen as a detached building.

Both timber and stone were used as building materials, but it is the stone ones which are the earliest to survive, and then only from the middle years of the twelfth century. Some of the oldest domestic buildings still standing in England are stone-built houses of two storeys in which the principal accommodation was on the first floor, where there is also a subsidiary, more private chamber called a solar, and a fireplace with a chimney stack built into one of the long sides. Such buildings include the Manor House at Hemingford Grey, for example, and the Hall of Christchurch Castle, both of about 1150–60, as well as Boothby Pagnell, in Lincolnshire, which dates from about 1200. Ground-floor halls of both timber and stone construction were also being built. In order to increase the floor area the roof was supported on double rows of posts or columns, to give aisles running parallel to the long sides. The hall of Oakham Castle, dating from about 1190, is a good example. Gradually, however, the use of aisles declines, and halls with a single-span roof are built, as at Penshurst in Kent, a substantial example dating from about 1340 and measuring 62 feet long by 39 feet wide, whilst the hall of Ightham Mote, built a little earlier, is altogether smaller, only 31 by 21 feet. The largest open-span hall by far is Westminster Hall, built at the end of the eleventh century for William Rufus. It measures 239 feet long by 67 feet wide. Its magnificent hammer-beam roof was built late in the fourteenth century and must rank with the octagon of Ely Cathedral as one of the most splendid examples of medieval engineering in timber. It still stands, although to some extent overshadowed by the nineteenth-century Gothic of the Houses of Parliament.

The hall throughout the medieval centuries was the principal room of a house, used for every domestic purpose. It was open to the rafters and heated by a single central hearth. Even before the Norman Conquest it was being subdivided in the interests of conveniency and privacy. Sometimes it was partitioned merely by a screen. Sometimes there was a passage behind the screen giving access to service rooms at the rear, and sometimes these service rooms were occupied by animals, since it was very common for man and beast to share the same roof. Kitchens, for much of the medieval period, were almost always detached buildings because of the danger of fire. Sometimes the hall was divided at both ends, giving three blocks, with service rooms and subsidiary accommodation at each end. During the course of the fifteenth century changing social and domestic habits saw the long, slow decline of the hall as the centre of the home and it began to be ceiled over, to give accommodation on the first floor. This meant that staircases had to be built to give access, and that the central hearth had to be moved and given a chimney stack. These developments appear first in the south and east of England. During the course of the fifteenth century some houses were being built with the subsidiary rooms at both ends of the hall projecting forward slightly, to give a shallow 'H' plan, the whole being covered by a single hipped roof. This Wealden-type house is widely distributed over much of southeastern England and, to judge from surviving examples such as Synyards, at Otham in Kent, they were being built for very prosperous farmers, merchants, and yeomen.

Substantial medieval hall houses, of great variety in plan, layout, and methods of construction, survive in considerable numbers the length and breadth of England, from Burton Agnes Old Manor in Yorkshire, of about 1170, to Clevedon Court in Somerset, of about 1320, and from Little Wenham Hall in Suffolk dating from about 1270 to Brinsop Court, Herefordshire, of about 1340. Houses of this kind must have been built for prosperous well-to-do members of society, whether called manorial lords or country gentry or successful yeomen farmers, since they are far removed in the size and comfort of their accommodation and in the quality of their construction from those peasant cabins described earlier in this chapter. They have often been much altered and added to in the centuries since they were first built. Their medieval core is often at first difficult to distinguish from later accretions, especially from the outside, so that a glimpse of the

25 The late-thirteenth-century manor house at Donington le Heath, Leicestershire. The hall is on the first floor and the site was once surrounded with a moat.

windows of the medieval hall which lies at the heart of the Old Parsonage House in Marlow, all but submerged in later additions, brings a shock of mild surprise at the recognition of a very much older layer to what is, at first glance, an eighteenth-century house. It is these layers which give to the British landscape its incredibly rich historical density and make endlessly rewarding the task of those who would explore it.

There are yet further occupation sites in the landscape which are medieval in their origins. Defended sites, often enclosed with nothing more elaborate than a single bank and ditch, have long been a common feature of the landscape, their roots deep in prehistory. A striking and unusual variation upon the theme appears during the course of the twelfth century, reaches maturity in the fourteenth, and fades from currency in the sixteenth. This is the moated site. They are very common over large areas of lowland England, being particularly numerous in the west Midlands and in a great belt of territory stretching from north Buckinghamshire and Bedfordshire through Hertfordshire into Essex, Suffolk, and Norfolk, although they are also to be found from Yorkshire to Dorset and from Lancashire into Kent. In all about 5,300 are known at present, including a number in Wales.

A moated site is essentially a homestead, with its ancillary buildings, set on an island which is surrounded with a water-filled moat. The island is frequently more or less rectangular, but circular and D-shaped ones are also known, as well as more complex ones with several islands and an interconnecting pattern of moats. The island can run to several acres in extent, and the moat is often 10 feet wide, sometimes 20 feet, crossed by a bridge or causeway. Sometimes there is a separate and distinctive gatehouse at the island end, as at Lower Brockhampton in Herefordshire, or else a gatehouse structure is incorporated in the main range of buildings, as at Little Moreton Hall in Cheshire and Ightham Mote in Kent. The buildings on the island were frequently substantial, and they appear to be what may be called manorial centres. There was almost always a hall house, with barns, stables, dovecotes, bakehouse, and even a chapel, although the actual layout and complexity of the site can vary considerably. Sometimes there were fish ponds in the vicinity, and excavation has shown that some islands had no buildings at all: they could very well have been gardens or orchards. Excavation has also revealed that very frequently a moated site was constructed over existing buildings, and at Clipston,

26 Little Moreton Hall, Cheshire, a splendid timber-framed moated house built between the end of the fifteenth and the end of the sixteenth centuries.

Walsall, and Little Gidding moated sites were laid out over older ridge and furrow.

Some moated buildings have stone walls, but the great majority seem to have been built in timber. Thus they could not have withstood any serious military attack, and if their primary purpose was defensive then it must have been against small bands of marauders rather than anything else. They seem to have been primarily dwelling houses, and fairly substantial ones, since they must have been expensive to construct. An island of about an acre in extent would need nearly 300 yards of moat, perhaps 15 feet wide and 6 feet deep, meaning that about 3,750 tons of soil would have to be excavated, and this for no more than an average-sized moat. It is thus very likely that an element of fashion is to be seen in their construction as well as the mental reassurance that the moat would have brought in a lawless age. They remain one of the commonest earthworks surviving from the medieval world, and also one of the more enigmatic.

Very much more strongly fortified occupation sites were also present in the medieval landscape. One of the first acts of William the Conqueror on landing in Sussex in 1066 was to order the building of a castle within the walls of the Roman fort at Pevensey. After the battle of Hastings he had others built at Hastings and Dover and then, when London had submitted, he went on to order the building of castles there, one where now the Tower

27 The east gate of Lincoln Castle. The tunnel-vaulted entrance is Norman; the other masonry visible here is largely fourteenth century.

of London stands, and two others, those which became Baynard's Castle and Mountfitchet Castle. Yet others followed rapidly throughout England as he consolidated his hold on the country and put down a succession of rebellions against his authority. Castles were built at Exeter, Warwick, Nottingham, Lincoln, Huntingdon, and Cambridge. There were two at York. In 1070 castles were built in Chester and Stafford, in 1071 at Ely, in 1072 at Durham, and his son Robert built one at Newcastle-upon-Tyne in about 1080. By 1086 Gloucester, Wallingford, Windsor, and Rochester each had one, and there were others, along the Sussex coast for example. Domesday Book records something of the impact that the construction of these castles could have upon the towns in which they were built. At Norwich, 98 messuages were empty in the town, being *in occupatione castelli*. At Cambridge, 27 houses were destroyed to make way for the castle, at Huntington only 21. At Lincoln however, where there were 1,150 inhabited houses in 1065, 166 were destroyed for the castle, and another 74 lay waste because of misfortune, poverty, and fire. At York there were seven wards or shires within the city, one of which was laid waste to make way for the castle.

These first castles were built very quickly, sometimes within a week, by gangs of forced labour, but they were also very simple structures: a ditch and bank, with a wooden palisade surrounding an oval-shaped area or bailey containing simple timber-built accommodation for the men and horses of the garrison, and a mound or motte of earth surmounted with a wooden keep which was sometimes on stilts and itself surrounded with a wooden palisade.

In due course these simple structures were replaced by stone ones of increasing complexity and sophistication. William the Conqueror rebuilt three, the White Tower in London and those at Colchester and Exeter. The White Tower still forms the central portion of the Tower of London. Three storeys high, 107 by 118 feet square, with walls 15 feet thick at the base, it must have been an astonishing sight in a city of thatch and timber, and a statement of power of stark brutality. It was both a fortress and a royal residence, since it included on the first floor both a great hall and a chapel, as does the only other castle of this period which can equal it, the keep at Colchester, which is even larger, 110 by 150 feet.

As the military defences of castles grew in complexity and sophistication so too did their residential accommodation. Thus the castle built by Edward I at Conway in 1284 had stables, kitchen, bakehouse, and brewhouse against the inner side of the north wall of the Outer Bailey, a Great Hall on the south side, with ovens in the thickness of the walls of two of the three nearest towers, whilst the King's Chambers were on the first floor in the Inner Bailey, with kitchens and a guardroom beneath.

Not all castles were built by the king. Roger de Montgomery built the motte-and-bailey castle at Hen Domen. This was replaced in about 1223 by the stone castle at Montgomery. Alan the Red built Richmond Castle, and Gundulf, bishop of Rochester, built the first castle in that city. William could tolerate these private castles, first because they were essential to the maintenance of his control over a hostile land and they relieved him of the burden of building them himself, and second because he was himself sufficiently powerful to prevent even the mightiest of his subjects from getting out of hand. When the royal authority was weak and divided, however, as during the reign of Stephen, 1135–54, then feudal lords built castles as they pleased. Large numbers were erected during the anarchy of Stephen's reign, the great majority no more than simple earthen motte-and-bailey structures. In all, nearly 800 castles were built between the Norman Conquest and 1189. Most did not survive for long and very few were ever rebuilt in stone. All that survives of them today are the grass-covered earthen mounds and hollows of their mottes and encircling ditches. They are very common in many districts of lowland England. There are well over a dozen in Buckinghamshire for example, at Weston Turville and Wing, Castlethorpe and Whitchurch, Little Missenden and Bradwell.

The first crusade, brought into being by the oratory of Urban II at a Church Council at Clermont Ferrand in 1095 and culminating in the capture of Jerusalem in 1099, brought western soldiers into close contact with the much more sophisticated military engineering of the Eastern Empire. This undoubtedly contributed to the growing scale and complexity of castle building in England. By the early years of the twelfth century massive square keeps of stone were being built, of which those at Norwich, built by Henry I, and Rochester, built by William of Corbeil, Archbishop of Canterbury, are splendid examples.

The castle as military stronghold reaches its climax, in Britain at any rate, in those built by Edward I in north Wales, at Rhuddlan, Conway, Harlech, Beaumaris, and above all at Caernarvon. Edward was a man of wide military experience, having spent long periods in France and Spain during his youth as well as going on crusade, and his knowledge of the most advanced fortifications in Europe and the Levant finds conscious echo in his work in north Wales, where the castles which he built were among the most sophisticated of his day. All were deliberate statements of his authority in the newly conquered lands of northern Wales. That at Caernarvon has an even greater significance. Just as work was about to begin, what were thought to be the bones of Magnus Maximus, the father of Constantine, the first Christian Roman Emperor, were discovered. The unusual banded masonry and polygonal towers of the castle were copied from the walls of Constantinople, which Edward would have assumed to have been the work of Constantine himself. The Eagle Tower, deliberately so named, was given three turrets to further reinforce the dignity of the man whose castle it was. Thus the whole conception of Caernarvon Castle

28   Tattershall Castle, Lincolnshire. A castle was first built here in 1231, but this splendid keep, begun in 1434, was built in brick by Ralph Cromwell, Lord Treasurer of England. It stands within a double moat.

was a deliberate statement of authority making a conscious appeal to Christian Imperial Rome for validation.

The castles of north Wales were among the last of the royal castles to be built primarily for military purposes. The improvements undertaken by Edward III at Windsor Castle in the middle decades of the fourteenth century were designed to turn it into a royal palace rather than a fortress, with display and ostentation the principal objectives.

The building of private fortifications as opposed to royal ones continued throughout the medieval centuries. The Crown sought to regulate them, and to make money out of them, by issuing licences to crenellate, that is to fortify either an existing house or a proposed one. These licences are known from the time of John, and some of the most picturesque of surviving medieval houses were fortified in this way: Haddon Hall in 1195, Stokesay in 1291 for example, Maxstoke in 1345, Bodiam, following a licence granted to Sir Edward Dalyungrigge by Richard II, and the manor house at Scotney, fortified by Roger Ashburnham from 1379.

By the end of the fifteenth century two important changes were taking place that would bring private fortification to an end. First of all the battle of Bosworth in 1485 brought Henry VII to the throne and inaugurated a long period of peace, stability, and strong central government in place of the often chaotic conditions of the fifteenth century and the Wars of the Roses. Both Henry VII and Henry VIII brought their over-powerful subjects to heel. Edward Stafford, third Duke of Buckingham, began building what is traditionally accepted as the last private fortified house built in England, at Thorney Castle in Gloucestershire, in the second decade of the sixteenth century. It made too many concessions to comfort and amenity to be seriously considered a fortress, but its high outer walls were crenellated, its gateways had gun ports and portcullises and, most serious of all, the duke kept a large household of private retainers. This was all too much for the jealous and suspicious Henry VIII, who had the duke executed in 1521 on trumped-up treason charges before Thorney could be finished. Other magnates quickly took the lesson to heart and were far more circumspect in what they built.

The second development was the introduction of gunpowder and artillery. This brought about a fundamental reappraisal of fortification during the course of the sixteenth century. Old castles became obsolescent. New ones had to be built, both to house artillery and to stand up to bombardment. Henry VIII built a series of low-lying fortresses with semi-circular bastions along the south coast in the 1530s, at Camber, Deal, and Walmer for example, severely practical in intent and quite unlike the fortress palaces of Windsor or Caernarvon. But technical developments, especially the introduction of the angle-bastion from Italy, made these out-of-date before they were finished. The fort built at Yarmouth in the Isle of Wight in 1546–7 and the fortifications begun at Berwick-upon-Tweed in 1558 show how rapidly the pace of change was accelerating. Only the Crown could bear the cost.

Developments in England and Wales are paralleled only partially in Scotland. The Anglo-Norman feudal lords encouraged to settle in Scotland by David I brought with them the motte-and-bailey castle. Over 250 are known, but the great majority are in remote areas such as Galloway, far from the Central Lowlands and the heart of royal power in Scotland. Most, as in England, survive as grass-covered mounds, as at Druchtag Motehill for example, Abington, and Carnwath, but there is a fine example at Duffus Castle, built in about 1150 by a Flemish adventurer already settled in Scotland called Freskin. The original buildings were replaced by stone ones in the fourteenth century and it is these which stand, albeit in ruins, today. Edinburgh Castle was also begun at this time, but only the chapel built by David I and dedicated to his mother, St Margaret, survives of this early work.

Castles were also built in the far north of Scotland by the Norsemen. On the little island of Wyre, in the Orkneys, stands the oldest datable stone castle in Scotland, built in about 1150 and almost certainly by Kolbein Hruga. Nominally under the suzerainty of the kings of Norway, the lords of the Western Isles and Highlands of Scotland were in fact largely independent and at liberty to build castles for themselves as and where they pleased, as at Sween for example, or Skipness of Kintyre or at Dunstaffnage, guarding the entrance to Loch Etive. Only very slowly did the Scottish kings extend their authority into this region, one of the first steps being the building, in about 1200, of the castle at Rothesay, on the island of Bute.

Towards the middle of the thirteenth century Walter of Moray, a

29   Gilnockie Tower, Eskdale, a largely intact mid-sixteenth-century Scottish tower house.

descendant of that Freskin mentioned above, began to build at Bothwell what would have been one of the finest castles in Scotland had it been finished. Its most striking feature is the great circular donjon, now in ruins, an idea almost certainly borrowed directly from France. The donjon continued to be a feature of Scottish castles, as at Tantallon castle for example, and that of Threave, built by Archibald Douglas in about 1370. It was of five storeys, with immensely thick walls. The ground floor was given over entirely to storage, and the whole was linked by a single spiral staircase. Threave Castle is traditionally accepted as the ancestor of the tower house, the peculiarly Scottish answer to the turbulent and unsettled conditions of the country for much of the fifteenth and sixteenth centuries and especially the violence which was endemic along the borders with England, where many were built as private fortified houses. Only during the last decades of the seventeenth century do they begin to relax their grim, closed-up, inward-looking demeanour. The Scots usually gave as good as they got, however, and tower houses are also to be found over much of northern England.

Hitherto the medieval occupation sites that we have been looking at have been essentially isolated ones, whether royal palaces and castles, manorial moated sites or substantial timber-framed yeomen's houses. Only the hovels of the peasants have constituted a larger social unit, namely a village, and even these have often comprised no more than ten or a dozen houses. At some stage in their history, however, some villages develop into towns, whilst yet other towns are deliberately established, both by kings and by lords, whether lay or ecclesiastical. The problem of an accurate dividing line between village and town is a perennial one, with different answers at different periods in time. We looked at some of the factors involved in Chapter 3 when discussing Roman towns. The conclusion there, that the difference is one of function, applies also to the difference between medieval villages and towns.

The long, slow decline of the fabric of Roman civilization in Britain brought all organized town life to an end by the last decades of the fifth century. This does not however imply the total desertion of all urban sites, and in London, York, and Canterbury, and probably in Lincoln and Carlisle, occupation almost certainly continued, but at a very much lower level of material well-being and with no continuity of municipal organization. The handful of fifth-century timber-framed buildings that have been found in Canterbury point to squatting rather than anything else. Many Roman buildings remained standing, and would do so for centuries, but the street plans and property boundaries have been almost entirely lost. Where Roman streets did for short stretches continue in use into the medieval centuries their survival seems to have been almost entirely fortuitous. Much more influential in the subsequent history of those English towns with a Roman basis has been the line of the Roman walls.

They were far too substantial, and far too useful, to be demolished save in short lengths, and they and their gates have exerted a profound influence on urban morphology ever since. Roman walls were much rebuilt in the medieval centuries, but those still visible today at Chester, York, Chichester, Exeter, and at basement level in London, follow the line of the Roman walls, and Roman gates still survive, at least in part, at Lincoln, Colchester, and Canterbury.

In 597 St Augustine landed in Kent to begin the conversion of the pagan English to Christianity. He met the King of Kent, Æthelberht, at Canterbury, described by Bede as the metropolis of the Kentish kings. What this implied at this date is still uncertain, but it brings together two of the most important factors making for the revival of town life in England, the church and royal administration. Augustine found just outside the Roman walls a building which Bede tells us had been used as a church since Roman times, and was the church in which Æthelberht's Christian wife, Bertha, had worshipped for at least thirty years before Augustine's arrival. The church is still to be seen and the present chancel is at least part of Bertha's church, although it is probably sub-Roman in date rather than anything earlier. Bede also tells us that Augustine 'recovered' a church in the northeastern corner of the walled area which he took as his episcopal seat, dedicating it to the Holy Saviour, that is Christchurch Cathedral. The immediate precinct of the cathedral may itself have been defended with a bank and ditch to form a *burh*, still commemorated in Burgate Street and the Borough, a short stretch of street immediately within Northgate. It seems very likely that at this time there was only very fragmentary occupation elsewhere within the line of the Roman walls. Slowly, however, the area filled up. A new gate was opened, the Newdingate, but the Roman street plan was lost.

Augustine also founded dioceses at Rochester and at London before his death shortly after 604. Again there is almost no evidence as to what was to be found in these places at this time, although it is worth recording that Councils of the Church held in 320 and 343 required bishops to have their sees in *urbes* and *civitates* and not in villages. In 625 a see was founded in York, its church being built in the northern part of the legionary fortress, much of which was still standing, with the *principia* still roofed. Similarly, almost the whole of the southeastern quarter of the walled area of Winchester was eventually given over to ecclesiastical and royal establishments, the Old and New Minsters, the Nunnaminster, the bishop's palace and a royal palace, which occupied the site of the forum. It was the tenth century, however, before this complex reached its fullest extent.

This juxtaposition of royal and ecclesiastical administration created demands and opportunities from which urban life was rekindled in seventh-century England. By the end of this century there is clear evidence for the existence of a number of settlements which were undoubtedly towns, however defined. Coastal trading centres were among the first to appear, almost certainly deliberately planned to serve centres of royal and ecclesiastical administration: *Hamwih,* now Southampton, for Winchester, Fordwich for Canterbury, and Ipswich for the kingdom of the East Angles, whilst both London and York, because of their favourable geographical locations, developed their own trading functions. The port of London is mentioned in that charter of 672–4 to Chertsey already referred to on p. 103, and Bede describes it as the mart of many nations resorting to it by land and sea. These places have all the attributes of towns: their streets are laid out to a regular plan, metalled with flint or gravel and lined with buildings. Their inhabitants are, from the archaeological record, engaged in a wide range of manufactures: leather and metal, textiles and pottery. Goods and merchandise of every kind were bought and sold, pottery from France, quernstones from the Rhineland, wine and silks from further afield, in all of which the demands of the newly established churches for materials of every kind, including glass, textiles, and metal goods, must have made an important contribution. These luxury goods, however, although of great value, were only a small portion of the total merchandise that passed through these places. Large numbers of cattle and sheep, for example, went through the slaughter-houses of *Hamwih* to provide the raw materials for the much more mundane but just as important textile and leather manufactures in the town, whilst the distinctive pottery manufactured in Ipswich was traded far and wide over southern England.

From this period on, towns appear in growing numbers and develop rapidly under a wide range of stimuli. They are centres of trade and manufacture. The market at Canterbury is mentioned in a charter of 762. They are the headquarters of royal and ecclesiastical administration, whether as cathedral towns or as the sites of minster churches. Many are deliberately planned, usually on royal initiative, with defensive ditches and banks and a gridiron street plan. Some reoccupy former Roman urban centres, where the walls must have offered ready-made defences. This occurred at Chichester, Exeter, and Bath for example, and at Winchester, where the evidence for deliberate planning is particularly clear, the new streets, over 5 miles of them, being uniformly surfaced in broken flint, in all about 8,000 tonnes of it. The Danish invasions and the English response under Alfred's leadership made defence of paramount importance in urban development in the late ninth century. A document of this time called the Burghal Hidage lists some thirty strongholds, or *burhs,* and gives details of the provision for the systematic manning of their defences. Some are newly fortified sites, others are old ones inside Roman fortifications. Some of the new ones will grow into important towns, Wallingford, Oxford, and Cricklade for example, whilst the defences built at Wareham are still conspicuous features of the town even today. Others, such as Halwell and Pilton, remained little more than forts. During the course of the tenth

30   The Anglo-Saxon fortifications at Wareham in Dorset.

century yet more towns were founded or refounded, as at Colchester for
example, and New Romney, founded before 960, although the evidence
for planning is often ambiguous, as at Nottingham, Hereford, Stamford,
and Bedford. Not all new towns were successful, however. A charter of
1007 is dated at the new town, *in novo oppido*, of *Beorchore,* a place which
cannot now be identified.

By the end of the tenth century there were in England probably nearly a
hundred places which could be called towns. There was a great deal of
individual variation between them, but certain broad characteristics can
already be discerned which will continue until the nineteenth century. The
area within the defences belonged at first to the king. It was divided up into
blocks, upon which individual tenants could build their houses. These
tenants were personally free. They paid rents in cash and could sell or
bequeath their property, which also included holdings in the fields and
meadows which surrounded the town. In other words a distinctive form of
land tenure, subject to the custom of the individual town, is emerging. By
the time of Domesday Book men subject to such tenure were being called
burgenses, burgesses. Custom implies a court to administer it, and borough
courts make their appearance in the documentary records during the tenth

and eleventh centuries. In those towns where Scandinavian influence was strong, Lincoln, Stamford, and Chester for example, there were groups of hereditary law-men, twelve in number, to perform these functions. Very frequently the blocks of land within a town were granted out to some lord, lay or ecclesiastical. Thus the Bishop of Worcester held most of Worcester itself. On these blocks individual lords built churches to serve their tenants, and it is to this that so many medieval towns owe their large numbers of parish churches: by the end of the eleventh century London had over a hundred, Norwich forty-six, Lincoln and York thirty-five each and Winchester perhaps fifty. These blocks were also subject to subdivision, producing in time the long narrow burgage tenements which were so prominent a feature of English towns until the combination of the bulldozer and compulsory purchase led to their disappearance in the years after 1945.

Trade, defence, manufacture, and administration, whether lay or clerical, continued to form the foundations of the distinctively urban functions of these places. By the early eleventh century it seems to have been axiomatic that every *burh* should also have a mint, and by the end of the tenth occupational specialization had developed to such an extent in Winchester that it gave rise to descriptive street names, including Tanner Street, Fleshmonger Street, and Shieldwright Street. This geographical concentration of occupations within well-defined quarters becomes a characteristic feature of most medieval towns, persisting down to the present in such street names as Fish Street, Milk Street, Haymarket, and the Shambles, to be found, for example, in York, Shrewsbury, Leicester, and London.

Finally, these places were becoming notable concentrations of population. It is notoriously difficult to calculate population totals from the figures given in Domesday Book, but it seems very likely that York may have had as many as 8,000 inhabitants, Norwich and Lincoln over 6,000 each, Oxford and Ipswich over 3,000, and Thetford over 5,000. Neither London nor Winchester appear in Domesday Book. Domesday Book also suggests that distinctive public buildings were also to be found in towns, since there is a reference to the guildhall of the burgesses at Dover, and there was a guild in Canterbury some two hundred years earlier.

The wealth of documentation for medieval towns as a whole that survives from about 1100 onwards means that much detail becomes available to expand and elaborate upon their role in the landscape, but there is no significant departure from that already discernible at the end of the seventh century. Very many more places develop urban functions. The rights and privileges of burgesses as individuals become more sharply defined, and towns incorporated as boroughs develop as distinctive legal entities. Their economic functions and the fluctuations in their wealth and prosperity become much clearer, but even at the end of the medieval centuries English towns were still small, whether by contemporary European standards or by the standards of the late twentieth century. London was undoubtedly the largest, with perhaps 50,000 inhabitants by 1500, and York and Norwich may have had 10,000 each, but many places which were undoubtedly fulfilling urban functions were very small indeed, with perhaps no more than 300 or 400 inhabitants, Wendover in Buckinghamshire for example, and Eye in Suffolk. This very small size means that town and country were intimately interconnected. Burgesses held strips in the open fields of their towns in just the same fashion as husbandmen in villages, whether in Leicester or Nottingham, Cambridge or Stamford, in some cases until the nineteenth century was almost over.

The tradition of royal town planning continues almost without a break after the Norman Conquest. Many places were created boroughs from the first, but many more were given markets without becoming boroughs, since it is clear that every borough had a market but that by no means every market town was a borough. Both kings and lords could create boroughs and markets but it is only at the end of the thirteenth century that Edward I finally established the rule that it is the prerogative of the Crown to establish boroughs and markets and that this can be done only by means of a royal charter. Those boroughs and markets already in existence were permitted to continue, it being presumed that they had lost their royal charters. One of the consequences of this is that the creation of seigneural boroughs and markets disappears almost completely save in Wales, where it continues until the sixteenth century. The Crown may on occasion have been moved by military and naval considerations in the founding of new towns, as at Portsmouth and Newcastle-upon-Tyne for example, but both king and lord hoped and expected to make money from their ventures, from property rents and from the tolls to be levied in markets and fairs. Sometimes they were outstandingly successful, as at Stratford-upon-Avon, founded by the Bishop of Worcester in 1196, or Bishops (now Kings) Lynn, found by the Bishop of Norwich in about 1095. Others failed to develop as expected and their very sites are now conjectural, as in the case of Newton, laid out in 1286 on the shores of Poole Harbour.

Some of the earliest new towns founded in the years immediately after the Norman Conquest were established at the gates of castles, as at New Windsor and Arundel. Others grew up at the entrances to monasteries, at Battle and at Bury St Edmunds, which grew rapidly in the years between 1066 and 1086, spreading out in a rectilinear grid plan over land which was once ploughed, and housing bakers, tailors, shoemakers, robe-makers, cooks, and ale-brewers to serve the needs of the monastic community. Yet others were more purely commercial in their origins, Boston and Liverpool as ports, and Dunstable and Stony Stratford as 'thorough-fare towns' on main roads. The great age for the creation of new boroughs, the founding of new towns and the establishment of new market centres was over by

1350, brought to an end by the economic blizzard precipitated by the devastating impact of the Black Death. By this time about 170 new towns had been planted in England and over 80 in Wales, and there were well over 600 boroughs and over 2,000 market places.

Urban topography has continued to be influenced down to the present by those factors which led to the rebirth of towns in the seventh century: trade, commerce and manufacture, defence and administration. Within individual towns these operate in unique combinations and with varying degrees of strength over time, but when seen within a national perspective their presence is permanent and all-pervasive. The legacy from Rome is largely confined to the constraints imposed by the line of the Roman fortifications and the location of gateways through them, the street plans of Roman towns being almost entirely abandoned. Gridirion street plans seem to be almost universal in the new towns of the Anglo-Saxon centuries, but far less common in the new towns of the post-Conquest period. Only one in seven medieval new towns seems to have been laid out in this way, with Stratford-upon-Avon and New Salisbury, laid out in 1220, among the best examples. In other towns the shape of the market-place was more influential, triangular as at Alnwick and St Albans, or running the full length of a long, wide street, as at Chipping Sodbury and Market Harborough. Very frequently this market-place becomes partially built over as market stalls become permanent buildings. This can be seen in the market-places at Maidstone, Ashbourne, and Bury St Edmunds for example, and it was deliberately encouraged by the Bishop of Lincoln in his new town at Thame, in order, it was recorded in 1279, to increase his rents. Sometimes a new town, complete with market-place and burgage plots, was added to an existing village. This seems to have occurred at Olney. Other towns were laid out in successive stages, something which appears to have taken place at Ludlow.

Over a hundred English towns were fortified or refortified during the medieval centuries, and these town walls and ditches exerted as strong an influence over the town plan as did their Roman predecessors. Much time and money went into medieval town fortifications and they were clearly a source of great civic pride. Those at Coventry took 200 years to finish, and Southampton built for itself an almost equally elaborate and expensive town wall, complete with 29 towers and 7 gates, of which 13 towers and 4 gates still survive. The new town of Kingston-upon-Hull was equally as ambitious. Early in the fourteenth century an elaborate defensive system was built, and at least one of the towers was built in locally made brick. Nothing now remains. Other towns had only a bank and ditch, as at Ipswich and Beverley, where there were however several imposing gates, including the North Bar, built in 1409–10, also in brick. It seems likely that gates of this kind were intended to serve as barriers and collecting points for tolls rather than for any serious military purposes.

31   North Bar, Beverley, built of brick in 1409.

Within the town, the streets marked off blocks upon which houses were built, individual plots often being long and narrow, sometimes quite large, as at Stratford-upon-Avon, where they measured about 60 by two hundred feet, and sometimes quite narrow, as at Alnwick, where they were little more than 6 feet wide. These plot boundaries have in their turn proved to be remarkably permanent features of the urban landscape, surviving in many instances down to the present. As with so many other features of a town, they impose their own constraints. Houses had to be fitted into them. Lack of elbow-room meant that many medieval town houses had either to spread back over their plots or else go up, and sometimes they did both. Houses of two and three storeys were appearing by the fourteenth century, and some of their more splendid sixteenth-century descendants can still be seen today, as at Ireland's Mansion, in Shrewsbury. The vast majority of medieval towns were built of thatch and timber-framing. Sadly, very little survives from before the sixteenth century, even in towns such as York, Norwich, and Shrewsbury, and probably the best impression of what a medieval town would have looked like is to be gained at Lavenham, in Suffolk, although the buildings themselves are today in a much better state physically than they would have been within a few years of being built, and the town itself is certainly much cleaner and sweeter-smelling than any medieval town would ever have been.

Some town houses were built of stone. They were being put up at the end of the twelfth century in Norwich, Southampton, Lincoln, and Canterbury for example, but they must have been expensive to build, and for long they remained rarities. Only in the later medieval centuries does stone come to be used on any scale, and then its use depended upon the availability locally of adequate supplies. Perhaps the best vernacular stone town is Chipping Camden, but even here much of what is visible is sixteenth and seventeenth century rather than anything earlier.

The origins of towns in Wales are at once very much more uncertain and much more clear-cut than they are in England. There is controversy as to

32 Aaron the Jew's House, Lincoln, a stone town house built in the late twelfth century.

whether or not towns had begun to develop in Wales before the Norman Conquest and also over the extent to which the Welsh princes had themselves begun to create towns before the conquest of Edward I. There is clear evidence for a Welsh castle and trading centre at Caernarvon before Edward I began his castle and new town in 1283, and he also had to move an existing trading community before he could found his new town and castle at Beaumaris. The inhabitants were sent off to found another new town, Newborough, some 12 miles away on the other side of Anglesey. It is also likely that the Welsh *maerdrifi*, that is royal or princely centres of administration, were in some instances beginning to show signs of an incipient urbanization, at Nevin and Pwllheli for example, but their overall contribution to the growth of towns in Wales was small. The establishment of towns in Wales is inseparably linked with the English and then Anglo-Norman penetration, and the association of castle and planted town with a market is particularly close. The impact of the castle as a symbol of lordship and dominion was apparent from the first, and the castle of Edward I at Caernarvon was obviously conceived in this way, but the market was even more important in the long-term if the community established about the castle was to have any future. Chepstow illustrates this admirably. It was known at first by the name of its castle, *Stroguil*, built by William fitzOsbern before 1071. From the early fourteenth century it was called *ceapstow*, meaning market place, its commercial importance now outweighing its military significance.

Only one Saxon *burh* is known in Wales, Clwydmouth, mentioned in 921. It may have been near Rhuddlan, but nothing further is known about it. The Earl of Chester had founded a 'new borough' at Rhuddlan by the time of Domesday Book, in which its castle, church, market and eighteen burgesses are described. Further towns followed as the Normans advanced into central and southern Wales: Brecon, Chepstow, Abergavenny, Cardiff, Monmouth, and Pembroke before 1100, Kidwelly and Carmarthen in about 1109, Swansea in 1116 and Haverfordwest at about the same date. Kenfig was established by the middle of the twelfth century and Cardigan by about 1165. Roger de Montgomery had built a castle at Hen Domen by the time of Domesday Book. In 1223 Henry III began a new castle and town about a mile and a half away, a town which in due course matured to become Montgomery.

These towns varied enormously in size. Cardiff, where the founder, Robert fitzhamon, refortified the Roman coastal fort, building a particularly fine motte in its northwestern corner, had 421 burgages in 1296. Chepstow and Haverfordwest had over 300. Even Kenfig had 142 in 1281, before the coastal sands began to engulf it. At the other extreme is Cefnllys, in Radnorshire, with 20 burgages in 1332, perhaps within the outer defences of the castle, or Dynevor, where occupation of the hill-top site may be Welsh in origin. It was chartered by Edward I, but had only 11 burgages in 1301, by which time Newtown had been founded on a lower site, with 44 burgages in 1308. Few towns could have been as short-lived as Dolforwyn, in Montgomeryshire, founded by prince Llewelyn in 1273 but destroyed by the English within the year.

The first foundations were by marcher lords. Henry I was the first monarch to intervene, bringing in Flemish immigrants and founding Carmarthen in 1109. Thereafter the role of the Crown became increasingly important, reaching a climax under Edward I. Edward was well acquainted, not only with the most advanced fortresses in Europe, but also with defended towns. Thus he would have known the great castle and fortified town of Carcassonne, and it was from another example of fortified urban planning, Aigues Mortes, that he embarked upon crusade in 1270. His memories undoubtedly contributed to his work in north Wales. His plantations fall into three distinct phases, influenced by the pattern of political events. Flint, Rhuddlan, and Aberystwyth were founded after 1277. Conway, Caernarvon, Harlech, Criccieth, and Bere form the second phase, in the years after 1282, whilst the last, Beaumaris, was not begun until 1294. Enormous sums of money were spent, and by the time the programme came to an end early in the fourteenth century Edward was almost bankrupt. At Flint a rectangular town, with one block reserved for the church and another for the market, was laid out within a banked and ditched enclosure outside the south gate of the castle, which could be reached from the sea at high tide. At Rhuddlan a canal was cut to enable ships to reach it, and Edward tried, unsuccessfully as it turned out, to transfer the see of St Asaph here. At Conway the town was planted on the site of the Cistercian monastery of Aberconway. The monks were moved to Maenan and the abbey church became the parish church for the burgesses. The town and castle were conceived as a whole, the castle and town walls being completed within four years. The same integrated plan is also to be found at Caernarvon, where the walled town was laid out at the foot of the castle. The town had three streets running more or less parallel from north to south and two further streets crossing them from east to west. Burgage plots measured 80 by 60 feet. Conway and Caernarvon were the most expensive of Edward's Welsh towns, the town walls of Caenarvon alone costing at least £3,500.

Edward's plantations were the most numerous and the most impressive in late thirteenth-century Wales. They were not the only ones. The Statute of Rhuddlan, already discussed in Chapter 4, created new counties and regrouped old lordships. The lordship of Denbigh came to the Earl of Lincoln, who founded a castle and town on so precipitous a site that within fifty years merchants and shopkeepers were establishing themselves in a more accessible spot outside the walls, which by the early years of the sixteenth century were empty. Lord Grey was granted the lordship of Ruthin and founded a town and castle, and the Earl of Surrey did the same at Holt, also in Denbighshire. By 1300 about seventy-five towns had been planted in Wales. About half a dozen more were established before 1350: Bala in about 1310, Adpar in Cardiganshire, and Abergwili and Llandilo, both in Carmarthenshire, before 1326, and Rhayader, perhaps the last, in Radnorshire. The heroic age of new towns then came to an end until the industrial revolution.

The origins and early development of towns in Scotland present an entirely different set of problems. Roman occupation of Scotland south of the Antonine Wall was brief, and Roman influence on the region slight. Only at Carriden, where the wall meets the Firth of Forth, is there evidence of a small civil *vicus,* associated with the fort. Those tribal *oppida* such as Traprain Law, which, as in England, might have served as the growth points for native urbanization, were deserted by the middle years of the fifth century. Stirling, Edinburgh, and Dumbarton do seem to have acquired some significance as tribal strongholds, although their nature is very uncertain. There seems to have been enough at Dumbarton for the Vikings to take the trouble to sack it in 780 and again in 870, but there is at present no evidence of a Viking town such as that which flourished so vigorously at York. It seems clear that Scottish burghs are deliberate plantations with no significant antecedents.

Scotland, largely owing to the depredations of the English, is particularly short of medieval documents. Only Aberdeen, for example, has any burghal records from before 1500, whilst urban archaeology has only just begun in Scotland. This means that the first centuries in the history of most Scottish towns are particularly difficult to explore. Nevertheless, in spite of all the problems, it is clear that there were burghs in existence in Scotland by the early years of the twelfth century. Many seem to owe their development, even if not their initial creation, to David I, a monarch particularly concerned to extend royal power in Scotland and with it the peace and stability within which trade and religion could flourish. To this end he encouraged both Anglo-Norman and Flemish settlers of every kind, whether to build motte-and-bailey castles or to engage in trade and manufacture. He became king in 1124, by which time he had already granted charters to Roxburgh and Berwick. He granted eleven more by the time of his death in 1153, including those to Edinburgh, Perth, Stirling, and Dunfermline. He had also given permission to the canons of Holyrood to found their own burgh of Canongate, between Edinburgh and their abbey. Most of these earliest burghs were founded under the shadow of a royal castle, and certainly for a time the chapel within such a castle had some parochial rights in the new town. This is certainly true for Perth, Stirling, and for Edinburgh, where the Church of St Giles in due course succeeded the castle chapel, its parish being carved out of that of St Cuthbert which lay to the west of the castle and once embraced the whole of the site of the city.

The establishment of castles, particularly royal ones, is one critical factor in the creation of Scottish burghs. The development of trade is the other. The most successful burghs were those whose location upon crossroads brought merchants, traders, and craftsmen of every kind together, and whose burghal privileges as granted in a charter protected and fostered the trading monopoly of those who were attracted to settle there. Scottish burghs had extensive trading monopolies, often within a large territory. Those monopolies were codified in a general charter of 1365 and not finally abolished until 1846. Royal burghs had exclusive rights to trade within their territories and should this extend to the sea then they could also have a port, since their monopoly included foreign trade. Thus Leith became the port for Edinburgh, Aberlady for Haddington, and Blackness for Linlithgow.

The first Scottish burghs were very simple: no more than a street or two with a back lane that gave access from the burgage plots to the burgh meadow, pasture, and arable, the latter being divided into strips. The original urban nucleus of St Andrews, founded in the middle years of the twelfth century, seems to have consisted of two streets, with a narrow back lane running between them. The name of the back lane in Edinburgh, Cowgate, describes admirably its purpose: to provide a route along which the animals of the burgesses could return each evening to their byres from the burghal pastures. Sometimes there was an open space set aside for a market, as at Haddington. Sometimes the principal street was sufficiently wide to allow it to be used for this purpose, as seems to have been the case with the High Street at Edinburgh. Burgesses paid rents for their plots and tolls were levied on goods coming into the town for sale. Such revenues could be extremely valuable. All the known revenues in money of David I came from this source. His enthusiasm for burgh planting is understandable.

In due course the first burgage plots were filled up. Further plots were then laid out, and the built-up area of the town gradually expanded, as at Ayr, at Haddington, where the market-place was encroached upon, and at St Andrews, where successive blocks were laid out to the west of the original urban nucleus. It seems very likely that the original urban nucleus of Edinburgh lay immediately to the east of the castle, along the Lawnmarket. A little later the Church of St Giles was established and the High Street was laid out, to meet the burgh of the canons of Holyrood at Netherbow, where Canongate begins, and already in existence by about 1150.

The founding of new towns has a much longer history in Scotland than in either England or Wales, where the impetus to found new towns came to an end by about 1350. In Scotland however new towns continued to be created until 1846, sixty-four for example in the years from 1600 to 1650. There is also, as we shall see, a remarkable outburst of the creation of new villages in the eighteenth century, when over 300 were established between 1720 and 1840.

The causes and processes behind this very long period of urban growth lie in peculiarly Scottish circumstances. The king himself could create burghs by means of a charter. These were royal burghs, and their privileges included a monopoly, at least in theory, of overseas trade and the right to send members to the Scottish Parliament. But Scottish lords could also found burghs if they so desired. These were burghs of barony. The great majority of Scottish burghs were of this kind, with only fifty-five royal burghs. This also means that the failure rate among burghs was much higher among burghs of barony, about 50 per cent, than among royal ones, where only three, Auldearn, Fyvie, and Roxburgh, failed, and Roxburgh only because it was burned three times by the English and was in English occupation for 178 of the 376 years between 1174 and 1550.

The earliest buildings in Scottish towns appear to have been of timber, with wattle-and-daub walls, but their rebuilding in stone seems to have been under way, at least in Aberdeen, by the end of the fourteenth century. Sadly, almost no medieval houses survive today in Scottish towns, at least above ground.

The thousand years covered in these last two chapters saw the landscape of Britain transformed, not by any cataclysmic earthquake, but by long, slow processes of change working within traditional social patterns through very limited technologies upon a landscape which had been settled for millennia. The coming of the English did not bring a dramatic break with the past: a new language, new laws, many new boundaries but probably comparatively few new men and women, many of whom seem to have fitted into existing structures without too much difficulty, a description which could probably be equally well applied to their prehistoric predecessors. Nowhere do the English succeed in blotting out the past, and their influence becomes progressively more diffuse in the western and northern parts of the island. The collapse of Roman authority at the beginning of the fifth century led to a sharp drop in material standards of living and it may have been accompanied by a fall in population. By the time the first historical documents begin to survive, that is from the seventh and eighth centuries, Roman Britain has become Anglo-Saxon England, and Wales and Scotland have gone their own separate ways; but the English, Scots and Welsh fields and farms, villages and towns which emerge from these documents have a very much longer history than that of the documents themselves, and neither were they established in a wilderness. Instead they were grafted on to existing stock. Unfortunately the full contribution of the old stock to the new growth must for ever remain hidden because of the almost total lack of documentary evidence for those crucial, all-important 200 years between the departure of Constantine III and the arrival of St Augustine in 597. The influence upon the subsequent evolution of the landscape of the religious ideals which he brought with him and of the organization through which they would find expression can scarcely be exaggerated. It is to the impact of Christianity on the medieval landscape that we must now turn.

6

Ideas:
the church in the
landscape

Of all the faiths, beliefs, and religions practised in Roman Britain it is
Christianity which has continued down to the present, although for many it
has never been more than a thin veneer, only half-concealing a world of
spirits, fairies, witches, magic spells and potions, horoscopes, lucky
charms, and holy wells. We saw in Chapter 3 that there is widespread
evidence of Christianity in Roman Britain, some evidence of a formal
Christian organization of bishops, but almost no firm evidence of the
existence of buildings which can be recognized as churches. The evidence
for the continuity of Christianity from Roman Britain into Anglo-Saxon
England is just as fragmentary and tantalizing as the evidence for other
modes and forms of continuity.

Among the most interesting materials for this continuity are the
place-names containing, under various disguises, the word *ecclesia*, in
origin a Greek word meaning a body, group, or assembly of Christians. It
was taken, directly or indirectly, into British, to give in modern Welsh
'eglwys', in Cornish 'eglos' and in Old Irish 'eclais'. It makes its way into
English place-names first of all simply as Eccles, of which there are six
recorded examples, and secondly as an element in a compound name such
as Eccleshall in Staffordshire and Exhall, near Coventry. There are getting
on for twenty of these names. There are in addition nearly thirty such
names in the eastern parts of Scotland, from Ecclefechan in Dumfriesshire
to the now lost place-name *Eglismenythok*, near Monymusk. It is very
unlikely that these place-names refer to a church building, and this for two
reasons. First of all there was, even in the fifth century, no specific word for
a church building as such, and secondly the Anglo-Saxons themselves
borrowed another word directly from the Greek to describe a church,
namely *cirice*, the ancestor of the modern English word church. What may

have happened is that *ecclesia* may have been adopted into late spoken British to describe a community of practising Christians who, because of their Christianity, stood out from their non-Christian neighbours. When the Anglo-Saxons took the place-name element over there is no real evidence to show that they understood fully its original meaning.

The story for the Scottish place-name is probably broadly similar. The Picts spoke a P-Celtic language intelligible to the British. Indeed the non-Indo-European branch of the Pictish language was probably to be found only to the north of the Mounth. It is very likely that much of southern and eastern Scotland had some Christian communities by the fifth century. Ninian was probably bishop of such a community centred on Whithorn early in the fifth century, and he may not have been the first. There are numerous cemeteries containing burials which have every appearance of being Christian, at Parkburn in Midlothian for example, and at St Ninian's Point, Bute. Thus it would not seem impossible that the word which Pictish Christian communities used to describe themselves eventually crystallized into a place-name, to survive the spread of the Scots from Ireland via Dal Riada, a people who had their own, Gaelic, word, *cell,* for a church, to give the very common place-name element *kil-.* A very similar story may lie behind the place-name element *papar,* to be found in the Northern Isles. It seems to be a Norse invention to describe places where monks or hermits were to be found. In these ways one of the most intangible elements of the landscape, a place-name, yet one of the toughest, can point to groups of men and women who, because of their unusual mental patterns, stood out from among their neighbours.

The Welsh place-name *merthyr* may also indicate the presence of early Christian communities but in a roundabout fashion since it appears to have been borrowed from the Latin *martyrium,* a technical term meaning a church or cemetery which contains the relics of a martyr or saint.

We saw in Chapter 4 that there were almost certainly two aspects to the Anglo-Saxon settlement of England: a slow, peaceful penetration by peasant farmers and the incursions of war bands. The first led to a patchy Anglicization in which a money economy had no place and towns as centres of trade were almost unknown. The second led to the creation of a number of new political organizations, including kingdoms and *regiones,* on the wreckage of Romano-British political structures, without however destroying them *in toto.* We have seen something of this wreckage, even in the south and east, the most heavily Anglicized parts of the country, in previous chapters. That some form of Christianity could also have survived is not impossible, although there is very little evidence for it. In the north and west, where English penetration was much slower, Christianity has undoubtedly continued from Roman times down to the present.

The centuries following the collapse of Roman authority were, in Wales, the great Age of the Saints, men venerated for the holiness and asceticism of their lives and their command over supernatural powers. Wells and streams with which they were associated became centres of devotion, as did relics of the saints themselves. Many were purely local men, whilst others had much wider connections. St Samson moved from Llantwit to Caldy and then to a cave near the River Severn in search of ever greater asceticism before going on to Cornwall and then to Brittany, to found the monastery in which eventually he died. They are often very shadowy figures, and we have almost no concrete evidence about them and often do not know exactly when they lived. This is also true of St Patrick. It is at present widely thought that he came from a Christian Romano-British family living in the Solway Firth area, and that he died in the second half of the fifth century. The Christian church that he left behind in Ireland was diocesan in its organization, and monasteries do not appear until after his death.

We saw in Chapter 3 the evidence for the existence of bishops in late Roman Britain. It seems very likely that the Christian Church in post-Roman Britain continued to be organized in dioceses, and that they probably had a fairly close association with the kingdoms and principalities into which post-Roman Britain divided, since there has always been a close connection between spiritual and secular authority, the one reinforcing the other. A new ecclesiastical organization finds its way into Britain by the end of the fifth century and this is the monastery.

33 Tintagel. The two rectangular buildings in the foreground form part of a loosely grouped cluster of similar buildings. It has been suggested that they form one of the earliest monastic sites in Britain, but this is not certainly proved.

The whole concept of the monastic way of life came from the Mediterranean, with which there were still direct links as late as about AD 500 via the western seaways from the Iberian peninsula to as far north as the Northern Isles. The monastery at Tintagel, in Cornwall, was almost certainly the first in Britain, and it seems to have been in existence by about AD 480. Its links with the eastern Mediterranean have been established by the excavation of pottery that could only have come from Egypt, Greece, Cyrenaica, and Roumania. Such pottery has also been found along the north Cornish coast and the coasts of Wales as far north as Bangor, often in close association with very early monastic foundations. Evidence for the earliest monasteries in Wales is very uncertain but some appear to have been founded by the early sixth century, with more during the course of that century, so that there were perhaps as many as fifty very small ones in the southeast, especially in Monmouthshire. Those at Welsh Bicknor and Llandinabo may have been established before the end of the sixth century, and those at Bellimoor and Garway early in the seventh, whilst there is more certain evidence for those at Llantwit, Caldy, Bangor-on-Dee, and St Davids in the seventh and eighth centuries. During the course of the sixth century the bishop became increasingly subordinate to the abbot, and a number of monasteries were founded by men who combined both functions, including Deiniol, Cadog, Illtud, and David himself.

These first monasteries were extremely simple. A bank and ditch, occasionally a stone wall, encircled a plot of land in which stood a church, invariably at first of wood, and a group of single-roomed cabins or cells in which the monks lived. Again place-names provide some help. The British word *lano-*, meaning flat, cleared space, was very quickly applied to a religious or sacred enclosure. It gives *llan* in Welsh and *lan* in Cornish. In Cornwall, Landocco, now represented by the large churchyard at St Kew, Lanpetroc, and Langorroc were all sites of early monasteries. From Wales the idea spread into Ireland and it was taken from Ireland into Scotland by St Columba, who founded his monastery on Iona in about 563. Here also the monastery was at first very simple, with a stone-faced bank surrounding the site, the individual monks living in cells of turf or stone. Other, similar, monasteries quickly followed: one was founded on the shores of Loch Awe, another at Applecross, in Wester Ross, a third at Kingarth, and, according to St Columba's biographer Adomnan, himself an abbot of Iona and writing about a hundred years after Columba's death, one was established on Tiree, although this site has yet to be discovered. Birsay, in Orkney, may date from the seventh century, and there are others on Canna and at Annait on the Isle of Skye, all marked by remains of the enclosing bank and ditch together with low grass-covered mounds to indicate where once were chapels and cells.

St Columba was not the only Irish missionary to what is now Scotland. St

34 The memorial stone in the Church of Llangadwaladr, Anglesey, to Cadfan, who died in about 625.

Brendan of Clonfert established in 542 a monastery on Eileach an Naoimh, the southernmost islet in the Garvelloch group in the Firth of Lorne and by tradition the burial place of the mother of St Columba, Eithne. St Moluag founded a community on Lismore at almost exactly the same date that St Columba landed in Iona, and he went on to found churches at Mortlach in Banffshire and at Rosemarkie, on the northern shores of the Moray Firth.

There is yet further evidence of the presence of Christianity in post-Roman western Britain. There are a number of memorial stones dating from the fifth, sixth, and seventh centuries, marked with epitaphs in Latin or in British and with distinctively Christian forms. The memorial stone from Llanerfyl in Montgomeryshire, for example, uses the overtly Christian IN PACE and from its style and lettering may be dated to the early fifth century. Another memorial stone, this time from Whithorn, records the death of Latinus, aged 35, and his daughter, aged 4, beginning with TE DOMINUM LAVDAMVS, a reference to Psalm 146. The memorial stone to Senacus, from Aberdaron in Caernarvonshire, uses the word PRESBYTER, and others have a cross clearly engraved, such as that to Catamanus, or Cadfan, king of Gwynedd, now built into the wall of Llangadwaladr church in Anglesey. The date of his death is uncertain but probably took place somewhere about 625. Similar stones are to be found in southern Scotland, at Kirkmadrine for example, where there is a memorial stone which seems to date from the fifth century, and the Yarrow Stone, which may date from the sixth.

St Columba died in 597, the same year in which St Augustine, journeying from Rome, landed in Kent to begin the conversion of the pagan English. By this time the Church in northern and western Britain had diverged markedly from the mainstream of Mediterranean Christianity, more especially over the calculation of Easter. It had its own long traditions and its bishops saw little reason to accept the authority of a newcomer to the island. It made its own attempts to convert the English. Aidan established a monastery on Lindisfarne in about 635. Some twenty years later Finan, Bishop of Lindisfarne, consecrated St Cedd as bishop of the East Saxons, and Cedd went on to build the church at Bradwell-on-Sea, the nave of which is still standing today. Bede also records that St Cedd built a church at Tilbury, beside the Thames, but this has long disappeared. An Irish monk and scholar, Maildubh, established a monastery at Malmesbury at about the same time. Aldhelm became its abbot in about 675 and he founded smaller houses at Bradford-upon-Avon and Frome. By this time, however, St Augustine had long been dead, the Church in southeastern England, after early successes, had suffered a number of reverses, and the Synod of Whitby held in 663, failing to reconcile the irreconcilable, had decided in favour of the Roman practice over the calculation of Easter, a decision which many northern and western religious communities refused for decades to accept. In 669 Theodore became Archbishop of Canterbury and he undertook with considerable skill the reorganization of the administration of the Church under his authority.

There were at this time only seven dioceses: Canterbury, London, Rochester, Dunwich, Winchester, Lichfield, and York, the last not becoming an archbishopric until 735. Theodore divided Dunwich into two, establishing a new bishopric at Elmham. He created a new one for Lindsey and two others, one for the *Hwicce* at Worcester and one for the *Magonsaetan* at Hereford. The medieval boundaries of these two last dioceses may well preserve the ancient boundaries of these tribal territories. At the same time one of the fieriest spirits of the English Church, St Wilfred, was Bishop of Ripon and also became Bishop of Selsey, which became the diocese for the south Saxons. By the early eighth century there was also a bishopric at Sherborne, as well as, in the north, at Hexham and Lindisfarne, and another was established at Leicester in 737.

By the end of the ninth century the fabric of the English Church had been largely destroyed by the Danish invaders, especially in eastern districts. The bishoprics at Dunwich, Elmham, Lindsey, Hexham, Leicester, and Lindisfarne had come to an end, and even the archbishopric of

York was little more than a shadow. The relics of St Cuthbert from Lindisfarne wandered over the north of England for nearly a century in the care of a community of monks until they were at last able to re-establish a settled form of life, first of all at Chester-le-Street, and then in 995 at Durham. By this time the reconstruction of the formal organization of the Church was well under way. A cathedral was built at Elmham for East Anglia in 956, and a diocese was established at Crediton to serve Devon and Cornwall, whilst Dorchester-on-Thames became the seat of a diocese which stretched from the Humber to the Thames. Further substantial changes were introduced in the years after the Norman Conquest. In about 1072 the diocese based in Elmham moved to Thetford and by 1092 it had moved again to Norwich. In about 1086 that at Dorchester-on-Thames was transferred to Lincoln, by which time Selsey had been moved to Chichester and Sherborne to Salisbury. A new diocese was created at Carlisle in 1133, although it was vacant between 1157 and 1203, and another new one was created at Ely by Anselm, who was Archbishop of Canterbury between 1093 and his death in 1109. The pattern of territorial dioceses thus created by the middle years of the twelfth century then remained without substantial change until the Reformation.

The establishment of bishoprics in Scotland is a much more obscure process. There is an almost total absence of documentary records and many long vacancies. The see at Glasgow may date from the seventh century, and there seems to have been a bishop at Dunkeld by 865, and one at St Andrews from the tenth century. St Andrews was formerly Kilrymont, and there is evidence of an abbot from the mid-eighth century. As in England it was the Viking invaders who destroyed this early ecclesiastical organization, and it was largely owing to the efforts of David I that the Church was re-established in Scotland upon a firm diocesan basis. By the middle years of the twelfth century there were bishops in Dunblane, Dunkeld, Brechin, Aberdeen, Moray, Ross, and Caithness. There was however as yet no archbishopric, and it was only in 1176 that the Archbishop of York was forbidden by the Pope to exercise any authority in Scotland. Not until 1472 was the bishopric of St Andrews made into an archbishopric, that of Glasgow following twenty years later. In the meantime Orkney and the Isles looked to Trondheim, in Norway.

The evidence is even more shadowy from Wales. There may have been a bishopric at Mynyw in the eighth century which was probably the precursor of St Davids. There was a bishop of Bangor by 800, and two early bishoprics in south Wales had been transferred to Llandaff by the early eleventh century, but a full diocesan organization seems to have been established at St Davids only in 1115, in Llandaff the following year, and at St Asaph in 1143.

At first a bishop had to care for his diocese almost single-handed. He was expected to preach, baptize, confirm, and otherwise provide for the

35 The late-seventh-century Anglo-Saxon cross in the churchyard at Bewcastle, Cumberland. The cross, the church, and the adjacent castle all lie within the site of a Roman fort, an outpost to Hadrian's Wall.

spiritual needs of his flock, and the life of St Cuthbert, who was for a short spell Bishop of Northumbria, shows how demanding this life could be. At first much preaching took place in the open air, the sites being marked by wooden crosses. In due course churches appeared, again of wood, and later both crosses and churches were rebuilt in stone. Fragments of stone crosses survive quite widely over northern and midland England and southern and western Scotland, of which at least two, those of Bewcastle, in Cumberland, and Ruthwell, in Dumfriesshire, are masterpieces of Anglo-Saxon sculpture. That at Ruthwell was broken into pieces by Scottish Covenanters in the seventeenth century and only reassembled and restored in 1887. There is also a fine late-eighth-century cross at Kildalton, on the island of Islay.

The first churches in England were established and endowed by kings at the central points of those great estates described in Chapter 4. These minster churches were staffed by a group of priests living together communally and serving the entire estate, which could be very large. Such minster churches have made their own contribution to the place-names of the English landscape, being commemorated in such names as Yetminster, Sturminster, Axminster, and Warminster, although there were certainly very many more minsters than the surviving minster place-names would suggest.

Almost from the same period other lords and estate owners were founding churches to serve the inhabitants of their estates. These private churches were endowed with property which in due course came to be called the glebe. It frequently lay scattered in strips throughout the open fields in just the same way as the holdings of a peasant farmer. Indeed for six days out of the seven there was often very little to distinguish a priest from a peasant.

These private churches also received the tithes of the inhabitants of the estate. Tithes were at first voluntary gifts made to support a priest, but they had become compulsory by the tenth century and their payment could be enforced at law. The payment of tithe became one of the most contentious matters in English rural life, and remained so until tithes were commuted by Act of Parliament in 1836. The priest also received payments for baptizing, marrying, and burying the members of his flock. These payments, together with glebe and tithe, meant that private churches became valuable pieces of property, and the landowners who founded them treated them as such. They were openly bought, sold, mortgaged, and divided into fractions. Some of the more bizarre consequences are recorded in Domesday Book. It is noted of Rickinghall, in Suffolk, for example, that fourteen freemen held a fifth of the church, but there is no further mention of the other four fifths. At Threekingham in Lincolnshire, two separate twelfths and a further sixth of the Church of St Mary are recorded, with nothing on the remaining two-thirds, and two separate sixths and one-third of the Church of St Peter there are also noted, but again there is nothing on the other third. The most notorious example of this mercenary attitude towards the church must relate to the Church of St Mary in Huntingdon. This, as Domesday records, was mortgaged by its original owner, the Abbot of Thorney, to the townspeople, given away by the king to two priests, sold by them to Hugh, the chamberlain, and then sold by him in his turn to the priests of Huntingdon. This buying and selling was not however without its beneficial side-effects for individual churches. An inscription over the south porch of the church at Kirkdale, in the North Riding of Yorkshire, records that Orm, son of Gamal, bought St Gregory's Church when it was all ruined and tumble-down and had it rebuilt from the foundations in the days of King Edward and Earl Tosti, references which date the rebuilding to the decade 1055–65. Churches have been built, rebuilt and allowed to fall into ruin ever since. The church at Netheravon in Wiltshire was said in 1086 to be ruined, roofless, and on the point of collapse, whilst that at Wilcot, also in Wiltshire, was said to be new, with an excellent house and a good vineyard.

It is because individual landlords built churches to serve their estates that the boundary clauses of so many Anglo-Saxon charters match those of ancient parishes. Estates for which churches had been established gradually hardened into parishes. Other estates, without a church, were absorbed into a neighbouring parish for spiritual purposes, retaining their identity for more mundane ones. The whole process is immensely complex and no easy generalization will cover it all. One example must suffice. The ancient parish of Horwood, in Buckinghamshire, was at one period divided into three estates. The Abbey of St Albans received one part late in the eighth century. This became the Parish of Little Horwood. Horwood is mentioned in Domesday Book but the entry refers to what became the Parish of Great Horwood, Little Horwood as such not being mentioned. Domesday Book also records the settlement of Singleborough, the third part of Horwood. This was clearly a separate estate when it came to paying taxes, but it never became a separate parish, remaining part of the Parish of Great Horwood.

It was the twelfth century before England had a comprehensive network of parishes, and even then the pattern continued to change, albeit very slowly, until the problems created by rapid industrialization and population growth brought extensive reorganization in the nineteenth century.

In Wales the creation of a parochial system came only after the establishment of dioceses, from the twelfth century onwards. In Scotland, many of the ancient 'shires' also became parishes, but again as compared with England the development of a parochial system is comparatively late and the result of Anglo-Norman feudal influence in the late eleventh century. Lay lords built and endowed churches which, as in England, they treated very much as private property, with much the same correspondence between parish and lay estate. Thus in the Clyde Valley parish and manor were often co-extensive, and a big parish like Wiston in due course broke up into four, corresponding with four lordships.

In this way, slowly, tentatively and hesitatingly, and from a combination of genuine religious feeling and close-fisted bargaining in varying proportions, the landscape of Britain was provided with one of its most enduring, best-loved and in due course most reviled institutions, the parish, and one of its most permanent building forms, the parish church, whilst both church and priest were part of a larger organization, the bishop in his diocese. Bishoprics were often used to reward able civil servants whilst parish priests were often only semi-literate. Both bishop and priest were often married, and their offices were sometimes in danger of becoming hereditary. The forebears of St Ailred of Rievaulx were hereditary priests of Hexham, and an inscription on an early tombstone at Llantrisant in Anglesey records that it was erected in memory of the loving wife of the *sacerdos* Rivatigirnus, herself a most holy woman. Nevertheless, the Church, whether as an organization or as a building, represents a projection into the landscape of some of the most profound aspirations of the human spirit. It is impossible to exaggerate its importance in the evolution of the landscape of Britain from the sixth century down to the present: it contributed a whole series of buildings, whether cathedrals, churches, monasteries, parsonages, or tithe barns, a hierarchy of territorial divisions, from the parish to the archdiocese, and, as we saw in Chapter 5, it did much, especially through medieval monasteries, to reclaim marshland, waste, and moorland.

The first churches were of wood. The church on Lindisfarne was built, as Bede writes, not of stone but of hewn oak and thatched with reeds. The oldest church at Glastonbury, the *vetusta ecclesia*, was said to have been built of timber-framing, wattle and daub, and to have been 60 feet long by 26 feet wide. It was destroyed by fire in 1185. Very many churches begin their history with a wooden structure, and church buildings are themselves, like every other facet of the landscape, a palimpsest of alterations, rebuildings, and extensions, of patching, mending, and restoration, the oldest surviving parts visible today almost always no reliable guide to the true age of the first building to be erected on the site for Christian worship, an important qualification since many churches occupy sites which have clearly had politico-religious significance since prehistoric times. The Church of St Laurence at Cholesbury, for example, is built within the defences of an Iron Age hill fort. However, of all the wooden churches which there must once have been in the landscape of England before the Norman Conquest only one now survives above ground, and this is the Church of St Andrew, at Greensted in Essex. The walls of the nave are made of tree trunks split in half and arranged in an upright position with

36 The west tower to the church at Earls Barton in Northamptonshire, built very late in the tenth century. Among its most striking features are the long and short quoining, the strip pilasters, the monumental doorway, and the unusual belfry window openings.

their flat surfaces facing inwards. Each trunk, of oak, had a tenon at the top and another at the bottom, to be fitted into mortises in the oak roof-plate and sill, as well as long grooves down each side to take tongues of wood which would have held them together and kept out the draughts. The church was restored in 1848, when the building was dismantled and then re-erected on a brick plinth. The chancel is Tudor, but excavation has revealed the former existence of two earlier wooden chancels.

Anglo-Saxon churches are particularly difficult to date at all closely, since there is little documentary evidence and there seems to have been almost no uniformity in stylistic development. Stone churches appear from the earliest times, sometimes to a very simple ground-floor plan of one or two cells, sometimes to a very elaborate one, with rooms on two or even three levels. St Wilfred caused a church to be built at Hexham in the years 672–8 which, according to his biographer Eddius, had a colonnaded nave with aisles, chapels, a crypt, and spiral staircases leading to rooms at first-floor level. The main body of the church was destroyed during the Danish invasions, but the crypt still survives today. The church at Brixworth, in Northamptonshire, dating from the same period, was probably just as splendid. It is still standing, save for the subsidiary rooms which formed aisles to its nave. Other churches were much simpler. That at Escomb, for example, has a nave over 40 feet long and 23 feet high, pierced only by a few small windows set high up in the walls, and a small chancel little more than 10 feet square. Two small rooms, on the south and the north, have disappeared. On the south wall of the nave is a sun-dial, something which is a characteristic feature of many Anglo-Saxon churches.

Two other characteristics do not make their appearance much before the end of the ninth century. These are the use of long and short quoining and pilaster strips, and the building of church towers, particularly at the west end, characteristics which come together in the splendid tower at Earls Barton in Northamptonshire. Surviving stone work from churches such as Breedon-on-the-Hill in Leicestershire, Barnack, and Bradford-upon-Avon as well as documentary evidence all point to Anglo-Saxon churches as having been often richly and lavishly decorated, not only with stone sculpture, but also with work in precious metals, paintings, vestments, and stained glass. Almost all of this has been lost, one of the most important survivors being the richly embroidered stole recovered from the Shrine of St Cuthbert and now to be seen in Durham Cathedral.

There are, even today, well over 400 churches containing Anglo-Saxon masonry, from almost complete buildings such as that at Escomb just described, to fragments such as the window still to be seen at Birstall Church, in Leicestershire. Some, such as that at Monkwearmouth, were monastic churches, but the status of most remains uncertain. Cathedral churches were undoubtedly built. Some, such as those at Canterbury and

Winchester, were on a grand scale, but for only one is there now anything standing above ground, and this is the church at North Elmham, in Norfolk. Here the ruins consist of a west tower with a turret stair, a nave with towers in the return angles of the transepts, and a small apsidal chancel. The buildings lie within a moated enclosure, itself set in the southwest angle of a much larger moated site. The whole complex presents a number of problems of dating and of usage, but it seems likely that some parts of the fabric are eighth century, with extensive rebuilding in the tenth, and with a house for the bishop built in the enclosure shortly after the Norman Conquest. The diocese was moved, as we have seen, from here to Thetford and then to Norwich.

It is very easy to underestimate the Anglo-Saxon contribution to the building of churches, monasteries, and cathedrals, since so much has disappeared, but excavations in recent years have revealed building on a large scale and of considerable technical achievement. At Canterbury, for example, at St Augustine's Abbey, there were two churches, SS Peter and Paul, and St Mary, built in line, with some 40 feet separating the eastern apse of SS Peter and Paul from the western end of St Mary. Abbot Wulfric, who was abbot between 1047 and 1059, planned an ambitious rotunda to fill this gap. It was never completed. At Sherborne the cathedral had a western tower with side chambers as well as a tower at the central crossing. In a land of thatch, wattle-and-daub, and timber-framing, such immense, many-storeyed stone buildings must have dominated both the landscape and the imagination of men in a way which we would find difficult to comprehend. Place-names may again provide a clue. Such great buildings as those at Sherborne, Winchester, and Canterbury were of course very rare, and even the most modest of stone churches would have been unusual. A new stone church, gleaming white in the sunshine, must have been very impressive, sufficiently impressive on a number of occasions to lead to the coining of a new place-name, Whitchurch, meaning white church. Nearly a dozen are known, stretching from Pembrokeshire to Berkshire, and from Devonshire to Shropshire, although the most famous of white churches, *Ad Candida Casa,* was built by St Ninian of Whithorn in Galloway, in the first half of the fifth century.

The Norman Conquest brought radical change into the Church in Britain. The pattern of diocesan organization was given a framework that would endure until the Reformation. Old monasteries were reformed and many new ones founded. Parochial organization crystallized out and, very slowly, the parish priest gained some independence from the lay patron at the same time as the bishop acquired increasing say in his appointment to ensure that he was a proper person for the office. The rules requiring priestly celibacy were slowly brought into force. The reforming zeal of the new Norman bishops and abbots, inspired by two remarkable Archbishops of Canterbury, Lanfranc, 1070–89, and Anselm, 1093–1109, was very quickly turned to the building and rebuilding of churches, cathedrals, and monasteries.

The history of English medieval ecclesiastical architecture has been a matter for intense and detailed research for at least 150 years, and this is not the place to repeat it, even in outline. The literature on the subject is immense and there are many very successful introductory accounts as well as a mountain of more specialized materials. Instead, some more general points may be made.

First of all, the Norman and later building and rebuilding absorbed immense resources in materials, money, and time, and demanded very highly skilled craftsmen of every kind. Only very rarely, however, was there complete demolition and rebuilding from the foundations in one sustained period of activity. In other words there are very few churches which were completed all of a piece and then have remained untouched down to the present. Every church in fact is in itself a palimpsest, reflecting successive changes in taste, ideals, attitudes, and technical advances in the handling of stresses, as well as changes in religious practices and the fluctuations in the economic fortunes of its region.

Second, medieval church building can be dated much more closely on stylistic grounds than can pre-Conquest building. This is because new ideas and techniques spread fairly quickly across Britain, carried by the highly skilled and professional craftsmen who moved readily and easily across the country from one project to the next, and not only over Britain but in northern Europe as well. Technical developments, changes in fashion and the interplay of ideas with European craftsmen, particularly those at work in the cathedrals of northern France, all played significant roles in the evolution of church building. Further, there is often abundant documentation of building work in many individual instances so that innovation can be dated exactly, and undocumented work dated by analogy and association. Finally there is of course very much more building surviving from after the Norman Conquest than there is from the centuries before, so that stylistic and technical developments are much more easily studied.

It is customary to divide medieval ecclesiastical architecture into periods, but it is important to appreciate that this compartmentalization and the labels given to it are the work of nineteenth-century scholars, not of medieval masons, and as such they serve only as convenient shorthand terms to describe successive changes in technique and style. The movement from Norman or Romanesque to Gothic, with its three subdivisions into Early English, Decorated and Perpendicular, certainly took place, but the labels themselves have about as much significance as the terms Mesolithic, Neolithic, Bronze Age, and Iron Age.

The rebuilding in the first century after the Norman Conquest is characterized by round arches and barrel-vaulted roofs requiring immensely thick walls to sustain the weight and thrust, with many major cathedral churches being built with very long naves, as at Norwich for example, and Ely. At Durham, where rebuilding began in 1093, one of the first major technical innovations took place, the use of rib vaulting, perhaps its first occurrence anywhere in Europe and one of the most important components of the Gothic style. The others, the pointed arch as opposed to the round arch, flying buttresses to take the weight and a strong sense of verticalism, all have their origins as much as a century earlier, but they all come together for the first time in the abbey of St Denis, near Paris, which was building from about 1140. The new style makes an early appearance in England, at Roche Abbey for example, and at Ripon, but its first full statement is to be found in the rebuilding of the eastern end of Canterbury Cathedral following a disastrous fire in 1174. The work was directed by a French master mason, William of Sens, until he fell from the scaffolding in 1178 and was badly injured, a story which illustrates first the way in which new ideas were transmitted and second the practicalities of building. Stone was cut in quarries, and a fair amount of the actual shaping was also done there in order to save on transport costs, which were enormous. Land transport was particularly difficult and so wherever possible stone came by water. When on site the stone was put into position either by hoists operated by men turning a capstan or else by men carrying it up ramps and ladders using hods and wheelbarrows. As work progressed

37 The splendid church at Iffley, near Oxford, built in about 1170 and a fine example of Anglo-Norman masonry at its best.

scaffolding was erected, made of poles lashed together and braced with diagonal struts tightened with tourniquets applied to the lashings at the intersections. The construction of a roof called for much heavy timber centring to support it whilst it was being built, and it requires only a moment's thought, inside the lofty nave of Winchester Cathedral for example, to yield to the modern observer a vivid appreciation of the courage and skill of medieval masons and carpenters working so far above ground.

The development of rib vaulting and the flying buttress meant that the weight of the roof could be progressively reduced and at the same time the remaining thrusts could be directed through the buttresses. In due course walls as such almost disappear. The Chapter House at Westminster Abbey, completed by about 1250, is a splendid early example of walls composed almost entirely of glass threaded together with stone tracery. Slightly later is Gloucester Cathedral's magnificent east end, which was being glazed in about 1350.

The opportunities offered by the square eastern ends to churches and the similar square ends to transepts were eagerly exploited. The great eastern window at Lincoln, begun in about 1256, is nearly 60 feet high. The apotheosis of the wall as window must surely be at King's College Chapel

38   The magnificent Parish Church at St Mary, Beverley. The west front is Perpendicular. The central crossing tower collapsed in 1520 and was rebuilt in the following decade.

39 Little Peover Church, Cheshire, a fourteenth-century timber-framed church, although much restored.

in Cambridge. The magnificent fan-vaulted roof appears to be poised on the most ethereal of vertical stone columns. In fact its weight is taken by external buttresses which are themselves half-concealed by continuous side chapels. The work here was finished by John Wastell between 1508 and 1515, just as two other almost equally as splendid late medieval chapels were being built, St George's Chapel, Windsor, and the Henry VII Chapel in Westminster Abbey, and just, too, as the faith which had inspired them was being seriously brought into question.

Work on cathedrals and on buildings for the royal court was often of the highest artistic and technical quality, reflecting not only the strength of the Christian faith which could command such resources but also the international character of the values and the craftsmanship which brought them into being.

The artistic and technical developments which lead from Romanesque through the Early English, Decorated, and Perpendicular styles can be traced in parish as well as in cathedral churches, although only occasionally, as at Holy Trinity, Hull, do they approach the dimensions of cathedral churches. Most parish churches show the same kind of pattern of building, rebuilding, patching, and alteration reflecting technical and socio-economic change that is to be found in cathedrals, the results often being just as splendid, even if on a smaller scale, as at Fenstanton and Lawford

40 The church at East Bergholt, built partly of brick and partly of flint in the late fifteenth century. The west tower was begun in 1525 but never finished.

41 The wooden bell-house in the churchyard at East Bergholt, probably built when the building of the west tower of the church was abandoned.

42 The Church of St Wendreda, March. The tower was built in about 1500.

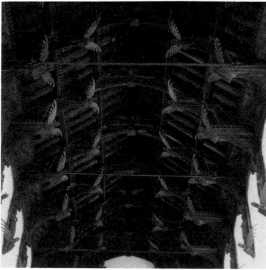

43 The magnificent roof to the church at March, added when the church was refurbished early in the sixteenth century.

for example, churches possessing magificent east windows which appear to be almost entirely composed of glass.

Parish churches often reflect more closely than do cathedral churches that intimate connection between buildings and geology which is so characteristic a feature of the British landscape. Those concerned to build cathedrals could often afford to import building materials from great distances. Parish churches usually had to make do with local materials. Thus flint and thatch were widely used in Norfolk and Suffolk. Flint is a difficult material to work, especially at corners, and so it became customary to build round towers to churches in East Anglia, such as that at Hales, in Norfolk, where a small twelfth-century church has a round flint tower and a thatched roof to its chancel and nave. Granite was used in Cornwall, whilst the fine golden limestones of the Cotswolds make their own distinctive contribution to the churches of the region, as do millstone grits to those of the Pennines. It is clear from surviving examples that timber was widely used in the construction of medieval parish churches, as at Little Peover, Marton, and Siddington, for example, in Cheshire, and at Claverley in Shropshire. There is a fine example of a timber-framed church at Hartley Wespall in Hampshire, and the tower to the church at Upleadon, in Gloucestershire, is also timber-framed. In Essex many churches have timber-framed belfries, as at Blackmore, Margetting, and Stock. Timber was also widely used for the roofs of churches, often with considerable technical skill, yielding work of great beauty. The roof to the nave of the church at St Wendreda, March, with its double hammer-beam roof and flights of angels must be among the most memorable of all English church roofs. There is a similar one at Needham Market. Both date from the end of the fifteenth century. The tradition long continued. The hammer-beam roof to the nave of the church at Handley, in Cheshire, is dated 1662.

Parish churches often show greater regional variation than do cathedral churches. Thus spires are a striking feature of many churches in the east midlands, especially in Huntingdonshire and Northamptonshire, as well as in Yorkshire, where Patrington has one of the finest of English parish churches, built in the first part of the fourteenth century, its splendid soaring spire being added a little later. In southeastern England spires are frequently covered with wooden shingles. Spires become something of a rarity in the fifteenth century, although this did not prevent the building of the highest, and last, medieval spire, to the church at Louth, in Lincolnshire, some 295 feet high and finished in about 1515. Towers became increasingly important instead, and a large majority of English parish churches had their towers built or rebuilt during the fifteenth century. Regional variations can also be detected here. The churches of Somerset are particularly noted for their towers, which show a marked emphasis upon vertical lines, as at Evercreech for example, whilst those of Gloucestershire often place equal emphasis upon horizontal divisions.

44 The church at Louth in Lincolnshire. The spire is 295 feet high. The tower was built late in the fifteenth century and the spire was added between 1501 and 1515 at a cost of £305 7s 5d.

The parish as a social unit had until well into the nineteenth century a cohesion which it is almost impossible now fully to appreciate, and the parish church was the focal point of almost every aspect of parish life, from the most trivial, as a centre for the distribution of news and gossip, through the mercenary, since many markets were once held in the parish church and its churchyard, to the most solemn, since it is here that those rites which mark the most significant stages in the life of the individual, baptism, marriage, and burial, are performed. Thus the fabric of the parish church reflects the fabric of the society which it serves. The simplest parish church comprised only two cells, the chancel and the nave. The chancel, often divided from the nave by the rood screen, was reserved for the priest and the mysteries of the sacrifice which lies behind the mass. Long tradition, but nothing more, dictated that the priest and his congregation should face to the east. Rising population and growing wealth could add to, alter and rebuild this original plan almost beyond recognition. Thus the parish church at Witney began in the twelfth century as a simple nave and chancel. In the late twelfth century a north aisle and porch were added. Transepts were built early in the thirteenth century. At the end of that century a south aisle was added, and the chancel, nave, and central crossing tower were rebuilt. In the fourteenth century three chapels were added, to the north aisle and to the north and south transepts.

The way in which this building and rebuilding of the parish church attracted the pride and the wealth of the parishioners reveals a great deal about the depth of their piety and devotion during the medieval centuries and the significance of the church in their lives. Thus the central tower to the church at Ludlow was rebuilt between 1469 and 1471 at the cost of the craft guilds of the town. The costs of rebuilding the nave of St Mary, Beverley, were met in the same manner, whilst the names of the 150 or so parishioners who contributed to the reroofing of the nave of the Church of St Lawrence, Reading, were recorded in the churchwardens' accounts. The wealth of individuals, as opposed to that of communities, and particularly that of wool merchants, was poured out in a similar fashion. John Fortey, who died in 1458, paid for the nave at Northleach. William Grevel, who died in 1401, paid for the rebuilding of the church at Chipping Camden, Thomas Spring and Simon Branch paid for Lavenham early in the sixteenth century, and John Barton for the rebuilding of St Giles, Holme, in Nottinghamshire, at the end of the fifteenth century. The churches upon which so much money was spent still survive today, monuments to the spiritual fervour of the donors, the skill of the craftsmen they employed, and the prosperity of the English wool trade.

But additions can also be demolished, as excavations in the now half-ruined church at Wharram Percy, in Yorkshire, have shown. Here was an Anglo-Saxon church of stone. This was substantially rebuilt in about 1080, and aisles were added in the late twelfth and early thirteenth centuries, only to be demolished in the late fifteenth century, when the length of the chancel was also halved. The ebb and flow of the building reflects the ebb and flow of the community which it served. In this, of course, Wharram Percy is by no means unique. The sixteen parish churches to be found in Huntingdon by 1265 had been reduced to four by the opening years of the sixteenth century, again reflecting fluctuations in the social and economic life of the town.

From the end of the thirteenth century parish churches begin to reflect in their structures two important social developments. First of all it was becoming increasingly fashionable to found chantries. A chantry was established by some wealthy person providing an endowment in his will for the saying of masses for his soul on some appropriate anniversary, usually the date of his death, and perhaps for the souls of other members of his family. There seems to have been a chantry in Lincoln Cathedral in about 1235, but the practice was given enormous stimulus by the masses said annually in Westminster Abbey on the anniversaries of the death of Edward I's beloved queen, Eleanor, who died in 1290. Second, religious guilds and fraternities were being established in increasing numbers. These were essentially social clubs providing mutual support and comfort during life and an appropriate funeral after death. Both of these developments called for special additions to be built to existing churches, additions which

45 The Bridge Chapel at St Ives in Huntingdonshire. The bridge was built in about 1415 and the chapel was consecrated in 1426.

could sometimes lead to substantial rebuilding. Thus chantry chapels were added early in the sixteenth century to the chancel of the fine parish church at Lavenham in Suffolk. At Chipping Sodbury the Guild of St Mary, founded in 1442, built a large chapel onto the south of the chancel, and the Church of St Michael at Coventry was particularly well-endowed with both chantry and guild chapels. Some men were sufficiently wealthy to found an entirely separate chantry college. Edward of Norwich founded one at Fotheringay in Northamptonshire in 1411, in fulfilment of the wishes of his father, Edmund, Duke of York. It was lavishly endowed, its properties including the castle, town, and manor of Stamford and the town and soke of Grantham. It had a master, eight clerks, twelve chaplains and thirteen choristers. Their duty was to pray for the souls of the members of the royal family.

Eventually there were more than 2,000 chantries, and some chantry priests also kept a school. Some of the religious guilds and fraternities also

46 The Guildhall built in Leicester for the Guild of Corpus Christi, founded in 1343. This, the north range, contains the Great Hall, dating from the middle years of the fourteenth century.

supported schools, as well as providing for the repair of roads and bridges, and at Wakefield and St Ives chapels were actually built on the bridges. The Fraternity of the Holy Cross at Abingdon, founded before the end of the fourteenth century, built a bridge over the River Thames, maintained the road from Abingdon to Dorchester-on-Thames, and founded an almshouse. Palmer's Guild, in Ludlow, founded in 1284, maintained a school in the town, and the Guild of Corpus Christi in Cambridge founded a college in the university. At Stratford-upon-Avon the Guild of the Holy Cross built a chapel separate from the parish church, and its own hall, and the chantry priest taught in the grammar school. The Guild of Corpus Christi, founded in Leicester in 1343, built its own guild hall, and this was being used by the corporation of the town for its meetings by the end of the fifteenth century.

The evolution of the parish church in Scotland follows a path which differs in a number of important respects from that in England. Parishes do not begin to appear in Scotland before the end of the eleventh century and they spread only very slowly into the Highlands and Islands, where small dependent chapels fulfilled many of the functions of parish churches. Four in five of Scottish parish churches were eventually impropriated to some monastic house, with the result that their fabrics were often neglected for years on end. This neglect, combined with the natural poverty of Scotland, means that there are very few Scottish parish churches which survive intact from the medieval centuries, and those that do are very simple in their layout, consisting of a nave and chancel, as at Birnie in Morayshire. The church at Dalmeny, in West Lothian, is the most complete twelfth-century church in Scotland, but it is quite exceptional. Many more survive only as ruins or else as broken fragments incorporated into later buildings. Thus Buittle Old Parish Church is now in ruins, a new one having been built in 1819. Both St Bride's, Douglas, and Bunkle Old Church are also in ruins, whilst all that survives of the twelfth-century church at Lamington is part of an arch incorporated into the church which was built in 1721, and the fine twelfth-century church of St Magnus, Egilsey, Orkney, is now roofless. The fifteenth and early sixteenth centuries saw considerable prosperity in Scottish burghs, and much rebuilding of their churches. The parish church of Edinburgh, St Giles, was rebuilt from the late fourteenth to the early sixteenth centuries. Both the Church of the Holy Rude in Stirling and St Michael's, Linlithgow still stand, but they are fifteenth century, having been built to replace older ones destroyed or damaged by fire. Others are now in ruins, partial or total. Thus the choir of the fine Church of St Mary, Haddington, built in the middle years of the fifteenth century, is now ruined, although the nave is still used.

The place of the chantry was often taken in Scotland by a collegiate church, usually founded by lairds and barons for much the same purpose as English chantries. One of the earliest was established at Maybole in 1382.

Sometimes they were founded in existing churches, sometimes entirely new buildings were erected, and occasionally the money ran out before they were finished. These new buildings were sometimes oblong, as at Castle Semple in Renfrewshire, founded in 1504, whilst others were cruciform, with polygonal-ended choirs, as at Seton, begun late in the fifteenth century. The most elaborately decorated collegiate building is that at Roslin in Mid Lothian, founded in 1447, but only the choir was ever finished.

Cathedrals and parish churches still stand in the landscape today as evidence of the strength of the Christian faith in the medieval centuries. The third building form which this faith took during these centuries survives now only in ruins. Norman bishops instituted rebuilding in cathedral and parish churches, Norman abbots in monasteries. There were by 1066 about forty monastic houses in England. English abbots were only slowly replaced by Norman ones, who brought with them a revitalized belief in the value of the monastic life and a desire to rebuild on a grand scale. To old institutions new ones were quickly added. William the Conqueror himself founded Battle Abbey, the high altar of its church standing over the spot where Harold fell at the Battle of Hastings. In 1077 William de Warenne founded Lewes Abbey directly from Cluny, the ultimate source of the wave of renewed enthusiasm for the monastic ideal which was then sweeping Europe, and by 1100 new abbeys had been founded at Colchester, Spalding, Selby, and Shrewsbury, whilst a small group of monks had moved from Cranborne to found what was to become one of the wealthiest monasteries in England, that at Tewkesbury.

It seems to be an inexorable law of monastic life that an initial period of ardour is followed by a long, slow decline into easy acceptance of the pleasanter side of conventual life, this in its turn to be galvanized into activity by some later movement of reform. The Abbey at Cluny had itself been founded in 910 on such a wave of reform, and for long it provided an astonishing example of fervent monastic life coupled with buildings of unparalleled architectural splendour. Another reform movement early in the twelfth century sought once again to return to the original fervour of the Rule of St Benedict by seeking a life that was both more rigorous and more retired from the world. The new movement was given extraordinary dynamism by one man, St Bernard of Clairvaux. He entered the monastery at Cîteaux, itself founded in 1098, in 1111, and Clairvaux was founded in 1115. From then until the general chapter at Cîteaux forbade further foundations in 1152 the Cistercian order spread like wildfire over western Europe, with some forty houses being founded in England and twelve in Scotland, beginning with the first, at Waverley in Surrey, in 1128 and going on to include Rievaulx, founded in 1131, its daughter house, Melrose, founded in 1136, Fountains, established in 1132, Jervaulx, founded in 1156

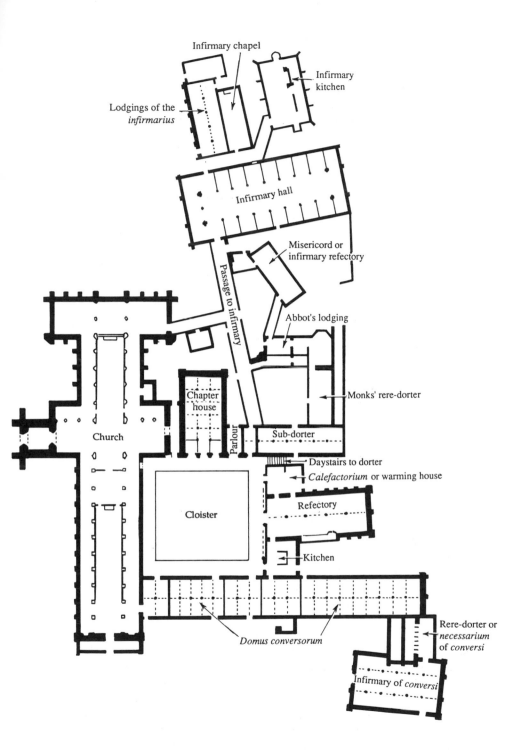

Figure 12 A plan of Fountains Abbey

after moving from Fors, together with Meaux, founded in 1151, Tintern in 1131, and Woburn, founded from Fountains in 1145.

Cistercian monasteries differed in a number of important respects from those of other orders. The rules of their order demanded that they be founded in desolate and uninhabited spots as far as possible from other human beings, the land itself to be cultivated solely for the use and advantage of the community. At the same time they were enjoined, at least in theory, to give up such feudal or manorial dues as bakeries, mills, fairs, and serfs. The aim of the monastic life anywhere was essentially spiritual, but in Cistercian houses more than usual emphasis was laid upon private prayer and reading. This meant that much of the physical labour involved in the cultivation of their lands was entrusted to *conversi,* lay brethren attracted by the comparative stability and security offered by such work but without the motivation to enter fully into monastic life. There were sometimes large numbers of *conversi,* and their dormitory became a distinctive feature of Cistercian monastic buildings, lying usually, as at Fountains, on the west side of the cloisters. Other *conversi* worked the outlying granges which were another distinctive feature of Cistercian organization.

Meanwhile the communities of canons who served cathedrals and minster churches were being increasingly urged to adopt a more stringent rule, more especially on the continent. Many individual communities did so, becoming known as regular canons. In due course the letter of advice

47 The west front of Fountains Abbey in Yorkshire, showing the long range of the *domus conversorum*, with the refectory on the ground floor and the dormitory on the first.

written in the fifth century by St Augustine of Hippo to a community in north Africa came to be adopted as the basis for a new order of Augustinian Canons, a name corrupted to Austin Canons. The rule prescribed a less austere daily life than that of most monastic orders and allowed greater liberty of movement in the outside world. Some existing houses of secular canons in England adopted the new rule, as at St Botolph in Colchester, and Henry I introduced them into a moribund house of secular clerks at Cirencester. He also established a new house at Carlisle in 1122, and this became the centre for the new diocese founded in 1133. Austin Canons also served the cathedral at St Andrews. Henry's queen founded Holy Trinity, Aldgate, in London, and from here further houses were established, at St Frideswide's, Oxford, at Dunstable, St Osyth, Launceston, and Plympton. Merton priory was founded in 1114 and a daughter house at Holyrood, just outside Edinburgh, in 1128. Other Scottish houses included Scone and Jedburgh. By 1350 there were over 200 houses of Austin Canons, although the great majority remained quite modest establishments, often with no more than ten canons. Their most famous house was at Walsingham, where the statue of the Virgin Mary was thought to work miracles, remaining an object of veneration throughout the middle ages and beyond, drawing pilgrims from all over Europe.

Early in the thirteenth century a new reforming movement swept through the spiritual life of Europe, taking its origins in the work of two remarkable men of completely opposing character and yet united in the religious fervour of their lives: St Dominic and St Francis of Assisi. St Dominic was an Augustinian Canon whose ideas were first formed whilst combating the heresies of the Albigensians of Languedoc. His Order of Friars Preacher, the Blackfriars, was formally approved by Innocent III in 1214. For the Dominicans the defence of the Catholic faith was all-important, and all else had to be sacrificed to this end. Thus his rule gave much greater room for the cultivation of the learning upon which this defence must rest, and to the art of preaching that would enable the faith to be more effectively spread among the laity. A party of Dominican friars landed in England in 1221 and immediately won the favour of the Archbishop of Canterbury, Stephen Langton. Their first foundations were at Holborn and at Oxford, where a seat of learning was rapidly developing, although there was a long delay before the English provincial chapter finally gave formal recognition to Oxford as a *studium generale* for the Order.

St Francis exacted from himself and demanded from his followers a perfect acceptance of the life of Christ, and although he was probably aware that few would be able to achieve such perfection he refused to compromise. All his followers were expected, by word and by example, to preach to all men. Nor were they to be bound to individual communities: a friar should have no permanent home since his life must be devoted to serving men in need wherever they might be found. He demanded absolute poverty, a refusal to accept any ecclesiastical preferment and a renunciation of all human learning. Such ideals made it impossible for him to draft a satisfactory rule for his Order, and in the last years of his life he withdrew more and more from the everyday affairs of his Order of Friars Minor, the Greyfriars, which Innocent III had approved in 1210.

In 1224 the first members of the Franciscan order, nine of them, landed in England. By 1256 there were forty-nine houses of Greyfriars, with 1,244 friars, by which time there were also about thirty-six houses of Blackfriars. Both orders were immediately and immensely popular throughout Europe, not least because they sought to bring Christianity into the world rather than to achieve their own spiritual salvation by retiring from it as the monks did. Both chose deliberately to settle in towns and in universities. Their first houses were small and extremely simple. Their rule of poverty forbade them to own property, and their first premises were often held in trust for them by the town in which they settled. As individuals they relied entirely upon alms-giving and begging, and even then they refused money and would accept no more than would suffice for one day. During the course of the thirteenth century they began to build their own churches, some of which were large but always plain and severe in style. There is only one complete friary church still left standing in England, that of the Dominicans in Norwich, now St Andrew's Hall. It is 250 feet long, with a nave 77 feet wide. Their conventual buildings seem to have followed no standardized plan, not least because of the awkward shape of their sites in towns. A friary always remained within the often cramped limits of its urban site and never came to control great landed estates in the way that the Cistercian houses so often did.

By the end of the thirteenth century even the friars were beginning to fall away from the ideals of their founders. Alms-giving and begging became institutionalized, conventual life became too attractive, they quarrelled amongst themselves and with the secular clergy. Nevertheless the friars always remained active as missionaries among the poor and as outspoken critics of worldly and complacent clerics.

Christianity has always presumed an educated priesthood, first in order to give instruction in the basic articles of the faith to the laity, and second to combat paganism and heresy. Schools for boys intended for the priesthood were attached to monasteries and cathedrals almost from their first beginnings in Britain. Bede had pupils in his monastery at Jarrow, of whom one was Egbert, in due course Archbishop of York and founder of a school there which acquired a European reputation. Egbert's own pupil, Alcuin, became master in 778 before being called to the court of Charlemagne to become head of the palace school, from there to make an invaluable contribution to the revival of learning in western Europe. The Viking invasions all but destroyed learning in Britain, but the thread was

not completely broken since Dunstan received his early education at the
school at Glastonbury. In due course he became head of the community
there and created from it the first regular monastery that had existed in
Britain for almost a hundred years. The revival of monasticism in England
which he fostered was but part of a European phenomenon, and schools
attached to both monasteries and cathedrals flourished during the tenth
and eleventh centuries. During the eleventh century it was the cathedral
schools of northern France which became particularly famous, their
reputations fluctuating with that of the masters who taught in them, more
especially at Bec, Laon, Chartres, and then Paris.

During the twelfth century some schools in England were acquiring
more than a local reputation, particularly those at Exeter, Northampton,
Lincoln, and then Oxford, where the existing religious foundations, the
secular canons in the castle chapel, established in 1074, the Augustinian
Priory of St Frideswide, refounded in 1122, and that of Oseney, founded in
1129, undoubtedly provided some stimulus. Lectures in theology were
being given by the middle years of the twelfth century. A *magister
scholarum Oxonie* is recorded in 1201 and the first Chancellor of the
University in 1221. At first much use was made of existing religious and
conventual buildings, especially St Mary's church for formal occasions.
Students rented rooms from townsmen, and disputes over high rents and
expensive, poor quality food began with the university and have continued
ever since. Masters soon began the practice of renting houses themselves
and providing both lodging and instruction for students. These halls were
progressively brought under the control of the university. Once very
numerous, only one, St Edmund Hall, has survived down to the present.
By the middle years of the thirteenth century the university was beginning
to attract gifts and benefactions. In about 1260 Sir John de Balliol agreed
to support a number of students. When he died the burden was assumed by
his widow and in 1282 she gave a permanent endowment and corporate
status. At about the same time Walter de Merton gave his estates at
Maldon, in Surrey, to a community of scholars who by 1270 were definitely
settled in Oxford, and a third college, University, came into existence in
about 1280, based upon a legacy of William of Durham who had died in
1249. Other foundations followed: Exeter College in 1314, Oriel in 1324,
Queens in 1341 and New College in 1379. This last college was founded on
a site immediately to the south of the town wall, still to be seen in the
college grounds. New College was the first foundation in Oxford to plan
and build a quadrangle specifically designed for collegiate life, and so its
buildings have a particular interest. The chapel and hall, backing
immediately on to the south side of the town wall, occupy the north side of
the quadrangle, with a kitchen in a wing projecting from the eastern end of
the hall and a muniment tower against its southeastern angle. To the west
of the chapel is the cloister, also used as a burial ground. On the western

48 New College, Oxford. The Great Quad. On the immediate left is the Chapel, and then the first floor hall, entrance to which is through the door in the Muniment Tower in the corner. The ranges of buildings about the Quad had a third storey and battlements added in 1674 and the windows had sashes inserted in about 1718.

side of the quadrangle is the main entrance, with a tower gateway. Here were the lodgings of the warden. The south side of the quadrangle contained lodgings for the fellows. On the east side was another gateway with the library over it, leading to a garden. In spite of sometimes extensive remodelling and some changes in purpose, the buildings around the Great Quad of New College still provide a faithful impression of what a medieval college must have looked like.

Yet further foundations followed during the fifteenth century, Lincoln College in 1427 and All Souls in about 1440. Up to this time the university as opposed to the colleges had almost no corporate property or buildings. In 1423 it was decided to build a Divinity School. It took nearly seventy years to complete, largely owing to a chronic shortage of money, and on its first floor were housed the books and manuscripts given by Duke Humphry of Gloucester, the existing library in St Mary's Church being overcrowded. The Divinity School has one of the finest medieval stone-vaulted roofs to be found anywhere in England.

The origins of the university at Cambridge are even more uncertain than those of Oxford. There are some, unsubstantiated, legends of lectures being given before the close of the twelfth century, but any institution that there might have been was given a firmer foundation by the migration of some students from Oxford in 1209 following riots and disturbances there between townsmen and scholars. A Chancellor is mentioned in 1226, by which time the university must have been well established. As at Oxford students were at first housed in lodgings provided by townsmen, with the inevitable brawls and riots over prices and, again as at Oxford, masters began to provide lodgings themselves in halls or hostels. By the middle years of the thirteenth century the university was attracting benefactions and the first college, Peterhouse, was founded in 1284. Corpus Christi College, granted a royal licence in 1352, is unique to both Cambridge and Oxford in that it was founded at the request of a guild of townsmen in Cambridge, the Guild of Corpus Christi, with the express purpose of providing prayers for the souls of departed members of the fraternity. The gild financed the buildings for its foundation and these were the first in Cambridge to be planned as a closed quadrangle, with the Master's Lodgings on the south side and blocks of other lodgings, on two floors, on the other three sides. There was at first no need for a chapel because the members of the college used the church of St Bene't, which was also the church of the gild which had founded and which continued to support the college.

The most splendid and most lavishly endowed medieval educational foundation was established by Henry VI in Cambridge in 1441. His ideas grew and developed and by 1445 a much larger college on an altogether more spacious site was planned. He acquired a substantial block of land between the river and the High Street, now the King's Parade. Here were numerous houses and shops, several streets, the Church of St John Zachery, the Salt Hithe on the river's edge, and a recently established college called Godshouse. All this was bought up and cleared for the new college. Building work began in 1441 on the range now called the Old Court. Work stopped when Henry changed his plans, demanding new buildings on an altogether grander scale for the very much enlarged site to the south. A quadrangle of unprecedented size was proposed, with a chapel on the north side, ranges of living quarters on the east and west, with the hall, service rooms and library on the south. Work began on the chapel and the eastern range. In 1461 Henry was deposed and building came to a standstill, to start again on a modest scale and on the chapel only in 1476. Both Edward IV and Richard III made gifts towards the cost, but it was only the generosity of Henry VII, who gave £4,000 in 1508 and another £5,000 in 1509, that enabled the work to proceed with any prospects of being completed. Further gifts from Henry VIII at last brought the chapel to a splendid conclusion with the magnificent rood loft, finished in 1536. The chapel was the only part of Henry VI's splendid scheme to be completed, although the footings of the work on the eastern range remained visible until the middle years of the eighteenth century.

King's College Chapel, Cambridge, makes a fitting conclusion to this chapter since it provides a magnificent summation of the artistic and technical achievements of the medieval centuries united in the service of the moral and spiritual values which dominated the lives of the men who conceived, planned, and built it. It is sadly ironic that it should at last have been completed just as the ideals and values which called it into being were under attack. The first session of what historians have come to call the 'Reformation' Parliament met on 3 November 1529.

This chapter does however require a coda. In our concern to re-create at least something of the ever-shifting and ever-changing patterns of the landscape of medieval Britain we have perhaps been over-concerned with the sizes and shapes of fields, the layout of peasant cabins and gentle manor houses, the building and rebuilding of churches and cathedrals, to such an extent that we have unconsciously looked at the world in which they belonged through late twentieth-century eyes rather than tenth- or fifteenth-century ones. We must, however, if we are to avoid too many anachronisms and too gross a misinterpretation of the record, endeavour to re-create not only the external physical world of the medieval centuries but also the mental world through which men sought to explain and rationalize what they saw about them. We have seen at least something of the way in which the external physical world differed from that of today, and we have also looked at some of the ways in which men regulated their rights of access to its resources, as through the complexities of the open-field system for example. But if this world has seemed strange, then how much more strange was their mental world.

The world picture held by that small minority of men who were literate and well read gave a remarkably coherent, logical, and emotionally satisfying view of the world and its purpose, based as it was upon the observation of natural phenomena with the naked eye, complex mathematical calculations and an extraordinary reliance upon authority, especially the Bible and, in due course as they were slowly recovered, the writings of Aristotle. The whole direction of medieval thought was spiritual and other-worldly, being turned towards the quality and the purpose of life and providing in the great work of synthesis of St Thomas Aquinas particularly satisfying and reassuring answers to some of the basic questions that human beings have always asked about their condition in life. Only at the Renaissance do men's minds turn from asking 'why?' to asking 'how?'.

The account of the creation of the world given in Genesis was accepted without question, as too was the story of the Flood, and since the world had been created, then in due course it would one day come to an end. The universe was composed of one basic material, the *prima materia,* which was possessed of four qualities: hot, cold, moist, and dry. These, when combined, gave the four elements of fire, air, water, and earth.

Earth, the heaviest, lay at the centre of the universe, a perfect sphere, with water and air on top. These were surrounded by pure, elemental fire, transparent and invisible, in a sphere just beneath the moon. All within the sphere, the sublunary world, was corruptible and transitory. Its elements were in perpetual conflict because they were out of balance and constantly striving to attain perfection. Only in gold was this perfection reached. All metals were a combination of sulphur and mercury produced within the ground by the action of heat and cold upon an underground watery vapour. If these natural processes could be speeded up and reproduced artificially then it should be possible to produce gold. Did not miners, working underground, encounter increasing heat, fumes, and water? When the galena (lead sulphide) which they dug out so laboriously was heated it gave off sulphurous fumes and yielded lead. When this was further heated, silver could be obtained by cupellation. From a combination of practical observation and reasoning by analogy, alchemy was born. The alembic of the alchemist was the womb of the earth. Add mercury, because it resembles silver, the metal closest to gold, and then sulphur, because it is yellow, and then some one further substance that would remove all impurities and resolve all discords, and the result should be gold. This one substance, the philosopher's stone, had to be sought for humbly and piously, with no trace of ambition, greed, or vice, since it was itself partly spiritual. Alchemy was widely believed and practised in the medieval centuries, as also were the opportunities it presents for fraud, as Chaucer makes clear in *The Canon's Yeoman's Tale.*

Beyond the corruption of the sublunary world lay a series of perfect, incorruptible and unchanging spheres. Each sphere supported one of the celestial bodies. These were made up of a fifth element, *quinta essentia,* which was itself perfect. The first seven of these spheres supported the Moon, Mercury, Venus, the Sun, Mars, Jupiter, and Saturn. Both the Moon and the Sun were then thought to be planets circling the earth. Beyond the spheres of the planets lay that of the stars, and then the *primum mobile,* the last sphere before Heaven and God. The spaces between the spheres were filled with light and with music. Before the Fall man had been able to hear this music, but now, because of his sins, he could not.

The influence of the Sun upon the lives of men was obvious and many Anglo-Saxon churches were provided with sundials to measure the passing of time. The other heavenly bodies must therefore influence man. From this belief astrology was born. Given the exact date, time, and place of a man's birth it was possible to construct his horoscope and so make an assessment of his personality and a forecast of the likely future of his life. Astrologers were always careful to point out that the influence from the heavenly bodies could be put to good or bad use, depending upon the proclivities of the individual. Not to have done so would have left no room for the free exercise of the will.

Thus the universe which God had created in six days was filled with purpose, light, movement, and music. In due course it would come to an end, and God would proclaim this with signs and portents, comets and great storms, plagues and pestilences.

The world itself was undoubtedly spherical, but there was little point in speculating as to whether or not men lived in the southern hemisphere because the equatorial zone was too hot for men to pass through. The world was filled with a wide range of animals and plants, but almost all medieval natural history was based upon the writings of Aristotle and Pliny rather than upon direct observation, and so medieval bestiaries are filled with marvellous and bizarre animals, although the decorations to such books as the Luttrell Psalter show that men were equally as capable of exact and realistic observation as they were of extravagant flights of fancy.

How far this complex cosmology penetrated beyond the small minority of literate men it is impossible to say. Some garbled version was probably held by many more. Similarly, it is very unlikely that the subtleties of theological debate penetrated much beyond the universities and monastic cloisters. Parish priests were often only semi-literate, capable of stumbling through the Latin mass but with no understanding of what it was all about, whilst ploughmen and craftsmen had little more than lurid wall paintings, such as that over the chancel arch in the church of St Thomas, Salisbury, to feed their minds and imaginations. Among the great majority of the inhabitants of Britain, Christianity was only dimly understood and certainly did not prevent widespread belief in spirits, good and evil, and the value and potency of lucky charms, holy wells, incantations, spells, the intercessary powers of saints and their relics, and the very real presence of the Devil and his imps. In a world in which natural phenomena were beyond control and beyond explanation men sought where they could for reassurance, protection, and comfort.

We have taken three very long chapters to describe the evolution of the landscapes of medieval Britain, from the collapse of the Roman Empire to the point where we stand on the brink of those great shifts in the patterns of human thought summed up in the words Renaissance, Reformation, and Scientific Revolution. This millennium sees the division of Britain into England, Scotland, and Wales. It sees the emergence of some of the most fundamental structures in the landscape: boundaries whether of parish or county; place-names; some of the oldest and most permanent buildings, especially churches; the development of some occupation sites into towns where, in spite of the ravages of later centuries, the main outlines of their morphology, first laid down during this period, can still be seen; and a second replanning of the rural landscape. All this, and much more, developed slowly, imperceptibly, and without serious break from the landscapes described in chapters 2 and 3, since the discontinuities between Roman Britain and Anglo-Saxon England are probably more a matter of evidence and interpretation than of substance. At the same time our understanding of the processes at work is immensely enriched by the survival of documents from which it is possible to reconstruct, at least in part, the attitudes, preconceptions, and values of those men and women who, in the course of their everyday lives, were creating and re-creating the landscape.

Much from this medieval world still remains, since no generation has been able entirely to blot out the contributions of its predecessors to the palimpsest which is the landscape, but the pace of change begins noticeably to quicken in the sixteenth century and it is to these changes that we must now turn.

Part III

TOWARDS
THE MODERN WORLD

7

Early modern Britain

The sixteenth and seventeenth centuries see profound and increasingly rapid changes in the landscapes of Britain. The dissolution of the monasteries, completed in England and Wales by 1540, was the consequence of a shift in men's spiritual values, a shift which led to the sudden collapse of the significance attached to certain kinds of buildings which had been part of the fabric of the landscape for generations. They suddenly became redundant, and were either demolished or converted into private dwellings, or were allowed to become quarries for building materials. Second, there were considerable changes in the rural landscape of Britain, brought about either by changes in the legal framework of man's relationship with the soil, or else by changes in his agricultural practices, and quite frequently by changes in both. Third, population growth, although erratic, brought increasing numbers of people into towns, especially to London, to ports and naval dockyard towns like Chatham, and to growing manufacturing towns like Birmingham and Manchester. Fourth, changes in men's patterns of ideas, values, and beliefs, summed up in the words Renaissance and Scientific Revolution, brought entirely new designs to buildings, designs which, it was thought, better expressed these ideals, and also entirely new kinds of buildings, of which the Royal Observatory at Greenwich is perhaps the best example.

Probably the single most important factor making for change in the rural landscape of England from the sixteenth century onwards is enclosure. We saw in Chapter 5 that there was much enclosure from the open fields, especially during the fifteenth century and especially in midland England, due to a large extent to a shift in the balance of profitability away from arable husbandry towards pastoral farming and particularly the rearing of sheep for wool. Opposition to enclosure persisted in government circles until the early years of the seventeenth century but was unable to prevent it altogether, and as an appreciation of the advantages of enclosure gradually emerged, together with a slowly dawning awareness that it need not necessarily be followed by large-scale depopulation, so hostility evaporated. There was also a steady movement towards enclosure by agreement amongst all those concerned rather than forcible enclosure at the will of the landlord. Sometimes enclosure extended to all the lands of the parish, as at Haselbeach in Northamptonshire for example, enclosed by agreement in 1599, or to only part, as at Rousham in Oxfordshire, where 120 acres of pasture were enclosed by agreement in 1645, the open arable fields remaining unenclosed until 1775.

Enclosure could lead to an almost complete redrawing of the landscape of a parish. The great open fields were divided up into small closes. Their boundary hedges were generally sinuous or gently curved. Rigidly straight field boundaries had to wait for the Parliamentary enclosure commissioners of the second half of the eighteenth century. New roads appeared, and gradually new, isolated, farmsteads as farmers moved out from the nucleated village into the middle of their newly consolidated farmlands. One of the most striking features of Laxton, in Nottinghamshire, where open-field agriculture is still practised, is the number of working farms still to be seen in the village itself. Enclosure could also lead to changes in land use. In the latter half of the sixteenth century it could be carried out as much in the interests of arable husbandry as of sheep farming. The open-field system was not as rigid as it is generally made out to be, and it was not impossible to insert turnips and other new crops into the traditional crop rotations, but enclosure made this much simpler, and as the range of new industrial crops such as woad, madder, and hops as well as cultivated grasses increased, so the pressure to enclose also mounted. At the same time cattle rearing, for meat, dairy products, and hides, was also becoming important, and the quality of stock could be improved only following enclosure.

Enclosure of this kind was a piecemeal, protracted affair, affecting sometimes hundreds of acres, sometimes only two or three. It provoked a great deal of controversy but in the long term it proved to be irresistible. It also went largely unrecorded. Numerous government commissions of inquiry provide us with individual examples of enclosure, but it is clear that many more escaped the net. Large numbers of agreements to enclose were enrolled in the central lawcourts, especially Chancery, but many more have left no documentary evidence of any kind. The extent of enclosure by private Act of Parliament in the eighteenth and nineteenth centuries is known fairly precisely. Some 6¾ million acres of land in England, almost 21 per cent of the total area, was enclosed in this way. If one can accept for a moment that the whole of England was 'unenclosed' at some point in time, and this is by no means certain, then 80 per cent, four-fifths, of the

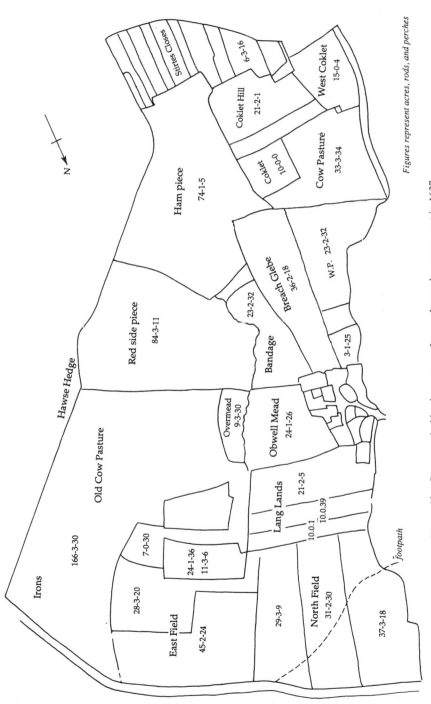

N

Irons
166-3-30

Old Cow Pasture

Hawse Hedge

Red side piece
84-3-11

Ham piece
74-1-5

Stirtes Closes

Coklet Hill
21-2-1

6-3-16

Coklet
10-0-0

West Coklet
15-0-4

Cow Pasture
33-3-34

23-2-32

Breach Glebe
36-2-18

W.P. 23-2-32

Bandage

3-1-25

Overmead
9-3-30

Obwell Mead
24-1-26

7-0-30

24-1-36
11-3-6

28-3-20

East Field
45-2-24

Lang Lands
21-2-5

10.0.1
10.0.39

29-3-9

North Field
31-2-30

37-3-18

footpath

Figures represent acres, rods, and perches

Figure 13 Greatworth, Northampton, after enclosure by agreement in 1637

total area must have been enclosed by non-Parliamentary means, and it is very likely that a great deal of this enclosure took place in the sixteenth and seventeenth centuries.

Much clearing and enclosing of woodland also took place, and there were also a number of proposals for large-scale fen drainage. A great deal of the enclosure of woodland and marshland was prompted by the financial difficulties of James I and Charles I, and Charles in particular sold off very large areas of woodland. The Royal Forests of Braden, Melksham, Pewsham, Hatfield Broadoak, Bernwood, Galtres, to name only a few, were all enclosed in the 1630s, the trees felled, the roots grubbed out, new farmsteads built and closes laid down to arable and pasture. This work was often accompanied by widespread riots, prompted by the loss to the local inhabitants of valuable grazing rights in the woods. Thus the Forest of Braden, in Wiltshire, an area of a little over 4,000 acres, provided grazing without stint for the inhabitants of fourteen villages. The Crown allotted only 390 acres as compensation for the loss of these rights. Disturbances in Wiltshire alone continued for nearly twenty years, and on one occasion soldiers sent to quell the riots sided instead with the rioters.

James I seems to have been less grasping than Charles I. When salt marshes were enclosed James took only one-fifth, but Charles insisted upon one-third, and the commissioners who carried out the enclosures returned to the Exchequer the names of those who had opposed or obstructed their efforts. Riots accompanied marshland enclosure in just the same way as they did woodland enclosure, and Charles was compelled to increase the allotment of land in compensation for the loss of grazing rights on a number of occasions, at Epworth for example, when Hatfield Chase was drained and enclosed.

The largest scheme of fen drainage, however, was begun by a group of private proprietors. In 1630 the Earl of Bedford agreed with a number of fenland landowners to drain that area of the southern fenlands which eventually became known as the Bedford Level. They were granted a charter of incorporation in 1634, and in 1663 an Act of Parliament created a corporation, the Governor, Bailiffs and Commonalty of the Great Level of the Fens, which was not dissolved until 1914. Within about thirty years some 350,000 acres of land could be declared drained and fit for cultivation. Crops of onions, peas, hemp, flax, oats, and wheat appeared, as well as rich meadows and pastures. But the project was not an unmitigated success. First of all it destroyed a traditional way of life based upon the skilful exploitation by the local inhabitants of the resources of the fens: fishing, wildfowling, reed cutting, and the grazing of cattle upon the rich summer pastures created by the winter floods. Riots and disturbances, accompanied by much destruction of the new drainage works, were the result, and it was many years before the new way of life could be accepted. Secondly the scheme ran into increasingly difficult technical problems. As the drainage took effect the level of the peat began to fall. By the last quarter of the seventeenth century many drainage channels ran at a higher level than the surrounding land and had to be embanked, and these banks, built from peat, were continually crumbling and needed constant attention. Horse- and wind-driven pumping engines only made matters worse since in draining one area they merely moved the water into another and threw great quantities of mud into the drainage channels. Thus in fact the success of the fenland drainage schemes was obtained only at very great cost, and remained very fragile until the coming of steam-powered pumping engines early in the nineteenth century put it on a surer footing.

There were almost as important and far-ranging changes in the Welsh rural landscape during the sixteenth and seventeenth centuries as there were in England, but in Wales peculiarly Welsh processes were at work. There was a great deal of enclosure taking place. The open-field arable husbandry characteristic of the lowlands of the Welsh borderlands and the coastlands of the south almost disappeared during this period, leaving very little to be enclosed by Act of Parliament in the eighteenth and nineteenth centuries. On the other hand this enclosure was very piecemeal in its nature, so that there are numerous surviving relics from the pre-enclosure landscape including, as at Rhosili in the Gower peninsula, some isolated areas still cultivated in strips.

Much enclosure of woodland, moorland, and mountain pasture also took place. Sometimes it was a matter of small plots of land, an acre or two at a time, nibbled away from the vast expanses of rough moorland grazing. On other occasions it was a matter of hundreds of acres at a time. However carried out the end-result was the same. Large tracts of land were cleared, enclosed, and cultivated, either as arable or as improved pasture. Thus between 1561 and 1573 piecemeal clearing and enclosing amounted to over 2,000 acres in the commote of Cyfeilig in Montgomeryshire alone, and this is but one isolated example of what must have been a widespread practice.

Much of this enclosure was prompted by a desire to improve agricultural practices, but there were other factors at work. In 1542 an Act of Parliament abolished the traditional Welsh tenures, described in Chapter 5, and in particular the practice of partible inheritance. At the same time estate surveyors and landlords were beginning to apply English law to unenclosed land by treating it as common land and therefore the property of the landlord, whereas in fact it was *cytir,* land held in common by coheirs and deliberately left open and unenclosed to make its management easier. These developments brought great uncertainty into the tenure of land. Enclosure was one way out, but often the parcels were too small to be profitable and so their owners had no course open to them but to sell up and move out. Those with money could buy up such parcels of land, consolidate them and build up substantial estates. Further enclosure would follow in order to improve the value of the land and pay off the purchase price. Woodland was a further resource being increasingly exploited commercially. Wales was undoubtedly very much more extensively wooded than it is today, but during the sixteenth and seventeenth centuries large areas were cleared. Some woodland was deliberately felled, with the timber going into shipbuilding, to make pit props and as fuel for the iron furnaces established in south Wales and Montgomeryshire, but also much disappeared through neglect and as a consequence of overgrazing, especially by goats.

Change came very much more slowly into the Scottish rural landscape than it did to either England or Wales. Scottish landed proprietors dominated the Scottish Parliament and it is clear from a number of Acts passed there that they were becoming increasingly aware of the benefits that enclosure and improvement could bring. Thus an Act of 1661 called upon proprietors to enclose at least 4 acres of land a year for ten years, with power to divert roads if necessary. Such land was to be exempt from taxation for nineteen years. The Act was renewed in 1685, with a renewal of the exemption from taxation. It is almost impossible to assess the importance of this Act, but it is clear from other evidence that Scottish proprietors were enclosing land in the immediate vicinity of their mansion houses from the early years of the seventeenth century, and it is very likely that innovation by example was more influential in the diffusion of new ideas and practices than any Act of Parliament, however well-meaning. Two further Acts were probably of more importance. One, 'Anent run-rig' (the Scottish equivalent of the English open field system), provided that proprietors of land held in run-rig could apply to the sheriff, justices of the peace, or lords of regality to have the lands consolidated and divided up into compact blocks. A second Act provided that any proprietor with rights of commonty could apply to the Court of Session to enclose common lands. Thus in Scotland there were by the end of the seventeenth century no legal barriers to enclosure, which could now be carried out at the wish of the individual proprietors without recourse to Parliament for the private Acts which were so important a feature of the English enclosure movement. It was well into the eighteenth century, however, before there were any substantial changes in that traditional pattern of infield/outfield cultivation described in Chapter 5.

The sixteenth and seventeenth centuries saw important changes taking place in men's expectations of what their houses should look like and of the values to be attached to them. Houses built to local, traditional patterns were gradually modified, altered, and adapted to reflect changes brought about by the slow diffusion of ideas best summed up in the word Renaissance. The new ideas came in only very slowly and unevenly, and there was neither a sudden acceptance of them, not least because their full meaning and implications were only very gradually realized, nor any widespread replacement of the medieval housing stock.

The vernacular tradition was a living, flourishing one in sixteenth- and seventeenth-century Britain, capable of adapting quickly to changing needs. By the early years of the sixteenth century the open hall, the principal, sometimes the only, room in a medieval house, was beginning to lose its importance as comfort and privacy became increasingly sought after, and it was ceiled over to provide first-floor accommodation. This presented two problems. First of all something had to be done about the central hearth. This led to the construction of chimneys, either against the through passage or against one of the walls. As the chimney was carried up through the first floor and out of the roof so it became possible to heat the first-floor rooms, and if the chimney was sited centrally within the house then it was possible to have hearths back to back, so that four rooms could be heated. Secondly, the problem of access to the first floor rooms led to the insertion of staircases. By the early seventeenth century a house of three ground-floor rooms and three first-floor ones, with a lobby entrance, chimney stack, and staircase placed axially, had become widespread in many areas of southeastern England. They were still timber-framed, unless local supplies of other building materials, stone, cob, or flint for example, were readily available, with wattle-and-daub infilling and thatched roofs, but they were certainly more convenient than anything which had gone

49   Sixteenth-century stone and thatched cottages at Alderton in Northamptonshire.

50 Townsend, Troutbeck, Cumberland, a remarkably well-preserved example of a prosperous Lake District yeoman farmer's house, built of stone with oak mullioned windows. The central, recessed block dates from the late sixteenth century. The wing on the right containing the kitchen was added in about 1623. The projecting wing on the extreme right is a dairy added in the nineteenth century. The wing on the left was added in the eighteenth century.

before, and by the same period glass was becoming cheap and plentiful so that windows could be glazed as a matter of course. Brick was also becoming more readily available. Much wattle-and-daub was replaced with brick, but it was a long time before housebuilders felt able to abandon the crutch of timber-framing and build entirely in brick.

In the north and the west of England, and particularly in Devonshire and the Lake District, the long house continued to be built and occupied throughout the period covered in this chapter. Substantial, well-built long houses of stone were erected, in which human beings and animals were now separated by a passage and stone walls, though they still shared a common entrance, the family turning in one direction into their living quarters and animals another into theirs. Such long houses continued to be occupied until well into the eighteenth century and even then they were not abandoned. Instead new byres were built for the livestock and the old ones were converted for human use.

The vernacular building tradition reflects complex reactions between geology, climate, and society. It is as much a part of the landscape of Wales and Scotland as it is of England. In the borderlands of Wales there was a strong tradition of fine craftsmanship in timber-framed building, a tradition that persists well into the eighteenth century. Over the rest of Wales, save in the towns, building was in stone, clay, or turf. The smallest, simplest houses were long, low buildings of only one storey and one room. Other, more substantial houses had two storeys and a number of rooms. A particularly interesting variation upon a theme is to be found in the 'unit' houses, in which two houses were built very close together, sometimes even touching at one corner, but with no internal communication. It is very likely that such houses represent one method of overcoming the problems set by the law of partible inheritance, under which property was divided between all the sons, a process which in a couple of generations could reduce a viable farm into small parcels of land which, individually, had almost no value. Two closely related families might have decided to manage a farm in common rather than subdivide it, and a second house, built close to the first, would enable this to be done without the two families being compelled actually to live together. We have already, in Chapter 3, looked at what may possibly be a similar arrangement in Roman villas. Any link, however, over a thousand years of considerable change, is probably nothing more substantial than the result of a similar problem prompting a similar response.

In Scotland, the distinction between landed proprietor and his tenants was much sharper than it was in either England or Wales, and it is a distinction which was reflected in their housing. The cabins which made up

51 A cottage at Torthorwald, Dumfriesshire. Built late in the eighteenth century, it is the last surviving example of a long tradition of cruck building in southwestern Scotland. There are three pairs of internal oak trusses, and the roof is thatched.

the Scottish ferm toun were almost without exception single-storeyed buildings, with walls of stone, clay, wickerwork and, on occasion, alternate layers of stone and turf. Larger houses were sometimes of the 'but and ben' type, composed of a kitchen/living room and a bedroom, the division between the two often no more than the wooden box beds which were universal in Scotland at the time. Only a small handful of pre-improvement cottages now survive in Scotland. Burns Cottage, Alloway, of about 1730, is one, a single-storeyed building containing but, ben, and byre and with a reed-thatched roof. The last surviving cruck-framed cottage in Galloway, again single-storeyed and of but and ben layout, is still to be seen at Torthorwald. Arnol Blackhouse, on Lewis, now a museum, was built towards the end of the nineteenth century, but so slow was the pace of change in northwestern Scotland that it still reflects accurately conditions as they must have been at least two centuries earlier, as do the South Voe Croft Museum on Shetland and the Corrigall Farm Museum on Orkney.

For the Scottish proprietor the turbulent and unsettled state of Scottish society and the constant threat of invasion from England meant that considerations of defence were overwhelming. The result was the tower house, whose origins we have already discussed in Chapter 5. It consisted

52   Queen Mary's House, Jedburgh, an example of a bastle, or fortified tower house, built in the late sixteenth century.

of a massive square stone tower block, sometimes four storeys high. The ground floor was a barrel-vaulted room used for storage. Living accommodation was on the first floor. The tower was surrounded by a walled enclosure, or barmkin, often used for herding cattle. As conditions gradually became more settled in the latter half of the sixteenth century so some concessions could be made to the growing taste for comfort. Windows became larger, and some lateral expansion, giving ancillary rooms, became possible. But living accommodation remained on the first floor, with access by a spiral staircase built in the thickness of the walls, and it was only at the end of the seventeenth century that the grim, stern tradition of the Scottish tower house began slowly to unbend.

By the fourth and fifth decades of the sixteenth century the first signs can be detected of new ideas and principles in building styles beginning to find their way into Britain, principles based ultimately upon the inexhaustible riches of classical architecture. They involved at first a rather superficial use of classical ornament and decoration, in particular such things as the classical orders to columns and pilasters and the use of classical pediments to doors and windows. These could be copied quite easily and they are to be found in Britain by the 1540s in the rebuilding carried out by Sir William Sharington at Lacock Abbey in Wiltshire, for example, and in the astonishingly precocious tomb of Sir Robert Dormer in the parish church at Wing, in Buckinghamshire, dating from 1552, as well as the north façade to the courtyard at Falkland Palace, built for James V between 1539 and 1542.

What took longer to learn were the underlying principles of classical architecture, namely the idea of a building as a complete, balanced, integrated whole, in which the building itself acquired a unity of spirit greater than the total of its parts, so that nothing could be added to it or taken away without destroying this unity. For the great Italian architect Andrea Palladio, who died in 1580 and whose buildings and writings were to be so influential, this unity was a reflection of the divine harmony, making architecture the queen of the arts. A growing awareness of this harmony is first visible in Britain with the increasing attention given to the regularity of the façade of a building, of which Longleat, completed in the last decades of the sixteenth century, is a splendid example.

During the course of the second half of the sixteenth century the new ideas flooded in, and the courtiers, politicians, civil servants, and merchants who surrounded Queen Elizabeth built houses upon a prodigal scale to embody at least some of the new ideas: Theobalds, Burghley, Hatfield, Wollaton, Hardwick Hall, Audley End, to name but a few. But the new ideas came through Flanders rather than directly from Italy and were transformed in the process so that the clarity and balance of classical architecture were submerged under a welter of extravagant linear decoration. It was Inigo Jones who returned to the fountain head. He

53 Hardwick Hall, Derbyshire, built between 1590 and 1597 for Bess of Hardwick, Countess of Shrewsbury, whose initials dominate the skyline. The house was almost certainly designed by Robert Smythson.

visited Italy in the company of the Earl of Arundel, taking with him his own copy of Palladio's book on architecture. He visited the sites that Palladio had studied, and he annotated his copy throughout his life. In 1615 he became Surveyor of the King's Works and in 1619, following a fire in the Palace of Whitehall, he was commissioned to design the Banqueting House, the first building in Britain to give full expression to the new principles of harmony, balance, and proportion which are the true foundations of classical architecture. Completed in about 1622, it must have seemed to contemporaries to be an astonishing break with the past, an alien intrusion into a world of thatch, brick, and timber-framing. But the example set by Inigo Jones, both here and in his other work such as the Queen's House at Greenwich, remained for many years without imitation, not least because of his close association with the court of Charles I which was becoming increasingly unpopular and isolated.

It was only in the years after the Restoration that his ideas find any following, and then largely as a consequence of the compulsory period of study in France and Italy forced upon many country gentlemen during the years of the Commonwealth. One of the most influential of these was Sir Roger Pratt. Between 1643 and 1649 he travelled extensively in France, Italy, and the Low Countries, returning to England to design, in about 1651, Coleshill, a country house in Berkshire, for his cousin. Coleshill was

54 Belton House, Lincolnshire, built from 1685 for Sir John Brownlow and a perfect
example of the classical English country house.

a long, rectangular block, with a hipped roof, dormer windows, cupola,
balustrade, and tall, prominent chimney stacks. It had two principal floors.
Its main entrance was in the centre of one of the long sides, approached by
means of a sweeping flight of steps. Inside, the hall was finally reduced to
being an entrance vestibule, with the main staircase rising out of it. A long
corridor ran the full length of both floors so that people could at last go
from one room to another without having to pass through intermediate
rooms, catching the occupants doing – literally – anything. A house of this
kind, set in an idyllic parkland setting, became the ideal country house for
the next century and a half, and even today, although the values upon
which it was based have now passed away, it seems the quintessence of the
English landscape.

By the end of the seventeenth century Coleshill was being widely copied
and imitated, and its influence had spread to Wales and to Scotland. Sir
William Bruce, Surveyor-General for Scotland, built his own version of
Coleshill for his own home at Kinross House, between 1685 and 1693.

Towns and cities were, even at the end of the seventeenth century, still
very small by the standards of the late twentieth. The largest by far was
London, with a population of perhaps 675,000. Next was Edinburgh, with
about 40,000 inhabitants, followed by Norwich with no more than 30,000.
Manchester and Birmingham may each have had 10,000, but it is unlikely
that either Swansea or Cardiff had more than 2,000 each. The small size of

towns meant that the dichotomy between urban and rural life, so marked a feature of late twentieth-century society, was far less noticeable than it is today. Fields and farms, hedgerows and cornfields, were at the back doors of most townsmen in this period. They kept pigs and chickens in their own backyards, and the better-off kept horses as a matter of course, so that stables, haylofts, and middens were part of their everyday lives. Further, many towns were still surrounded by their open fields, and the craftsmen, shopkeepers, and tradesmen of Leicester, Nottingham, Cambridge, Stamford, and Stony Stratford, for example, were also farmers, cultivating their strips of arable and turning their livestock into the stubble in just the same way as any village husbandman.

We discussed the importance and the difficulty of drawing a dividing line between town and village in Chapter 3. The problem is a perennial one, and has been from Roman times down to the present, since any criteria that might be used to sharpen the distinction clearly change over time. Sixteenth- and seventeenth-century towns were very small, but, as with Roman towns, it is their function as marketing and distribution centres which marks them off from villages, even if in individual instances the line is difficult to draw consistently.

In spite of their small size, sixteenth- and seventeenth-century towns did

55   Mid-eighteenth-century town houses in Appleton Gate, Newark.

have a certain density of population, even if their houses occupied no more than two or three streets. Buildings in British towns have been altered, rebuilt, demolished, and rebuilt again and again over the centuries, but the town plan itself, the actual pattern of streets and blocks of buildings, has proved to be remarkably durable. We have seen in previous chapters that the town plan is medieval in origin, and that many towns reached the limits of their pre-industrial extent by the end of the thirteenth century. From this time until the middle decades of the eighteenth century most towns showed few or no signs of physical expansion. There were of course exceptions, notably London, but places like Norwich, Ipswich, Gloucester, and Nottingham saw little addition in the sixteenth and seventeenth centuries to their medieval street plans. In Glasgow there were eight streets to the medieval town. Candleriggs was laid out in 1662, King Street in the 1720s, but development and building was very slow. No new street was laid out in Leeds between 1634 and 1767. Queen Square, laid out in

56 The market cross at Beverley, built in 1714.

Bristol in 1700, took nearly thirty years to fill up, and until the second half of the eighteenth century St Helens was no more than a chapel at a country crossroads.

There was however much rebuilding, patching, and alteration in towns during this period, and their own traditions of vernacular building were affected by the same range of ideas from Renaissance Italy that touched country houses of every kind. Most towns had one public building, either a town hall or a market hall, sometimes both, and sometimes a building which combined both functions and occasionally provided accommodation for a school. In its traditional form such a building usually had an open ground floor with a first storey supported on rows of columns. The ground floor provided a covered market-place and the first floor room served for council meetings and for a school. A fine timber-framed example, built in 1633 by John Abel, the King's Carpenter, survives at Leominster. In due course however the traditional form is clothed in decent classical garb, with columns, pilasters, and cupolas. What must be the most splendid of all these seventeenth-century town halls is that at Abingdon, built between 1678 and 1680 to designs by Christopher Kempster, who had worked with Sir Christopher Wren on the rebuilding of a number of churches in the City of London after the Great Fire.

The Scottish equivalent of the town hall is the tolbooth, and there is the same story here of a traditional building-form slowly adopting a new dress. By the end of the sixteenth century a tolbooth was a complex structure including a bell tower, council chamber, courtroom and prison. At Glasgow the ground floor of the tolbooth was divided up into stalls and booths, the rents from which helped towards the upkeep of the building. Often the first floor of a tolbooth was approached by an external flight of stairs, with a cross on the landing. This was a relic of the mercat cross, which was common in medieval Scottish towns and still widely distributed at this time. There is a splendid example at Prestonpans. Built early in the seventeenth century, it has a circular, drum-like base divided into eight compartments, two of which have doors. One door opens into an internal chamber, the other on to a narrow staircase which leads to a platform on the roof of the drum, on which stands a column crowned by an heraldic beast.

Traditional houses in towns could, as in the country, vary enormously in size, from one-roomed cabins to mansions of thirty or more rooms. Again as in the country, town houses were built of timber-framing, with wattle-and-daub walls and thatched roofs, unless local supplies of other building materials were readily and cheaply to hand. Even when stone was plentiful it was not uncommon to use timber-framing for decorative purposes. Houses provide shelter for the basic unit of human society, namely the family and household, and so in its plan the house reflects the needs of this unit. In pre-industrial society the family was the unit of

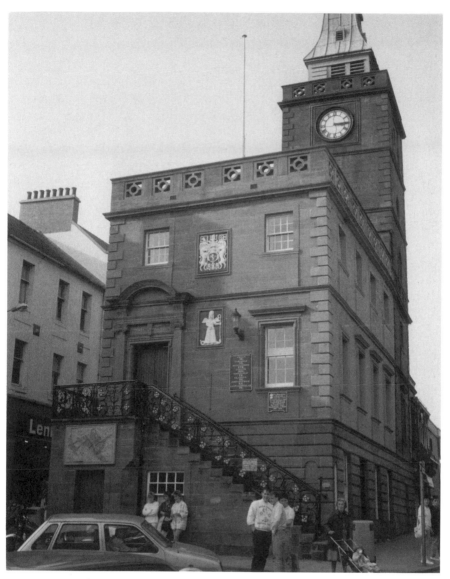

57 The Mid Steeple, or town house, at Dumfries, finished in 1707 to replace a sixteenth-century predecessor. It was designed by the Liverpool architect John Moffat. The main entrance is reached by the external staircase, with a wrought-iron balustrade. As originally designed it contained a council chamber, clerk's chamber, several prison cells, a tron or weights office and a magazine for the town's arms and ammunition. The panels on the south entrance front include a royal armorial, a figure of St Michael and a mileage panel of 1827, recording, *inter alia*, the distances to Edinburgh, 72 miles, London, 330 miles, and to Huntingdon, 272 miles, then one of the most important centres in eastern England for the cattle drovers of Galloway.

58 Staple Inn, Holborn, London. Heavily restored in 1937 this is nevertheless one of the few surviving reminders of what London before the Great Fire must have looked like. The block of five gables on the left was built in 1586, that on the right is slightly later.

production for almost every kind of economic activity, and so the house, in addition to providing purely residential accommodation, also contained retail shops, workshops, offices, warehouses, tenter yards, dye houses, stables, pig sties, and rooms for servants and apprentices. Houses in towns were subject to pressures which are largely absent in the countryside. Towns by their nature have relatively dense populations. This means that building plots are expensive. When towns were laid out the plots were long and narrow with the short end facing on to the street. The houses built along the street formed one continuous façade, and they could expand only by building upwards or else by filling in the long tail of the plot, and often both. By the sixteenth century town houses, especially in the centres of towns, were often three or four storeys high, their plots filled with a huddle of sheds, workshops, stables, brewhouses, and warehouses, often surrounding an open courtyard where there was a well. Access was by means of a back lane, and often too through an arched gateway on to the street. Raw materials were brought on to the premises, stored in warehouses, made ready for sale in workshops and sold by retail through the shop at the front, and all this within the same domestic unit. This meant that the journey to work was unusual at this time, since so many manufacturing and commercial processes took place under the same roof as the residential accommodation of those who were engaged in these processes.

The social geography of towns also differed markedly from that of today. Well-to-do merchants and shopkeepers lived in large houses in the centre of the town, whilst the poor lived in smaller cottages in the suburbs or on awkwardly shaped plots between the larger houses. There was too a growing practice of allowing the sheds and outhouses to the rear of large premises to be divided up and used as dwellings, especially for poor immigrants into the town. Town authorities did all that they could to remove these 'inmates', because there was a real danger that they would become a charge on the poor rate, but the frequency with which the regulations against them are repeated in town records of the period must indicate widespread evasion. Thus, because almost everyone literally lived over the shop, the centre of a town was as much residential as it was commercial. The Central Business District of towns at the end of the twentieth century, crowded with shoppers and business people during the day and almost deserted at night save for those in search of entertainment, is essentially a creation of the second half of the nineteenth century and was not completed in many towns until after 1945.

There was a great deal of rebuilding in towns in the sixteenth and seventeenth centuries but, apart from London, very little real expansion in the actual urban area. Much of this rebuilding followed traditional vernacular patterns, and Renaissance ideas came into the towns only very slowly before the Restoration. Because so many buildings in towns were of timber and thatch, and because so many industrial processes in towns needed fires and furnaces, occupations like brewing, baking, and dyeing, towns very frequently saw outbreaks of fire which on occasion could be on a disastrously large scale. Rebuilding following a fire invariably followed the ancient pattern of streets and building plots, and this in spite of growing interest in the concept and design of the ideal city after the long hiatus of the later medieval centuries.

The first tentative steps towards conscious city-planning were taken in London by Inigo Jones. In 1631 he designed the Covent Garden scheme for the Earl of Bedford, an open square surrounded on three sides by three- and four-storeyed houses of uniform façade and with arcaded ground floors. For the fourth side he designed the church of St Paul, a severely simple building of entirely classical design. The scheme was laid out over an area of pasture land. After the Restoration further schemes were devised, both to the east and to the west of the built-up area of London, St James's Square for example, and Soho Square, but the opportunity presented by the Great Fire of London for the large-scale replanning of the city was not followed up.

The Great Fire of September 1666 destroyed 13,200 houses, 87 parish churches, St Paul's Cathedral and the Royal Exchange, making perhaps 200,000 people homeless. It was a national disaster on an unprecedented scale and the greatest single opportunity for urban replanning before 1939. The Act for Rebuilding, passed in the February of 1667, laid down stringent regulations for the new houses which were to replace the old. They were to be in brick or stone. Wood, save for window casements and doors, was banned from exteriors. There were to be four kinds of houses, and detailed provision was made in the Act for the number of storeys, the interior heights of the rooms, the thickness of the walls, and the scantling of interior timbers for all save the fourth kind of house, 'mansion houses . . . of the greates bignes'.

Charles II took great interest in the rebuilding and at first was in favour of a completely new plan. Dr Wren, John Evelyn, and at least four others drew up new ground plans, but as the scale of the disaster began to be more fully appreciated they were abandoned in the face of the urgent need to rehouse people as quickly as possible and to start business going again. That the city was largely rebuilt in its old form tells us a great deal about the balance of power in Restoration Britain.

The new London which emerged from the rubble and the ash proved to be immensely influential, and the rows of solid, commodious brick-built terraced houses which began to appear were echoed in many other towns in Restoration Britain. At the same time a variety of attempts, tentative and small-scale, were being made to improve the appearance of towns. Cambridge, Ipswich, and Windsor obtained Acts of Parliament in 1554, 1571, and 1585 respectively to pave their streets. A public walk was laid out in Exeter in 1612 at the Northernhay, and an arcaded walk was built in Reading in 1620. A public garden, called the Prospect, was laid out in Ross-on-Wye at the very end of the seventeenth century, and in 1719 the municipal authorities in York planted trees to 'beautify' the Lord Mayor's Walk, which lay just outside the city walls. Bowling greens were also constructed in many towns; there were seven in Cambridge in 1688. It seems very likely that at least some quarters in some towns in late seventeenth-century Britain were marginally cleaner, sweeter-smelling, safer and more comfortable to live in than they had been in the opening decades of the sixteenth century.

The chapters in this book on the medieval landscape were preoccupied with place-names, fields and farms, towns, churches, and monasteries, and certainly the pages given over to the last two kinds of buildings reflect the concern of so much medieval thought and speculation with religious beliefs and practices. This is not however to deny the presence of industry and manufacture in the medieval landscape, although it is probably better to speak only of manufacture, in its literal sense of being concerned with things made by hand, rather than of industry, with its late twentieth-century overtones of factories, mass production, and crowds of workers. Things were made during the medieval centuries: locks and hinges, weapons and implements, bricks, tiles, pottery, glass, and textiles, and coal, iron, and clay were mined or quarried, but it was all done on a small-scale domestic, hand-made level. It is unfortunately the nature of all mining and manufacturing enterprises to destroy the evidence for their earliest beginnings. This means that although the sites of many medieval forges, furnaces, and quarries of every kind are known, almost nothing remains visible above ground. The sixteenth and seventeenth centuries saw a number of important technical advances, but even at the end of the seventeenth century many manufactures, textiles for example, and nail making, remained essentially domestic in their organization. The largest industrial enterprise in Britain at the end of the seventeenth century was the royal naval dockyard at Chatham, employing about 1,500 men during King William's wars with France.

Coal is to be found at or near the surface in many parts of Britain, and it has been worked since Roman times. Much surface coal was mined by sinking open, bell-shaped pits into the seam, or else by digging into the hillside. The earliest pits were comparatively shallow, perhaps no more than 20 feet deep. During the course of the sixteenth and seventeenth centuries the pits went deeper and deeper, reaching over 150 feet by the 1690s. This meant that coal-mining was becoming progressively more complex, more technically demanding and also more dangerous. Pit shafts were square, and lined with timber. Both men and coal were brought to the surface by means of a windlass turned by up to four men or else a horse. Ventilation and drainage presented increasingly demanding problems. Sometimes a separate shaft was dug and a fire lit at the bottom to provide an updraught of hot air. This could be fairly effective but increased enormously the risk of explosion from igniting fire damp. Flooding was also a serious problem. It was sometimes possible to drive an adit from the lowest point in the mine to an outfall lower down a hillside so that water would drain away by the force of gravity. Sometimes men or horses turned a wheel to hoist buckets to the surface, but such devices were very inefficient and expensive to maintain. In the 1650s the Marquess of Worcester was experimenting with a steam-engine to pump out water from his mines at Raglan, but without success. It was not until the very end of the seventeenth century that the combined efforts of Savery and Newcomen overcame the technical problems involved and it was only in 1712 that the first working steam-engine anywhere in the world was built to pump out a coal-mine near Dudley in Staffordshire. It was grossly inefficient, using about a quarter of 1 per cent of the thermal power of the coal it burned in its furnace, and it kept breaking down, but it was also very much more powerful than any man- or horse-driven pump, and when it was working it could go for days on end. It was the harbinger of an entirely new world and an entirely new landscape.

The other great problem facing coal-mine owners was transport. Land carriage costs could double the price of coal over 10 miles, and those pits near navigable water had an immense advantage over more inland ones. One solution was a railway, an idea almost certainly imported from Germany. By 1598 a railway, with rails made of wood and the wagons pulled by horses, was running from the coal pits of Sir Francis Willoughby at Wollaton in Nottinghamshire down to a wharf on the Trent. By the end of the seventeenth century they were quite common in British coalfields, by which time, too, coal was being widely used as a fuel in such industries as salt boiling, brick, tile and glass making, brewing and dyeing, as well as for domestic purposes. It could not however yet be used in iron making.

Coal-mining was probably the most important extractive industry in Britain in the sixteenth and seventeenth centuries. It was by no means the only one. Clays, sands, and other minerals are widely distributed over Britain and formed the basis of a number of important manufactures.

Brick, pottery, and tile manufacture was very extensive, and it is clear that pottery manufacture was very much more widespread than the standard histories of the industry, with their emphasis upon Burslem and the Wedgwoods, would have us believe. Thus there were in Essex in 1595 at least forty-six pottery and tile kilns at work, and there is no reason to believe Essex to have been particularly favoured or unusual. There is even evidence to suggest regional and local specializations: thus kilns in Cornwall, Devon, and south Wales made large earthenware pots in which pilchards were preserved, and Burslem first began to acquire a more than purely local importance when it started to supply butter pots to the market at Uttoxeter.

Important technical developments took place in pottery manufacture during this period. A round single-flue kiln, perhaps 6 feet in diameter and about 8 feet high, built of stone bonded with clay and lagged with turf, had been in use for centuries. From the second half of the seventeenth century such kilns were being housed in a permanent brick or stone bottle-shaped structure fired with coal wherever possible. These bottle kilns became ever larger and more numerous until they dominated the skyline of the pottery towns of north Staffordshire in the nineteenth century, only to disappear almost completely in the years since 1945.

Glass making was another industry that grew rapidly throughout the period covered in this chapter. Glass furnaces in the middle years of the sixteenth century were perhaps 12 to 20 feet long and 6 or 7 feet wide, with projecting wings at each corner. Glass needs to be heated three times during its manufacture, and it seems likely that all three processes were carried out in the same furnace. Glass furnaces were first established in Surrey and Sussex, and then they spread to London, Staffordshire,

Gloucestershire and Herefordshire and the Stour valley, and in due course to Newcastle-upon-Tyne. Much of the technical knowledge and skilled labour was provided by immigrant craftsmen, especially from Normandy and Lorraine. By the end of the seventeenth century the timber-framed structure which housed the furnace was being replaced by the cone-shaped brick building which became the typical glasshouse of the eighteenth century.

Brick, tile, and glass manufacture contributed enormously to the successive waves of building and rebuilding which swept over Britain in the sixteenth and seventeenth centuries, making living conditions increasingly warmer, more convenient and undoubtedly very much cleaner. Perhaps their greatest achievement was the rebuilding of London after the Great Fire.

Iron manufacture was transformed during the sixteenth and seventeenth centuries by the spread of one of the most important technical advances ever to take place in the industry. This was the introduction of the blast furnace. The first one to be built in Britain was erected at Newbridge, in Sussex, in 1496. By the end of the seventeenth century the blast furnace was a tall, square structure of masonry, well over 20 feet high. It was fed at the top with charcoal and iron ore by men wheeling barrows up an inclined slope. As the fuel was consumed and the iron melted so the charge moved slowly down the shaft of the furnace to meet the blast of heat from the hearth at the bottom. Here it was tapped from time to time, the molten iron running out into moulds of sand to produce pigs, or bars, of iron. This was cast iron, and with a carbon content of anything up to 5 per cent it was extremely brittle. It had to be reheated and then hammered to remove the impurities. This was done in a forge. Almost from the beginning both furnace and forge were water-powered in that a pair of bellows operated by a waterwheel was used to provide the blast of air required to reach the necessary temperatures. A waterwheel was also used to power the hammers in the forge. The operations in furnace and forge were quite distinct. Sometimes they were carried out on the same site, sometimes on quite separate ones.

Thus the first need of the iron industry was water power. The second was for plentiful supplies of wood to make into charcoal. This was the only fuel which could be used since coal contained so many impurities that iron made in coal-fired furnaces was unusable. Endless experiments were carried out during this period to use coal, but it was only in 1709 that Abraham Darby, in his furnace at Coalbrookdale, at last succeeded in using it successfully, and then only after he had converted the coal into coke. Supplies of iron were only the third, and the least important, constraint upon the industry at this period. When all three factors came together, as in the Sussex Weald, then blast furnaces and forges were quickly established and became highly successful. There was plenty of

59   The furnace at Coalbrookdale in which Abraham Darby succeeded, in 1709, in using coke to smelt iron.

wood, which could be coppiced to produce a regular supply of charcoal, and there was, then, also plenty of iron. Small streams were dammed to produce a head of water that would drive the all-important bellows. A survey of 1574 lists forty-nine furnaces and fifty-eight forges. Only seven furnaces were outside the Weald. In the second half of the sixteenth century the industry spread rapidly, to Cannock Chase, to Glamorganshire, West Bromwich, Sheffield, Rievaulx, and, by 1610, to the shores of Loch Maree in the Highlands, always to spots where wood and water came together in abundance.

Although the furnace itself was of necessity built of stone and lined with brick, the ancillary buildings were almost always timber-framed with thatched roofs, even the gallery and covering to the mouth of the furnace itself. Sheds for storing charcoal, iron ore and tools and equipment, together with houses for the workmen, formed part of the furnace or forge complex. Fires must have been common occurrences, from sparks and burning debris and from insufficiently quenched charcoal in storage sheds. When in operation, and furnaces were generally fired during the winter months, they would remain in blast for weeks on end. The site must have been noisy, very hot, and smoke-filled to an almost unbearable degree, as well as very dangerous. Nevertheless it was all, in modern terms, on a very small scale. A dozen men could keep a furnace in blast.

Of all this almost nothing now remains visible above ground. The sites of numerous furnaces and forges are known precisely. They are marked today by heaps of slag, the footings of the furnace and perhaps a little of the stone work, as at Upper Soudley in the Forest of Dean, by silted watercourses and above all, especially in the Weald, by the hammer ponds, made by damming small streams to create a reservoir of power to drive the bellows. The woods have grown around them again, as at Hawkings Pond, Mannings Heath, in Sussex, and at other sites there is a string of such ponds, as at Wakeners Wells, on the Hampshire/ Sussex border, but their tranquillity today makes it almost impossible for a modern observer to re-create mentally the heat, noise, and fumes which once must have surrounded them.

There was a great deal of activity in the mining of non-ferrous metals in the sixteenth and seventeenth centuries, especially tin, lead, zinc, and copper. Much time and money was spent, and much was wasted, since veins of these metals occur very erratically, and their exploitation was fraught with problems and difficulties, often beyond the technology of the time. Two companies were established by Royal Charter in 1568 to mine these minerals. The first, the Company of Mines Royal, was established to search for gold, silver, and copper in Wales and the north of England. It had some initial success in opening up a copper mine near Keswick, bringing in German miners to provide the technical skills, but the mines could not be made to pay, their buildings and equipment were destroyed by Parliamentary soldiers in 1651 and the location of the mine was then very quickly forgotten. The second, the Society of Mineral and Battery Works, was established to introduce the manufacture of brass and iron sheeting into England and to search for copper and zinc outside the areas assigned to the Company of Mines Royal. It built a works for making and drawing wire at Tintern. This took a long time to become properly established, and in 1646 the iron master Thomas Foley took over its management. It was quite prosperous by the end of the seventeenth century and it did not finally close until the end of the nineteenth. Eventually, following a lawsuit over the opening of a lead and silver mine at Bwlch yr Esgairhir, the two companies lost their monopolies. They merged in 1710, and after an insurance group took a controlling interest they embarked upon a new career as the Royal Exchange Assurance.

Much lead and tin mining, in spite of the monopolies of these two companies, was in the hands of small-scale miners who were often also farmers. This is particularly true of Derbyshire and the Mendips. In the High Peak and Wirksworth districts the miners were closely regulated under their own ancient customs. Individuals searched for veins of lead, and when one was found it was registered with an official called the Barmaster, and all disputes were settled in a special court called the Barmoot. The veins, or 'rakes', exploited in this way snaked across the Derbyshire moors, sometimes petering out within yards, sometimes going on for a mile or more. The miners followed the veins by digging pits in close succession, and trails of disused pits and spoil heaps around Winster, Bonsall, Sheldon, and so on remain today as evidence of the efforts of these men. Lead mining in the Mendips was organized in a rather similar fashion and has, around Priddy for example, left similar scars in the landscape.

Mines, whether for coal, tin, or lead, got deeper and deeper during the course of the sixteenth and seventeenth centuries. Furnaces and forges became larger and larger. Glasshouses and pottery kilns developed their own specialized forms. The end-result was a marked improvement in the standard of living of many of the inhabitants of Britain. By the end of the seventeenth century an enormously varied range of metal goods of every kind, of pottery, cutlery, and glass, whether wine glasses, tea cups, or scissors, was available, and available very cheaply. In the first decades of the eighteenth century some of the most serious technical problems would be solved: steam power was adapted to pumping out mines and the secret of using coal for smelting iron was at last discovered, although use of the process spread only very slowly. But in spite of these innovations and in spite of the astonishing increase in the range and variety of manufactured goods, much remained unchanged from an older, medieval world. Most industrial buildings were still timber-framed and thatched. Much still depended upon human or animal muscle, or else upon wind and water power. Horses still met almost all of the energy demands of the period. They pulled carts, wagons, and ploughs. They plodded patiently round in circles to wind up men and coal from ever greater depths. They pulled barges. They carried messengers, post boys, news, and letters. Both windmills and water-mills were very common features of lowland Britain at this time. Most parishes had one of each kind, and many had two or three. They ground corn. Their machinery had been adapted to grind rape seed for its oil, and flint for the pottery industry. Waterwheels provided the power to drive bellows and hammers in iron furnaces and forges, to crush and smelt tin ore, to make paper, saw timber, and grind the constituents of gunpowder. During the seventeenth century windmills appear in increasing numbers to pump the water from fenland drainage schemes. Both windmills and water-mills were indispensable and ubiquitous in the landscape and they retained their place until the early twentieth century.

Landscape is the autobiography of society. It reflects every aspect of the social and economic preoccupations of successive generations of men. It also reflects, equally vividly, their moral and spiritual values, and changes therein. The sixteenth and seventeenth centuries are marked by particularly profound and radical changes in the patterns of men's beliefs and ideals, and these in turn are echoed in the landscape. We have seen some of these new ideas at work on the design and form of buildings, as from the ferment that is the Renaissance the concepts of form and balance and symmetry in architecture took increasing hold of men's minds. The second grouping of these profoundly radical ideas is summed up in the word Reformation. Under its impact buildings which had expressed some of the highest ideals of the human spirit were devalued into quarries for building materials.

During the course of the middle ages men went to extraordinary lengths to give physical expression to their view of a moral, spiritual, eternal world lying beyond the perils and miseries of this one. The spiritual crises of Martin Luther prompted a profound reappraisal of this pattern of values. His demand that men should place their trust in the infinite mercies of God meant that the forest of intercessary practices which had developed about the medieval Catholic Church suddenly became unnecessary, and indeed represented a barrier to salvation. Pilgrimages, chantries, masses for the dead, the relics of saints, even the monastic ideal, were all irrelevant. It was the individual conscience which was all-important, the Bible its only guide. Almost from the first some reformers saw that this implied a literate laity, vernacular translations of the Bible and religious toleration. It also exposed the considerable wealth of the monasteries to the rapacity of those with the will to seize it.

Monastic houses had been dissolved before in England, notably the alien priories at the time of Henry V and those closed by Cardinal Wolsey to endow his school at Ipswich and his college in Oxford. Nevertheless, in the 1530s there were 502 monasteries, 136 nunneries, and 187 friaries in England, many quite poor and with few members, but many also well-endowed with extensive landed estates, although it is now impossible to arrive at accurate estimates of this wealth.

This is not the place to examine the causes and progress of the Reformation in England, or the mix of motives which led to the dissolution of the monasteries. It is sufficient to say that the financial difficulties of Henry VIII in the 1530s undoubtedly played a large part, and it is not without significance that within weeks of the passing in 1536 of the Act dissolving those monasteries with an annual income from lands of under £200, another Act was passed for the establishment of 'a certain court commonly to be called the Court of the Augmentations of the Revenues of the King's Crown'. The Act for dissolving the remaining monasteries was passed in 1539. The friaries were never formally abolished. Instead a visitation was carried out during the course of 1538 and 1539 and their voluntary surrender was actively encouraged. None could resist the scarcely veiled pressure.

As individual houses surrendered an inventory was made of the movable goods, much of which was sold locally. Plate and jewels were sent to the Master of the King's Jewel House, most of it to be melted down for the bullion. The lead was stripped from the conventual buildings and this also was melted down, usually on site because of the weight. The buildings themselves were often defaced in order to make them unusable. It was assumed from the beginning that almost everything was for sale, including the landed possession of the monasteries. There does not seem to have been any real scramble for monastic lands, nor did the Crown give very much away. Almost all was sold at the prevailing price for land, twenty years' purchase, that is twenty times the assessed annual value, although this assessment was often based upon out-of-date rent rolls. Nor does the sale of so much land appear to have depressed prices to any great extent. By 1547 the Crown had disposed of some two-thirds of monastic lands, and almost all had gone by the time of James I. Had the Crown resisted the temptation to treat capital as income then it would have acquired an immense source of extra-Parliamentary revenue, and the course of history in the seventeenth century might have been very different.

The fate of the monastic buildings varied enormously. The fourteen monastic cathedrals, including Canterbury, Norwich, and Durham, were secularized. New dioceses were created at Chester, Oxford, Peterborough, Gloucester, and Bristol on the basis of monastic foundations. A sixth, at Westminster, lasted only ten years. About a hundred monastic churches became, or continued to be, parish churches, the corporation at Tewkesbury paying £403 for one of the most splendid Norman churches in England. Other monastic buildings were converted into private residences. At Titchfield Sir Thomas Wriothesley rebuilt the nave of the church as a gatehouse and turned the frater into the great hall of his new house. At Newstead the cloistral buildings were converted into a private dwelling. At Fountains the magnificent conventual buildings were stripped of everything saleable and what was left was used as a quarry from which to build a new house, Fountains Hall.

In England and Wales the death of the monasteries was fairly swift. In Scotland it was much more protracted. Scottish monasteries were already in a sorry state owing to the practice of commendation, under which the revenues of a house were granted to some powerful lay figure. He was then expected to allow the monks a 'portion', but this was invariably far too small even for everyday expenses. Buildings were neglected and their decay was aggravated by a succession of English invasions in the early years of the sixteenth century. Jedburgh was burnt in 1523 and 1544, Holyrood in 1547, Melrose in 1545. By the time the Scottish Crown annexed the monasteries in 1587 there was little left. Much of their property was already in lay hands and most of the buildings were empty. The monks were not turned out; they were instead forbidden to recruit

new members. There was not the concerted attack upon monastic buildings
that there was in England, however, with the result that for many Scottish
monasteries much of their ancient fabric remains in the landscape today.
No English town, for example, is dominated in the same way as Jedburgh is
by the ruins of its abbey.

In this way, and within a comparatively short period of time, buildings
which had for generations been an integral part of the landscape and the
focus for the devotion and piety, not only of their members but also of
many lay men and women, lost their meaning. The other religious
buildings in the landscape, churches and cathedrals, could however be
more easily adapted to the new requirements, and they did not suffer to the
same extent as the monasteries.

By the end of the fifteenth century Britain was well stocked with
churches and comparatively few new ones were added during the sixteenth and seventeenth centuries. Those which were came from two
directions. First of all there were those provided for new parishes created
to meet population change. This is particularly apparent in London,
where new parishes were carved out of old ones in both the West End
and the East End to meet the needs of expanding suburbs. Thus St
Paul's, Covent Garden, and St Anne's, Soho, were both created out of St

60   The Quaker Meeting House at Alston, Cumberland, built in 1732.

Martin-in-the-Fields, and Wapping and Shadwell were created out of Stepney. All were provided with new churches.

The second direction from which new churches came was the consequence of the religious controversies of the period and the slow emergence of the idea of religious toleration. Nonconformist meeting houses began to appear early in the seventeenth century. There is a Baptist chapel dating from 1623 in Tewkesbury, and another of about 1653 in Loughwood, near Axminster. By the end of the seventeenth century they had become quite numerous, and toleration was being extended yet further. The Jewish synagogue at Bevis Marks, in London, was built in 1700.

The repair and rebuilding of existing churches was however an almost continuous process throughout the period. Many were obviously poorly maintained and roofs seem to have been leaking almost permanently. Storms often caused great damage. The spire of Buckingham Church, for example, was blown down in 1699 and never rebuilt. The Civil War also brought destruction and damage to individual churches, but the greatest single outburst of church rebuilding followed a natural disaster, the Great Fire of London. In all, eighty-seven churches and old St Paul's were destroyed. An Act of Parliament of 1670 increased the tax on coal coming into London to pay for the rebuilding of fifty-one churches, since a number of parishes were amalgamated. The work was to be supervised by three Commissioners, the Archbishop of Canterbury, the Bishop of London, and the Lord Mayor, with Dr Christopher Wren as Surveyor General. For the next forty years Wren drew plans, saw to the making of wooden models, supervised masons and bricklayers and checked accounts. From his marvellously inventive mind came a succession of plans, each one unique, each one fitting a church into an often awkward and difficult site. By 1686 most of the work on the churches was completed, although he continued to design and build steeples for several years. Work continued on St Paul's Cathedral until 1711. This was his masterpiece, and one of the finest buildings of any kind or of any age, a serene, harmonious embodiment of the principles of classical architecture reproduced in the heart of late seventeenth-century London.

The Reformation also brought important changes into the provision of education in Britain in the sixteenth and seventeenth centuries, and again these changes find their reflection in the landscape. The reformers were from the first aware of the importance of education for the proper instruction of children in the principles of true religion, and the need for a properly educated clergy if this true, reformed religion was to be protected from its enemies. From the 1550s many individuals and institutions, particularly town councils, sought to establish new schools with these objectives in mind, and the movement continued well into the seventeenth century. Some were certainly refoundations of medieval schools attached

61   The school at Tuxford, Nottinghamshire, founded by Charles Read in 1669.

to chantries, institutions which were abolished by Act of Parliament in 1547 because they represented beliefs now regarded as superstitious. Others were founded from local pride as well as individual piety. Many of these new schools were provided with purpose-built accommodation, as at Shrewsbury for example, founded in 1552, or Blundells School at Tiverton and that at Guildford, where splendid buildings surrounding a courtyard were completed in about 1586.

The universities of Oxford and Cambridge were seen as bulwarks in the defence of the reformed religion. Their statutes and curricula were revised, the study of Greek was introduced and that of canon law dropped. Henry VIII founded Trinity College, Cambridge, in 1546 'for the increasing of pure Christian religion, the extirpation of error and the education of youth in piety and knowledge'. Emmanuel College, Cambridge, was founded with the express purpose of training clergymen, and its statutes were taken as the model for those of Sidney Sussex College, founded in 1589. University education became increasingly sought-after in the years before 1640, and there was much building and rebuilding to accommodate the new students, at Wadham College, Oxford, for example, founded in 1610, and at Gonville and Caius College, Cambridge, refounded in 1559. Sir Christopher Wren made his own contribution to both universities,

62 The Sheldonian Theatre, Oxford, and the first architectural design of Sir Christopher Wren. It was provided by Archbishop Sheldon to serve as a centre for university ceremonies. On the left is the Clarendon Building, designed by Nicholas Hawksmoor and built from the profits from the publication of Clarendon's *History of the Great Rebellion*, published in 1702–4. On the right is the original Ashmolean Museum, built between 1678 and 1683.

designing the Sheldonian Theatre at Oxford and the library at Trinity College, Cambridge, completed in 1684 and one of his most satisfying masterpieces.

The history of schools and universities in Scotland is quite different. Most burghs in Scotland had a grammar school, encouraged by an Act of the Scottish Parliament of 1496. Scottish reformers were as aware as those in England of the importance of education in the defence of the reformed religion. *The First Book of Discipline* of 1560 called for a schoolmaster to be attached to every church. In 1616 the Scottish Privy Council called for the establishment of a school in every parish, and another Act of the Scottish Parliament in 1696 required the building of a schoolmaster's house. Nevertheless, in spite of these measures, schools spread only very slowly over Lowland Scotland and were almost entirely absent from the Highlands. School buildings were often small and thatched, although, in contrast, Edinburgh Royal High School moved into substantial stone buildings in 1578. There were five universities in Scotland in this period, in contrast to the two in England. St Andrews was founded in 1411 and Glasgow in 1451, to be virtually refounded in 1577 by Andrew Melville. There were two in Aberdeen, founded in 1494 and 1593, although they were both very small, and Edinburgh was established in 1582. That at Edinburgh was very much under the control of the town council, which appointed the staff, decided upon the courses, granted the degrees and provided much of the accommodation, both for the students and for the university.

In these ways the spiritual crisis of Martin Luther brought profound changes into British landscapes. Monasteries, chantries, and friaries as institutions ceased to exist. Their buildings were demolished, converted into other uses or allowed to fall into ruins. The fanaticism of many of the first reformers produced its own long, slow reaction, and religious toleration was at last reluctantly accepted, a development leading to its own building forms, as Nonconformist and Dissenting chapels made their quiet, self-effacing appearance in the landscape, whilst the need to defend the new beliefs led to the provision of new schools and of new university and college buildings. At the same time, those new churches which were built, and they are more numerous than at first would appear, incorporated those newly rediscovered principles of classical architecture first embodied in the Banqueting House of Inigo Jones. Thus a church like St James's, Piccadilly, fuses together on one site two of the three movements in ideals and values to be found in the centuries covered in this chapter, those embodied in the words Renaissance and Reformation, since in the harmony of its design and in the detail of its interior decoration it reveals the mastery of its architect, Sir Christopher Wren, over the principles of classical architecture, and in the absence of a chancel it is witness to the demands of the new, reformed religion for congregational participation in the act of worship and the emphasis which it gave to a preaching ministry.

The third intellectual and spiritual movement of the sixteenth and seventeenth centuries, the Scientific Revolution, is slower to make its impact upon the landscape, but it is the one which has had the most profound long-term implications, since it is the consequences which have flowed from it which have shaped the landscape of the late twentieth century.

The medieval world picture outlined in the previous chapter was under increasing strain from the second half of the sixteenth century, and by the end of the seventeenth it had been replaced by an entirely new one. It was undermined from several directions. The great voyages of discovery opened up entirely new mental as well as physical horizons. Here was a world of men, animals, and plants hitherto quite unknown. Men could clearly survive a journey through the torrid zone. The new animals and plants prompted renewed curiosity about those in Europe. The new plants were much sought-after for their medicinal qualities, and botanical gardens were established to further this study. The one founded in Oxford in 1621 still survives. The collection and study of plants, animals, fossils, and curiosities of every kind became increasingly systematic, and in 1683 the first English museum was opened, the Ashmolean, in Oxford. Many traditional assumptions about the natural world were thrown into confusion by the new discoveries, and new attitudes slowly emerged, including the idea of a sympathetic rather than a hostile Nature.

The voyages of discovery also prompted renewed interest in map-making, in astronomical observations and in mathematics, and this for purely practical reasons. If sailors were to return from their new-found lands, or even to find them again, then they would have to learn to navigate their ships accurately. At the same time the ferment of ideas produced by the Renaissance placed increasing emphasis upon man as the centre of the world and master of his own destiny, whilst the Reformation shattered for ever many traditional certainties of religious belief.

By about 1512 Copernicus had arrived at the conclusion that the earth revolved round the sun. He spent the next thirty years making increasingly accurate and careful observations, still with the naked eye, of the movements of the planets and the stars. When he finally published his work, in 1543, as *De Revolutionibus,* his heliocentric theory was largely ignored, but his observations and measurements were quickly adopted. By the end of the sixteenth century a succession of brilliant astronomers had established the truth of his theory. Tycho Brahe, Galileo, and Kepler completed the destruction of the traditional world picture, Tycho Brahe unwittingly, Galileo and Kepler fully conscious of what they were doing. Galileo, by discovering with the telescope which he had made for himself the satellite moons of Jupiter, shook to the foundations the authority of Aristotle, who did not know of them; and Kepler, following an astonishing intellectual feat, realized that the paths of the planets through the skies were eliptical about the sun, not circular about the earth. The traditional world picture was now under serious threat and its guardian, the Church, moved to its defence. In 1616 the theory that the earth together with the other plants moved round the sun was declared heretical and the writings of Copernicus were placed upon the Index.

It was left to Sir Isaac Newton to construct a new world picture. His *Principia Mathematica* was published in 1687. It was the force of gravity which kept the earth and the planets swinging for ever in their paths about the sun, and the solar system was itself but one small part of an infinite universe. Only very slowly could the full implications of endless time and infinite space be accepted, and Newton himself still found room for an Intelligent Agent as the moving spirit in the new world picture, and for much of his working life he took a keen interest in alchemy. There is never a clean break between the old and the new.

The revolution in astronomy was matched and complemented in a thousand more mundane and practical ways. Astronomers found their mathematics eased beyond measure by the rapid adoption of Arabic as opposed to Roman numerals. Decimals were devised and published as a system in 1585. Logarithms were invented in 1614, and within ten years were being calculated to fourteen decimal places. These advances meant that surveying and map-making became more accurate, and the pictorial element rapidly disappeared from maps and plans. Estate maps of remarkable detail and accuracy were being made by the end of the sixteenth century, and the first road maps designed specifically for travellers were published by John Ogilby in his *Britannia* in 1675, all meaning that men were looking at their world with a fresh eye, an approach reinforced by the discovery of the rules of perspective by Italian painters in the fifteenth century.

Men slowly learned to think in new ways: to measure, observe, weigh, and experiment rather than to rely upon tradition and authority. St Thomas Aquinas was interested in the laws of motion. Objects, he thought, move because they are in a state of potentiality, and since everything seeks to perfect itself, objects will move in a straight line towards their own proper goal in order to achieve this perfection. That everything had a purpose was the essence of the medieval world view. Galileo, through an intellectual wrench which it is almost impossible now fully to appreciate, ignored all this, and after repeated measurement arrived at a mathematical formula to express the acceleration of moving bodies. A quantitative approach to the world replaced a qualitative one. From this new mental attitude gradually emerged the idea that it might be possible to improve the lot of men during their lives here on earth. This was the great contribution of Francis Bacon. A propagandist rather than a scientist, he urged that mechanical and practical arts should be employed 'to the endowment and benefit of man's life'. The Royal Society was founded in 1662 largely to give expression to his ideas and for many years it adopted enthusiastically numerous utilitarian and practical projects, some genuinely useful, others undoubtedly trivial. It also assumed a vague responsibility for the management of the Royal Observatory, founded at Greenwich in 1675 and provided with buildings by Sir Christopher Wren, the first significant manifestation of the Scientific Revolution in the landscape.

The organization and structure of the British landscape changed profoundly during the hundred and fifty years covered in this chapter. Many open fields were enclosed, forests felled, and marshes drained. But many more still remained open, unfelled and undrained. New furnaces and forges appeared, and there was much domestic rebuilding in both town and country. The despoliation of religious buildings, especially monasteries, was completed during the early part of the period, but new types began to make their appearance towards its end. Continuity remains the hallmark of the landscape, although the tempo of change is noticeably quickening. The really significant changes occur in men's values, attitudes, and vision of their environment, changes in which the ferment of the Renaissance, Reformation, and Scientific Revolution are given physical expression, whether in the symmetrical façade of some country house, the quiet unassuming anonymity of a brick-built Nonconformist chapel, or the increasing accuracy with which the strips of an open field could be surveyed and mapped. Once again however the extent of the changes must not be exaggerated. It is impossible to measure the depth of the penetration of the new ideas. Palladianism did not lead everywhere to a total rebuilding of the housing stock of seventeenth-century Britain, and in any case it will in due course itself be rejected. Monastic ruins, reviled as symbols of superstitious tyranny, will in time come to be valued for their picturesque qualities. By the end of the seventeenth century, many educated men had come to reject witchcraft, but astrology still exercises a powerful fascination over many minds, even today.

8

Georgian Britain

This chapter covers a period in which the pace of change begins to accelerate across the entire fabric of the landscape of Britain. It is a period which begins with the building of the first steam-engine, for pumping water from a coal-mine at Dudley in Worcestershire, in 1712. These engines were at first stationary, grossly inefficient and could be used only for pumping. But technical improvements accumulated so rapidly that within little more than a hundred years steam-engines could provide rotary motion and their weight and size had been so reduced that they could be mounted on wheels. The period closes with the building of the first railway, in 1830, using steam-powered locomotives and carrying both passengers and goods.

It is important, however, not to exaggerate either the pace or the extent of these changes. There was in 1712 only one working steam-engine throughout the whole of Britain, and indeed throughout the world, and however much, from the vantage point of the late twentieth century, it may appear to symbolize the beginnings of the industrial revolution and all that this means, in fact change took place only very slowly and its impact remained diffuse and uneven. Patterns of life in both town and country altered only in a particularistic, small-scale, local fashion, although for the individuals concerned the consequences could often be far-reaching. In the opening years of the eighteenth century it is probably true to say that no more than a quarter of the inhabitants of Britain lived in towns. Only in 1851 are there for the first time more people in towns than in the country and even then it is by no more than the narrowest of margins, 51 per cent to 49 per cent, figures that may serve as very crude indicators of the slow, localized and very uneven spread of the changes that the first steam-engines inaugurated.

The protracted nature of the processes at work is nowhere more apparent than in the organization of the rural landscape. Those traditional structures for the cultivation of the land that we have looked at in previous chapters continued in many individual villages and townships without interruption and with scarcely any perceptible change. Villages such as Padbury and Maids Moreton, both in north Buckinghamshire, are classic examples of open-field communities, with three or four great fields stretching on all sides to the parish boundaries and with only very restricted areas of common waste, meadow, and woodland. They remained almost entirely unchanged until the very end of the eighteenth century, when the passing of a private Act of Parliament for their enclosure brought, within four or five years, a complete remodelling of their landscapes. In neighbouring villages, however, piecemeal change, affecting in some years no more than two or three acres and in others two or three hundred, had been going on for centuries. Both Padbury and Maids Moreton must have seemed slightly old-fashioned in the last years of the eighteenth century.

The most important single process making for change in the rural landscape was enclosure. We have seen in previous chapters that enclosure within individual townships and parishes had been going on at least since the thirteenth century, and we have seen too that it could be prompted by a variety of motives and carried out in a variety of ways. By the end of the seventeenth century it is likely that enclosure by agreement amongst all the parties concerned, followed usually by an enrolment of the agreement in the records of one of the courts of law, had become the most usual method in England, and it continued to be used in isolated instances until the early years of the nineteenth century.

By the early years of the eighteenth century the disadvantages of enclosure by agreement were becoming apparent. The agreement of everyone was necessary, it could be disputed in a court of law, even a generation or more later, and so instead recourse was had to a private Act of Parliament. Between the first, for Radipole in Dorset, of 1604, and the last, passed in 1914, there were in all 5,265 enclosure Acts for England, affecting a little over 6¾ million acres of land, almost 21 per cent of the total area. The most important periods for the passing of these Acts were the years from 1760 to 1780, and then from 1793 to 1815, during which two periods 80 per cent of all enclosure Acts were passed.

Parliamentary enclosure brought about the third replanning of the English rural landscape. It affected commons, waste, moorland, and fen as well as arable. Of the total acreage affected, some 2,307,000 acres were in fact common and waste, not arable. Each Act had to be promoted by a group of proprietors for the lands of a single parish or township. There was never any form of government control over the movement and open-field agriculture has never formally been abolished. There could be, and often was, considerable opposition, usually on the part of small proprietors, unconvinced of the benefits and only too well aware of the costs. In

Figure 14 Islip, Oxfordshire, after enclosure

Quainton, Buckinghamshire, for example, opposition held up the passing of the enclosure Act for almost forty years, from 1801, when it was first proposed, until 1840, when it was at last passed.

Each Act appointed a small group of commissioners and gave them considerable powers. They had to reallocate land held in small strips scattered the length and breadth of the parish into compact blocks. They could straighten, or close, old roads, and lay out new ones. They could allocate lands for use as sand or gravel quarries. The Act itself often laid down detailed regulations for the construction of roads, fences, gates, and hedges. The enclosure commissioners could apportion costs among the new proprietors, and levy a rate to pay their own expenses. Parliamentary enclosure commissioners have been much reviled, unjustly, because all the evidence points to their having carried out their duties with scrupulous attention to the legal rights of all concerned. Individual commissioners often had extensive practices, and were frequently on five or six commissions at any one time. They must count as among the most influential of all of those who have shaped the English landscape, and yet as individuals they remain almost anonymous.

Within two or three years of the passing of the Act the landscape of the parish concerned could be transformed. An open, bare landscape of huge fields divided into furlongs and strips but lacking any extensive fencing or hedges, had been divided up into compact, rectangular blocks marked off by straight fences in which young hawthorn seedlings were already becoming established. Roads were straight, often with wide grass verges. At the same time new farmsteads were already appearing on sites away from the village since it was now more convenient for individual farmers to have their houses and farm buildings in the middle of their farms, which were now compact blocks of land surrounded with a ring fence, than to stay in the village. Where this enclosure was part of a long-term policy of estate improvement, as on the Norfolk estates of Thomas Coke of Holkham for instance, then by standardizing the layout of farm buildings and by insisting that farmhouses and cottages should have distinctive decorative features, a landlord could give an unmistakable character to his estates, a process reinforced by the appearance of architects who specialized in farm buildings.

Enclosure and improvement became both profitable and fashionable in the last decades of the eighteenth century, but it was by no means the exclusive prerogative of the great landlord. Many smaller proprietors were also well aware of the benefits that enclosure could bring. Nor did it produce mass unemployment or migration. The new roads, hedges, fences, and farm buildings provided a great deal of employment, and it is the 1840s and 1850s before rural depopulation really begins.

In Scotland enclosure and improvement were entirely the work of the landlord. His task was both more difficult and easier than that of his contemporaries in England. It was more difficult because the Scottish terrain is steeper and rougher. Soils were often thin, acid, and water-logged. Boulders were strewn everywhere. The climate is harsher. Scottish roads were very much worse than those in England and wheeled traffic was almost unknown outside the towns. Finally, there was no long tradition of agricultural improvement in Scotland as there was in England. On the other hand there were fewer obstacles: very few trees, no well-built cottages or roads, no rights of common of pasture over the arable, and the landlord himself could abolish run-rig. Thus there were no legal difficulties in the way of enclosure. The landlord could carry it out himself, and neither agreement nor Act of Parliament was necessary.

An improving landlord in Scotland, and there were growing numbers of them from the last decades of the seventeenth century, often began with his Mains, or home farm, and it was not unusual, as in England, for these to be run at a loss, at least at first. Attention was also paid to the grounds, or policies, surrounding the mansion house. Shelter belts of trees were planted, and, again as in England, it was not unknown for entire villages to be moved to improve the view. Atholl, for example, was moved when Blair Castle policies were improved in the 1750s. Tree planting was done on a large scale in the barren Scottish landscape. At Monymusk Sir Archibald Grant spent a long life slowly improving his estates. He had his own nursery for raising trees from seed, and he bought acorns, fir and pine cones as well as elm seed. By 1754 he estimated that he had two million trees on his estates. Not the least impressive aspect of a life such as that of Sir Archibald is the vision, foresight and patience that could even contemplate raising oak and elm trees from seed. There was no quick profit to be had here.

The processes of enclosing, planting, ditching and draining, paring and burning, liming and ploughing, slowly and gradually transformed the landscape of lowland Scotland. Big square fields replaced run-rig. Boulders collected from the surface of the land went into boundary dykes, which were often very substantial. The Kingswell Dyke, west of Aberdeen, is half a mile long and anything from 6 to 20 feet wide. At the same time new crops were introduced, including the ubiquitous turnip, and new breeds of livestock emerged, of which Ayrshire and Aberdeen Angus cattle are the best-known.

The structure of traditional Scottish rural society presented Scottish landlords with a very real problem. Enclosure meant that large numbers of sub-tenants could find themselves homeless as traditional ferm touns were replanned. The benevolent paternalism so characteristic of eighteenth-century society, reinforced in Scotland by particularly strong ties of kinship and patronage, meant that landlords felt obliged to provide for the dispossessed. Large numbers of new towns and villages, perhaps as many as 350, were established during the eighteenth century, at Grantown on Spey, Tomintoul, Brydekirk, New Keith, and Ballater for example. John Cockburn was laying out a new town at Ormistoun by 1735. He provided building plots and materials and required that the new houses should be two storeys high, in itself a break with tradition. Landlords built sawmills, paper mills, breweries, and waulk mills, and laid out bleach fields, giving every incentive to artisans and craftsmen to settle in the new towns. Newcastleton, in Roxburghshire, is a particularly fine example, founded in 1793 by the Duke of Buccleuch to house handloom weavers.

By the end of the eighteenth century agriculture in the Scottish Lowlands was generally as good as, and in some respects better than, English agriculture. Ferm touns, composed of a huddle of appallingly insanitary one- or two-roomed cabins, had been replaced either by isolated farmsteads or else by nucleated villages of two or three streets of

63 Douglas Square, Newcastleton, Roxburghshire, an estate village founded in 1793 by the Duke of Buccleuch to house handloom weavers. The stone column with the domed top in the centre is the public well.

substantially built two-storey houses. In the Highlands, however, conditions were approaching crisis point. A steadily rising population had become dependent upon three things: the kelp industry, the potato, and cattle raising. Kelp, obtained by burning seaweed, was almost the only source of sodium carbonate, essential in the manufacture of glass and soap. During the Napoleonic Wars prices soared. Whole communities became dependent upon kelp for their livelihood. In 1825 the manufacture of Leblanc alkali began in Glasgow, and the kelp industry collapsed. At the same time, the potato had largely come to replace oats as the mainstay of the diet of most Highland communities. In the 1840s the potato crop failed. Finally, the price of cattle began to fall steeply after 1815, and sheep became more profitable. Sheep rearing required large grazing grounds and much capital. A new, commercially orientated form of animal husbandry came into headlong collision with an ancient traditional form of subsistence agriculture.

Many landlords, only too well aware of the problems that rising numbers of people were causing, did what they could, sometimes with disastrous consequences. The notorious Sutherland clearances were part of a well-meaning attempt to improve the estate for the benefit of all concerned. Between 5,000 and 10,000 people were moved to coastal towns between 1808 and 1821, and much money was spent on laying out Helmsdale as a fishing port. But the project went appallingly wrong. The factor to the Countess of Sutherland, Patrick Sellar, was unable to comprehend the fierce attachment of the Highlander to his traditional way of life. He still has not yet been forgiven for his ruthless firing of the houses of Strathnaver, when at least two elderly people met their deaths.

After 1815 emigration was actively encouraged, although it had been going on for many years. Thousands of Highlanders left their homes, to go into Lowland Scotland or else to North America. Deserted, roofless, tumble-down stone cottages, at Bourblige, in Ardnamurchan, for example, or at Invea, overlooking Calgary Bay in the island of Mull, are gaunt reminders in the landscape today of a particularly unhappy episode in Scottish history.

The eighteenth century witnessed an astonishing outburst of building and rebuilding of country houses and the reshaping of their parks, gardens, and policies. This movement closely reflected changing attitudes to nature, art, philosophy, and aesthetics, and even political ideas, as men sought, with ever-increasing sophistication and often at enormous cost, to reshape their environments in order to create an ideal world that would reflect their taste, their judgement, and their knowledge and appreciation of classical art and architecture.

The new movement began with the almost inevitable reaction against Sir Christopher Wren's interpretation of classical architecture and a return to what was considered a much more truthful view, more especially as exemplified in the work of Andrea Palladio and Inigo Jones. The movement was patronized almost from the first by the Earl of Burlington, and his circle of friends included some of the most important names in English literary and cultural circles: Alexander Pope, William Kent, and Thomas Coke. Palladianism dominated almost every area of English building for half a century, and some of the largest English country houses were built or rebuilt under its influence: Holkham Hall, Wanstead, Wentworth Woodhouse, Prior Park, whilst Mereworth Castle in Kent was built as an almost exact replica of the Villa Rotonda.

Palladianism, which began as the fad of a coterie of rich, fashionable young men, spread rapidly throughout Britain, carried forward on a tide of pattern books which provided country masons and bricklayers with a wealth of examples of mouldings, decorations and details of the classical orders together with some guidance in the handling of proportions, something which lay at the heart of Palladio's work. Some provincial builders, such as John Carr of York, could handle the new style with taste and distinction. Others copied or imitated where they could, and hundreds

64   The south front of Kedleston Hall, designed by Robert Adam and built between 1760
and 1770, and modelled on the Arch of Constantine in Rome.

of smaller country houses, rectories, and town houses still survive today as
testimony to their more or less successful attempts to introduce the
principles of an Italian architect into the British landscape.

Although Palladianism was born from a return to the inexhaustible well
of classical architecture, interest in medieval architecture never really died
out in England, and a renewed enthusiasm can be detected in the same
circles as those in which Palladianism was first nurtured. Alexander Pope
and Lord Bathurst designed, in the latter's park at Cirencester, what
eventually came to be called Alfred's Hall. By the time it was finished, in
about 1732, the Earl of Strafford had built a ruin, Stainborough Castle, on
his estate in Yorkshire. The craze for follies, whether ruined castles or
abbeys, had begun. Only very few men were as lucky as William Aislabie,
who in 1768 was able to buy Fountains Abbey and include its splendid
ruins, in a suitably well-groomed setting, into his park at Studley Royal. It
was however the example set by Horace Walpole which really stimulated
interest in 'Gothick' architecture. For thirty years, from 1748 onwards, he
progressively adapted and altered his house at Strawberry Hill, adding
rather amateurish imitations of genuine medieval architectural features
to create a house whose self-conscious, studied irregularity, as opposed
to the equally self-conscious regularity of Palladian architecture, was increasingly admired, contributing enormously to the development of the
Picturesque. Strawberry Hill became one of the most visited country

65 Osterley Park, Middlesex. The original house was built by Sir Thomas Gresham in the 1570s. It was then remodelled by Robert Adam, who added the splendid portico, finished in about 1773, as a screen across the mouth of the courtyard to the original house.

houses in England and Walpole had to restrict visits to certain afternoons of the week.

Just as Palladianism took its origins from a rediscovery of the work of Palladio, prompted in part by the publication of an edition of his book, *I Quattro Libri dell'Architettura,* in 1715, so some of the major developments of the second half of the eighteenth century were stimulated by the publication of important books on architecture. *The Antiquities of Athens* was published in 1755 by James Stuart and Nicholas Revett. In 1757 William Chambers published *Designs of Chinese Buildings,* and in 1764 appeared *Ruins of the Palace of the Emperor Diocletian at Spalato,* by Robert Adam. All of these are important, first because they show a genuine concern for historical accuracy, and second because they also show a remarkable extension geographically and chronologically in the range of ideas and themes available to builders and architects. Sir William Chambers's book created what amounted to a craze for things Chinese, of which the Pagoda in Kew Gardens is one of the best-known examples, and the dairy built for the Duke of Bedford at Woburn Abbey is one of the more bizarre, whilst the interest in things oriental led eventually to the splendidly ornate Royal Pavilion at Brighton.

Robert Adam made lavish use of his own liberal interpretation of classical architecture, of which he had a considerable and exact knowledge. Much of his time was taken up in completing the work of others or else in remodelling existing buildings. Thus at Kedleston, in Derbyshire, he added a replica of the Arch of Constantine to the south front of an existing house. At Osterley House he added a double portico to an Elizabethan dwelling, and at Syon House he decorated a series of rooms in an extraordinarily rich and astonishingly varied style.

The scholarship lavished upon the study of classical architecture was only slowly applied to that of medieval buildings, and the two were often merged to give results that were sometimes bizarre, sometimes pretty, and occasionally perverse. At Inveraray Castle, designed in 1745 by Roger Morris for the Dukes of Argyll, a four-square block with a classically regular façade and classical interior has crenellations and pointed windows. At Downton Castle, built for Richard Payne Knight between 1774 and

66 Nether Winchendon House, Buckinghamshire, an early sixteenth-century house Gothicized at the very end of the eighteenth century when the screen and battlements were added.

1778, a deliberately irregular layout, complete with towers and crenella-tions, again conceals a classically decorated interior. Perhaps the oddest of all is Castle Goring, completed in about 1798 for Sir Bysshe Shelley. It has a brick south front in classical garb, and a flint north front, with turrets, battlements, and pointed windows. From this curious *mélange* of styles emerged the Picturesque, of which Richard Payne Knight and his friend Uvedale Price were the chief protagonists. All that was irregular, uncultivated, and wild was now to be sought out for its own sake. Country cottages were discovered to be picturesque, and John Nash built a number, with half timbering, thatched roofs, and wrought-iron balconies with verandas, an idea that came from India. This was also the golden age of the 'Gothick' novel, at which Jane Austen poked fun in *Northanger Abbey*.

Country houses were not however conceived in isolation. Each house was set in its gardens and park, and as much attention was paid to this framework as was given to the house itself, and it has a similar history of change in response to new ideas, tides of fashion, and changes in taste. At the beginning of the eighteenth century gardens were formal, rigid, and mannered in their design and layout, something which the contemporary Stephen Switzer called 'La Grand Manier'. The model was the work of Le Nôtre in France, and especially the immense formal gardens he laid out at Versailles for Louis XIV, where long straight rides were cut through immense belts of woodland, much use was made of water and fount-ains, and elaborately designed parterres composed of intricate beds were laid out near the palace in order that they could be seen from the windows. Everything was done on the grandest scale, with the deliberate intention of impressing visitors with the power, splendour, and authority of the Sun King, and even today something of this splendour still shines through.

All who could attempted to emulate the Sun King, but no English nobleman had the authority of Louis XIV, and although formal, elaborate gardens were created at Chatsworth, Blenheim, and Longleat at the end of the seventeenth century none could approach the scale of Versailles. Early in the eighteenth century, however, a change can be detected. Formal gardens, with their rigid straight lines, were increasingly thought to be a symbol of the authoritarian regime of Lous XIV. More relaxed, informal gardens were symbols of liberty, and in particular the Whig version of it. Landscape gardening came to have political overtones and nowhere is this more apparent than at the great gardens at Stowe, in north Buckingham-shire. Here Lord Cobham spent thirty years progressively softening the straight lines of the formal seventeenth-century garden which once surrounded the house, at the same time putting up a series of garden buildings loaded with political meaning. Here was a Temple of Ancient Virtues and a Temple of British Worthies, a Gothic Temple dedicated to

67 The Temple of Piety at Studley Royal, Yorkshire. The grounds were laid out by John Aislabie between about 1720 and 1740. It was his son William who incorporated Fountains Abbey into the grounds in 1768.

the liberty of our ancestors, and a Temple of Friendship. The straight edges of lakes and canals became curved and sinuous. Trees were no longer cut into fantastic shapes but were allowed to grow naturally.

It was also becoming increasingly apparent that the elements of a garden could be composed into a picture and that the best gardens were those in which carefully planned walks led from one picture to the next. The first to give full expression to this concept of movement in a garden was William Kent, and the best surviving example of his work is to be found at Rousham in Oxfordshire. The fullest 'picture' garden must however be that at Stourhead, created by Henry Hoare in the years after 1741. Here is an idealized landscape rich in allusion to a wide range of literary and artistic sources: the poetry of Virgil and Horace, the description of the Garden of Eden in *Paradise Lost*, the evocative paintings of Claude.

Such 'literary' gardens were often overloaded with temples, grottos, obelisks, and bridges and they were not to everyone's liking. The Duchess of Portland complained in 1744 that the gardens at Stowe were overcrowded with buildings and this was well before they were all complete. There was the inevitable reaction. The greatest of English landscape gardeners, Lancelot Brown, began his career at Stowe. He married there in 1744, and finally left for good in 1751. He quickly established his reputation and until his death in 1783 he dominated landscape gardening as no one has ever done, either before or since. He used only three elements: grass, water, and trees. From these, and often working on the grandest scale, he created landscapes which, now that they have matured, as at Petworth for example, have an almost palpable aura of serene tranquillity. Such was his contribution to the making of the English landscape that it is almost impossible either to grasp fully the extent of his achievement or to realize that older, much more ancient landscapes everywhere underlie his work. In his last years he was increasingly criticized and after his death his reputation fell away almost to nothing. Taste at the end of the eighteenth century found his landscapes too monotonous when what was really meant was that, relying as they did almost entirely upon line and mass, they were too subtle. By the end of the century, prompted by the rising flood of new trees and plants being brought from North America, South Africa, and China, and under the guidance of Humphry Repton, flowers, statues, and buildings were reappearing in gardens. By the time Repton died, in 1818, the formal flower bed had once more become established in gardens, greenhouses permitted the cultivation of tender, exotic plants and gardens were once again as formal as anything which might have been seen at the end of the seventeenth century.

Just as the fabric of the rural landscape of Britain was changing at an accelerating pace during the eighteenth century so too was that of the towns and cities of Britain, and more especially in those towns such as Manchester and Birmingham which were experiencing the first stages of industrialization.

We looked in the previous chapter at the social structure and physical layout of the pre-industrial town in Britain. Change in either or both came to individual towns at differential rates governed by purely local, particularistic factors. In no sense was there any kind of overall national direction for what was taking place, not least because what was happening in Britain during the eighteenth century was happening for the first time anywhere in the world. Almost all urban development was left to private individuals or groups of them. Very frequently they had to obtain a private Act of Parliament before they could lay out new streets or make any satisfactory arrangements to pave, cleanse and light old ones. Thus Acts of Parliament were passed in 1711 and 1726 to enable the Grosvenor Estates, and more especially that part of it called the Hundred Acres lying to the south of Oxford Street and east of Hyde Park, to be laid out. Lord Burlington had to obtain similar Acts in 1718 and 1734 before he could begin building on land to the north of Burlington House, in Piccadilly. An Act of 1746 permitted the development of the Colmore Estate in Birmingham, and one of 1768 was required before the Pulteney Estate in Bath could be developed. These Acts were necessary because the land involved was subject to a strict settlement, and the eighteenth century gave punctilious regard to every kind of property right, however remote.

The Grosvenor Estate was laid out on a lavish scale, with the centrepiece, Grosvenor Square, itself extending over eight acres. Building in other towns was much less spectacular. Piecemeal enclosure to the north and east of Leeds had created a pattern of small closes in individual ownership. No new street was laid out in the town between 1634 and 1767, but when expansion did begin it came by way of small-scale building, one close at a time, and the ancient pattern of field boundaries within which the builders were compelled to work could be recognized beneath the streets and terraces of the nineteenth-century industrial city until modern redevelopment swept them all away.

It was the landlord, great and small, who released land for building purposes during the eighteenth century. His reward was an increasing income from ground rents. The actual building was almost always carried out on a small scale by an army of masons, carpenters, and bricklayers. It was quite usual for a mason to begin to build a couple of houses on his own account, subcontracting for much of the specialized work, which was often done on a barter system with very little money actually changing hands. If he could sell or lease the properties fairly quickly all was well, but many overstretched themselves and bankruptcies were very common. The Adam brothers had to hold a lottery in order to get themselves out of the financial mess that the building of the Adelphi scheme in London had landed them in. Some prosperous townsmen were drawn into property speculation from other trades. Richard Paley, a soap boiler of Leeds, was in 1800 the second largest property owner in the town. Three years later he was bankrupt. Charles Spackman, a wealthy coach-builder who financed the building of Lansdown Crescent in Bath, and Thomas Sambourne, a Sheffield attorney drawn into property development, fared rather better. Before the end of the eighteenth century money was being channelled into building projects by means of building societies. In origin they were concerned to finance a particular scheme, and were then wound up. Permanent societies, which lent money to their members, appeared first of all in the West Riding and in Lancashire, spreading to the rest of the country after 1800.

Even when the land was found and the main pattern of streets laid out, the actual completion of schemes could take many years. The Grosvenor Estate took half a century to finish. Daniel Laurie bought 47 acres of land on the south bank of the Clyde in 1801–2, intending to build a high-class residential district. But he was always short of money and what emerged after seventeen years of effort was one of the most insalubrious districts in Glasgow. In Bristol the Queen Square and King Square projects each took nearly thirty years to complete, and the George Square scheme in Glasgow twenty-five years.

Almost all of these new schemes were based on a rectilinear, gridiron

68 Charlotte Square, Edinburgh, designed by Robert Adam in 1791; a fitting climax to Edinburgh New Town, begun in 1767, and the only part planned as a single harmonious scheme.

pattern of streets and squares. The Grosvenor Estate in London, the Aytoun and Mosley districts of Manchester, and the George Square area of Glasgow were all laid out in this way. Probably the most rigid of these gridiron schemes is to be found in Edinburgh. The old city occupies a very cramped site, from the Castle Hill on the west to Holyrood House on the east, with the Nor'Loch on the north and another shallow loch on the south. Plans to improve the city were published in 1752. It was the end of the century before the scheme was completed. Both lochs were drained, and on the bed of the Nor'Loch three long straight streets were laid out; Princes Street, George Street, which had a square at both ends, St Andrews and Charlotte Squares, and finally Queen Street. These three principal streets were linked by a series of cross streets. Building began at St Andrews Square and moved slowly westwards. The scheme was from the first under the control of the town council, which imposed ever-stricter controls over the designs of the buildings which were put up. Only in 1791 did building reach the western end of the scheme, and here Robert Adam produced a plan for uniformly designed house frontages to the four sides of Charlotte Square. The result was a splendid example of spacious, harmonious town planning.

By the time Charlotte Square was finished, however, squares and straight streets were commonplace and old-fashioned. An entirely new concept was introduced into the urban landscape by the work of the Woods, father and son, in Bath. John Wood the elder settled in Bath in

69   The Crescent, Buxton, Derbyshire, built to designs by John Carr in the 1780s as part of
the attempts of the Duke of Devonshire to make Buxton a rival of Bath.

1727. His grandiose plans for a rebuilding of almost the whole of medieval
Bath were rejected by the town council, and so he turned to an estate lying
almost due north of the town. He secured a series of 99-year leases from
the owners, the Gay family, and laid out on a magnificent scale a physical
embodiment of his almost mystical vision of classical architecture. The
King's Circus is composed of two perfect circles, one inside the other, a
symbol of the divine perfection, broken into three equal segments to
represent the Trinity. The splendour of what is almost a processional way,
from Queen Square to the Royal Crescent, represents an astonishing
projection of a mental landscape into the environment of eighteenth-
century Britain.

Crescents and circuses became increasingly common in the second half
of the eighteenth century. John Carr of York built the Crescent at Buxton
for the Duke of Devonshire between 1779 and 1781. Atholl Place, in Perth,
was laid out at the very end of the century. The Royal Crescent was built in
Edinburgh between 1820 and 1823. At the same time control over the
design and construction of the actual buildings became increasingly strict as
landlords and their architects sought to emulate the monumentality that
uniformity of façade had brought to the Royal Crescent at Bath.

The work of the Woods in Bath is the summit of town planning and
building in eighteenth-century Britain. At the other extreme are the rows
of back-to-back dwellings being built in Nottingham and elsewhere to

provide cheap accommodation for the immigrants that rapid industrialization was drawing into many towns in the midlands and the north. The
physical expansion of towns was not controlled in any way. It was left to
landlords and builders to decide what to put up. Cheap housing sold more
quickly than more expensive. Between about 1745 and 1780 about 5,000
houses were built in Birmingham. The great majority, with no more than
two or three rooms, sold for less than £100. The only crescent in the town,
planned in 1788, was to have twenty-three houses costing £500 each. It was
still only half finished at the end of the century.

The eighteenth century is marked by increasingly rapid industrialization.
In order to place this movement in perspective two important points must
be made. First of all the household remained not only the most important
unit of manufacturing and commercial enterprise throughout the century,
but also the most important unit in agricultural activity, as well as being the
fundamental unit of social structure. Almost everything, even at the end of
the eighteenth century, was still made in workshops which occupied either
a room, or sometimes a whole floor, in a house, and it was not unknown for
blocks of terraced houses to be built with a communal workshop stretching
the entire length of the block, or else in a huddle of sheds and outhouses in
what were once gardens and back yards. Specialized purpose-built mills
and factories were rare at the beginning of the eighteenth century and still,
on a national scale, uncommon at its end. Matthew Boulton's Soho
factory, finished in about 1765, Richard Arkwright's Cromford mill, the
industrial complex at Coalbrookdale, were quite exceptional at the time
and astonished contemporaries for this very reason.

The second important point is that the principal source of energy, even
at the end of the eighteenth century, was not the steam-engine but the
waterwheel, one of the earliest machines devised by man and certainly in
use in Roman Britain. It was common and widespread during the
Anglo-Saxon centuries, over 5,000 being recorded in Domesday Book.
There are two principal ways in which water can be used to turn a wheel. It
can pass under the wheel, to give the undershot mill, or it can pass over it,
to give the overshot mill. A third kind was confined to the Northern Isles.
Here the wheel was placed horizontally in the water, housed in a small
building of drystone construction, and often there were several of these
watermills strung along one stream. There are three at Huxter for
example, and nine along the Clumlie burn at Troswick, both in the
Shetlands.

By the thirteenth century the watermill had been adapted to power the
fulling mill, in which woollen cloth was felted and shrunk, and in due
course it came to be used to crush ore, seeds, and other raw materials,
including flints and clay for the pottery industry, as well as grain for flour.
In 1759 John Smeaton communicated to the Royal Society his discovery
that the undershot wheel was about 22 per cent efficient and the overshot

70 The watermill at Leek, Staffordshire, where James Brindley worked in his early years.

about 63 per cent. He then went on to design and construct iron components for waterwheels, and by the early years of the nineteenth century the watermill had become a remarkably powerful and efficient source of energy. The North Mill at Belper, built in 1803–4 by William Strutt, was five storeys high and 127 feet long. It was powered by a single waterwheel, 18 feet in diameter and 23 feet wide, driven by the Derbyshire Derwent.

Water power was the single most important determinant of the location of industry in the eighteenth century. In the Lake District an astonishingly wide variety of manufactures was powered by water: iron forges and furnaces, slitting, rolling and boring mills, bobbin mills, woollen, cotton, flax and silk mills, pencil and gunpowder mills. The Derbyshire Derwent by the middle years of the century was lined with mills for slitting and rolling iron and copper sheets, for lead smelting as well as iron foundries and gypsum, plaster, and colour mills. The six miles of the River Frome from Garston to Beckington was said in 1800 to have 200 mills along it, whilst there were water-powered iron works in Hampshire, gunpowder mills at Faversham in Kent, and the mill that made the paper for the Bank of England stood on the banks of the Test, near Laverstoke in Hampshire.

Water power was essential to eighteenth-century Britain. There was no alternative before the 1780s and it was long before contemporaries could think in other terms. Richard Arkwright bought a steam-engine for his mill at Cromford in 1780, but it was used to pump the water back over the wheel, not to drive the machinery.

Windmills, one of the most remarkable achievements of the medieval engineer and carpenter, first appeared in Britain in the first decades of the twelfth century. The earliest kind was the post mill, in which the main body of the mill, carrying the sails and the machinery, pivots on an immense upright post, strengthened by quarterbars and resting on cross-trees. The tower mill, in which the machinery was housed in a fixed tower and only the cap which supported the sails actually turned, was a later development, of which the smock mill, an eight- or twelve-sided structure clad in clapper boarding, is a variation. Windmills were used chiefly for grinding corn, but in due course they too were adapted to grind and crush lead ore, flints, seeds, and dyes, and also to pump water. By the opening years of the eighteenth century they were very common over much of England and in the eastern lowlands of Scotland, and were even to be found on North

71 The windmill at Skidby, Yorkshire, built in 1821.

Ronaldsay and Papa Westray. Many parishes had both windmills and watermills, and often several of each kind.

Both windmills and watermills suffer from a number of disadvantages. Frosts in winter and droughts in summer mean an uneven or interrupted supply of water. This could be overcome to some extent by building dams and reservoirs, so that the supply of water could be controlled by weirs and sluices. This was done at the Old Furnace at Coalbrookdale, for example. The power supply to windmills is even more erratic and uncertain, and there was no way in which it could be stored. Great skill and dexterity were required to keep the sails into the wind, and a strong gust from the wrong direction could spell disaster.

Windmills and watermills were complemented to some extent in the eighteenth century by the horse gin. A horse, plodding patiently round in a circle, pulled with him a wheel that was geared to a driving shaft. This could be used to wind up coal, lead, and men from underground mine shafts. Horse gins were in use in the Derbyshire coalfields until the end of the nineteenth century. Many horse gins were also used to drive agricultural machinery, especially the threshing machine, invented in 1786 by Andrew Meikle. They could also power other machines. Samuel Unwin built a cotton mill at Sutton-in-Ashfield in about 1770. The machinery was driven by horses and oxen harnessed to rotating beams. In due course they were replaced by a waterwheel, and Unwin built a windmill on the roof of his mill to pump back the water so that it could be used again. Horse power lives on into the age of the internal combustion engine since James Watt, when trying to measure the power of his steam-engine, devised a unit he called a 'horse', namely the energy required to lift 33,000 pounds through 1 foot in 1 minute. This unit has been used ever since, although it is in fact about one and a third times the power of a horse.

At the very end of the seventeenth century a more reliable alternative to wind and water power was at last discovered. This was the steam-engine. There had for long been much theoretical interest in the power which atmospheric pressure could exert, more especially through a piston beneath which a vacuum had been created. There were also, for much of the seventeenth century, desperate attempts made to find some method of pumping water out of mines. The two threads came together in the work of Thomas Savery, who in 1698 took out a patent for an engine for raising water 'by the Impellent Force of Fire'. His engine worked by condensing steam in a cylinder. This created a vacuum, which in its turn was filled by water being sucked up into it. Steam was then used to force the water out again, and the cycle began once more. He used two cylinders, which were filled and emptied alternately. He was in fact using steam at high pressure, and contemporary engineering and metalworking skills could not cope with the energy which he had unleashed. Working quite independently, Thomas Newcomen, a Dartmouth ironmonger, developed an engine which used steam at atmospheric pressure. The two men seem to have come to some kind of agreement, and the first steam-engine in the world was erected in 1712 at Dudley Castle, Worcestershire, for pumping water from the coal-mines there. It could raise 120 gallons of water per minute from a depth of 150 feet. It was grossly inefficient and it was always breaking down, but even so it was much more efficient than any windmill or watermill, and by the time Newcomen died in 1729 his steam-engine was being widely used, not only in Britain but also in France, Germany, and the Low Countries.

James Watt worked for a number of years in the 1760s on the problem of improving the efficiency of Newcomen's engine, and in 1769 he took out his patent for a separate condenser. In 1774 he entered into a partnership with Matthew Boulton and in 1775 they obtained an extension of the patent until 1800. Boulton & Watt engines were over twice as efficient as those of Newcomen and much more reliable. They were, however, still used only to pump water from mines and were only very slowly adapted to other purposes. In 1776 the Shropshire ironmaster John Wilkinson used one to supply the blast for his iron furnace at Willey and another to drive a forge-hammer at his forge at Bradley, also in Shropshire. By 1781 a number of patents had been taken out for devices to provide rotary motion, and further refinements followed. Only now does the Age of Steam really begin. In 1785 a steam-engine was built to provide the power for the machinery in a textile mill at Papplewick, in Nottinghamshire. From this time onwards the use of the steam-engine as the prime mover spreads rapidly. Supplies of coal now become of the first importance and so industrialists looking for new sites for their factories and mills turn to the coalfields rather than to the river valleys of the Cotswolds or Derbyshire. Watermills were not abandoned overnight however, and it was not until the slump of 1825 that there was any significant drop in the number of water-powered textile mills in Wiltshire and Gloucestershire.

Throughout the sixteenth and seventeenth centuries almost the whole of manufacture and commerce was domestic in its structure and organization. Nails, textiles, shoes, cutlery, farm implements, wagons, furniture, spoons, pottery, were all made in a huddle of workshops close to the purely domestic accommodation of those engaged in the trade. Merchants and shopkeepers lived over their counting houses and warehouses. Even for iron and glass furnaces the workforce, never very large, lived near by. Simple and comparatively inexpensive machinery could be erected in attics and barns and garrets, and much weaving, stocking-knitting, and lace-making took place in the homes of craftsmen and women. Things began to change when water power was harnessed to manufacturing processes, especially to cotton-spinning. The more machines that could be harnessed to the prime mover the more profitable the whole enterprise would become. At the same time the drawbacks of the domestic system were

72 Stocking-frame knitters' cottages at Calverton, Nottinghamshire, built in the first half of the nineteenth century. They have long windows on the ground floor in order to give as much light as possible to the machinery.

becoming increasingly apparent, especially in the textile industry. Quality control was very difficult. Theft and embezzlement were common. It was almost impossible to introduce new processes and technical improvements or to guard them against imitators. From these parents the factory was born. Its evolution was a protracted affair, and the distinction between domestic workshop and factory was for long almost impossible to draw. In the last decades of the eighteenth century rows of two- and three-storey houses were being built in Nottinghamshire and in Lancashire with special rooms, often on the top floor and sometimes running the whole length of the block, to house weaving machinery and stocking frames, and it was only in 1802, after some fourteen years in business, that Peter Stubs of Warrington built workshops of his own and brought some of his employees together under one roof in order to streamline his file-making business, hitherto carried out on a contracting-out basis in the houses of those who worked for him.

Perhaps the first building which would be recognizable as a factory was the silk mill built in Derby in 1702 by Thomas Cotchett. This was followed by Lombe's mill, also for silk and also in Derby, built in 1717 and big enough to house about 300 employees. But the idea was taken up only very slowly. By the 1730s some Nottingham frame-work knitters had as many as forty poor apprentices at work in the same premises, although the frames were still operated by hand. Several small mills appeared in Derby in imitation of Lombe's silk-throwing mill, and there was one of four storeys in Chesterfield by 1757; but it was Richard Arkwright who was the first to exploit the opportunities that the factory offered. He built his first water-powered cotton-spinning mill at Cromford in 1771. It was very successful, and he went on to build further mills in Derbyshire, at Rocester in Staffordshire, at Keighley and in Manchester. He visited Scotland in 1783 where he met David Dale, a wealthy banker. The two became partners and established a mill, together with a village to house the workers, at New Lanark. In 1798 Robert Owen became the managing partner, marrying Dale's daughter in the same year. Owen was at once a highly successful businessman and a benevolent, enlightened and in some ways autocratic employer. He gave up employing children under 10 years old. He built a school, a church, and a New Institution intended for the educational benefit of all his employees. The complex of buildings at New Lanark became one of the sights of Europe, attracting visitors from far and wide. In spite of extensive internal modernization and a fire in 1882, much still survives today of what was once one of the largest and most influential industrial complexes in Britain.

The first factories, whether at New Lanark or Cromford, Derby or Nailsworth, were water-powered and, as we have seen, water power remains of the first importance until well into the nineteenth century. Only very slowly was steam power introduced, the first purpose-built steam-powered textile mill being the Revolution Mill, built by Major Cartwright at Retford in 1788. All were engaged in the textile industry, and especially in cotton spinning, and it was this branch of the industry which grew with astonishing speed in the very last decades of the eighteenth century. For many, the huge gaunt cotton mills of Oldham or Paisley seem to be the epitome of the worst excesses of the industrial revolution. It is however important to put them into perspective. The textile industry is, after all, only one industry and large steam-powered mills were concentrated in Lancashire, Lanarkshire, and the West Riding, so that wide areas of Britain were entirely without them. Many mill-owners were benevolent employers, building houses, churches, and schools for their workers, like those that Richard Arkwright put up at Cromford, houses which were certainly cleaner, warmer, and more sanitary than the timber-framed and thatched cottages which their occupants had left behind.

Nevertheless, even with these reservations made, the factory was by the end of the eighteenth century beginning to make an increasingly dramatic impact upon the fabric of the landscape as well as the fabric of the society with which the landscape is so intimately linked. In spite of some attempts to make factories look like country houses – Cressbrook Mill, Miller's

73   The factory as Georgian country house: Cressbrook Mill, Derbyshire, rebuilt in 1815.

Dale, Derbyshire, built in 1779 and rebuilt in 1815 after a fire, has a pedimented central section and a classically regular façade – they were large, severely plain, utilitarian, intrusive additions to the landscape. Manufacture slowly ceased to be domestic and machinery began to disappear from the home, although the houses built by Richard Arkwright at Cromford had unusually wide windows to the second floors to provide light for the stocking frames which were housed there, because he employed women and children in his factory whilst the male members of the household continued to work at home at stocking-knitting. Nothing new has ever been able to make an entirely clean break with the past.

    We have hitherto in this book tended to look at individual facets of the landscape in isolation, almost as though woods, farms, towns, and churches each had a separate existence. This is in some ways forced upon us by the very nature of historical writing, which can only put one word after another, whereas what is really required is a diagram representing the full range of all the interrelationships between the various strands of the landscape together with an added chronological dimension showing how the parts change over time. Perhaps in due course a computerized program will be devised in which the history of the landscape will appear upon a screen as a multi-dimensional diagram with a built-in time-lapse mechanism. But this is speculation.

Historical analysis may lay bare the roots and causes of change, but it can also obscure and destroy many of the more subtle interrelationships between the parts. The fields, farms, churches and cottages, castles and gardens of the landscape are not discrete entities but the constituent elements of a dense historical matrix, linked in the minds of men and women by assumptions, values, and preconceptions, sometimes formally codified, often nothing more than practices informally recognized through custom and long usage. Such linkages can only be formed and maintained through physical and intellectual contacts between people, and such contacts depend for their existence upon a communications network. Men have always been great travellers, from Mesolithic times down to the present, and Roman Britain, as we saw in Chapter 3, was provided with an efficient transport system. The justification for leaving any further account of transport in the landscape of Britain until a chapter on the eighteenth century must be because it is only then that there is at last any significant change in or addition to methods of transport which had been in use since post-Roman times.

The Romans left behind them an extensive network of roads, a network which penetrated into every corner of the parts of Britain under their occupation. Even in the most remote and mountainous parts of Wales there could have been few points which were more than 4 or 5 miles from a road. The network was provided with posting stations and mile-posts and was regularly and carefully maintained. The main roads of Roman Britain, in spite of much alteration, neglect, rebuilding, and local deviation, have provided the backbone of the road system of Britain until the building of the motorways in the twentieth century.

The collapse of Roman power in the fifth century meant also the collapse of the engineering and surveying skills which had brought the network into existence and maintained it once it was built. The extent to which the English made use of Roman roads is uncertain and controversial, but there is a growing body of evidence to show that they did make widespread use of it, although often in a rather incoherent way. No Roman names for their roads survive, even for the major ones, which are known today either by English names, Akeman Street, Watling Street, and Ermine Street, or else by a name for which there is at present no satisfactory explanation, such as Ryknield Street, a name containing the same element as is found in Icknield Way, or else from a Latin word, *fossa*, which may have come into English through British to give the Fosse Way.

The English had a wide vocabulary for different kinds of roads, as they

74   Wansford Bridge, Northamptonshire, built and rebuilt at various times between
1577 and 1795.

did for almost every other feature of the landscape. The word 'road' itself
seems to come from a word meaning 'to ride', and so it may perhaps
indicate a road which could be ridden by men on horseback. This may be
compared with the word *pæth,* giving 'path', a word which seems to have
been applied particularly to roads over moorland and heath, with the
compound *hærepæth,* meaning literally 'army path' and seemingly meaning
main road, a word occurring quite frequently in the boundaries of estates
and occasionally surviving down to the present in such local names as
Haresway Field, found in Aston Clinton in Buckinghamshire, in a survey
of 1581. *Weg,* becoming 'way', appears to have been the usual term for a
road, whilst the Old Norse word *gate,* found chiefly in the Danelaw and in
the north of England, was applied principally to streets in towns in the
form '-gate'. Perhaps the most interesting Old English word in this context
is *stræt,* from which the modern word street descends. It appears to be a
loan word from the Latin *via strata,* meaning paved road, and where it is
used in major settlement names it seems to indicate the presence of a
Roman road. Its meaning does however seem to shift in the later
Anglo-Saxon period, when it was being used in the names of important
streets in towns.

75 Stockley Bridge, Cumberland, a stone packhorse bridge of uncertain date.

Travel was undoubtedly difficult and dangerous, and the great majority of men and women probably did not go far in the course of their lives. But the ability of men to travel great distances must not be underestimated. Both Alfred and Cnut went to Rome, as did Aldhelm, and Benedict Biscop went four times. Archbishop Theodore had studied in Athens. Bede, on the other hand, spent almost all of his life in the monastery at Jarrow, going no further afield than York and Lindisfarne. Kings and bishops were not the only people who wanted to go to Rome; the widow Werthryth did, selling her estate at Cleeve Prior in Worcestershire to Cuthulf, the king's thegn, perhaps to finance the journey, according to a document to be dated to the end of the ninth century.

Travel implies the existence of roads of every kind, of bridges, fords, and ferries, wagons and carts, ships, ports and havens. By the time the earliest documents start to survive, that is at the end of the seventh century, it is clear that all of these elements are present in the landscape, and as a matter of course, with the proviso that bridges may have been comparatively rare at first, since the place-name element *brycg* does not occur in those place-names recorded before 730, so that bridges may have been built only slowly to replace fords. There is one recorded instance of a place-name ending in '-bridge' replacing one ending in '-ford'. Redbridge, in Hampshire, was called *Hreutford* by Bede in about 730 but had become *Hreodbrycg* in 956, by which time London Bridge had also been built, and there are documentary references to bridges at Ducklington in Oxfordshire and Chetwode in Buckinghamshire. A charter of 944 relating to an estate at Badby, in Northamptonshire, refers in the perambulation of the boundaries to a stone bridge which can be identified with that near Everdon Manor House, and shortly afterwards the arrangements for the repair and maintenance of the long bridge over the Medway at Rochester were formalized. The bridge had nine piers. The first and third were the responsibility of the Bishop of Rochester, the others fell to certain estates and manors within the Lathe of Aylesford.

Bede refers to 'public roads', and the concept of at least some roads being the special responsibility of the king appears to be very ancient. Law books of the twelfth century list Watling Street, Ermine Street, the Fosse Way, and Icknield Way as being royal roads, *chimini regales,* and under the king's special protection. They should be wide enough for two wagons to pass or sixteen armed knights to ride abreast. This again almost certainly represents a very ancient tradition, and the king's protection extended to many other roads. In east Kent, for example, those obstructing the roads had, according to Domesday Book, to pay a fine of 100s to the king. In due course the idea of 'the king's highway' was extended to all main roads, and their maintenance and the protection of those who used them became a matter of public concern. Many purely local attempts to provide for the upkeep of short lengths of road were made, and malefactors of every kind were punished when they could be caught, whether for highway robbery or for ploughing up the king's highway, an offence which speaks volumes for the state of the road concerned. The Statute of Winchester of 1285 ordered that highways leading from one market town to another should be broadened so that there was neither dyke, tree, nor bush where a man could lurk to do harm within 200 feet of either side of the road, although this did not extend to great oaks or beeches provided it was clear beneath them, it being the responsibility of the lord to see this done.

Travellers went on foot, on horseback or, together with their goods and merchandise, in wagons and carts which were pulled either by horses or by oxen. In 732 Æthelberht II, King of Kent, granted to the Church of St Mary at Lyminge, in Kent, land by the river Lympne as a site for boiling salt, together with 120 wagonloads of wood to fuel the furnaces. The king's burgesses in Wallingford had, according to Domesday Book, to perform carrying services as far as Reading, Blewbury, and Bensington, and the burgesses of Cambridge complained that they had provided neither carrying services nor carts in the time of King Edward but that now, that is at the time of the compilation of Domesday Book, the sheriff was demanding these services of them. Domesday Book also records the tariffs charged for carrying away salt from the Cheshire brine pits: 4d if the cart was drawn by four oxen or more, only 2d if only two, and at Northwich the charge was 4d for a cart with two or more oxen from another shire, and only 2d for a man from the same shire, and the Geld Inquest of 1084 records that the king had 509 pounds of his geld in his treasury at Winchester, the men who brought it having 40s for their maintenance, they paying 9s 8d to the wagoners.

The first real attempt to make provision on a national scale for the repair and maintenance of roads in England came in 1555. An Act of Parliament of that year imposed responsibility for the repair of roads upon the parish through which the road passed. The Act required that parishioners should elect two surveyors of highways each year. These surveyors could then call upon their fellow parishioners to work on the roads in the parish, at first for four days in each year and then, from 1563, for six. The Act was made perpetual in 1586 and in 1662 the surveyors were empowered to levy a rate in order to meet the expenses for repairs over and above that possible with the six days' compulsory labour of the inhabitants. In 1697 another Act of Parliament gave county justices of the peace authority to set up signposts, although the first milestone to be erected in Britain since Roman times was not put up until 1729, on the London road out of Cambridge. The surveyors themselves lacked technical knowledge and skill, and any practical experience they might have gained during their year in office could not be extended or built upon. Suitable road-mending materials were often not available locally, and the parishioners themselves made very reluctant labourers. The overall result was that roads varied enormously in quality from one parish to the next and were almost completely at the mercy of the weather. Ruts and pot-holes made during the winter months, when the ground was wet and muddy, baked hard in the summer. Accidents were frequent. Both men and horses drowned in the potholes, or broke legs in the ruts. The burden on individual parishes varied enormously. In a remote rural parish the system may have worked fairly well within the expectations of the times, but parishes along the Great North Road found the burden intolerable. In 1660 the parishioners of Stanton, in Hertfordshire, appealed to Parliament for help. In 1663 their petition was renewed, with support from other parishes in Cambridgeshire and Huntingdonshire. The result was the first Turnpike Act. Toll gates were to be erected at Stilton, Caxton, and Wadesmill. Receipts from the tolls were to be applied to the repair of the road, although this did not absolve the parishioners from their liability for statute labour. In 1665 the Act was extended for twenty-one years. No further Acts were passed until the 1690s, when the roads from Colchester to London, Wymondham to Attleborough, and Reigate to Crawley were turnpiked, among others. All gave powers to the county justices to appoint surveyors to view the roads, erect turnpike gates, and charge tolls. A new development occurred in

1706, when a private Act of Parliament provided for the first time for the creation of a body of trustees with powers to manage a stretch of road between Fonthill and Stony Stratford independently of the county justices. This Act served as the model for the turnpike trusts of the eighteenth century. By 1830 there were over 1,100 of them with responsibility for 22,000 miles of road.

Turnpike trustees could appoint salaried surveyors and hire labour in place of the unwilling statute labourers. Their administration was often lax, jobbing was common, roads were often carelessly maintained. Further, their powers were granted for twenty-one years only, and so at the end of this period they had to seek another Act, with all its attendant expense and delay, to renew their powers. Often they failed to do so, and so a road could remain without trustees for years together. Engineering knowledge remained sketchy. Nevertheless, for all their faults, turnpike trustees did bring improvements slowly into the English road network. In 1720 they were required to measure and signpost their roads, and this in itself must have brought enormous savings in time and energy. They had power to widen and straighten roads, and this they did, as well as lowering the gradients of roads on hillsides. In all they brought a thousand minor improvements of a purely local nature to English roads, improvements which were cumulative in their results, so that road travel by the end of the eighteenth century was undoubtedly easier, swifter, and safer than it was at the beginning.

The real improvement in the construction of roads came only at the very end of the eighteenth century with the work of McAdam and Telford. McAdam became general surveyor to the Bristol Turnpike in 1816. This gave him the opportunity to put his theories of road construction into practice. Within three years he and his sons were advisers to thirty-four trusts. His roads were certainly well built and properly drained, but much of his success was undoubtedly due to his skills as a publicist. Telford became county surveyor for Shropshire in 1786. Between 1802 and 1828 he was surveyor to the Commissioners of Highland Roads, and it was in the Highlands of Scotland that he made his reputation. In 1815 he was appointed surveyor to the Commissioners for Improving the Holyhead Road. His methods were much more expensive than those of McAdam, but they also led to better, more solidly constructed roads, and he gave much more attention to the layout of his roads and the reduction of their gradients.

Roads in Scotland were very much worse than those in England, and there were no roads at all west of the Great Glen. Only after the Jacobite rising of 1715 was a programme of road building in the Highlands begun, General Wade constructing about 242 miles of road, including one linking Fort William, Fort Augustus, and Inverness along the line of the Great Glen. The programme was extended after the 1745 rising and after 1784 the roads were gradually turned over to civil rather than military purposes. The Commission for Highland Roads and Bridges was established in 1802, with Telford as the surveyor. In all he built 920 miles of roads and 1,117 bridges, including the coastal road from Inverness to Wick and Thurso. By 1847 a London Sunday newspaper could be in Skye by the following Thursday.

As the roads themselves were slowly improved so change also came to the methods by which they were travelled. By the end of the fourteenth century a public carrier's wagon was making a regular run between Oxford and London. By the end of the sixteenth century a regular network of services covering the country had come into existence, with the longest run said to have been that from Kendal to London. Wagons were heavy, four-wheeled vehicles pulled by a number of horses. Given the state of the roads they could do severe damage to road surfaces, and numerous attempts were made during the seventeenth century to regulate the number of horses which could be used, and the breadth of the wheels. A minimum breadth of 4 inches was imposed, in the hope that such wheels would roll the roads rather than churn them up as narrower ones would do. An enormous range of merchandise went the length and breadth of the country by the carrier's wagon. Alexander Dent kept a shop in Kirkby Stephen in the middle years of the eighteenth century. He drew his tea, sugar, buttons, cloth, paper, books, and magazines from Kendal, Manchester, Newcastle, and London. It all came by the carrier, the journey from London taking about a fortnight, and goods rarely went astray. The second Keeper of the Ashmolean Museum in Oxford, Edward Lhwyd, who died in 1709, had an extensive correspondence with clergymen, antiquaries, and naturalists over much of Wales. They sent him botanical specimens by the carrier, who was asked to 'besprinkle a handful or two of water every night' over the contents of the boxes in order to keep them fresh, and he also received birds' eggs by the same method. William Stubs of Warrington, the file maker who has been mentioned earlier in this chapter, drew his supplies of steel rods from Sheffield by the carrier's wagon and sent his finished products all over England in the same way.

The carrier's wagon was not the only vehicle to be seen on the roads of seventeenth- and eighteenth-century Britain, and where wheeled vehicles could not go, in mountainous districts, for example, then packhorse trains went instead, and until well into the nineteenth century. Four-wheeled coaches were first seen in England in the 1560s and their use spread rapidly. Hackney coaches were to be found in London by the 1620s and they were being licensed by 1637, which is also the year in which the first recorded service of a coach from London to a provincial town took place, to St Albans. The network grew rapidly so that by 1658 a coach travelled to Salisbury in two days and to Exeter in four, with a coach once a fortnight to Edinburgh. The network grew and contracted very rapidly as individual coachmasters opened up what they hoped would be profitable routes and closed down unprofitable ones. The turnpiking of roads undoubtedly benefited stage-coaches and the times taken over journeys came down steadily. In 1754 the journey from London to Manchester took four and a half days. By 1825 it could be done in under twenty-four hours. The Golden Age of stage-coaching was crammed into the fifty years from about 1780 to 1830, the year in which the first passenger railway was opened. Coaching traffic was dense, and brought much prosperity to inns, coachmakers, and coachmasters. By 1830 there were eight coaches a day between Leeds and Sheffield, thirteen between Leeds and Wakefield, and the same number between Leeds and Manchester. It was coaching traffic which made modern Slough, for almost all of its history little more than a hamlet in the parish of Upton, in south Buckinghamshire. Growing traffic along the Bath road brought increasing prosperity to its innkeepers. By 1830 between sixty and eighty coaches a day were passing through the town, which grew accordingly.

The contribution of road transport to the fabric of British history must

76 The Haycock Inn, Wansford, a splendid late-seventeenth-century inn built when the Great North Road passed in front of its door.

never be underestimated, even in the earliest post-Roman centuries. Nevertheless it always remained slow and hence comparatively expensive, and was often very hazardous. Water transport, where it was available, was much to be preferred, especially for moving bulky goods, and the first surviving documents make it clear that ships, havens, wharves, and ferries were nothing unusual in the English landscape at the time. That invaluable charter of about 672 to Chertsey Abbey which has been referred to so often in this book speaks of the Port of London where ships come to land, and a grant of Cnut in 1023 to the monks of Christchurch, Canterbury, includes the haven at Sandwich, all the water dues and the ferry, still in the hands of the monks in 1127. Domesday Book records ferries at Fiskerton, Southwell, and Gunthorpe and gives details of the harbour dues for ships at Chester, Arundel, Pevensey, and Southwark. The burgesses of Dover supplied twenty ships for the king's service for fifteen days, the king's messenger paying 3d for the passage of a horse in winter and 2d in summer, the burgesses finding a steersman and one other helper. Hugolin the steersman held Hampstead Marshall, in Berkshire. The mill built recently at the entrance to Dover Harbour was said to cause great damage to shipping by its disturbance of the sea. A ferry is mentioned at Stockton on Tees in 1184, and another at Houghton, in the Isle of Wight, in 1102. In the following year the bridge at Steyning was said to be impeding shipping. In 1110 the monks of Abingdon had confirmed to them the rights which they had exercised in the time of King Edward to take tolls from shipping passing on the River Thames, either in herrings or in the right to buy merchandise from the ships' cargoes. At the same time all the property of the monks was quit of all tolls, customs and ferry duties throughout England, a valuable privilege much sought by other monastic houses. In about 1127 the reeve of Southampton was ordered by Henry I to restore to the monks whatever he had taken from their goods by way of toll or customs dues.

Most English rivers and many of their tributaries were navigable after a fashion during the medieval centuries, but there were many hazards and difficulties. Rivers froze over in winter and could lose almost all of their water in summer droughts. Fishermen built traps and weirs to catch fish, millers built dams to conserve supplies of water for their mills. The conflicting interests led to many disputes and squabbles, often ending in violence and the destruction of boats, cargoes, weirs, and mill dams. By the early years of the sixteenth century there was a growing interest in the problems and opportunities for river navigation. An Act of Parliament was obtained in 1539 for 'mending of the Ryver of Exetor', although it was not until 1563 that work at last began on what was to be the first canal in England, just under 3 miles long, joining Exeter to the sea at Topsham and bypassing the obstructions on the river. It was two hundred years before it was copied.

Increasing attention was given, especially during the seventeenth century, to the improvement of rivers, the Warwickshire Avon for example, and the Wey from Guildford to Weybridge, where it joins the Thames. Two Acts of Parliament, in 1605 and 1623, provided for the improvement of navigation on the Thames, which was eventually made navigable as far as Oxford. Pound locks were built, and the wharf at South Bridge, in Oxford, had a crane and a wet dock. The river became very busy, with cargoes of coal, wine, sugar, tobacco, and other merchandise going up in exchange for grain and timber, and towns like Henley and Marlow became flourishing river ports. The Severn and the Trent were if anything even more important as navigable waterways, the Severn in particular having one great advantage in that an Act of Parliament of 1532 had made it toll-free. It was also a particularly dangerous river to navigate, with extensive shoals and rapids made worse by the tidal bore.

There were, however, limitations to what river improvement could do. Cuts were already being made to shorten the meanders of rivers, and it could not be long before someone would abandon all connection with a natural waterway and build an entirely artificial one. By the middle years of the eighteenth century the problem of the coal supplies for Liverpool was becoming acute, and a solution had to be found. In 1754 the Corporation of Liverpool ordered a survey to be made of the Sankey Brook. They petitioned Parliament for an Act to make it navigable, and this was passed in 1755. The Sankey Brook was the merest trickle of water and could never have been made navigable. An artificial waterway must have been in the minds of the promotors from the first. The actual building of the canal went unrecorded but in November of 1757 it was complete. Within five years it had been extended north to the coalfields near St Helens and south to the Mersey. It was an outstanding success in every way, although this success has been overshadowed by the even more successful Bridgewater Canal. The third Duke of Bridgewater owned an extensive estate near Manchester, including coal-mines at Worsley, some 10 miles away. The transport of coal from these pits into Manchester was very expensive, doubling the price of coal by the time it reached the town. In 1759 the duke obtained an Act of Parliament to enable him to build a canal, and a second Act of Parliament in the following year authorized him to build an aqueduct over the River Irwell. The first cargo of coal arrived in Manchester in July of 1761.

The Bridgewater Canal was an astonishing feat of engineering, more especially the Barton Aqueduct, and ambitious schemes of canal building were drawn up, with the advice and experience of the duke's engineer, James Brindley, being eagerly sought. In 1766 Acts of Parliament were obtained authorizing the construction of a canal linking the Trent and the Mersey, with a branch from Great Hayward to the Severn. James Brindley was the engineer. He designed and built 118 locks, four aqueducts, and the Harecastle Tunnel, 2,880 yards long.

This first enthusiasm for canal building was followed by a long period of inactivity, the consequence of the outbreak of the American War of Independence. With the restoration of peace in 1783 came a dramatic upsurge of activity, culminating in the early 1790s in the Canal Mania, a period of feverish excitement and much speculation. Between 1791 and 1794 no less than forty-four Acts for the building of canals were passed, with an authorized capital of £6,661,700, and these were only the ones which Parliament approved. Some of the canals projected turned out to be expensive failures. It took fifty-four years to complete the canal between Hereford and Gloucester, and that from Salisbury to Southampton was never finished, and yet it is almost impossible to exaggerate the contribution made by the canals to almost every facet of the landscape. Their actual construction introduced into the landscape entirely new engineering works of dazzling ingenuity and vision, of which the great aqueduct designed by Thomas Telford to carry the Llangollen branch of the Ellesmere Canal 121 feet above the River Dee at Pontcysyllte must rank as the most astonishing. Wharves, locks, tunnels, and towpaths were built, and wherever the canal passed then every opportunity was taken to seize the advantages which it offered. At least five entirely new towns were created by the canals – Runcorn, Grangemouth, Goole, Stourport, and

77 Canal locks and wharves at Stoke Bruerne, Northamptonshire, built for the Grand Junction Canal just to the south of the Blisworth Tunnel which, when opened in 1805, completed a waterway link between London and the midlands.

Ellesmere Port – and many more owe at least something to them. At Fenny Stratford, for example, and at Louth and Blisworth, Loughborough and Aylesbury, the rather gaunt factory blocks which are still to be seen are striking reminders of just how powerful the influence of the canals could be.

James Watt steadfastly refused to use steam at anything more than a few pounds per square inch above atmospheric pressure, and so he failed to take advantage of its full potential. His patents expired in 1800. Within months Richard Trevithick was experimenting with a high-pressure steam-engine, and within a couple of years he had an engine working at 145 pounds per square inch with a cylinder no more than 7 inches in diameter, sufficiently small to be mounted on wheels. He built a steam locomotive in 1804, and in 1813 George Stephenson built his first locomotive for a colliery near Gateshead. A group of coal owners were so impressed with his engines that when they planned a horse-drawn railway 27 miles long from their mines at Darlington to the sea near Stockton-on-Tees they used steam locomotives to haul the trains over at least part of the line. The project was a great success and attracted much attention. Visitors came from all over Britain, including a group of Liverpool and Manchester businessmen, anxious to improve the communications between their two cities. In 1826 they obtained an Act of Parliament for the construction of a railway line. From the first it carried both passengers and goods in trains powered entirely by steam locomotives. When the line opened on 15 September 1830 a new era began.

9

Victorian Britain

All ages are periods of transition, but the twenty or thirty years ushered in by the opening of the Liverpool to Manchester Railway in September of 1830 are particularly so, and not least because contemporaries seem to have become suddenly and acutely aware of the revolutionary changes which were taking place on every side and in every facet of the fabric of Britain. John Stuart Mill wrote in 1831, 'mankind have outgrown old institutions and old doctrines, and have not yet acquired new ones'. The transition was, in his eyes and in those of Matthew Arnold, Carlyle, Dickens, and many more, not so much from the immediate past of the late eighteenth century as from a medieval, feudal world of a fixed and ordered social hierarchy based upon a landowning aristocracy and upon shared certainties in religious and political principles and in matters of taste, all based in their turn upon an economic system in which peasant farming was more important than manufacture, something which in any case should be domestic and small-scale in its organization. Such a world picture was of course an idealized view of the past, one which conveniently overlooked the nastiness of much of medieval life, the bloodshed of the Civil War and the shock of the Scientific Revolution. It was nevertheless a genuine reaction against the ugliness and squalor which industrialization seemed everywhere to bring in its wake, and in its uncritical turning towards a lost medieval Golden Age it has left its own traces in the landscape through the high moral purpose which it came to attach to the revival of Gothic architecture. It was also a world picture which had long been under attack, at least since the Renaissance and the Reformation, but it was really only the outbreak of the French Revolution together with the changes following upon rapid and large-scale industrialization as epitomized in the railway that brought these new developments suddenly and forcibly into the open.

The old certainties were being replaced by new ideas and concepts, bringing chaos and confusion where once, it seemed, there had been peace and tranquillity.

The year of the opening of the Liverpool to Manchester Railway was one of intense political excitement. In July the reactionary government of Charles X in France was overthrown. At the end of June George IV died, and the general election which constitutional custom then demanded should take place upon the demise of the Crown was held under the influence of the news from France. Parliamentary reform was once more in the air, together with widespread rioting in southern England and strikes in northern towns. The first Reform Bill was introduced in March 1831. The political struggles which attended its passage through Parliament and the riots which accompanied it outside are not our concern, but the passage of the Bill in June 1832 and its long-term consequences are, since it is one of the principal themes of this book that landscape is the product of the interaction between man in society and his environment. In the short-term the Great Reform Bill opened the way first to changes in some of the most ancient structures in the landscape, and second to the first tentative steps towards remedying some of the worst environmental abuses that indus-

78   The workhouse at Arclid, Cheshire, built in 1844.

trialization was creating. In the long-term it led to increasing state participation in an ever-broadening range of affairs, so that by the end of the period covered by this chapter it is probably true to say that central government had become the single most powerful body influencing landscape change. Let us look at some of the ways in which these changes begin to make their appearance.

In 1834 the Poor Law Amendment Act provided for the creation of unions of parishes for the better administration of the poor law, a measure which was accompanied by the building of union workhouses, many of which are still to be seen in the landscape today, as at Sleaford in Lincolnshire, built in 1838, or Winslow in Buckinghamshire and Stockport in Cheshire, built in 1841, although later changes in the law have led to their being put to more humane uses than those so savagely portrayed in *Oliver Twist.* The unions thus created emerged as new administrative units and became the basis for urban and rural sanitary districts and then urban and rural district councils, areas of local government which disappeared only in 1974.

The ancient boroughs of England and Wales and the burghs of Scotland had become increasingly corrupt during the course of the eighteenth century. A committee was set up in Edinburgh in 1783 for the reform of Scottish burghs, but the bill introduced into the House of Commons by Sheridan failed to pass. Burgh reform Acts – there were three – were passed in 1833 and the franchise for Scottish municipal elections was extended to £10 householders. In 1835 the Municipal Corporation Act reformed the government of 178 of the 246 boroughs which were identified at the time in England and Wales. All four Acts brought very much more liberal constitutions to the reformed boroughs and burghs but did little to improve the efficiency of their administration. Local Improvement Commissioners, both in Scotland and in England and Wales, where there were about 300, a third in metropolitan parishes, appointed under local Acts of Parliament, were under no compulsion to surrender their powers to cleanse, light, and pave the streets of their towns, and this division of responsibility persisted for many years. In Birmingham, for example, it was the Street Commissioners, first appointed under an Act of Parliament of 1769, who built the splendid town hall in the 1830s, and their powers only passed to the new corporation, itself founded in 1838, after a further Act of Parliament of 1851. Indeed several towns which possessed only Improvement Commissioners were better governed than many with the full array of borough institutions; Birkenhead, for example, which was said in the 1840s to have the best sewer system in the country, or Bournemouth, where Improvement Commissioners were first introduced in 1856 under a local Act of Parliament, whilst Manchester had a Police Commission which, after its reform in 1828, administered the town remarkably efficiently within the standards of the time.

At the same time as the ancient borough corporations were being reformed, equally ancient borough boundaries were being redrawn. The Commissioners appointed for this purpose wrote in 1837 that they attempted to exclude large agricultural areas from boroughs, but this, they found, did not give 'unmixed satisfaction to the inhabitants of every Borough to which it applies', not least because there would be fewer properties to contribute towards the rates. Thus the boundary of the borough of Andover was 20 miles in circumference, enclosing 7,670 acres. This was reduced to an area of a mile and a half square. Boston was reduced from 4,574 acres to 1,100, Beccles from 1,877 to 350, whilst Brecon lost the Ward of Trecastle, some 10 miles distant from the town.

Thirdly, a succession of statutes, beginning in 1818, led to the extensive reshaping of parish boundaries, among the most ancient elements in the landscape, as we saw in Chapter 4. The redrawing of parish boundaries had of course been taking place ever since they first appeared in the landscape. Great and Little Loughton, in Buckinghamshire, were amalgamated in 1409 for example, and Fulmer, in the same county and once a chapel annexed to Datchet, became a separate parish in 1553. Hawkshead, in Westmorland, became a separate parish only in 1578, and Ambleside in 1675. Nevertheless it was in the nineteenth century that the process became at once more radical and very much more far-reaching. Thus, to choose examples from Buckinghamshire once more, Lillingstone Lovell was transferred to that county from Oxfordshire in 1844, the same year in which Caversfield was transferred from Buckinghamshire to Oxfordshire. Seer Green was made a separate parish from Farnham Royal in 1847. Gerrards Cross was created a separate parish from Chalfont St Peter in 1861. In 1868 Latimer was carved from Chesham, and in 1875 Ashley Green was also removed from Chesham and made into a separate parish, whilst in 1886 Helsthorpe, a detached portion of Drayton Beauchamp, was incorporated into the parish of Wingrave.

The first tentative steps were also taken to reshape diocesan boundaries, again in order to provide for the rapid growth in the population of industrial towns. An Act of 1836 created the bishoprics of Ripon and Manchester, although violent opposition to the proposals meant that it was 1847 before the first Bishop of Manchester was appointed. Since the number of bishops sitting in the House of Lords could not be increased, the dioceses of Bristol and Gloucester were amalgamated, only to be separated once more in 1897 when this particular dilemma had been overcome.

In these ways a traditional network of local relationships of the most delicate and particularistic nature was disrupted in the interest of rationality, ease of administration and an earnest attempt to provide for the gross distortion of the traditional fabric which the astonishing population explosion of the nineteenth century was bringing about.

The nineteenth century was the great age for the collection of statistics, and as the methods became increasingly accurate and the range of topics covered increasingly sophisticated, so by the end of the century there were very few corners of the national life which had not been counted, weighed, or measured in one way or another.

The population of England and Wales grew from 8.9 million in 1801 to 32.5 million in 1901, whilst that of Scotland grew from 1.6 million to 4.4 million in the same period. The population of Greater London rose from 1,114,000 in 1801 to 7,252,000 in 1911. In 1801 London was the only town with more than 100,000 inhabitants. By 1901 there were thirty towns of this size. In 1851 the agricultural workforce was at its peak, 1.88 million, and over one in five of adult males were thus employed. In the same year, for the first time, more people lived in towns than in the countryside. In 1811 it is estimated that agriculture contributed 35 per cent of the national income of Great Britain. In 1901 78 per cent of the population of England and Wales was urban and only one in eleven of the adult male workforce was employed in agriculture, which now contributed only 6.4 per cent to the gross national income. In 1800 total United Kingdom coal output was about 11 million tons a year. In 1913 it was 287.4 million tons a year. In 1830 there were 71 miles of railway track open to traffic. In 1912 there were 16,223 miles of track in England and Wales, and at the same time there were 175,000 motor vehicles.

We may be forgiven for asking, as the Lord did of Ezekiel: 'can these bones live?', but these figures, when aggregated, conceal a profound transformation of almost every strand of the fabric of the British landscape, as population growth and industrialization added to it an ever-increasing burden of houses, streets, factories, warehouses, viaducts, railway stations, and gas holders. At the same time, however, it is important to appreciate that they also conceal wide local and regional variations and much fluctuation over time. The processes of change were in some districts swift and dramatic, in others they were slow and protracted, making only very little impact on traditional ways of life, especially in rural areas, before the end of the nineteenth century. Oxen were still being used for the plough in Sussex as late as 1926, for example.

Contemporaries were astonished at the transformation which was taking place at ever-increasing speed in and around Manchester, Birmingham, Leeds, Glasgow, and in the upper reaches of the Taff valley. Thus Edward Baines, writing of Oldham in 1824:

Manufactures have grown in this place with astonishing rapidity. Sixty years ago there was not a cotton mill in the chapelry; at present there are no fewer than sixty-five, of which all, except two, have been built during the present century. These mills, which are wholly employed in spinning cotton, are all worked by steam, and there are, within the same limits, one hundred and forty steam engines, used in the various processes of manufacturing and mining.

> (E. Baines, *History, Directory and Gazetteer of the County Palatine of Lancaster,* Vol. 2, London, 1825: pp. 440–1)

Oldham at this time was at once a township and a parochial chapelry, itself composed of two other townships, Chadderton and Crompton, and another chapelry, Royton, all of which were part of the parish of Prestwich. Only after 1832 would this administrative tangle start to unravel. But, as Baines pointed out, 'the descendant has so much outgrown the parent that the chapelry has begun to take precedence of the parish'. In 1801 the population of Oldham was 12,024; by 1821 it was 21,662. Baines goes on to add that two streams, the Irk and a branch of the Medlock, had

> formerly contributed in a material degree to the manufacturing prosperity of the place, and they are still of considerable utility, but the general introduction of steam engines has diminished the necessity for water power, and supplied its place by a more potent and an unfailing agency.

Here in Oldham and in the comments of Baines are to be found an epitome of those changes which were already transforming the landscapes of Britain. Ancient, traditional, long-established patterns of life were proving incapable of containing the new structures which were crystallizing with such astonishing and such disturbing speed. Men were pouring new wine into old bottles as fast as they could, and the bottles were breaking, the wine was running out and the bottles were perishing. The wine was a fierce, heady compound derived from two sources, a rapid growth in population and the application of scientific and technical knowledge to everyday problems across the whole spectrum of society.

The population of Britain had begun to grow again from the beginning of the second half of the eighteenth century, and between 1801 and 1911 it multiplied almost fourfold, with much the largest increase, a little over 18 per cent, coming in the ten years between 1811 and 1821. Within the long-term view of the history of Britain, population growth took off like a rocket during the nineteenth century, bringing with it problems and consequences of an hitherto unknown scale and complexity.

The fact of this rapid growth in the numbers of the inhabitants of Britain is incontrovertible. The reasons for it remain much less clear. Population grows either because the birth-rate is rising or because mortality rates are falling, or because of a combination of the two. Both birth- and death-rates have always been high in pre-industrialized societies and Britain was no exception. The birth-rate continued at a comparatively high level for much of the nineteenth century. The death-rate started to fall only in the second half of the century, and this in spite of very high mortality rates in some of the larger towns, in Manchester and Liverpool for example, where the expectation of life at birth was between 24 and 26 compared to a little over 40 for the country as a whole. There are still no satisfactory explanations for the long-term trends, although it is clear that there were very wide regional differences.

Not only were towns growing rapidly in size during the nineteenth century, but the proportion of the population living in towns was also growing. In 1801 only one in five of the inhabitants of England lived in towns with populations of more than 20,000, and if London is excluded the proportion falls to about one in fourteen, whilst in Wales no town even reached 20,000 inhabitants. In the 1820s and 1830s population was growing almost everywhere, and the 128 parishes in the Highlands of Scotland reached their maximum total population in 1841. By the 1840s the exodus from the countryside had begun, and by 1851 many rural communities, in Leicestershire and in Dorset for example, were smaller than they had been in 1831. In the Highlands of Scotland fifty-three parishes were declining by 1831, whilst five, Farr in Sutherland, Laggan in Inverness, and Craignish, Kilninver and Kilmelfort, and Lochgoilhead, all in Argyll, were at their maximum in 1801 and have declined ever since. In 1851, for the first time, the number of people living in towns in England and Wales as then defined exceeded the rural population, and then only by the smallest of margins, 9 million to 8.9 million. The transition occurs somewhat later in Scotland, between 1881 and 1891. In the last half of the nineteenth century a great swathe of England, from Devon and Cornwall in the southwest to East Anglia, eastern Yorkshire and the northern Pennines, almost the whole of Wales away from the coalfields, together with the Highlands of Scotland, experienced a fall in population ranging from the slight to the precipitous.

The published census returns are essential reading for every student of the British landscape, since the population changes which they chart are written across it in bold and unmistakable characters. More people meant more houses, shops, churches, and streets: 320,000 new houses were built in England alone between 1841 and 1851, and in Sheffield 156 new streets were built or projected between 1831 and 1836. A map of Manchester and Salford made in 1804 shows a compact built-up area, although the population of the two townships had already reached 84,000. By 1851, 367,000 people lived there, whilst the population of what today would be called the Manchester conurbation exceeded one million inhabitants, with the roads out to Oldham, Ashton-under-Lyne, Hyde, Stalybridge, and Dukinfield already continuously built up. In 1820 there were 126 warehouses in Manchester. By 1829 there were more than a thousand. Whole new towns were created, from Goole and Swindon to Crewe and Wolverton, where there were 218 inhabited houses in 1841 and 367 in 1851. In 1853 there were 604 houses in Rhyl. In 1881 there were 1,329, as well as

115 uninhabited ones and 17 building. Industrial towns like Middlesbrough and seaside towns like Blackpool and Southport grew with astonishing speed, although the fastest growth of all took place in Brighton, where between 1811 and 1821 the population increased by 102 per cent, the greatest percentage increase for any town in Britain during the nineteenth century.

For many Victorians, intensely proud of the undoubted achievements of their era, the nineteenth century was the Age of Great Cities, since the speed with which cities multiplied the numbers of their inhabitants and spread outwards in all directions was obvious to all. By the 1830s, however, they were also becoming aware of the appalling living conditions which this breakneck growth had created, so that attitudes towards towns became increasingly ambivalent. Many town dwellers, of whom a large proportion must have been first generation townsmen, could not reconcile themselves to town life, and hankered after an idealized, often sentimentalized, rural life, although both George Eliot and Thomas Hardy were at pains to point out, from *Adam Bede* to *Far From the Madding Crowd*, that country life was not a rural idyll, but could be just as strenuous, violent, and treacherous as anything in the towns. Nevertheless increasing public awareness of and reaction to the squalid conditions which so many people had to endure in the cellars of Liverpool or the back-to-back houses and courts of Nottingham led very slowly to a gradual amelioration of town life, although in spite of a piecemeal standardization of a growing range of facets of life in Britain, each town and city retained its own individuality and its own distinctive characteristics. A minority, largely confined to south Lancashire, the West Riding, the west Midlands, and the lowlands of Scotland, were rapidly and profoundly transformed by industrialization and population growth. Others, York for example, were affected very much more slowly, and yet others, Buckingham for example, were scarcely touched at all much before the end of the nineteenth century. All this makes generalization particularly difficult.

London has always been *sui generis* in that it has always been by far and away the largest city in Britain and has always contained within its boundaries every facet of urban life, so that it is possible to illustrate every trend of every fashion, from the banal to the bizarre, from London alone. By 1830 it contained some of the worst slums to be found anywhere in Britain, Jacob's Island, in Bermondsey, for example, and Seven Dials in Holborn, together with new streets and terraces epitomizing every subtle social gradation up to the most elegant and fashionable residential districts in and about Grosvenor Square. It was, throughout the nineteenth century, the largest single concentration of industry and manufacture in Britain, although much was centred in workshops rather than in large factories. It was also Britain's largest port, and indeed the largest and busiest port in the world, a role which, from the last years of the

79   Terraces of houses built by Thomas Cubitt in Pimlico, London, in the 1840s and 1850s on
an area once given over to market gardening.

eighteenth century, created an industrial landscape quite the equal in size, complexity, and exuberant self-confidence to anything to be found in the Black Country, Leeds, or Manchester. Wet docks had been built from the end of the seventeenth century, but it was only at the end of the eighteenth that docks, fully enclosed with high brick walls and surrounded with bonded warehouses, make their appearance. The West India Dock was built between 1799 and 1806. The London, East India, and Surrey Docks followed in quick succession. St Katharine's Dock was built between 1825 and 1828, enclosed on almost all sides by a splendid series of warehouses supported on magnificent colonnades. The contractor, Thomas Cubitt, used the materials excavated from the dock itself to turn the marshy ground lying to the west of the gardens of Buckingham Palace into suitable building land, upon which he proceeded to lay out and then build up the streets and squares which in due course came to be known as Belgravia.

From the late eighteenth century both banks of the Thames below London Bridge became built up with row upon row of docks and warehouses, of massive size and construction, making use of the latest materials and techniques. Warehouses, sometimes seven storeys high, were built on columns of cast iron, and both cast- and wrought-iron trusses were in use by the early nineteenth century, whilst corrugated-iron sheeting was being used by about 1830 to provide lightweight roofing material. This new landscape appeared with astonishing speed, prompted by the immensely complex range of political and economic factors which had precipitated Britain into the position of world leader as an industrial and commercial nation. It has disappeared with equally astonishing rapidity and for equally complex reasons, to be replaced by even more massive blocks of offices in concrete and plate glass. It is however still possible to recapture at least something of nineteenth-century dockland, in Wapping for example, and in Rotherhithe and Bermondsey, where Shad Thames is still a dark and narrow canyon of a street between massive six- and eight-storey warehouses, interconnected by wrought-iron bridges which cross and recross the street at every level. Another group of warehouses survives in Rotherhithe, where the medieval Church of St Mary, rebuilt between 1714 and about 1740, and the building of about 1700 which once housed Peter Hills School are amongst the fragments which survive from a yet older landscape.

Towns and cities throughout Britain were transformed during the course of the nineteenth century and this transformation affected both their social and their physical topography. The two factors worked together in the most subtle and complex manner, and the processes were often not completed in some towns before 1945.

For much of the early decades of the nineteenth century the social topography of the centre of a town remained as it had been in medieval times. Well-to-do merchants and tradesmen lived in premises which often combined shop, workshop, warehouse, counting house, and residential accommodation, whilst the poor lived where they could, either in small houses and tenements fitted on to cramped central sites which no one else could use, or else in straggling suburbs, such as Frankwell, just outside Shrewsbury. Mr Gardiner, the uncle of Elizabeth Bennett, the heroine of *Pride and Prejudice,* lived in Gracechurch Street within sight of his own warehouses. At the census of 1801 the City of London had a population of 128,000. During the course of the nineteenth century and with growing momentum in the second half, city and town centres lost their permanent residents and instead were given over to shops, offices, banks, and other commercial and industrial premises. By day the city centre would be thronged with people; by night it would be almost deserted save for residential caretakers. The process developed first and most rapidly in London, where much remained from the rebuilding after the Great Fire. During the twenty years or so from about 1857 the City was almost rebuilt as banks and insurance companies competed for prestigious sites and even more prestigious façades, frequently in a classical or Italianate garb, with an occasional incursion into Gothic. By 1901 the population of the City of London had fallen to 27,000. Once again much has disappeared in the

80   The Prudential building, Holborn, built to designs by Alfred Waterhouse between 1899
and 1906 on the site of Furnival's Inn.

years after 1945, so that in Gracechurch Street, for example, all that Mr
Gardiner would recognize today is the east front of the Church of St Peter,
Cornhill, built by Sir Christopher Wren between 1677 and 1681. The
buildings which replaced his own house and warehouses have themselves
disappeared and nothing is now to be seen which is earlier than 1914, save
the main façade to Leadenhall Market, built from 1881 onwards. Beneath
both the market and Gracechurch Street, however, lie the remains of the
great basilica of Roman London, a huge aisled hall 505 feet long and 150
feet wide. The site has been in almost continuous use for commercial
purposes for nearly 2,000 years. Technical and social changes have in their
turn brought changes into the ways in which this commerce is carried on,
and hence in the building forms which it requires. The nineteenth century
sees this process of replacement, under the stimulus of technological
innovation, accelerate rapidly.

   Where did the heirs and successors of Mr Gardiner go? They went to the
suburbs, and as population grew so too did residential suburbs expand, a
process hastened and strengthened by improvements in transport, from
railways to trams and finally the motor car. Railways brought with them

both industry and working-class housing, and the actual building of the railway, particularly mainline stations, meant that large numbers of houses were demolished to make way for them. Little attention was given however to housing those displaced, and so poor-quality housing was made even worse as it became overcrowded. Slums could develop very quickly and those who could afford to do so went ever further out into newly built and more salubrious suburbs. Nineteenth-century suburban extensions are to be found around almost all British towns and cities, great and small. In London, plans were made to lay out new streets on 600 acres of land at Paddington in 1795. It was the 1840s before the scheme was finally completed, when it was described as an 'elegant and recherché' district. Bayswater was built up in the 1840s and Kensington and Hammersmith in the 1850s. Thomas Cubitt laid out Clapham Park as an estate of large detached houses from 1825 onwards. Victoria Park, Manchester, was planned from the 1830s as a district of large detached villas enclosed within a wall, with gates that were locked at night. Bold Street, Liverpool, was planned in the 1780s as a quiet residential district, and Abercromby Square and Rodney Street were being laid out in the second and third decades of the nineteenth century. The railway reached Kingston-upon-Thames in the 1840s and an entirely new suburb emerged, called Kingston-upon-Railway, later Surbiton. It acquired its own Improvement Commissioners in 1855. Such examples can be multiplied *ad nauseam,* but the example of Birkenhead illustrates almost all of the points which have been made in previous paragraphs.

At the beginning of the nineteenth century Birkenhead had a population of 110. The lord of the manor, impressed with its location and the safety and regularity of the newly established ferry across the Mersey to Liverpool, laid out a few streets and built a hotel and a church. In 1824 a Scotsman, William Laird, established a boiler-making factory and then a shipbuilding yard. He employed James Graham to lay out a regular gridiron pattern of streets focusing on Hamilton Square. The buildings put up round the square were built of stone with a regular façade, giving them an aura of grave dignity which they have not entirely lost, even today. Sir Joseph Paxton laid out the park in 1843, the first ever to be provided at public expense, as well as two areas of well-to-do villas, at Clifton Park and Claughton. In 1844 docks were excavated, the population began to mount, and the social character of the town began to change. The quality of the housing declined, and what had begun as a quiet residential district rapidly became a bustling industrial and shipbuilding town.

The piecemeal nature with which so many suburbs developed, the nice social distinctions implied by the total absence of front gardens, small front gardens to terraced houses, large front gardens to semi-detached ones, a housing form which first appeared in St Johns Wood in London in the 1790s, and the seclusion of large detached houses in tree-filled gardens, the presence or absence of bow windows, of decorated barge-boards, and the happy Victorian practice of putting dates on everything, makes a walk through almost any suburban district a particularly rewarding experience for the landscape historian. Some are laid out on a regular gridiron pattern, others incorporate crescents and squares, whilst beneath it all lies an ancient pattern of fields and closes, since property developers could often do no more than buy one field at a time, with the result that its boundaries have come to exert a permanent influence on the shape and layout of the streets which now fill its place.

At the same time that the transformation of the centres of towns and cities was taking place, replacing the mansions and warehouses of well-to-do merchants and tradesmen with banks, shops, and offices, the physical topography of towns was also being transformed. The appalling overcrowding which characterized the slums of urban Britain created health and sanitation problems on an unprecedented scale. Slowly and tentatively steps were taken to put things right. The technical and engineering problems involved in providing clean water and sewers had themselves to be solved, whilst the property rights of all affected, however indirectly, in any proposed changes were carefully safeguarded. The long-term benefits of improved water and drainage facilities had often to be spelled out in pounds, shillings and pence, and it took several cholera epidemics before the connection between polluted water supplies and disease was widely accepted, and decades before the problems of waste disposal were overcome. The Public Health Act of 1875 gave for the first time to the municipal corporations reformed in 1835 the powers necessary to put things right, powers which some had exercised by private Act and which in other towns had long been exercised by Improvement Commissioners. Several London parishes, especially in the western suburbs, had their own Improvement Commissioners, but it was only in 1855 that it was finally recognized that the metropolis as a whole had problems which could only be resolved at a metropolitan level. The result was the creation by Act of Parliament of the Metropolitan Board of Works, of which the Chief Engineer until 1889 was Sir Joseph Bazalgette. Its first major work was the building of two main sewers, running from west to east, one north and one south of the Thames, culminating in two splendid pumping stations, at Crossness, to the east of Woolwich, opened in 1865 and equipped with four Watt beam-engines, and Abbey Mills, in Newham, opened in 1868. The work on the north bank was associated with the improvement of the riverside itself, the Thames Embankment. This in turn was part of a major programme of new street construction, including Queen Victoria Street, leading to the Mansion House, and Northumberland Avenue leading to Charing Cross. All were marked by an astonishing variety of building styles and materials, revealing Victorian architecture at its best and its worst. The same can be said for Shaftesbury Avenue, laid out and built up between

1879 and 1886. Similar schemes of improvement, varying in detail and scale, are to be found the length and breadth of Britain, from the Corporation Street scheme in Birmingham to Hawick, in Scotland, where a number of new streets and bridges were laid out during the nineteenth century, including the High Street, complete with a new town hall in Scottish baronial style, built between 1884 and 1886.

Improvements in water supplies brought change into the countryside, since reservoirs for the storage of water had to be built. The first ones were provided with earthen dams, and occasionally these could fail. That at Dale Dyke collapsed in 1864 with the loss of 244 lives. The first high masonry dam built in Britain was put up at Vyrnwy for Liverpool Corporation between 1881 and 1889. Three dams were built in the Elan valley for Birmingham Corporation between 1893 and 1904, and Manchester Corporation acquired Thirlmere, in the Lake District, in 1894. This was fenced off from the public, the water-level was raised, the catchment area was afforested and an aqueduct, 96 miles long, was built to bring water into Manchester. The Lady Bower reservoir scheme was begun early in the twentieth century with the building of the Howden and Derwent dams between 1906 and 1907.

Soaring numbers of people in the major industrial regions of Britain meant that places which once had been rural villages rapidly became towns and in due course acquired their own sense of civic pride, to be given expression in the building of town halls, whilst older towns and cities rebuilt theirs on a grand scale in order to give appropriate physical form to their new-found wealth, size, and importance. Sir Charles Barry wrote in 1859 that a town hall should dominate other public buildings in a city being 'the means of giving due expression to public feeling upon all national and municipal events of importance'. Thus Stalybridge, in Cheshire, where the first cotton mill was built in 1776, acquired its town hall in 1831, and that at Hyde, its near neighbour in the Manchester conurbation, was built between 1883 and 1885. Bradford was one of the fastest-growing towns in Britain in the first half of the nineteenth century, but it was not incorporated until 1847. Almost immediately plans were made for building a giant assembly hall, St George's Hall, lit by gas and capable of accommodating over 3,000 people. The rivalry between Bradford and Leeds was intense, and Leeds was not to be outdone. In 1850, even before St George's Hall had been started, plans were laid for a similar hall in Leeds. The plans were changed again and again, and eventually it was decided to build a new town hall. The competition for the design was won by a hitherto unknown young architect, Cuthbert Brodrick. The cost soared. The contractor went bankrupt. It was still unfinished when it was formally opened by Queen Victoria in 1858. When finally complete it had cost £122,000, three times more than the original estimates. The town hall at Manchester cost even more, over £1,000,000, before it was finished, a

81 The town hall at Hyde, Cheshire, built between 1883 and 1885 to designs by
J. W. Beaumont.

masterpiece of Victorian civic Gothic, built to designs by Alfred
Waterhouse between 1868 and 1877, and a fitting symbol of Manchester's
sense of its own importance as a world centre of commerce and industry.
To explore fully the reasons for the building of the town halls in Leeds and
Manchester is to lay bare the immensely subtle network of assumptions,
values, and preoccupations which underly one of the most important
Victorian contributions to the landscape.

The building and rebuilding of town halls all over Britain during the
nineteenth century was in many respects but a manifestation of a sense of
civic pride which, in spite of a series of metamorphoses prompted by
changes in religious and social values, can be detected almost from the
beginning of towns in Britain, whether through Roman basilica and forum,
medieval town walls, or sixteenth-century Scottish tolbooths. Manchester
Town Hall is undoubtedly a masterpiece of Victorian Gothic. It is also an
ancient building type in Victorian fancy dress. Even more interesting from
the point of view of landscape change are the entirely new types of
buildings which increasingly rapid social and technological development
were adding to the environment of nineteenth-century Britain: gasworks,

82   The gas holders just outside St Pancras Station, London.

fire and police stations, cemeteries, municipal offices, sewage pumping plants, whilst building forms which once had been very unusual, such as museums and art galleries, public libraries, public parks and open spaces, multiplied enormously. Each type has its own history, representing in physical terms a complex pattern of social change and technological innovation. Thus William Murdock, who was employed at the Soho works of Boulton & Watt, had succeeded in using gas to light the foundry there by 1803. In 1807 the offices of the Manchester Cleansing and Lighting Commissioners were being illuminated by gas. Its use spread so quickly that by 1830 few towns over 10,000 inhabitants did not have at least their main streets lit by gas. Kendal, for example, had a gas works in 1825, and Banbury one soon after, whilst the splendid gas holders just outside St Pancras Station date from the 1860s.

Other, older and more traditional forms of land use take on new directions. The ghastly conditions in urban cemeteries revealed by social reformers in the 1820s and 1830s led to the creation of entirely new ones. The London Cemetery Company laid out a cemetery on 51 acres of land at Kensal Green, in Paddington, in 1833, and went on to build more at Highgate, Abney Park, Stamford Hill, and Nunhead. The South Metropolitan Cemetery Company was incorporated in 1836, acquiring 39 acres of land at West Norwood. Two chapels were built, one Church of England and the other Nonconformist, both designed by Sir William Tite, who also designed the splendid cast-iron railings at the entrance in Robson Street. The chapels to the new cemetery at Ince in Makerfield, in Lancashire, were designed by Alfred Waterhouse and built between 1855 and 1857, whilst Macclesfield got a new cemetery in 1866. Perhaps the most dramatic of nineteenth-century cemeteries is that of St James, in Liverpool, laid out in an abandoned quarry between 1825 and 1829. Perhaps the most bizarre is to be found at Brookwood, about 2 miles south of Bisley, in Surrey. Here a cemetery was laid out in 1854 on 2,400 acres of heathland. It was originally intended as a national necropolis. It was served by its own railway line and one of the two plain white wooden stations still survives.

The nineteenth century was also the great age for the building of public libraries, museums, and art galleries, although all three were not unknown before. The library amassed by Sir Robert Cotton before his death in 1631 proved an embarrassment both to his descendants and to the nation. An Act of Parliament of 1700 recognized its importance, describing it as 'the

83 The National Gallery, built between 1832 and 1838 to designs by William Wilkins.

84 The Albert Memorial, London, designed by Sir George Gilbert Scott and built between 1863 and 1872.

best of its kind now extant', and providing that upon the death of Sir Robert's grandson it should be vested in trustees. A further act of 1708 vested Cotton House in the Crown. A disastrous fire in 1731 was followed eventually by an Act of Parliament in 1753 creating the British Museum, with the Cotton Library as one of the founding collections. A lottery was organized to raise £10,000 with which to buy the manuscripts from the library of Edward Harley, Earl of Oxford, and a further sum bought Montagu House, in Bloomsbury, as a suitable repository for the collections. Here the British Museum gradually took shape. The splendid Ionic colonnade encompassing the entire façade to Great Russell Street and designed by Sir Robert Smirke in 1823 was not finished until 1847. By this time the National Gallery had been built to house the collection of pictures formed by John Angerstein, a wealthy London merchant, who had died in 1823. Trafalgar Square had been laid out in 1820 by John Nash, replacing the Royal Mews and an area of very poor housing, especially in the immediate vicinity of the Church of St Martin-in-the-Fields. It was intended that the National Gallery should provide a suitable climax to the new square, something which it has lamentably and obviously failed to do.

85   The Albert Hall, London, designed by Captain Fowke and built between 1867 and 1871.

Perhaps the single greatest concentration of buildings illustrating the seriousness and earnestness with which the Victorians approached educational and cultural self-improvement is to be found in South Kensington. Here, on a site purchased with the profits of the Great Exhibition of 1851, appeared first of all the Albert Memorial, erected between 1863 and 1872 to commemorate the man who embodied so many of the most characteristic Victorian moral and spiritual attitudes. This was followed by the Albert Hall, finished in 1871, the Royal College of Organists, the Royal College of Music, the Natural History Museum, designed by Alfred Waterhouse, the City and Guilds Institute, the Imperial Institute, the Victoria and Albert Museum, the Imperial College of Science and Technology, and finally the Science Museum, begun in 1913.

Both free and subscription libraries were not unknown before the nineteenth century. There was one in Ipswich by the opening years of the seventeenth century, and Humphrey Chetham founded one in his college in Manchester in 1653, whilst the Portico Library, a subscription library in Manchester, was built between 1802 and 1806. Nevertheless it is only following the passage of the Public Libraries Act of 1850 that public

libraries begin slowly to make their appearance in the landscape, since the
Act was, like so much Victorian legislation, merely enabling rather than
compulsory. Many libraries depended for their buildings upon private
benevolence. Thus Sir Henry Tate provided a number of public library
buildings in south London, at Brixton, for example, in 1893 and in South
Lambeth in 1888, whilst Miss J. Durning Smith paid for the Durning
Library in Kennington Lane in 1889. Many other towns had to wait for the
munificence of Andrew Carnegie before they acquired public library
buildings, Kendal in 1908 for example and Knutsford in 1903–4. At
Wigan, however, the public library was built in 1878 to designs by the
indefatigable Alfred Waterhouse.

The appearance of these buildings in the nineteenth-century landscape is
evidence of widespread efforts to improve the quality of life of
townspeople, whether by providing better drainage and street lighting or
by providing opportunities for spiritual and cultural betterment. Almost
everything, however, was left to local, often individual initiative, so that,
although towns and cities in nineteenth-century Britain followed broadly
similar patterns of change, no two were exactly alike and each retained its
own very marked consciousness and individuality. One of the most

86 The florist's shop was built at the end of the nineteenth century by Andrew Carnegie as a
public library at Jedburgh.

splendid groups of nineteenth-century public buildings is to be found in Liverpool. St George's Hall, designed as a concert hall and lawcourts in direct rivalry of Birmingham's town hall, was built between 1841 and 1856, and remains one of the finest neo-Grecian buildings in Britain. Sir William Brown, a wealthy Liverpool banker, paid for the building of the public library and museum, built between 1857 and 1860. The Picton Reading Room of 1875–9 commemorates another benefactor of the city, Sir James Picton, whose *Memoirs of Liverpool,* published in 1873, can still be read with profit, whilst Sir Andrew Walker, a rich brewer, paid not only for the art gallery which bears his name but also for the science laboratories of the university, founded in 1881, with Alfred Waterhouse as the architect for the first buildings. The whole group, hall, library, museum, art gallery, and reading room, have a remarkable coherence, reinforced by their restrained classical style. They constitute an outstanding monument to all that was best in Victorian civic pride and private philanthropy.

A Select Committee on Public Walks, reporting in 1833, found no public open spaces in Bradford, Blackburn, Bolton or Sheffield, Birmingham, Bristol, or Hull. The reason, it thought, was that the very great increase in population of recent years had led to a rapid rise in property values and much enclosure, leaving no room for open spaces for public recreation. In Bolton it found much building in all directions. In Sheffield, Sheffield Park, on the southeastern side of the town, was wholly enclosed and in the hands of agricultural tenants of the Duke of Norfolk. The breakneck speed at which building was taking place around so many towns in Britain was imposing ever-increasing ranks of narrow courts and back-to-back houses between the opportunity for recreation in fresh air and open countryside and those most in need of it. The committee thought that there was a genuine requirement for public parks and open spaces 'fitted to afford means of exercise or amusement to the middle or humbler classes'. The committee not only highlighted the need but also the difficulties in satisfying that need. Land had simply become too expensive to be set aside as public parks.

London was more fortunate than most. Hyde Park had been enclosed as a deer park by Henry VIII. It was first opened to the public in 1637 and the Serpentine was created in 1730. The leper hospital of St James, set in an isolated and poorly drained spot, was dissolved in 1532, the marsh was drained and St James's Palace built. Charles II laid out the Mall soon after the Restoration, dividing what came to be known as St James's Park and Green Park. Landscaping of St James's Park began in 1828 and the Select Committee of 1833 wrote that it had been lately planted and improved with great taste and was now open, with Kensington Gardens, 'to all persons well-behaved and properly dressed'. William III bought a house from the Earl of Nottingham in 1689 and, with the aid of Sir Christopher Wren, transformed it into the quiet, unostentatious, brick-built Kensington

87   Derby Arboretum, given to the town by Joseph Strutt in 1840 and laid out
by John Loudon.

Palace. Gardens were laid out and an Orangery built. The landscaping of
the former palace kitchen garden into what is now Kensington Palace
Gardens began in the 1840s.

Public parks and open spaces came very slowly into other towns, at first
almost entirely due to private benevolence. The Duke of Rutland laid out
botanical gardens in Bakewell in 1814 as part of his attempts to turn the
town into a fashionable resort that would rival Buxton. In 1832 John
Loudon laid out botanical gardens in Edgbaston, then developing as a very
select residential suburb of Birmingham, and in 1839–40 he designed the
Arboretum at Osmaston Road, Derby, given to the town by Joseph Strutt.
In 1834 the Jephson Gardens in Leamington Spa were opened, and in 1843
a private Act of Parliament was obtained for a public park in Birkenhead,
laid out over 180 acres of land at a cost of £120,000 to designs by Sir Joseph
Paxton. But none of these, not even that at Birkenhead, can be said to
have met the needs of the working classes. Instead they were provided in
what were essentially middle-class residential suburbs. Industrial towns
still had long to wait. Queen's Park in Bolton dates from 1866, and Mesnes
Park, Wigan, from 1878. Battersea Park was constructed between 1854 and
1861, and Kennington Park was carved from what was left of the common
in 1851.

In the latter half of the nineteenth century the creation of public parks became part of a growing movement towards conservation rather than exploitation, and as a result, as we shall see at the end of this chapter, increasingly strenuous and increasingly successful attempts were made to preserve open spaces, and many of the commons, Hampstead for example, and Wandsworth and Tooting, still surviving in suburban London, were saved from property speculators. By the end of the nineteenth century most towns had a municipal park, often with bandstand, boating lake, and bowling green, set with flower borders whose formal rigidity and use of masses of bedding plants of violent and garish colours reveal Victorian gardening at its worst; but at least those of 'the middle and humbler classes' who strolled there of a Sunday afternoon with their families could get some fresh air on one day of the week.

We saw something in Chapter 5 of the great wave of town planning which swept over medieval Britain. It came to a standstill in the years following the Black Death in 1348 and revived only very slowly during the latter part of the seventeenth century and the eighteenth, and then, unlike so much medieval town planning, as a result of private rather than royal initiative. Medieval town planners hoped to make money from property rents and from the tolls of markets and fairs. The greatly increased rents to be drawn from lands which had been built over, as opposed to agricultural land, were always among the strongest motives behind the willingness of landlords to lay out new towns or new suburbs to old ones, but others were increasingly tempted by the profits to be made from coal-mining and from other industrial enterprises. The physical growth of old towns came almost to an end in the sixteenth and seventeenth centuries save for London, where the planning and building of suburbs to the east, the north, and the west of the medieval city proceeded at an accelerating pace in the years after the Restoration, receiving an enormous stimulus in the enforced exodus from the city caused by the Great Fire.

A handful of new towns was founded in the seventeenth and eighteenth centuries, largely to exploit newly discovered coalfields. The first of these was Whitehaven, laid out by Sir John Lowther as a coal port upon a simple gridiron pattern from the 1680s onwards. At about the same time Sir Robert Cunningham opened up his coal pits at Stevenston and built a harbour at Saltcoats, also to handle the trade in coal. Maryport was renamed as such by Humphrey Senhouse, after his wife. He laid out a very simple gridiron pattern of streets in the hope that the town would develop as a coal port, but it never achieved the success of Whitehaven.

Both the canals and the railways created new towns, the former at Goole for example and the latter at Crewe. Both were entirely 'company' towns in that the town was planned, its houses built and its services, ranging from churches through schools to gasworks, were all provided by the company which built the canal or railway in the first place. Industrialists, whether cotton-mill owners or ironmasters, often found it necessary to provide

88   Houses built by the Butterley Iron Company at Ironville, Derbyshire, in the 1850s, to house its workforce.

housing for their workforce, especially for skilled ones. Sir Richard Arkwright built his mill at Cromford in 1771, adding to it a row of houses, North Street, the Greyhound Inn in 1778, and a church, built between 1792 and 1797. Arkwright was for ten years in partnership with Jedediah Strutt, and they built a mill at Belper in 1776. When the partnership came to an end in 1781 Strutt concentrated his efforts in Belper. More mills were built, together with rows of houses for his employees, in Long Row for example, and in the appropriately named William, George, and Joseph Streets. The Butterley Iron Company built stone houses in Golden Valley between 1797 and 1813 and then went on to build brick ones at what came to be called Ironville, in Derbyshire, from 1834 onwards, adding a school in 1850, a church in 1852, and a recreation ground.

Such housing, whether of brick or stone, was often of a substantial quality within the expectations of the time, and several employers, of whom Robert Owen at New Lanark is perhaps the best known, took a benevolent though often patronizing and sometimes despotic interest in the welfare of their workers. Other industrialists, however, paid little or no attention to housing their workers, and property speculators filled the gap. Cheap, jerry-built housing of poor-quality workmanship and without even the most basic drainage facilities, often huddled together in closes and courts at factory gates, was the result. Unskilled and casually employed workers could neither afford to rent anything better nor to live beyond walking distance from their place of work. The slums of Liverpool, Manchester, Nottingham, and Glasgow became notorious from the reports of social reformers in the 1830s and 1840s but it was the end of the century before the long, protracted attempts to put things right at last began to bear fruit.

Robert Owen was undoubtedly the most successful of the first generation of benevolent industrialists in that he was able to make philanthropy pay, but his ideas were not followed up, first because they were obviously unpractical and second because his proposals for social reorganization were too radical. Much more influential was the model town built at Saltaire by Sir Titus Salt. He moved his alpaca and mohair mills out from Bradford on to a new site in the countryside. The new mill was opened in 1853 to a blaze of publicity. By 1872, 820 houses had been built, in four main streets and twenty-one minor ones. The houses themselves were arranged in regular blocks, with sixteen cottages in a row, each of two storeys. He built a school and an institute, Methodist and Congregational churches and even laid out a park of 14 acres. Although the scheme attracted much attention it remained for many years an isolated example. Even more important was the new town built by George Cadbury at Bournville. The Cadbury brothers moved their chocolate factory out from the centre of Birmingham in 1879, in search not only of more hygienic conditions for food manufacture but also the opportunity to provide better housing for their employees. The scheme took a long time to get started. It was 1893 before George Cadbury began to lay out a model town. By 1900 over 300 houses had been built and a trust was created to administer the project. It was altogether different in concept from Saltaire in that through the trust it was administered quite separately from the factory and so its residents did not have to be drawn exclusively from company employees. The architects also paid much more attention to visual appearance than was ever done at Saltaire. Houses were either semi-detached or else arranged in blocks of four, most being built in brick with slate or tile roofs. Exteriors were made as varied as possible, using gables, bay windows, and dormers, all done quietly and without ostentation or unnecessary expense. Every house had a garden, and trees and flowers were to be found everywhere.

Bournville is in many ways perhaps the most influential of nineteenth-century housing schemes, although it must be recognized that it came at the end of a long period of experiment and speculation on ways of improving housing conditions, some promoted by philanthropic bodies such as the Society for Improving the Condition of the Labouring Classes and the Peabody Trust. The latter, founded in 1862, was responsible for some particularly cavernous blocks of tenement flats, in Greenman Street, Islington, for example, equalled perhaps by the Sandringham buildings put up in 1883–4 following the opening up of Charing Cross Road after an Act of Parliament of 1877. The motives of earlier industrialists cannot be doubted. Their schemes, however modest, all called for considerable capital investment upon which there could be no return for many years, and all were supported by a well-established and prosperous manufacturing enterprise. Nevertheless it is Bournville which both summarized almost a century of experiment and set new standards for the future. The concepts of town planning and of the garden city were in the air. Ebenezer Howard published his book, *Tomorrow*, in 1898, revised and reissued as *Garden Cities of Tomorrow*. In the following year he founded the Garden City Association, and in 1903 bought a site of nearly 3,800 acres at Letchworth in Hertfordshire. His ideas were both comprehensive and practical. Letchworth Garden City was not a company town. Its principal aim was to provide good living conditions for working people. Howard was well aware that people had to work for their livings and so he made suitable provision for shops and for industrial undertakings. The plan avoids a rigid gridiron layout. Streets are gently curved, with plenty of trees and small open spaces. By 1914 the town had a population of over 9,000.

In 1909 the first Town Planning Act was passed. In itself the whole concept of planning future urban development was very new, but the Act grew out of an awareness of the long-term costs of putting right the consequences of the haphazard way in which towns had grown during the nineteenth century and of the need to provide amenities. The Act was very limited in its scope. It applied only to new suburban developments. It was optional and it gave no powers for compulsory purchase. It was nevertheless a beginning. By 1915 the preparation of 105 schemes under the Act had been authorized by the Local Government Board.

We concluded the previous chapter with the opening of the Liverpool to Manchester railway in September 1830, an event marking the culmination of at least two centuries of scientific and technical effort, since wooden railways had been in use in mining districts from the end of the sixteenth century in England and from 1722 in Scotland, and the power of atmospheric pressure had been a matter for scientific curiosity since the seventeenth. It also marks the beginning of the end of centuries' old traditions and ways of life whose contributions to the rich fabric of the British landscape had almost always been cumulative rather than destructive. It is impossible to exaggerate the impact of the railways upon every strand and thread of this fabric. Within twenty years almost 6,000 miles of railway track had been built, so that by 1852 the only major towns in England without a railway station were Hereford, Weymouth, and Yeovil. There were already two routes from England into Scotland, one from Carlisle to Glasgow and the other from Berwick to Edinburgh. Several lines had been built in the Central Lowlands, and one had already reached Aberdeen by way of Perth and Dundee. In Wales there was a line from

Chester along the north coast to Holyhead, although in the south there were only four or five unconnected lines running north from the coast. By 1875 the network had doubled, and by 1912 it had almost trebled, reaching 16,223 miles in England and Wales alone.

By the middle years of the century the railway had become an accepted part of life and had already begun to affect profoundly every community which it touched. Thus the growth of the population of Kilwinning, in Ayrshire, from 5,251 in 1841 to 6,359 in 1851 was attributed, in the 1851 Census Report, 'to the advantages of railway communication', and a similar explanation was given for similar patterns of growth in Kilbirnie and Dalry. In contrast, the population of Great Missenden in Buckingham-shire fell from 2,225 in 1841 to 2,097 in 1851, 'due to the discontinuance of two boarding schools and the removal of families in consequence of the want of railway communication'. The direct impact of railway communi-cation upon the population of towns and villages, large and small, continued throughout the century. It was reported in the 1911 Census that the growth in the population of Chalfont St Peter from 1,402 in 1901 to its present 2,802 was due 'mainly to building development consequent upon improved railway facilities', whilst the population of Wolverton had grown from 5,323 to 7,384 in the same period because of extensions to the railway engineering works and the printing works in which railway timetables were produced.

The actual building of the railways introduced many new, often alien, elements into the landscape and dislocated many ancient ones. Railway companies often sought sites for their stations as near to the centres of towns as possible. This frequently led to large-scale demolition of existing buildings of every kind. Thus when King's Cross Station was built in London – it was completed in 1852 – it required 45 acres of land, for which streets of slum dwellings and at least two fever and smallpox hospitals were swept aside. Stations were entirely new building forms and the styles in which they were built reflect first the uncertainty experienced for much of the century about what to do in such circumstances, second the by now enormous range of styles and building materials available to architects and builders, and third a not altogether unjustified pride in their achievements to which many railway companies wished to give expression in physical form. Some railway stations were built in late Elizabethan and early Jacobean styles, as at Stowmarket, and that at Wansford, built in 1845, is a particularly fine example. The North Staffordshire Railway Company favoured this style, and at Winton Square, in Stoke-on-Trent, the square, with the station on one side and the North Staffordshire hotel on the other, forms a particularly impressive and satisfying group. Yet other companies favoured classical styles, of which the most splendid example by far was at Euston, deliberately planned on the grand scale as the gateway to the north, a composition crowned by a magnificent Doric arch at the main

89   The railway station at Wansford, built in 1845.

approach way. Its destruction when the station was rebuilt in 1969 remains an act of quite unforgivable vandalism. The very long Tuscan colonnade at Gosport, built in 1841, still survives, although the station itself is now closed. The little station at Market Harborough, built in 1884, is a very pleasant imitation of what was then thought to be Queen Anne style. In contrast the Bedford Railway Company, during its very brief existence as an independent company, built four stations, at Ridgmont, Millbrook, Fenny Stratford, and Woburn Sands, all opened during the course of 1846, in what is best described as the *cottage orné* style with much use of decorative half-timber work, gables and dormer windows with fretted barge-boards.

Tunnels were among the most impressive of the engineering works which the railways created, and their entrances provided splendid opportunities for architectural extravagance. One of the earliest and finest examples must be the western entrance to the Box Hill Tunnel, built in 1841 to designs by Isambard Kingdom Brunel. Here is a great classical portico in Bath stone with sweeping side walls. In contrast, the north entrance to the tunnel at Clay Cross is Victorian medieval castle style,

90 A ventilation shaft to the Kilsby Tunnel, Northamptonshire, 1 mile and 682 yards long and built in 1838.

complete with towers and crenellations, as is the entrance to the Clayton Tunnel, on the line to Brighton, completed in 1841. Medieval or Gothic architecture was always much favoured by the Victorians, whether it be the crenellated towers and parapets at Conway or the less than convincing Gothic arches to the viaduct at Tilt, near Blair Atholl. The railway companies shared the Victorian delight in ostentatious and grandiose building schemes, and were as capable as anyone else of producing work that ranged from the impressive to the meretricious. They could also on occasion be as parsimonious as they were extravagant, building small simple stations in wood, as at Plumpton, near Lewes, and Little Kimble, in Buckinghamshire, buildings which are as much a monument to the Victorian age as St Pancras Station itself.

The railway companies frequently added hotels to their stations. St Pancras Station was designed by W. H. Barlow, and his glass and iron roof, spanning 240 feet, is still an entirely admirable masterpiece of Victorian engineering. Sir Gilbert Scott was commissioned to design the enormous hotel building, which is structurally quite separate from the station and yet masks it from the road. The hotel block was completed in 1873, and controversy has swirled around it ever since. Whatever its architectural merits it is undoubtedly sensational. Scott was as lavish on the interior as he was on the exterior, and its reputation as 'the most sumptuous and

91   The magnificent roof to St Pancras Station, London, built in 1868, the ironwork being
manufactured by the Butterley Iron Company.

best-conducted hotel in the Empire' was entirely justified. It had central
heating and hydraulically operated lifts, both then very recent innovations.
Much of its interior decoration still survives, although it has long ceased to
be used as a hotel.

Most of the other railway termini in London acquired hotels, as at
Paddington and Charing Cross for example, though not at Waterloo, as
well as at many other stations throughout Britain, at Crewe for example,
and Bradford, Ayr, and Holyhead, whilst others were built at ports to
provide accommodation for travellers going on by sea, as at Dover and
Parkeston Quay.

The impact of railways in the countryside was as great as anything in the
towns. Ancient patterns of fields, hedgerows, and lanes were sliced
through and permanently disrupted by the new lines. Tunnels, bridges, and
viaducts enabled the lines to ignore all but the most intractable of physical
obstacles. Railway lines strode across rivers and valleys and bored through
hills and mountains, often with an engineering skill coupled to an
astonishing self-confidence in the mastery of man over his environment
that cannot fail to impress even today. The viaduct on the western side of
Durham is one example, that which strides over the centre of Stockport is

92   Derby Midland Hotel, built in 1840 and the first railway hotel in Britain.

another, and the Royal Border Bridge, built by Robert Stephenson to carry the line over the Tweed, is an impressive third.

The completion in 1835 of the Birmingham to Liverpool Junction Canal brought almost to an end the era of canal building which had begun some eighty years before. Some minor work was carried out, especially in the Black Country, and a link from the Bridgewater Canal to the Weaver was built, as was the Slough branch of the Grand Junction, but the only major inland waterway of the second half of the nineteenth century was the Manchester Ship Canal, opened in 1894.

Many canals flourished during the 1830s and 1840s by transporting railway construction materials, but once the railways were built competition intensified dramatically. The tonnage actually carried by canals often rose, but tolls had to be sharply reduced, so that total revenues fell. The profits made by the Bridgewater Canal amounted to £47,650 in 1830. They fell to £17,473 in 1833. At the same time maintenance costs were rising. The result was that some companies went into voluntary liquidation, and several simply faded away as company meetings ceased to be held and wages remained unpaid. Railway companies bought up others, and found ways of controlling yet more, so that, for example, all three trans-Pennine canals were under railway control at one time, and the water-borne trade in finished textiles came to an end.

Only a few canals remained profitable and then only with vigorous management and technical improvement. The Aire and Calder Navigation was perhaps the most successful in combatting the competition from the railways. Steam tugs were in use from 1831 and in the 1880s the company embarked upon an extensive programme of rebuilding and widening locks.

The only major canal undertaking of the last half of the century was the Manchester Ship Canal. Planning began in earnest in 1882, but the passage of the enabling Act through Parliament was violently opposed and the first issue of shares failed, so that it was 1887 before construction actually began and 1894 before it was opened for traffic. The first major engineering work of the canal era, Brindley's aqueduct over the Irwell at Barton, had to be demolished and replaced with a swing aqueduct in order that ships might pass, yet a further example of the way in which, in the latter part of the nineteenth century, social change and technological innovation were replacing elements in the landscape, elements which, within the long-term perspective of landscape history, were themselves only comparatively new.

A Royal Commission on Canals was appointed in 1906 and it presented its massive report, in twelve volumes, in 1911. It made a number of sensible recommendations for improving and enlarging the trunk canals which formed the 'Cross': those which joined the Thames, Severn, Humber, and Mersey, the centre of the network being at Birmingham. The Commissioners thought, however, that the costs involved were beyond private financial resources and so they recommended nationalization, with a Waterways Board to manage the system. The outbreak of war in 1914 effectively put an end to any prospects of the proposals being implemented, whilst yet further technical innovations were already threatening both railway and canal alike. The first patents for motor cars were taken out in 1886. A factory for the manufacture of Daimler motor cars was opened in Coventry in 1896. Herbert Austin opened his Longbridge factory on the outskirts of Birmingham in 1905 and within two years was employing 800 workers.

By the third decade of the nineteenth century the redrawing of the rural landscape embodied in the phrase 'the Parliamentary enclosure movement' was almost complete. Of the 5,265 Acts of Parliament passed for the enclosure of common lands of every kind in England, only 187 were passed after 1830. Open arable land had all but disappeared by that date, although some very large, but by now quite isolated, areas still remained: 1,717 acres at Totternhoe in Bedfordshire, for example, were not enclosed until 1886; over 1,000 acres surrounded Nottingham and were not enclosed until the award was signed in 1865, twenty years after the enclosure Act was passed; and 1,593 acres of the open fields of Stamford were not enclosed until 1875. The last enclosure award was made in 1918 for 628 acres of land at Elmstone Hardwicke in Gloucestershire. Save for the living fossil at Laxton, in Nottinghamshire, one of the most complex systems ever devised for the exploitation of the natural resources of the land, a system which had been widespread over large tracts of lowland Britain since at least the tenth century if not before, finally came to an end, and with it the third great replanning of the rural landscape since the end of the last ice age.

Although the enclosure of open arable land was almost complete by 1830, much common waste, moorland, forest, and fenland still remained open. Thus 32 per cent of Northumberland, 46 per cent of Westmorland and 47 per cent of Caernarvonshire were enclosed between 1800 and 1873. Some 2,800 acres of Matterdale Common, in Cumberland, remained unenclosed until 1882, 10,000 acres at Knaresdale in Northumberland were enclosed in 1859, and 12,000 acres of Bowes Moor in the North Riding of Yorkshire were enclosed in the same year. Many miles of stone boundary walls were built, and isolated farmsteads in more sheltered and congenial spots. Some areas of waste and moorland were improved by stripping, burning, and liming, and were then converted to improved pastures, but these attempts were not everywhere either successful or permanent, and large areas in remote and inhospitable districts remain as rough pasture even today.

By the 1830s most remaining Royal Forests had long ceased to function as such, and were often areas of open heathland and scrub, overstocked by the inhabitants of the surrounding villages, who turned their animals into the forest without stint. Each Royal Forest has its own unique history, so that to look briefly at the fate of one during the course of the nineteenth century does less than justice to the others, although it does illustrate many of the factors making for change in the nineteenth-century landscape.

The Forest of Delamere, in Cheshire, had been reduced by long centuries of piecemeal enclosure and overgrazing to about 10,000 acres of poor heathland on a ridge of sandstone and glacial outwash. This remaining area was enclosed by Act of Parliament in 1812 as part of a nationwide drive by the Commissioners of Woods and Forests, a body set up to ensure an adequate supply of timber for ships for the Royal Navy. Of the 7,600 acres covered by the award, 4,000 acres were allotted to the Crown. By 1823 almost the whole of this had been divided up and planted with trees, mainly oak, but with some Scots pine to afford shelter to the young trees, together with chestnut, larch, and ash. By 1854 the fears of timber shortages had largely faded before technical improvements in the making of iron plate, and it was stated categorically that oak trees should never have been planted, the soils being totally unsuitable. It was decided to clear some 2,400 acres of woodland and by extensive marling to convert them into agricultural land. The first area to be reclaimed, about 240 acres surrounding Hondslough Farm, was marled during the course of 1860, a special light railway being built to convey the marl from the newly opened pit at Waterloo Gate. The work was a success, and both here and at Delamere Lodge Farm and Organsdale Farm fertile arable lands were created which have remained in cultivation ever since, lands which in the regularity of their layout are characteristic of nineteenth-century agricultural practices. Some woodland remained. A report of 1908 described nearly 2,000 acres, of which just over a quarter had been replanted in the previous fifteen years. Much was of poor quality, and a proposed replanting programme recommended the use of conifers rather than oak, and it is plantations of Corsican and Scots pine which dominate the landscape today. Some oaks remain, silent reminders of the speed with which technological developments had made them redundant long before they were mature. The first paddle steamer was built for the navy in 1822, but both steam and iron plating came in very slowly. The first iron-clad, HMS *Warrior,* was launched only in 1860, and then largely in reaction to the French building four iron-clad warships. After 1866, however, no large wooden-hulled ship was laid down for the Royal Navy.

Whereas the creation of the open-field system, perhaps from the eighth century onwards, seems to have been accompanied by the nucleation of settlement, not least because, if the individual parcels of lands which went to make up a farm lay scattered the length and breadth of the lands of a community, it was probably more convenient for the individual farmer to live at a central point, so enclosure and consolidation, as soon as they appear in the historical record, in the later twelfth century, were accompanied by the slow dispersal of settlement as it became more convenient for farmers to live in comparative isolation, away from the village, in a farm at the centre of their newly consolidated farms. New and very often substantial farmhouses and farm buildings make their appearance in increasing numbers in the rural landscape of Britain. Much thought and experiment went into the design and layout of these new farms and a number of architects came to specialize in this branch of the profession. G. A. Dean, for example, had an extensive practice, and Samuel Wyatt designed many farm buildings on the Holkham estates in Norfolk. Farm buildings became increasingly elaborate, so that by the 1860s for example, the farms on the Sneyd estate, at Keele in Staffordshire, had fixed steam-engines, separate accommodation for hay, turnips, straw, and grain, and implement sheds and tanks for storing liquid manure. Perhaps the most elaborate farmstead of all is to be found at Eastwood Manor Farm, at East Harptree in Somerset. The entire complex is completely enclosed, with two arched and glazed domes surmounting two bullock yards, dairy, stabling, granaries, store rooms, and a basement slurry tank with a capacity of 3,000 gallons into which everything drains, including rainwater from the roof. The whole structure was completed in 1858.

Much of the encouragement to improve came from great landowners who poured a great deal of money and even more enthusiasm into their model farms. The last farm to be built on the Holkham Estates in Norfolk, Egmere Farm, cost £5,458 for example. The lead came from the very top, since the enthusiasm of George III for things agricultural was continued by the Prince Consort, who built the Flemish Farm near Windsor, completed in 1858, and the Royal Dairy at Frogmore, an extravagant essay in Renaissance style with an astonishing expanse of decorated tiling inside. Few could afford to follow the royal example, but the home farm of the Lowther estate in Cumberland, with its Gothic tower and crenellations, is one of the more remarkable examples, as is the octagonal dairy to the model farm at Arundel Castle.

Many landlords also turned their attention to rehousing their agricultural labourers, who often lived in conditions of appalling squalor, even by nineteenth-century standards. Timber-framed cottages with wattle-and-daub infilling and thatched roofs proved particularly insanitary, and were badly lit and ventilated, totally lacking in any form of drainage or water supply, whilst the practice of building ramshackle, poor-quality housing on wastes and commons seems to have persisted for much of the nineteenth century.

Landlords often did much to improve these conditions. Thus Mr Tyringham was said, in 1867, to have built four pairs of very good brick and slate cottages at Tyringham in Buckinghamshire, for £230 the pair, each containing three bedrooms, living room, scullery, pantry, privy, and ash pit. Three bedrooms became a standard feature of much improved housing in the later nineteenth century, on moral grounds, since it provided one bedroom for parents, one for boys and one for girls. Lord Overstone made similar improvements on his estates, the cottages at Aston Abbots being considered model dwellings for the time, and the Rothschilds on their estates in central Buckinghamshire did a great deal to improve the housing of their tenants. A report of 1842 describes cottages in Waddesdon as being particularly liable to damp, with roofs of thatch which speedily decayed, yielding a gas of the most deleterious quality. Fever of every kind was said to be endemic in the parish. The cottages and houses built by the Rothschilds to replace these hovels are still to be seen today, marked by the family crest, a hand grasping a bundle of five arrows, the name given to the splendid inn built at the entrance to Waddesdon Manor itself.

Such landlords were of course at liberty to build in whatever architectural style they chose. The Picturesque style was very popular for cottages in the earlier part of the nineteenth century. In 1810 John Nash designed nine cottages at Blaise Hamlet, in Henbury, near Bristol, for a wealthy banker. Each one was different, an extravagant mix of thatched roofs, dormer windows, rustic porches, elaborate brick chimneys, and dark pokey accommodation for the inhabitants. They were enormously influential for much of the first half of the century. At Edensor, near Chatsworth, the Duke of Devonshire was very much more eclectic in his

93 Estate housing at Edensor, Derbyshire. The village was moved out of sight of
Chatsworth and then rebuilt by the sixth Duke of Devonshire in the 1830s.

choice of styles, with everything from mock Tudor to imitation Swiss
chalets. Other landlords were much more utilitarian, as on the Northamptonshire estates of the Duke of Grafton. The Prince Consort was as much
concerned to improve the housing of agricultural labourers as he was to
improve farming practices, and model villages at West Newton on the
Sandringham Estate and at Whippingham on the Osborne estate in the Isle
of Wight were the result. He also designed a pair of model cottages for the
Great Exhibition of 1851. They were taken down and rebuilt after the
exhibition and now form the Lodge at the Kennington Road entrance to
Kennington Park, in south London. They were very unusual for their time
in having built-in water-closets with internal access, not only on the ground
floor but on the first floor as well.

Many landlords were undoubtedly well-meaning in their efforts, but few
could help imposing their own moral attitudes and social values, sometimes
by forbidding public houses, sometimes by demanding regular attendance
at church. The villages of Ardington and Lockinge, in Berkshire, were
almost completely rebuilt by Lord and Lady Wantage from the 1860s
onwards, and everything was provided, including allotments, a reading
room, a co-operative grocery store, a bakery, schools and churches, even a

public house. But although Lord Wantage could never have been accused of openly exerting any improper pressure upon any of his tenants, the indirect pressures to conform were enormous and the two villages were described as being politically dead in the last years of the century.

The vernacular tradition in building was not completely dead, however, and in the West Riding of Yorkshire economic and social factors peculiar to the hills and dales of the eastern Pennines produced a new house-type, the laithe house. A laithe house combines human accommodation with cattle byre and barn under one roof, and differs in its layout in a number of respects from the plan of the ancient longhouse. Laithe houses seem to have been built in direct response to the enclosure of waste and commons from the latter part of the eighteenth century onwards. The farms thus created, with the laithe house as their centre, were often quite small, rarely over 14 or 15 acres. This meant that the occupants had to turn to other trades, especially woollen textile manufacture and stone-quarrying, as well as farming in order to make a living. Several hundred laithe houses are still to be seen, some now in ruins and others converted into country homes for well-to-do Yorkshire industrialists, evidence of a local response to local demands.

The wealthiest landlords often built or rebuilt their own country houses on the most lavish scale, the money coming as much if not more from urban ground rents or industrial and mining profits as from more traditional agricultural rents, whilst the older aristocracy and landed gentry were joined by newcomers anxious to give respectability to fortunes acquired in banking, commerce, or industry by buying a country estate and building a house that would reflect their pretensions if not their standing. The ideal of the Victorian country gentleman was given an astonishing aura of deference and respect. Sir Gilbert Scott wrote that 'he has been placed by Providence in a position of authority and dignity, and no false modesty should deter him from expressing this, quietly and gravely, in the character of his house.' The Duke of Westminster seemed, in the last quarter of the century, to be the embodiment of this ideal; grave, dignified, benevolent, and immensely rich. There were of course many who did not match up to this ideal, which was why the sale of the contents of Stowe on the bankruptcy of the Duke of Buckingham was considered to be so scandalous.

Victorian country houses were built in an astonishingly wide range and mixture of styles, although by the 1860s more than half of those then building were in what may loosely be called Gothic, with much emphasis upon vertical lines and a marked asymmetry, together with a welter of decorative detail. The overall effect is often one of strain rather than repose. Harlaxton Manor, in Lincolnshire, was built for George Gregory in the 1830s. Much he designed himself, but he had the assistance first of the young Anthony Salvin and then of William Burn. Together they

94 Belvoir Castle, Leicestershire. A castle was built here in the late eleventh century. It was almost demolished during the Civil War and much rebuilt between 1654 and 1668. It was rebuilt again between 1801 and 1830, during which period parts were destroyed by fire. It is very much the early-nineteenth-century romantic, idealized, medieval castle.

produced one of the most extravagant of nineteenth-century country houses, an extraordinary essay in Victorian Jacobean, with themes drawn from Burghley House, Cobham, Montacute, and Audley End. Even more extravagant was Eaton Hall, built for the Duke of Westminster between 1870 and 1882 by Alfred Waterhouse at enormous cost, well over £600,000. It was 'the most ambitious instance of Gothic Revival domestic architecture anywhere in the country'. It lasted less than a hundred years, all save the chapel, clock tower and stables being demolished in 1961. At the same time that Waterhouse was at work at Eaton Hall Hippolyte Destailleur was building Waddesdon Manor for Baron Ferdinand de Rothschild, a remarkably successful re-creation in the Buckinghamshire countryside of themes drawn from Chambord, Blois, and Azay-le-Rideau.

Considerable thought and ingenuity went into the planning of the internal layout of these houses, revealing indirectly a great deal about the values, attitudes, and assumptions of the society which created them. The smooth running of the household was based upon a careful analysis of the tasks involved, so that, for example, dirty linen went in at one end of a laundry department, made its way through washing and mangling, drying, ironing and folding rooms, to emerge ready for use at the other. Kitchens were equally elaborate in their organization, and every effort was made to keep kitchen smells away from the main living quarters. A small army of servants was required to keep one of these houses running, and yet they could not be allowed to be seen in the main part of the house. The work had to be done, but it must not be seen to be done. At the same time there was an elaborate hierarchy within the servants themselves, from the butler and housekeeper, both of whom would have had their own sitting rooms, downwards. Male and female servants were rigidly separated in their own quarters.

Georgian country houses were arenas for public display. Victorian country houses became increasingly private, and by the 1820s houses were being built with a private family wing. The first seems to have been at Blairquhar, in Ayrshire, built in 1820 by William Burn, a Scottish architect who came to have the largest country-house practice in Britain and who brought to perfection the carefully arranged and minutely subdivided plan which became so characteristic of the Victorian country house.

During the 1830s an exclusively male area of the house began to develop, again a reflection of Victorian moral attitudes. As the cult of the 'pure and angelic woman' began to emerge, itself a facet of that idealized, highly romanticized medieval world picture with its overtones of chivalry hinted at in the opening paragraphs of this chapter, so an area in which men could talk without having to watch every word 'because there are ladies present' became increasingly desirable. It was centred first round the billiards room, and then the smoking room. The Prince Consort had one built at Osborne in 1845, but perhaps the most elaborate of all Victorian smoking rooms is that at Cardiff Castle, built for the enormously wealthy third Marquess of Bute. By the 1870s the gun room was making its appearance and the male wing became as nicely subdivided and as exclusive as the servants' wing.

Conservatories were becoming a popular feature of country houses by the end of the eighteenth century. Improvements in the manufacture of iron and glass and in heating techniques made them ever larger in the nineteenth century. Joseph Paxton designed the great conservatory at Chatsworth in 1836. It measured 277 by 123 feet and covered exactly an acre. He then designed one at Capesthorne, on a slightly smaller scale, and there was an immense winter garden at Somerleyton built in about 1855 and measuring 125 by 90 feet. Conservatories housed the exotic, tropical plants and ferns that Victorian botanists were bringing back from South America, southern Africa, and the Far East. They were, however, difficult to maintain and expensive to heat. Those at Capesthorne and Somerleyton have long since disappeared, and that at Chatsworth was demolished in 1920.

The gardens which surrounded country houses shared their characteristics: they were elaborate in their design, eclectic in their style and just as restless in their use of brightly coloured bedding plants and exotic trees. Thus the araucania, or monkey-puzzle tree, was widely planted from the 1840s. Sir Charles Barry developed what he called 'architectural gardening', in which he made use of a succession of formal gardens linked by terraces and balustrades to the house. Some of his most characteristic work was to be found at Shrubland Park near Ipswich, and in the gardens he designed for the Duke of Sutherland at Trentham Park in Staffordshire. William Nesfield became particularly skilful at designing elaborate parterres, rivalling any Elizabethan knot garden in their geometrical complexity but making use of a much wider range of plants and shrubs, together with statuary, sculpture, evergreens, and topiary work, as at Stoke Edith in Herefordshire and Crewe Hall in Cheshire, and the enormous Perseus fountain and gardens at Witley Court, Worcestershire, laid out for the first Earl of Dudley.

Such extravagance provoked the inevitable reactions. Some gardens were laid out as historical reconstructions, as, for example, at Hewell Grange, Worcestershire, where Lord Windsor in the 1880s laid out what he was pleased to call a garden in 'early Jacobean English Renaissance style'. Sir Frank Crisp, in his gardens at Friar Park, Henley, re-created gardens based upon medieval illuminations, of which he had a collection of over 600. But the eclecticism of Victorian gardening is illustrated admirably in this same garden: Sir Frank used 7,000 tons of stone to build a scale reconstruction of the Matterhorn to house his collection of alpine plants. Different types of gardens, whether alpine, water, Dutch, French, or Chinese, were built. James Bateman laid out the gardens at Biddulph Grange in Staffordshire in the 1840s and 1850s, and succeeded in creating an integrated landscape from a wide range of disparate parts; there was a rose garden, a long narrow dahlia walk, a pool, masses of rhododendrons, and an Egyptian court enclosed in yew trees clipped into pyramidal shapes.

Gardening in Britain took a further direction in the last quarter of the nineteenth century. In 1870 William Robinson published his book *The Wild Garden*. He objected strongly to what he called 'pastry-work gardening', the elaborate beds filled with half-hardy annuals so characteristic of the work of Barry and Nesfield. Instead, he advocated wide, sweeping lawns, much more shapely, gently curved beds of plants and shrubs, and the use of creepers over buildings and walls in order to soften their harsh outlines. In about 1875 he met Gertrude Jekyll, and by the 1880s she was designing gardens using woodland and water much more 'naturally' than had been done for a generation. She developed a particularly sensitive approach to planting, choosing flowers and shrubs for the subtlety of their colours and textures, drawing much of her effects from the juxtaposition of plants of similar, but muted, colours. Before the end of the century she had met the young Edwin Lutyens, and together they pioneered an altogether new approach to the design and layout of house and garden, the two being carefully linked through materials, textures, and the interrelationship of the parts in order to construct a harmonious whole. This geometrical approach to gardening was taken a step further by Reginald Blomfield in his book *The Formal Garden in England,* published in 1892, the first time the word 'formal' was actually applied to gardens in Britain.

The period from the 1860s to the outbreak of war in 1914 was the Golden Age of the country house, but even as it reached its apogee its economic base was crumbling. In 1868 four-fifths of the food consumed in Britain was home-grown. The gradual improvement in living standards in the first half of the century meant a growing demand for livestock products. Although many great country houses drew their support from industry, the majority were founded on the prosperity of Victorian agriculture. Change came suddenly and dramatically in the 1870s. The decade was marked by seven bad harvests out of ten, that of 1879 being the worst of the century. Foreign imports of grain were drawn in to fill the gap and prices moved down rather than up. The import of both grain and of meat doubled in twenty years, stimulated by the construction of railways in the United States and the introduction of refrigerated ships on the run from Australasia. Cereal growing was particularly hard hit, and much arable land went out of cultivation as the acreage of land under the plough fell, from 15 million acres in 1870 to nearly 11 million in 1914. Cattle rearing continued to be fairly prosperous, but the number of sheep fell from 21.6 million to 17.2 million, not least because the market for wool and woollen textiles was itself changing rapidly. The impact of the agricultural depression was of necessity very uneven. The heavy arable lands of southern England, from Wiltshire to East Anglia, were particularly badly hit. The clays of Essex proved to be unsuitable for pasture and much became derelict. The movement from arable to pasture, even in those areas best suited to pastoral farming, was slow, hindered by a lack of capital and by the natural conservatism of so many hitherto well-established farmers. Landlords found that they had to remit rents or have no tenants at all, and rents overall fell by about a quarter between 1870 and 1900, thus cutting capital investment just when it was needed most. The situation was not universally gloomy, however, and those farmers who were prepared to experiment often fared quite well as market conditions changed. Large numbers of Scottish farmers moved south and acquired a reputation for hard work and the ability to pull success from disaster. Nevertheless, agriculture slowly lost its pre-eminence in the economic life of Britain. The number of agricultural labourers fell from 900,000 in 1871 to 660,000 in 1911, and as the agricultural interest declined, both relatively and absolutely, so the political power and influence of the landowning classes also declined. By the end of the century large country houses and their dependant estates were coming up for sale in increasing numbers and they were proving increasingly difficult to sell. Land was no longer the investment that it was, even for purely political and social motives.

The rapid industrialization which was taking place in Britain from the 1780s was led by the cotton industry. A series of important technical innovations, beginning with Arkwright's water-frame, patented in 1769, multiplied again and again the capacity of cotton spinners. By the end of the eighteenth century Hargreaves' spinning jenny, patented in 1770, could take 120 spindles. The benefits of scale became increasingly apparent and the machines were moved into factories. Their location was for long dictated by the need for water power, since the waterwheel was both more powerful and more reliable than the first generation of steam-engines, and such waterwheels, once built, were expensive to replace so that many continued in use until well into the second half of the nineteenth century.

Steam power was first applied to cotton manufacture in 1785, at Papplewick in Nottinghamshire and, slowly at first, steam power began to replace water power, with the result that, because of the cost of transporting coal, the industry came to be concentrated in the northwest of England, from Stockport in Cheshire to Preston in Lancashire, and more especially on the south Lancashire coalfield. Few mills in Oldham, for example, were more than a quarter of a mile from a coal pit. Canals had little impact upon the location of the industry and the railway came too late to bring any substantial change to an industry which by the 1830s was showing all the signs of immobility born of maturity. By 1838 four-fifths of cotton mills were steam-powered and 1,200 out of 1,600 mills in England were to be found in Lancashire, where local and regional specializations were already well established, with spinning and weaving towns developing their own characteristics.

The phenomenal growth of the cotton industry is marked by the rise in the quantity of raw cotton imported: an average of 8.7 million pounds weight per year for the period 1781–3, 16.1 million per year for 1784–6, and for 1829–31 no less than 249 million pounds weight per year. The causes for this astonishing growth in the demand for raw cotton, and the social consequences of a flood of cheap, easily laundered cotton cloth upon the home market, are matters for economic history, whilst the springs of the sudden burst of technical innovation which made it all possible still remain beyond satisfactory explanation. The impact upon the landscape, however, in some parts of Britain was dramatic in the extreme. Cotton mills of ever-increasing size were built, sometimes in plain brick, sometimes extravagantly decorated, together with villas for their owners and cottages for the workers. In Manchester, which was the commercial hub of the industry, equally enormous warehouses were built. Thus the Sedgwick Mill, Redhill Street, in Salford, built by about 1820, was eight storeys high. Dixon's Mill, Junction Street, Carlisle, when finished in 1836, was seven storeys high, 225 feet long, with a 300-foot high chimney. At the time it was the largest cotton mill in England. At Reddish, near Stockport, Sir William Houldsworth's mill, finished in 1865, is composed of two five-storey blocks. He also planned several streets of cottages for his employees, but only a few terraces of houses were built. The church of St Elisabeth was built at his expense, to the designs of Alfred Waterhouse, who also designed the rectory, a school, and a working men's club.

Cotton mills continued to be built throughout the nineteenth century. The Swan Lane Mills, just outside Bolton, were said at the time of their completion in 1905 to be the largest in the world. The Manchester warehouses were equally as massive. The largest, Watts Warehouse, in Portland Street, finished in 1851, was nearly 300 feet long and 100 feet high, built in an elaborately decorated Italianate *palazzo* style. After all, were not Manchester businessmen the nineteenth-century equivalents of Italian merchant princes? Perhaps the most fantastically decorated nineteenth-century factory is to be found in Glasgow, where Templeton's carpet factory, a gorgeous confection finished in 1889, is loosely, very loosely, derived from the Doge's palace in Venice.

The cotton industry, as it reached its maturity, became increasingly dependent upon abundant supplies of cheap coal. The opening of the Liverpool to Manchester railway served to multiply demand yet further, both directly, in the need for good steam coal for the locomotives, and indirectly by stimulating the manufacture of iron and bricks, both of which depended upon coal for their furnaces. Industrialization created, and was created by, a most subtle and complex network of interlocking parts. Each retained its own individuality and each created its own regional and local landscapes, and yet the links between the parts were deep and strong.

The rising demand for coal, together with the building of railways, led to the opening of many new coal-mines. Improvements in mining techniques meant ever-deeper pits, and by 1835 Monkwearmouth colliery shafts had reached 1,590 feet. By 1853 some 1,704 collieries were officially recorded, producing 47 million tons of coal a year, an unprecedented figure. A quarter came from the Northumberland and Durham coalfield, where the coming of the railway had dramatic effects. At the beginning of the nineteenth century coal-mining was narrowly confined to the immediate vicinity of the Tyne and the Wear. Gateshead Fell was still unenclosed common, and settlement had scarcely begun to spread to the north and west beyond the medieval walls of Newcastle-upon-Tyne. Individual pits were on a small scale and depended upon wagonway links to navigable water. One of the longest of these wagonways ran from South Moor to the Tyne near Gateshead, a distance of about 7 miles. Fields and farms were the dominant landscape features rather than coal pits or iron furnaces. By the 1820s the seams along the Tyne were becoming exhausted and new mining hamlets were developing to the north of the Ninety Fathom Dyke, a geological fault which runs inland from the coast near Cullercoats to cross

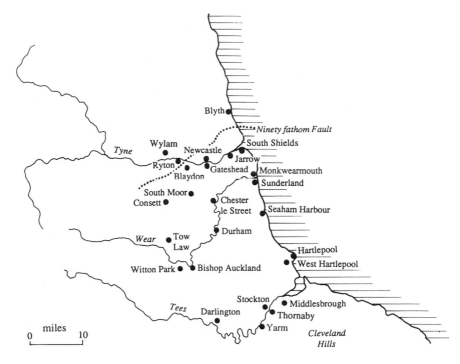

Figure 15   North-east England in the early nineteenth century.

the Tyne above Ryton. The coming of the railway, of which the earliest in the northeast was the Stockton to Darlington line, opened in 1825, led to a rapid extension of mining to the north of Newcastle, to the east of Durham, where Seaham harbour was built in 1828 to handle the traffic, and about Bishop Auckland. Almost every pit had its own railway link. At the same time local supplies of iron ore led to the building of blast furnaces at Wylam, Witton Park, Consett, and Tow Law. Further south, the Tees below Stockton was improved in 1808 by cutting across a meander. It was yet further improved in 1828 and 1830. This was but tinkering with the problem of getting the coal to the coast and hence on board ship for transport to London, and so in 1830 the railway company chose a site yet further to the east of Stockton, at the mouth of the Tees. Here a plot of 32 acres was laid out in a severely gridiron plan on a virgin site, and the first houses of what was to become Middlesbrough were built. Supplies of iron ore were discovered in the nearby Cleveland Hills and in 1852 the first blast furnaces were erected. In 1856 there were twenty-one in blast. Shipyards for the building of iron-clad ships followed quickly. At the same time the shipment of coal from the entirely new town of West Hartlepool began in 1835. Within less than fifty years completely new industrial landscapes had been imposed upon very ancient, rural ones. No wonder contemporaries were astonished and not a little bewildered at what they saw.

The story for the south Staffordshire coalfield shows the same intimate links between geology, topography, and technology. The south Staffordshire coalfield is marked by two geological features which have dictated the course of the evolution of its landscape. The first of these is the Thick Coal seam or Thirty Foot seam, which lies in a great arc, and no more than 400 feet beneath the surface, from Dudley to Bilston, Darlaston, and Wednesbury. It is often 30 feet thick; hence its second name. The second is the Bentley Faults, which lie from east to west a little to the north of Walsall, effectively separating the coal seams of south Staffordshire from those of Cannock Chase. Ironstone and fireclays were also to be found. From the early years of the nineteenth century large numbers of shallow pits were opened in the northeastern areas, just to the south of the Bentley Faults, with much very wasteful exploitation. At the

Figure 16 The South Staffordshire Coalfield.

same time iron making developed with equal rapidity. In 1800 there were
about 26 furnaces in blast. By 1823 there were 84 and by 1865 the number
had risen to 172, of which 114 were actually in blast. From the early years
of the nineteenth century what had still been essentially a rural landscape
rapidly developed into one of the most desolate and dehumanized
industrial landscapes to be found anywhere in Britain. The Black Country
was born in these years. Population grew dramatically. Bilston grew from
about 3,000 in 1780 to 23,500 in 1851. Entirely new villages were created,
Coseley for example. Housing was of the most squalid kind and suffered
severely from the effects of mining subsidence, something which also
wrecked the natural drainage, producing stinking pools known locally as
'swags', whilst slag heaps and waste tips were to be found everywhere,
many of them still smouldering, amidst a tangle of canals and railways. In
1843 Thomas Tancred was given the unenviable task of reporting on the
midland mining industry. His description of the landscape of the Black
Country has often been reprinted, but it is so vivid that it deserves to be
quoted in full:

> In traversing much of the country included within the boundary of red
> sandstone the traveller appears never to get out of an interminable
> village, composed of cottages and very ordinary houses. In some
> directions he may travel for miles and never be out of sight of numerous
> two-storied houses; so that the area covered by bricks and mortar must
> be immense. These houses, for the most part, are not arranged in
> continuous streets, but are interspersed with blazing furnaces, heaps of
> burning coal in process of coking, piles of ironstone calcining, forges,
> pit-banks, and engine chimneys; the country being besides intersected
> with canals, crossing each other at various levels; and the small
> remaining patches of the surface soil occupied with irregular fields of
> grass or corn, intermingled with heaps of the refuse of the mines or of
> slag from the blast furnaces. Sometimes the road passes between
> mounds of refuse from the pits, like a deep cutting on a railway; at
> others it runs like a causeway, raised some feet above the fields on either
> side, which have subsided by the excavation of the minerals beneath. In
> one place, observing that the turnpike road sloped a good deal to one
> side, I asked the driver if it would not be repaired, to which he replied
> that they were still working the coal beneath it, and that they would
> probably wait to see if the road would not right itself by sinking on the
> opposite side and so become level again.
>   . . . The whole country might be compared to a vast rabbit warren. It
> is matter of everyday occurrence for houses to fall down, or a row of
> buildings inhabited by numerous families to assume a very irregular
> outline from what they term a 'swag', caused by the sinking of the
> ground into old workings. . . . There is an instance in the parish of

Sedgley of a church and parsonage-house recently erected composed of wooden frame-work, which will admit of their being screwed up into the perpendicular again whenever they may be thrown out of it. Cellars beneath dwelling-houses are occasionally filled with choke-damp arising from old workings to a degree which makes it dangerous to enter them. On one occasion a gentleman remarked that, perhaps I was not aware that the steps by which I entered his house (in a town) were built on an arch covering the mouth of an old coal-pit. Early potatoes for the London market are raised in ground near Dudley, heated by steam and smoke which proceed from an old colliery which has been on fire for many years, and which may be observed bursting through the crevices of the rock on the side of the road close to the town.

(Midland Mining Commission, First Report.
British Parliamentary Papers, Vol. XIII, 1843, pp. iv–v.)

No landscape ever stands still, however, and that of the Black Country is no exception. By the middle years of the century it was becoming clear that the great Thirty Foot seam was almost exhausted, and so new pits were opened, first to the north, beyond the Bentley Faults into Cannock Chase, and second to the southeast in the area around West Bromwich and Oldbury, where shafts were becoming progressively deeper. In 1873 Sandwell Park Colliery was opened with a shaft driven through overlying strata to reach the Thirty Foot seam, here thrown to a depth of 1,200 feet by the Eastern Boundary Fault.

In the 1850s and 1860s the Black Country iron industry was at its peak. In 1865, 2,100 puddling furnaces were in operation, producing an immensely wide and varied range of wrought-iron goods, in plates, sheets, bars and rods, and in an equally wide range of qualities, from 'common merchant iron' to 'best best best'. The whole edifice was erected upon the manufacture of wrought iron; it collapsed as a result of one of those technological innovations which by now were flooding in an ever-broadening stream into every corner of British society and economy and hence into the landscape. In the middle years of the nineteenth century steel was still very expensive to produce. In 1856 Henry Bessemer patented his converter process, by which molten iron is converted into steel by passing a blast of very hot air through the molten metal. In the same year Frederick Siemens obtained a patent for his heat regeneration process for the making of steel by the open hearth process. Steel, with all its advantages over wrought iron, could now be made cheaply and easily. Few Black Country ironmasters converted their works to making steel, and the wrought-iron industry began slowly to decline. By 1911 only two major iron works remained in the region, and by the same time coal production had been halved.

Coal had been mined where it reached the surface in Cannock Chase

Figure 17 Cannock Chase in the early nineteenth century.

since medieval times, particularly in Beaudesert Park and around
Brereton, and, as in the Black Country, by means of small and shallow
pits. A similar pattern was to be found around Great Wyrley and
Bloxwich, where the drift cover was either very thin or else non-existent.
The building of a canal from Wolverhampton through Great Wyrley to
Essington, authorized in 1792, provided the opportunity for some
development but the real expansion of mining came only after about 1850.
In 1852 the Uxbridge colliery near Hednesford was opened and by about
1875 the whole region was being exploited and entirely new mining
communities were being created, Brownhills for example, and Heath
Hayes, Chase Town and Chase Terrace, whilst Cannock itself grew from
2,913 inhabitants in 1861 to 17,125 in 1881. At the same time the areas of
open heath and common of the Chase itself were shrinking rapidly. By

1900 they had largely disappeared to the south of Beaudesert Park and had been much reduced to the north. By 1905 the southern areas of the Cannock coalfields were in their turn becoming exhausted, and further development was concentrated in the centre and the north, where the Littleton colliery was successfully sunk in 1897.

The story of the exploitation of the south Wales coalfields follows different lines. Iron furnaces and forges had been erected in the sixteenth century, but by 1750 there were only seven furnaces in south Wales. In 1759 a partnership, which included John Wilkinson, the Shropshire ironmaster, took a lease of a remote rural site at Dowlais with liberty to mine coal and ironstone and build a furnace and forges. In 1763 a second works was started, and in 1765 a third, at Cyfarthfa. Here, on the northern edge of the coalfield, coal was easily accessible, either as surface outcrops or by means of levels driven into the steep valley sides. Ironstone was also available, together with limestone, needed as a flux in the furnaces. In the 1790s the Swansea, Neath, and Glamorgan canals were built, making the transport of coal and of iron goods, hitherto carried almost exclusively by packhorse, both cheaper and easier. Mining developed rapidly. The Swansea Canal led to the sinking of new pits, at Brynmorgan and Ynyscedwyn for example, and the Neath Canal stimulated the working of deeper seams, as at the Bryncoch and Bryndewy pits. The ironmasters of the Merthyr district did not enter the coal trade, and it was left to others to exploit the advantages presented by the Glamorgan Canal. In 1811 Walter Coffin built a link to the Glamorgan Canal from his mine at Dinas, the first shaft sunk in the Rhondda Valley. By the 1820s the demand for coal for the furnaces, not only of the iron works in and around Merthyr but also of the tin-plate works near Swansea and the pumping engines of the Cornish tin and copper mines, themselves developing at breakneck speed producing the ores for the Swansea non-ferrous metal industries, meant a soaring demand for coal and a corresponding growth in its export. In the 1830s Thomas Powell began mining coal at Gelligaer, in the Taff Valley, and in 1842 he sank the Duffryn pit at Tyr Founder in the Aberdare Valley. In 1841 the Taff Valley Railway from Cardiff to Merthyr was built, and in 1846 a branch line to Aberdare was opened. Powell went on to open a string of pits in the Aberdare Valley, including Lower and Middle Duffryn and Cwmpennar. In 1845 Admiralty trials had shown that Welsh coal, and especially that from Aberdare, was by far and away the best for raising steam. As the Royal Navy slowly converted to coal, so the Admiralty built a worldwide string of coaling stations. Private shipowners, impressed with the prestige that this recommendation brought, followed suit, and the export trade in Welsh coal grew at an astonishing rate, especially from the Aberdare Valley pits. Mining in the Rhondda Valleys developed more slowly and it was 1875 before output from these two valleys equalled that of Aberdare. Between 1872 and 1883 twenty-three pits were opened in the

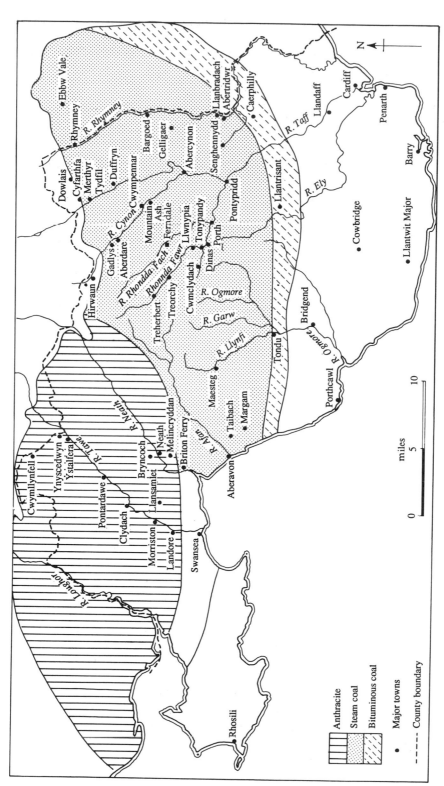

Figure 18 The South Wales Coalfield.

Rhondda, and demand meant that mining spilled over into other valleys, Llynfi, Ogwr, and Garw, and in the 1890s pits were opened at Senghennydd and Abertridwr, in the Aber Valley between Caerphilly and Pontypridd, hitherto entirely rural.

Canal and railway made the movement of coal to the coast cheap and easy. The Glamorgan Canal from Merthyr, built in 1794, terminated in a tidal basin just to the south of the medieval walled town of Cardiff, which then had less than 2,000 inhabitants. A canal and dockyard community grew up at Bute Town, but the primitive facilities for handling the expanding coal-trade became hopelessly congested. In 1839 the second Marquess of Bute ordered the construction of the West Bute dock. In the following year exports of coal from Cardiff amounted to 166,000 tons. In 1841 the Taff Valley Railway was built, adding further to the congestion, and the population of the town reached 10,000. The marquess died suddenly in 1848, leaving a 3-year-old son, and the further development of his estates devolved upon trustees. The East Bute dock was built in three stages between 1855 and 1859, but improvements in facilities always lagged behind the enormous expansion in the export trade in coal. In 1874, 3,780,000 tons of coal were shipped out of Cardiff, and by 1913 the total had multiplied by six. By 1901 the population of Cardiff had reached 164,000. Right in the heart of the town was Cardiff Castle and its park. In 1868 the third marquess came of age and, in conjunction with William Burges, he set to work to restore the castle, creating, at enormous expense, one of the most lavishly decorated monuments of Victorian architecture to be found anywhere in Britain. It was still unfinished at the time of his death in 1900.

The iron works on the northern rim of the south Wales coalfield reached their peak in the 1840s and 1850s, and the long, slow decline began, for reasons very similar to those that produced the decline in the Black Country. First of all the local iron ores became increasingly expensive to mine, and in the 1850s ore began to arrive from Spain. The Dowlais iron works took a licence to use the Bessemer process within weeks of its being announced, but the actual production of steel was a very difficult matter and the company moved only very slowly into steel manufacture. Nevertheless it fared better than other iron works in the region. The great Cyfarthfa works had become almost derelict by the 1870s and only after very considerable investment in plant for the manufacture of steel did it return to life. In 1902 the Dowlais and Cyfarthfa companies merged, and in 1910 Cyfarthfa closed. Only Dowlais and Ebbw Vale remained in production of all those iron works which once had dominated the northern rim of the coalfield. In the meanwhile, the advantages of a coastal location for steel making were becoming increasingly apparent. Tin-plate making had been established in and around Swansea since the end of the seventeenth century, and in 1863 a steel plant opened at Landore. By 1875 it was making mild steel strip plates which proved to be ideally suited for tinning, and steel production and tin-plate making became increasingly integrated. In 1898 the docks at Port Talbot were rebuilt and an entirely new steel works was started on a site near by.

The first canals and railways, iron works, and coal pits were the work of practical men who solved problems as they arose, often after a great deal of painstaking experiment on a trial-and-error basis. Fundamental scientific research was itself in its infancy and at first learnt more from the work of the pioneers of the industrial revolution than it could contribute. This situation changed during the course of the nineteenth century and at an accelerating pace. We have seen something of the impact of technological innovation upon the landscape in the effects which the discovery of methods of making steel cheaply had upon the industrial landscapes of the Black Country and South Wales. Entirely new industries were created during the nineteenth century and their visual impact has been even greater and certainly much more widely diffused.

In 1800 Alessandro Volta succeeded in making what amounted to an electrical battery. The electric arc which it created became increasingly a matter for scientific curiosity and by 1845 attempts were being made to use it for lighting purposes, but a great deal of experiment was necessary before the technical problems involved could be successfully overcome. Faraday announced the discovery of electro-magnetic induction in 1831, but it was a Frenchman, Hippolyte Pixii, who first successfully demonstrated a practical electric generator. In 1858 the South Foreland lighthouse was being lit with electric arc lamps, but it proved to be an immensely expensive undertaking. In 1870 a Belgian, Zenobe Gramme, made the first practical dynamo, and it was widely manufactured. In 1875 the Gare du Nord railway station in Paris was being lit with electric arc lamps. In 1878 Joseph Swan perfected his incandescent filament lamp. Manufacture began in 1881 and by the end of the year the House of Commons, the Savoy Theatre in London, two ships, and a train on the London to Brighton line were being illuminated by electricity. In January 1882 the first electric power station was built, at Holborn Viaduct, and the use of electric lighting spread rapidly. In 1887 Sebastian de Ferranti began to build a power station at Deptford, the first to generate electricity for transmission over a long distance, namely to London's West End. One wall of this power station is still to be seen at Deptford East Power Station.

The first electric telegraph line was put up in 1839, from Paddington to West Drayton. In 1850 the first submarine cable was laid, between England and France, and by 1858 a trans-Atlantic submarine cable had been successfully laid, by which time there were some 6,700 miles of telegraph line in Britain. In 1878 the first telephone system was installed, in Chislehurst, and in the following year the first telephone exchange was built, in London. In 1895 Lord Rutherford succeeded in transmitting a radio message over a distance of three-quarters of a mile at Cambridge. Marconi arrived in England in the following year, took out English patents and founded the Wireless Telegraph Company. In 1901 he succeeded in transmitting a message between Cornwall and Newfoundland.

By the 1820s two-wheeled hobby-horses, a German invention, were to be seen in the streets of London. By about 1840 some were being propelled by a system of treadles and cranks. In 1861 pedals were being attached directly to the wheels, and in 1869 a factory was opened in Coventry for their manufacture. Such machines came in a bewildering range of sizes and shapes. In 1885 the Rover safety bicycle, propelled by pedals and a chain, was introduced. Solid rubber tyres were in use from 1845, when a patent for a pneumatic tyre was also taken out, but it was only after John Dunlop took out his patent in 1888 that pneumatic tyres became commercially successful.

In 1859 the first successful engine powered by means of a gas mixture ignited from an electric spark was made. Numerous experiments followed. Gottlieb Daimler made a small high-speed gas engine in the 1880s and in 1885 he patented a surface carburettor to enable it to use petrol. He fitted his engine to a bicycle in 1886 and to a four-wheeled vehicle shortly afterwards, by which time Karl Benz of Mannheim had built the first three-wheeled motor vehicle. It was F. W. Lanchester who designed a motor-driven vehicle from first principles, and by 1897 they were achieving speeds of up to 20 miles an hour. By this time also Herbert Austin was working for the Wolseley Sheep Shearing Machine Company, and the first four-wheeled Wolseley motor car was built in 1899, two years after the English Daimler Company opened its first factory for the manufacture of motor vehicles in Coventry. Austin opened his Longbridge factory, near Birmingham, in 1905. In Greengate, Salford, there is still to be seen a building of about 1900 with the words 'Motor Garage' carved on its façade.

The dates and names mark the principal stages in the creation of entirely new industries, the product of much basic scientific research and a great deal of practical experiment, drawing upon novel concepts and hitherto unexplored resources. Their physical impact upon the landscape was clear and unmistakable, creating new building forms that reflected both the new inventions themselves and the social consequences of their introduction. Motor buses appeared in the streets of London, and electric trams, with their attendant maze of tracks and overhead cables, in Birmingham and Leeds. Bicycle and motor cars meant that roads had to be improved, and garages and petrol stations began to make their appearance. Electric power stations, the telegraph and the telephone meant cables and poles, illuminated streets and street signs.

The names of these pioneers also reveal that the effort which went into the creation of these new industries was an international one and this in its turn was to lead, albeit indirectly, to yet further changes in the landscape.

By the 1860s there was growing concern in Britain at the very serious deficiencies which by then were apparent not only in the provision for scientific research and technical training but also in basic education. A Select Committee of 1868 stated that 'the facilities for acquiring a knowledge of theoretical and applied science are incomparably greater on the Continent than in this country, and such knowledge is based upon an advanced state of secondary education'. There was still much widespread distrust of state intervention and equally widespread religious inter-denominational rivalry over the provision of schools, and change came only very slowly. The National Society for Promoting the Education of the Poor in the Principles of the Church of England was established in 1811 and the British and Foreign School Society in 1814. The aims of the first are apparent from its name. The second sought to give religious instruction without denominational bias. Both made entirely commendable efforts to combat illiteracy and ignorance but were severely hampered by lack of funds, since both had to rely entirely upon private subscriptions. Nevertheless the National Society, between 1811 and 1833, established nearly 7,000 schools and by 1846 this number had risen to 17,000.

In 1833 the state made its first tentative contribution towards the cost of education by providing the sum of £20,000 to the two societies for spending on school buildings. A National School, built in 1834, is still to be seen in Barker Gate in Nottingham, and a water-powered textile mill at Cuckney in Nottinghamshire was converted into a National School at the expense of the Duke of Portland in 1844. There is a British School in Queen Street, Hitchin, in Hertfordshire, and many others are still to be seen throughout England.

State control over education grew slowly. In 1838 a Committee of the Privy Council was established, the grant was increased, reaching £100,000 in 1846, and the first school inspectors were appointed, among whom, from 1851, was Matthew Arnold. Such measures could do little more than tinker with an immensely complex problem. The Education Act of 1870 made the first systematic and nationwide attempt to find a solution. Responsibility for the provision of schools was entrusted to locally elected School Boards. All children up to the age of 13 were expected to attend, but it was 1880 before enough places had been built for this to be enforceable. Interdenominational rivalry found its way into the School Boards, and progress was often difficult and slow. Schools were built, however, and the example set by E. R. Robson, architect to the London School Board from 1871 to 1889, was of the first importance. He turned from Gothic to what can best be described as Queen Anne style, and gave much thought to the internal layout of schools. The pupil-teacher system then in vogue, and the desperate storage of trained teachers, meant that it was impossible at first to introduce the Prussian system of separate classrooms for each class; although a school incorporating this kind of internal plan was built at

Jonson Street, Stepney, as an experiment, it was the 1890s before the system was widely adopted. Board Schools became common throughout England. The architects William Martin and J. H. Chamberlain built no less than forty-one for the Birmingham School Board between 1873 and 1898, and many still survive, at Oozells Street for example, now the Birmingham College of Food and Domestic Arts, and Stratford Road, Sparkbrook, built in 1885. They even designed the School Board Offices, in Edmund Street, built in about 1875 There is a Board School at Lovers Lane, in Newark, built in 1889, and another in Heanage Road, Grimsby, built in 1876.

Improvements in the provision of secondary, technical, and higher education came even more slowly. In the 1820s Mechanics' Institutes were widely established to give what amounted to evening classes in technical subjects to adults, but they quickly ran into severe problems. They had to rely upon members' subscriptions, and the lack of even the rudiments of education among so many of their members made for very heavy going. Nevertheless there were by mid-century over 600 in England and Wales. Dr George Birkbeck came to London to establish one in 1823, and the buildings of a number of the others still survive, although now long converted to other purposes. In 1828 the University of London was founded and from the first it was deliberately non-denominational. King's College was established in the following year as an Anglican counterpoise, and in 1836 the two were incorporated as the University of London and the original institution became University College. In 1850 Owens College, Manchester, was established, and in 1875 Mason College in Birmingham. Almost from the first they were able to prepare students for London external degrees. In 1884 the Victoria University was established, made up of colleges at Manchester, Liverpool, and Leeds and with the power to confer its own degrees. It split up into its component parts in 1903–4, and the colleges at Birmingham, Sheffield, and Bristol became separate universities at about the same time. In the meanwhile science and engineering subjects had slowly been introduced to Oxford and Cambridge. Oxford built science laboratories between 1855 and 1860, and the Duke of Devonshire paid for the Cavendish Laboratory at Cambridge, opened in 1871, whilst he was Chancellor of the University.

In 1854 a Department of Science and Art was founded, taking over from the Board of Trade the responsibility which that office had held since 1837 for administering grants to schools of design. The department was also enabled to make payment to schools offering classes in mathematics and scientific subjects. Successive Select Committees and Royal Commissions, in 1868, 1872, and 1884, reveal just how slowly the department made any impression. At last, in 1889, came the Technical Instruction Act. It empowered local authorities to set up technical schools and to subsidize science in secondary schools. Real progress followed from an Act of the

95 University Museum, Oxford. This building, erected between 1855 and 1860, was designed by Benjamin Woodward to house a museum, laboratories, and lecture rooms and was built under the intense personal scrutiny of John Ruskin. It was the first university building in Britain to be devoted to scientific research and teaching.

following year, the Taxation (Customs and Excise) Act. This made a large sum of money available to local authorities from the excise duties upon beer and spirits, a sum which by 1901–2 amounted to £859,000. The technical schools and colleges thus slowly and painfully brought to birth are still to be seen in the landscape today: at Derby for example, where a municipal technical college was built in Green Lane in 1876, in Birmingham, where a technical school, now demolished, was built in Suffolk Street in 1893–5. At Bury, in Lancashire, technical schools were built in Broad Street in 1894, and the Royal Technical College was opened in Salford in 1896. Warrington acquired a School of Art in 1883 and a technical school in 1900–1, about five years after the public library and technical school in Wigan were finished. The first buildings of Battersea Polytechnic were put up between 1890 and 1891, and the technical college in Great Horton Road, Bradford, was built between 1880 and 1882. The first buildings of the Woolwich Polytechnic Young Men's Christian Institute were erected in 1890.

But the tentative involvement of the state in the provision of education was propelled by very much wider considerations than the need to keep up with international competition. Much more important was the spiritual and

96   Bilston Technical School, built in 1896.

moral welfare of the population, especially children, and it was the religious dimension to the provision of state education that provoked so much controversy. The fervour and enthusiasm of the Victorian religious revival cannot be doubted. It affected all classes and kinds of people, and in the broadest terms Victorian moral earnestness made itself felt across very many aspects of the landscape, but nowhere more plainly than in the building and rebuilding of churches.

One of the most disturbing features of industrialization in the eyes of contemporaries was the entirely lamentable impact it had upon the religious practices of the people who were flocking into the growing industrial towns. Many were entirely ignorant of the basic tenets of the Christian faith and many more gave up the public practice of their religion and refused to go to church. What appeared to be a moral and social crisis, the 'melancholy, long, withdrawing roar' of the Sea of Faith, was made worse by the obvious inability of the traditional organization of the Church of England to cope with the new conditions. The ancient parishes of the industrializing districts were swamped by a population explosion on an unprecedented scale. At the beginning of the nineteenth century Liverpool, with a population of 94,000, had church seating for 21,000, and

Manchester and Salford, with a combined population of 79,000, could seat about 11,000. In London, with a population of over a million, the Church of England provided about 150,000 seats in its churches. Something clearly had to be done if the population was not to turn to dissent or, even worse, to anticlericalism, even deism and the revolutionary principles of Jacobin France. In 1817 a Church Building Society was formed. In the following year it persuaded Parliament to pass a statute granting one million pounds for the building of new churches. The Act also provided for the creation of new parishes. This had hitherto been enormously difficult, not least because of the controversy it always provoked over the division of glebe, tithe, and pew rents. The Act provided that inhabitants of the new parishes had to pay church rates to their old church as well as their new one for a period of twenty years, and that 20 per cent of the seats in the new church should be free of pew rents. Commissioners were appointed to see to the administration of the Act, and between 1818 and 1856 they divided 1,077 parishes and built 214 new churches, a further half million pounds being voted by Parliament in 1824. There was at the same time an enormous surge of private giving towards church building and restoration. Voluntary effort raised at least £6 million for this purpose between 1813 and 1833, and between 1840 and 1876, 7,144 churches were restored and 1,727 new ones built, at a total cost in excess of £25 million. Between 1860 and 1885 the Church of England alone raised from voluntary contributions the sum of £80 million, of which £35 million was spent on building, restoring, and endowing churches. Nonconformists always maintained that their efforts were greater, and they may well have been right.

In 1851 a unique Religious Census was taken of all those present at places of worship on one particular Sunday. Its results and their interpretation aroused much controversy when they were published, and they have done so ever since. They were also profoundly depressing. As the report said, 'a sadly formidable portion of the English people are habitual neglecters of the public ordinances of religion'. Two-thirds of available Church of England seats were empty. The Established Church provided less than half of the available seating and attracted 3.7 million worshippers, whilst the Roman Catholics and Nonconformists had 3.4 million worshippers between them. Even more depressing was the evidence which showed that the enormous efforts made to provide new accommodation had been largely unsuccessful. It was estimated that between 1801 and 1851 the Church of England had increased its seating by 24 per cent, that is just over a million seats in 2,698 places of worship, but the population had increased by over 100 per cent. Other denominations, however, had added 16,689 new places of worship with four million seats, of which over half had been provided by the Methodists.

This enormous effort on the part of organized religion probably absorbed more of the disinterested enthusiasm of more Victorians, of every class, occupation, and status, than any other achievement of the century. It was carried out in an atmosphere of intense rivalry, polemic and controversy. Much that was done in its name seems now, at the end of the twentieth century, to be mawkish, sentimental, narrow-minded, sanctimonious, and hypocritical, whilst the physical embodiment of the movement, namely its chapels and churches, are often as remarkable for their bad taste and sometimes downright ugliness as for anything else. Now that so many of these buildings are redundant, and either demolished or converted to other uses, the movement may appear to have been a failure, but its success is probably to be found in a dimension which lies beyond the landscape historian, namely in the hearts and minds of innumerable individuals who had the burden of a harsh working life a little relieved on one day of the week by contact with great literature, however narrowly interpreted, and with music, however poorly performed.

The Commissioners appointed under the 1818 Act had to provide as many churches as possible as cheaply as possible. This last condition was sometimes difficult to keep to: the church of St Thomas, Wellington Road

97 St Mary's Church, Oxford Street, Bilston, a Commissioners' church built between 1827 and 1829.

South, Stockport, for example, built between 1822 and 1825, cost over £15,000. Some of the earlier ones were mildly Greek in their design, as at St John, Waterloo Road, Lambeth, finished in 1824, not nearly so good an example of Greek Revival as the church at St Pancras, proposed in 1816 and completed in 1822, but an entirely private venture into church building, incorporating details from the Erechtheum and other monuments in Athens. The flirtation with Greek was only very transient, however. The great bulk of the Commissioners' work was done in Gothic, and a peculiarly anaemic, drab, etiolated Gothic at that. St George's church, Hyde, finished in 1832, is an example, and the church of St John the Baptist at Hampton Wick, built in yellow brick, another. Cast iron was used, both to reproduce decoration and to provide the supporting pillars for galleries, and the plan was often no more than a simple rectangle dominated by the pulpit, with the alter in a slight recess at the east end, a pale shadow of the chancel of a medieval church.

Such churches could scarcely escape criticism by contemporaries, and the most scathing was Augustus Welby Pugin, who raised the debate about the merits of these churches to an altogether higher plane by accusing them of lack of serious moral purpose amounting almost to sacrilege, at the same time condemning classical designs for churches as pagan. Many of his ideas and strictures were taken up and expanded by the Cambridge Camden Society, founded in 1839 and re-formed as the Ecclesiological Society. Through its journal, *The Ecclesiologist,* it became enormously influential, calling, among other things, for the use of 'real' materials, stone, for example, rather than plaster, for decoration, denouncing the use of brick and calling for a full-length chancel. Its most important convert was Sir George Gilbert Scott. Until his death in 1878 he worked tirelessly to restore and rebuild existing churches and cathedrals, including Chichester, where the spire collapsed in 1861, Salisbury, Chester and Ripon, and Doncaster, where he rebuilt the church of St George, destroyed by fire in 1853, in what was considered the 'best' Gothic, that is Early Decorated, producing one of his finest parish churches.

Neither Scott nor the Commissioners were the only architects and patrons of new churches. In London Bishop Blomfield established a Metropolitan Churches Fund in 1836, and, as we have seen earlier in this chapter, both industrialists and landlords felt compelled to provide churches. Thus the second Marquess of Westminster built several churches on his estates in Cheshire, at Aldford for example, and Holy Trinity, Castle Street, Northwich, also in Cheshire, was built in 1842 by the Trustees of the Weaver Navigation for the watermen. Sir George Gilbert Scott built what he considered to be his best parish church, All Saints, Boothtown, Halifax, in 1856–9 at the expense of Colonel Akroyd as part of Akroyd's industrial complex comprising mills, cottages for the workers, and his own splendid Italianate villa. At the same time the interpretation of Gothic was becoming increasingly 'free', using Norman, Italian, and Romanesque motifs, together with polychrome brickwork. One of the earliest and best examples of this new movement is to be found at Christchurch, Streatham Hill, finished in 1842. Both William Butterfield and G. E. Street made use of structural polychromy, under the influence of a growing acquaintance with the multicoloured, striped medieval buildings of Italy. Brick was also increasingly used, a material particularly associated with J. L. Pearson and James Brooks. Even the ecclesiologists were converted to brick following the publication in 1847 of a description of the brick-built medieval cathedral at Albi, in France. Butterfield's most striking, or perhaps most strident, use of polychromy is to be found at All Saints, Margaret Street, London, finished in 1859, whilst his most comprehensive, most earnest statement of his own ideals and those of the Camden Society is Keble College, Oxford, built between 1868 and 1882, an

98 Keble College, Oxford, built between 1868 and 1882 as a monument to John Keble and the Oxford Movement to designs by William Butterfield, and the most serious statement of his architectural ideals and objectives.

astonishing display of virtuosity in the handling of brick and a wide range of polychrome materials. The overall effect is overwhelming: whether it is also aesthetically pleasing is another matter.

The last quarter of the nineteenth century is marked by an increasing eclecticism as the architects drew their themes and ideas from an ever-widening range of sources. Thus Truro Cathedral, begun in 1879, is basically thirteenth-century French Gothic, whilst Westminster Cathedral, begun in 1895, is essentially Byzantine. At the same time the interior furnishings of churches become increasingly rich, reflecting a growing ritualism among some Anglican clergymen, leading in its turn to a re-emphasis of the altar as the centrepiece of a church. Thus Sir Ninian Comper brought back the baldacchino, a canopy of stone, wood, or metal that served to cover the altar, as well as the screen to separate chancel and nave, often blending classical and Gothic in a fashion which at its most successful can be extraordinarily rich, as at St Mary, Knox Road, Wellingborough, a church which occupied much of his time between 1906 and 1930.

By the middle years of the nineteenth century Nonconformists were beginning to abandon the mild, discreet classicism which had hitherto characterized their places of worship, even when rebuilt on a large scale, as Great George Street Congregational Church, Liverpool, rebuilt after a fire in 1840. They became increasingly aware that something grander was called for, but at the same time they often sought to avoid Gothic as a style too closely associated with the Church of England and with Rome. One of the earliest Nonconformist churches rebuilt in the new fashion is Mill Hill Unitarian chapel, City Square, Leeds, built in 1847 in what could be called Perpendicular Gothic. It has a chancel but no tower. All too frequently, however, Nonconformist chapels descended into a debased Italianate style that beggars all description, as in the Buckingham Street Methodist Church in Aylesbury, built in 1893.

Sir George Gilbert Scott had an enormous practice. He was grossly overworked and simply did not have the time to supervise adequately all of the work done from his office. Much of his restoration work was undoubtedly insensitive, heavy-handed, and ruthless. St Mary's Church, Aylesbury, is a good example of his restoration work at its worst, although it must be said in his defence that many churches were by the nineteenth century in a particularly bad state of repair, and it was often a matter of almost total reconstruction if the buildings were to be made safe. He was by no means the only ham-fisted Victorian restorer, however, as witness the disastrous restoration of Hexham, or the equally inept conversion of the eighteenth-century Church of St Andrew at Wimpole, in Cambridgeshire, to Decorated style in 1887.

The clumsy restoration of so many medieval buildings in the middle years of the nineteenth century provoked its own inevitable reaction.

Ruskin was one of the first to condemn what was being done. In *The Seven Lamps of Architecture*, published in 1849, he wrote:

> Neither by the public, nor by those who have the care of public monuments, is the true meaning of the word restoration understood. It means the most total destruction which a building can suffer: a destruction out of which no remnants can be gathered: a destruction accompanied with false description of the thing destroyed . . . it is impossible, as impossible as to raise the dead, to restore anything that has ever been great or beautiful in architecture . . . do not let us talk then of restoration. The thing is a Lie from beginning to end. Take proper care of your monuments and you will not need to restore them. A few sheets of lead put in time upon the roof, a few dead leaves and sticks swept in time out of a water-course, will save both roof and walls from ruin . . . it is again no question of expediency or feeling whether we shall preserve the buildings of past times or not. We have no right whatever to touch them. They are not ours. They belong partly to those who built them, and partly to all the generations of mankind who are to follow us.

His words contributed to a growing movement towards conservation as the need to protect the ancient fabric of the landscape from the worst ravages of industrialization became increasingly recognized. Up until the latter part of the eighteenth century the contribution of each generation to the making of the landscape had been cumulative rather than destructive. Only with the advent of industrialization did men develop sufficient power to destroy their environment as well as add to it. The railway companies were particularly crude and insensitive. The Ludgate Hill railway bridge destroyed the prospect of St Paul's Cathedral, and that over Friargate, Derby, built in 1878, is nearly as bad. The railway station at Berwick-upon-Tweed was built on the site of the medieval castle. Railway lines were built straight through the ruins of Lewes Priory and the medieval town of Flint, and only the efforts of a local antiquary, Charles Warne, saved Maumbury Rings from the London and Southwestern Railway. Wordsworth's indignation at the proposal to build the Kendal and Windermere Railway is well known, although some of his reasons read strangely today, namely 'that the imperfectly educated classes are not likely to draw much good from rare visits to the lakes . . . and . . . on their own account it is not desirable that the visits should be frequent'.

In 1855 the Society of Antiquaries of London established a Conservation Fund with the object of forming a catalogue of historic buildings and monuments. Ten years later the Society for The Preservation of the Commons of London was founded. In 1871 alone it saved Wimbledon and Putney Commons from property developers, saw the passing of the Hampstead Heath Act and another to save Wandsworth Common, this last only after a railway line had cut it in two. In 1877 William Morris founded the Society for the Protection of Ancient Buildings with the express object of saving them from Sir George Gilbert Scott and his like. In 1882, after much effort, Sir John Lubbock obtained an Act for the Preservation of Ancient Monuments, the first tentative step on the part of the state in the direction of conservation rather than exploitation. Sir John himself was a man of very wide interests, achieving distinction as a banker, naturalist, and archaeologist as well as a philanthropist. It was owing to his efforts that the first Bank Holidays Act was passed in 1871, and in his book, *Prehistoric Times*, published in 1865, he did much to popularize the division of prehistory into three stages, the Stone Age, the Bronze Age, and the Iron Age, basing his work upon that of Danish archaeologists, particularly C. J. Thomsen, and coining the term 'Palaeolithic'. He married as his second wife Alice, the daughter of General Pitt-Rivers, who, from a series of brilliant excavations in Wiltshire and Dorset, was establishing the outlines of British prehistory. The National Trust was founded in 1895 by Sir Robert Hunter, Canon Hardwicke Rawnsley, and Octavia Hill. The first building that it acquired, for £10, was the fourteenth-century Clergy House at Alfriston, in Sussex, then in a tumbledown condition. An Act of Parliament passed in 1909 gave the Trust the power to declare its lands and buildings inalienable. It was many years before it began to take an interest in post-medieval buildings, however. The idea of green belts around large cities was first suggested in 1901 and the first Town and Country Planning Act was passed in 1909. In 1908 the Royal Commission on Historical Monuments was created, to begin its magisterial way through the counties of Britain listing and describing buildings and monuments of historical importance and of every kind, but it was not until after the Second World War that it started to list buildings dating from after 1714.

In these ways, slowly and tentatively, something was at last being done to protect the age-old fabric of the British landscape, with its accumulated evidence of ten thousand years of human history, from the destructive powers suddenly thrust into the hands of the last two or three of those innumerable generations who had contributed to its making.

The hand of the nineteenth century lies particularly heavily across the landscape of Britain, and hence across this book. It added whole new towns, from Middlesbrough to Swindon, and immense suburbs to old ones, whether to London or Birmingham, Manchester or Glasgow. The third great replanning of the rural landscape since the end of the last ice age was completed during this period. Advances in science and technology added not only entirely new kinds of buildings, from gasworks to petrol filling stations, telegraph poles, and telephone boxes, but also new institutions such as scientific laboratories in which yet further additions would be hewn from the infinite riches of the natural world. At the same time, every shade of the moral values and material aspirations of Victorian people was deeply engraved across every facet of the landscape: in the lavish building of new churches of every architectural style and for every religious denomination, in the bright red terracotta decoration of a Carnegie public library, and in the grim rows of cottages huddled about the massive block of a Lancashire cotton mill.

The Victorians added the best-documented and in many parts of Britain the most obvious text to the palimpsest which is the landscape, and it is this superabundance of their contribution which makes it so difficult at times to see the contribution of earlier generations, especially in places such as Manchester and central London, not least because this contribution is in its turn being rapidly replaced. It is this superabundance which must be the justification for the length of this chapter, as it is the entirely new dimension given to landscape history by the profound and far-reaching changes precipitated by the outbreak of war in 1914 which is the justification for making it the last.

Further reading

The history of man in the landscape is the total history of every facet of his life since his first appearance on the earth. This means that no aspect of his activities, whether social, spiritual, or physical, is without some impact upon his external environment. It also means that very few books, however old or old-fashioned, recondite or obscure, are without some interest for those who would study the evolution of this environment. In other words it is impossible to compile a comprehensive reading list, so that all that can be offered here are some preliminary suggestions, especially of books which themselves have good bibliographies, together with a note of those which have been of particular value for the themes covered in each chapter.

There are many general histories of Britain, of which the *Oxford History of England* can be especially recommended, together with the *Edinburgh History of Scotland*. The volumes of *The Victoria County Histories of England* are invaluable, as are the volumes in the 'Buildings of England' series edited by Nikolaus Pevsner, and the publications of the Royal Commissions on the Ancient and Historical Monuments of England, Wales and Scotland. The series *Exploring Scotland's Heritage*, edited by Anna Ritchie for the Royal Commission on the Ancient and Historical Monuments of Scotland and published in seven volumes in 1985–6, has proved especially useful. The *Making of the English Landscape* volumes, edited by W. G. Hoskins and Roy Millward, are almost as valuable, as are the volumes in the 'Regions of Britain' series, such as *The Peak District* by R. Millward and A. Robinson (1975). There are also a number of important volumes in 'The New Naturalist' series, including *The Lake District* by W. H. Pearsall and W. Pennington (1973). For Scotland there is *The Making of the Scottish Landscape*, by R. N. Millman (1975), as well as *The Making of the Scottish Countryside*, edited by M. L. Parry and T. R. Slater (1980). Wales is less well provided for, although there is *The Making of the South Wales Landscape* by M. Williams (1975). Also of great value are *A New Historical Geography of England*, edited by H. C. Darby (1973), *An Historical Geography of England and Wales*, edited by R. A. Dodgshon and R. A. Butlin (1978), *An Historical Geography of Scotland*, edited by G. Whittington and D. Whyte (1983), *An Historical Geography of Scotland after 1707* by D. Turnock (1982), and *Studies in Field Systems in the British Isles*, edited by A. R. H. Baker and R. A. Butlin (1973). Since one of the principal themes of this book is the interaction of man in society on the landscape, and since his mechanical ingenuity has been just as important as his political opinions or his religious beliefs in the evolution of the man-made environment, the magisterial *History of Technology*, edited by C. Singer and others, and published in seven volumes between 1954 and 1978, has been of immense value for every chapter of this book. Finally, the volumes of the English Place-name Society need to be mentioned. They contain a mass of material relating to the landscape at a crucial point in its evolution, the exploitation of which has scarcely begun, although Margaret Gelling's book, *Place-names in the Landscape* (1984), is a brilliant pioneering attempt, revealing just how much can be wrung from particularly intractable material.

1   The land of Britain

Clapham, A. R. (ed.), *Upper Teesdale: the Area and its Natural History*, 1978.

Curtis, L. F., Courtney, F. M., and Trudgill, S. T., *Soils in the British Isles*, 1976.

Embleton, C. and Thornes, J., *Process in Geomorphology*, 1979.

Godwin, H., *History of the British Flora*, 2nd edn, 1975.

Harley, J. L. and Lewis, D. (eds), 'Symposium on the flora and vegetation of Britain: origins and changes', *New Phytologist*, 98 (1984).

Lamb, H. H., *Climate, Present, Past and Future*, 1977.

McVean, D. N. and Ratcliffe, D. A., *Plant Communities of the Scottish Highlands*, 1962.

Oxburgh, E. R., 'The plain man's guide to plate tectonics', *Proceedings of the Geologists' Association*, 85 (1974), 299–358.

Parry, M. L., *Climatic Change in Agriculture and Settlement*, 1978.

Price, R. J., *Scotland's Environment during the Last 30,000 Years*, 1983.

Read, H. H. and Watson, Janet, *Introduction to Geology*, vol. 2, *Earth History*, 1975.

Sissons, J. B., *The Evolution of Scotland's Scenery*, 1967.

Trueman, A. E., revised by J. B. Whittow and J. R. Hardy, *Geology and Scenery in England and Wales*, 1971.

Whittow, J. B., *Geology and Scenery in Scotland*, 1977.

Windley, B. F., *The Evolving Continents*, 2nd edn, 1984.

Woodell. S. R. J. (ed.), *The English Landscape: Past, Present and Future*, 1985.

2 The first men

Atherden, M. A., 'Impact of late prehistoric cultures on the vegetation of the North Yorkshire moors', *Transactions of the Institute of British Geographers*, n.s. 1 (1976), pp. 284–300.

Bowen H. C. and Fowler, P. J., *Early Land Allotment in the British Isles,* British Archaeological Reports 48, 1978.

Clark, J. G. D., *Excavations at Star Carr,* 1954, repr. 1971.

Cunliffe, B., *Iron Age Communities in Britain,* 1974.

Cunliffe, B. and Rowley, T. (eds), *Oppida in Barbarian Europe,* British Archaeological Reports, Supplementary Series 11, 1976.

Evans, J. G., *The Environment of Early Man in the British Isles,* 1975.

Evans, J. G., Limbrey S., and Cleere, H. (eds), *The Effect of Man on the Landscape: The Highland Zone,* Council for British Archaeology, Research Report 11, 1975.

Feachem, R., *A Guide to Prehistoric Scotland,* 2nd edn, 1977.

Fowler, P. J., *The Farming of Prehistoric Britain,* 1983.

Jones, M. and Dimbleby, G., *The Environment of Man,* British Archaeological Reports, British Series 87, 1981.

Laing, L., *Orkney and Shetland,* 1974.

Limbrey, S. and Evans, J. G. (eds), *The Effects of Man on the Landscape: The Lowland Zone,* Council for British Archaeology, Research Report 21, 1978.

May, J., *Prehistoric Lincolnshire,* 1976.

Megaw, J. V. S. and Simpson, D. D. A., *Introduction to British Prehistory,* 1979.

Renfrew, C. (ed.), *British Prehistory,* 1974.

—— (ed.), *The Prehistory of Orkney,* 1985.

Royal Commission on Historic Monuments (England), *Long Barrows in Hampshire and the Isle of Wight,* 1979.

Simmons, I. G. and Tooley, M., *The Environment in British Prehistory,* 1981.

Spratt, D. A. (ed.), *Prehistory and Roman Archaeology of Northeast Yorkshire,* 1982.

Tallis, J. H. and Switsor, V. R., 'Forest and moorland in the south Pennine uplands in the mid-Flandrian period. I. Macrofossil evidence of the former forest cover', *Journal of Ecology,* 71, (1983).

Taylor, J. A. (ed.), *Culture and Environment in Prehistoric Wales,* British Archaeological Reports 76, 1980.

Williams, C. T., *Mesolithic Exploitation Patterns in the Central Pennines: A Palynological Study of Soyland Moor,* British Archaeological Reports 139, 1985.

3 Roman Britain

Frere, S., *Britannia*, 1967.
Frere, S. and St Joseph, J. K., *Roman Britain from the Air*, 1983.
McWhirr, A. (ed.), *The Archaeology and History of Cirencester*, British Archaeological Reports 30, 1976.
Miles D. (ed.), *The Romano-British Countryside*, British Archaeological Reports 103, 1982.
Percival, J., *The Roman Villa*, 1976.
Rivet, A. L. F. and Smith, C. *The Place-names of Roman Britain*, 1979.
Rodwell, W., *Temples, Churches and Religion: Recent Research in Roman Britain*. British Archaeological Reports, British Series 77, 1980.
Rodwell, W. and Rowley, T. (eds), *Small Towns of Roman Britain*, 1975.
Salway, P., *Roman Britain*, 1981.
Thomas, C., *Christianity in Roman Britain*, 1981.
Todd, M. (ed.), *Studies in the Romano-British Villa*, 1978.
Wacher, J., *The Towns of Roman Britain*, 1975.
—— *Roman Britain*, 1978.
—— (ed.), *The Civitas Capitals of Roman Britain*, 1966.

4 People: English, Scots, and Welsh

Addyman, P. and Morris, R., *The Archaeological Study of Churches*, Council for British Archaeology, Research Report 13, 1976.
Barrow, G. W. S., *The Kingdom of the Scots*, 1973.
Campbell, A. (ed.), *The Charters of Rochester*, 1973.
Cantor, L. (ed.), *The English Medieval Landscape*, 1982.
Darby, H. C., *Domesday England*, 1977.
—— (ed.), *The Domesday Geography of Eastern England*, 3rd edn, 1971.
Darby, H. C. and Campbell, E. M. J. (eds), *The Domesday Geography of Southeastern England*, 1971.
Darby, H. C. and Finn, R. W. (eds), *The Domesday Geography of Southwest England*, 1967.
Darby, H. C. and Maxwell, I. S. (eds), *The Domesday Geography of Northern England*, 1962.
Davies, W., *Wales in the Early Middle Ages*, 1982.
Drewett, P. L. (ed.), *Archaeology in Sussex to A.D. 1500*, Council for British Archaeology, Research Report 29, 1978.

Ekwall, E., *The Concise Oxford Dictionary of English Place-names,* 4th edn, 1960.

Finberg, H. P. R. (ed.), *The Early Charters of the West Midlands,* 1961.

—— (ed.), *The Early Charters of Wessex,* 1964.

Gelling, M., *Signposts to the Past,* 1978.

—— (ed.), *The Early Charters of the Thames Valley,* 1979.

Hart, C. R. (ed.), *The Early Charters of Eastern England,* 1966.

—— (ed.), *The Early Charters of Northern England and the North Midlands,* 1975.

Henderson, I., *The Picts,* 1967.

Hooke, D., *Anglo-Saxon Landscapes of the West Midlands: The Charter Evidence,* British Archaeological Reports, British Series, 95, 1981.

McNeill, P. and Nicholson, R., *An Historical Atlas of Scotland,* 1975.

Reed, M. (ed.), *Discovering Past Landscapes,* 1984.

Rees, W., *An Historical Atlas of Wales,* 1967.

Robertson, A. J. (ed.), *Anglo-Saxon Charters,* 2nd edn, 1956.

Sawyer, P. H. (ed.), *Anglo-Saxon Charters: An Annotated List and Bibliography,* 1968.

—— (ed.), *Medieval Settlement,* 1976.

—— (ed.), *The Charters of Burton Abbey,* 1979.

—— (ed.), *Domesday Book: A Reassessment,* 1985.

Taylor, C., *Village and Farmstead,* 1983.

Whitelock, D. (ed.), *English Historical Documents, 500–1042,* 2nd edn, 1979.

Wilson, D. M., *The Archaeology of Anglo-Saxon England,* 1976.

5   *Places: fields and farms, villages and towns*

Aberg, F. A., *Medieval Moated Sites,* Council for British Archaeology, Research Report 17, 1978.

Adams, I. H., *The Making of Urban Scotland,* 1978.

Barley, M. W. (ed.), *The Plans and Topography of Medieval Towns in England and Wales,* Council for British Archaeology, Research Report 14, 1976.

Beresford, M. W., *New Towns of the Middle Ages,* 1967.

Beresford, M. W. and Hurst, J. G. (eds), *Deserted Medieval Villages,* 1971.

Beresford, M. W. and St Joseph, J. K., *Medieval England: An Aerial Survey,* 2nd edn, 1979.

Brooks, N. P. and Whittington, G., 'Planning and growth in the medieval Scottish burgh: the example of St Andrews', *Transactions of the Institute of British Geographers,* n.s. 2 (1977), 278–95.

Conzen, M. R. G., 'The use of town plans in the study of urban history', in
    H. J. Dyos (ed.), *The Study of Urban History*, 1968.
Darby, H. C., *The Medieval Fenland*, 2nd edn, 1976.
Dunbar, J. G., *The Historic Architecture of Scotland*, 1966.
Gordon, G. and Dicks, B., *Scottish Urban History*, 1983.
Laing, L. (ed.), *Celtic Continuity*, British Archaeological Reports 37, 1977.
Mercer, E., *English Vernacular Houses*, 1975.
Naismith, R. J., *Buildings of the Scottish Countryside*, 1985.
Platt, C., *The English Medieval Town*, 1976.
—— *Medieval England*, 1978.
—— *The Castle in Medieval England and Wales*, 1982.
Rowley, T. (ed.), *The Origins of Open Field Agriculture*, 1981.
Smith, P., *Houses of the Welsh Countryside*, 1975.
Tabraham, C., *Scottish Castles and Fortifications*, 1986.
Wood, M., *The English Medieval House*, 1965, repr. 1981.

6   Ideas: the church in the landscape

Barley, M. W. (ed.), *Christianity in Roman Britain*, 1968.
Clifton-Taylor, A. *English Parish Churches*, 1974.
Cook, G. H., *Medieval Chantries and Chantry Chapels*, 1947.
Donkin, R., *The Cistercians: Studies in the Geography of Medieval
    England and Wales*, 1978.
Fawcett, R., *Scottish Medieval Churches*, 1985.
Knowles, D., *The Religious Orders in England*, 3 vols, 1948–59.
—— *The Monastic Orders in England*, 2nd edn, 1963.
Platt, C., *The Parish Churches of Medieval England*, 1981.
Rodwell, W., *The Archaeology of the English Church*, 1981.
Rodwell, W. and Bentley, J., *Our Christian Heritage*, 1984.
Taylor, H. M. and Taylor, J., *Anglo-Saxon Architecture*, 3 vols, 1965–78.
Thomas, C., *The Early Christian Archaeology of North Britain*, 1971.
Webb, G., *Architecture in Britain: The Middle Ages*, 1956.

7   Early modern Britain

Barley, M. W., *The English Farmhouse and Cottage*, 1961.
Darby, H. C., *The Draining of the Fens*, 2nd edn, 1956.
Dunbar, J. G., *The Historic Architecture of Scotland*, 1966.
Mathias, P. (ed.), *Science and Society, 1600–1900*, 1972.
Owen, G. D., *Elizabethan Wales*, 1962.

Rees, W., *Industry Before the Industrial Revolution*, 1968.
Sanderson, M. H. B., *Scottish Rural Society in the Sixteenth Century*, 1982.
Summerson, J., *Architecture in Britain, 1530–1830*, 1953.
Thirsk, J. (ed.), *The Agrarian History of England and Wales*, vol. 4, *1500–1640*, 1967.
Webster, C. (ed.), *The Intellectual Revolution of the Seventeenth Century*, 1975.
Whyte, I. D., *Agriculture and Society in Seventeenth Century Scotland*, 1979.

8 Georgian Britain

Buchanan, R. A., *Industrial Archaeology in Britain*, 1972.
Butt, J., *The Industrial Archaeology of Scotland*, 1967.
Caffyn, L., *Workers' Housing in West Yorkshire, 1750–1920*, 1986.
Chalklin, C. W., *The Provincial Towns of Georgian England*, 1974.
Fenton, A. and Walker, B., *The Rural Architecture of Scotland*, 1981.
Hadfield, C., *British Canals*, 6th edn, 1979.
Handley, J. E., *Scottish Farming in the Eighteenth Century*, 1953.
Hussey, C., *English Country Houses: Early Georgian, 1715–1760*, 1955.
—— *English Country Houses: Mid-Georgian, 1760–1800*, 1956.
Moore, D. (ed.), *Wales in the Eighteenth Century*, 1976.
Naismith, R. J., *Buildings of the Scottish Countryside*, 1985.
Pawson, E., *Transport and Economy: The Turnpike Roads of Eighteenth Century Britain*, 1977.
Turner, M. E., *English Parliamentary Enclosure*, 1980.

9 Victorian Britain

Ashworth, W., *The Genesis of Modern British Town Planning*, 1954.
Briggs, A., *Victorian Cities*, 1963.
Carter, H., *The Towns of Wales*, 1966.
—— *The Study of Urban Geography*, 3rd edn, 1981.
Chadwick, O., *The Victorian Church*, Pt 1, 1966, Pt 2, 2nd edn, 1972.
Clark, G. Kitson, *The Making of Victorian England*, 1962.
Dyos, H. (ed.), *The Study of Urban History*, 1968.
Dyos, H. and Wolff, M. (eds), *The Victorian City*, 2 vols, 1973.
Flinn, M. (ed.), *Scottish Population History*, 1977.
Forsyth, A., *Yesterday's Gardens*, 1983.

Girouard, M., *The Victorian Country House*, 1971.
—— *Life in the English Country House*, 1978.
—— *Cities and People*, 1985.
Hadfield, M., *A History of British Gardening*, 1969.
Lawton, R., 'Rural depopulation in nineteenth century England', in R. W. Steel and R. Lawton (eds), *Liverpool Essays in Geography*, 1967, 277–56.
Metcalf, P., *Victorian London*, 1972.
Mingay, G. (ed.), *The Victorian Countryside*, 2 vols, 1981.
Pugin, A. W. N., *Contrasts*, reprinted with an Introduction by H. R. Hitchcock, 1969.
Robson, E. R., *School Architecture*, 1874, repr. 1972.
Simpson, E. S., 'The reclamation of the Forest of Delamere', in R. W. Steel and R. Lawton (eds), *Liverpool Essays in Geography*, 1967, 271–92.

Index

Since this book concerns the landscape of Britain before 1914 all places are given their pre-1974 county locations.